SAMUEL BECKETT

The Grove Centenary Edition

SAMUEL BECKETT
The Grove Centenary Edition

SAMUEL BECKETT
The Grove Centenary Edition

Volume III

Dramatic Works

Paul Auster, Series Editor

Introduction by Edward Albee

Grove Press
New York

Printed in the United States of America

FIRST GROVE PRESS EDITION

Design and textual supervision by Laura Lindgren

front cover illustration by Laura Lindgren, based on a photograph by David H. Davison

Library of Congress Cataloging-in-Publication Data
Beckett, Samuel, 1906–
    [Selections. 2006]
    Samuel Beckett : the Grove centenary edition / series editor, Paul Auster—1st ed.
        p.   cm.
    Contents: v. 1. Novels. Murphy ; Watt ; Mercier and Camier / introduction by Colm Tóibín — v. 2. Novels. Molloy ; Malone dies ; The unnamable ; How it is / introduction by Salman Rushdie — v. 3. Dramatic works / introduction by Edward Albee — v. 4. Poems, short fiction, and criticism / introduction by J. M. Coetzee.
    ISBN-10: 0-8021-1819-4   ISBN-13: 978-0-8021-1819-6   (v. 3)
    ISBN-10: 0-8021-1831-3   ISBN-13: 978-0-8021-1831-8   (boxed set)
    I. Auster, Paul. 1947–   II. Title.
    PR6003.E282A6   2006
    848'.81409—dc22   2005055078

Grove Press
an imprint of Grove/Atlantic, Inc.
841 Broadway
New York, NY 10003

DISTRIBUTED BY PUBLISHERS GROUP WEST
WWW.GROVEATLANTIC.COM

06 07 08 09 10   10 9 8 7 6 5 4 3 2 1

Poet, novelist, short-story writer, playwright, translator, and critic, Samuel Beckett created one of the most brilliant and enduring bodies of work in twentieth-century literature. In celebration of the one hundredth anniversary of his birth, the four volumes of this new edition bring together nearly every word Beckett published during his lifetime.

Nearly every word, but not all. Because these volumes are intended for English-language readers, and because Beckett wrote in both English and French, a number of untranslated French poems and short critical essays have not been included. Those with a knowledge of French can find them in *Collected Poems in English and French* and *Disjecta*, both available from Grove Press.

In the case of the poems, I was sorely tempted to translate them myself, but then I recalled a series of letters I exchanged with Beckett in the late seventies and early eighties. I was then in the process of putting together *The Random House Book of Twentieth-Century French Poetry*, a six-hundred-page anthology that contains the work of forty-eight poets. Beckett generously allowed me to use his translations of Apollinaire, Breton, and Eluard. When I broached the subject of including him as a *French* poet, however, he hesitated, claiming that he had neither the energy nor the inclination to revisit those old works from the late thirties. When I suggested that I translate them instead, he thought it over for a while, then said no. Only he could do the translations—and he didn't feel up to the task. So I let the matter drop.

With any other poet, I might have insisted more strenuously, but Samuel Beckett was and is a special case. Apart from some early collaborative efforts (notably with Richard Seaver on the stories "The End" and "The Expelled" and with Patrick Bowles on the novel *Molloy*), Beckett served as his own translator. But "translator" hardly does justice to the nature of the job he took upon himself. Beckett's renderings of his own work are never literal, word-by-word transcriptions. They are free, highly inventive adaptations of the original text—or, perhaps more accurately, "repatriations" from one language to the other, from one culture to the other. In effect, he wrote every work twice, and each version bears his own indelible mark, a style so distinctive that it resists all attempts at imitation. No matter how deft or skillful my translations might have been, they never would have come out sounding like Beckett.

This edition, then, does not constitute a Collected Works. Beckett scholars and astute bibliophiles will also note the omission of two posthumously published books, which the author blocked from appearing in print while he was alive: his first novel, *Dream of Fair to Middling Women*, completed in 1932 at age twenty-six (certain passages of which he later plundered and reworked into *More Pricks Than Kicks* and *Murphy*), and his first play, *Eleuthéria*, written in French in 1947. Both are available from other publishers (Arcade and Foxrock), but in my opinion they do not form an essential part of the Beckett canon.

What one will find between the covers of these four volumes are the works on which Samuel Beckett's reputation rests, everything that qualifies him as one of the great literary artists of our time, all the books and plays that will continue to be read and performed for generations to come. From the dazzling early essay on Proust to the revolutionary *Waiting for Godot*, from the uproarious prose of *Watt* to the austere minimalism of *How It Is*, from the poetic murmurs of *Texts for Nothing* to the tender, heartbreaking *Company*, from the mordant recollections of *Krapp's Last Tape* to the tragic feminine Mouth of *Not I*, everything is here: seven novels, thirty-two dramatic works, thirty poems, fifty-four stories, texts, and novellas, three pieces of criticism. Open anywhere and begin reading. It is an experience unequaled anywhere in the universe of words.

PAUL AUSTER

INTRODUCTION

You have in front of you one of the most important books of the second half of the twentieth century—the collected plays of Samuel Beckett. There are other writers of this period who "matter," of course—Borges, Nabokov, not to make a list but to name two—but Beckett is special in that he was equally a master in more than one field of literature—drama and the novel, in his case. I would go so far as to say he reinvented both forms. Certainly his great trio of novels (*Molloy*, *Malone Dies*, and *The Unnamable*) are of a stylistic and thematic achievement far greater than the work of many of Beckett's more popular fellow Nobel Prize winners. Did the novel seriously "end" with these three pieces of Beckett? Well, no, but avenues were certainly closed or—to be generous—blockaded.

And what about the play as a form; did Beckett close this down, too? No, but he made it harder to take seriously most of what passes for drama these days, and he gave those of us who try to make serious theatre a far harder task, forcing us to be pertinent and inventive in ways unlike those of the master, for it is always the case that the greatest writers, while they teach and embolden us, are singular in that while their influence is profound, imitation is laughable. As an example, Pinter and I have both learned much from Beckett—clarity, simplicity, precision, the use of language as sound, as music, if you like—but if one can say of a piece of ours, "Oh, that's just like Beckett," then we have failed. An imitation of Beckett is folly, for he wrote Beckett better than anyone did, or could.

I have directed Beckett frequently—*Happy Days*, *Krapp's Last Tape*, *Ohio Impromptu*, as examples—and the experience has taught me so much about both directing and writing. Beckett heard and saw his plays onstage as he wrote them, and his stage directions need be followed precisely, for the simple reason that they are exactly on target and approximation or departure from them leads to a lesser experience of the play. In general, the better the play, the least departure from the author's instructions is needed. In a lesser play the director and actors must be creative to compensate for the author's imprecisions. With Beckett, just assume that he knows what he's doing.

I am always deeply puzzled when people say of Beckett, "Oh, he's so difficult!"—or avant garde, or complex, or . . . ambiguous. It is the profoundest nonsense, for Beckett is perhaps the most naturalistic playwright I know of, as well as the clearest and least obscure. The "obscurity" resides in the assumption of obscurity. I know that if Beckett's outdoor plays were set on suburban terraces, and the indoor ones just inside those terraces, in suburban living rooms, everyone would be the wiser, certainly the less puzzled. We are most comfortable with the familiar.

While there isn't a play in this collection that any sane playwright would not be proud to have written, we all have our favorites. To my taste, Beckett kept getting better as he wrote and, while *Waiting for Godot* and *Endgame* are head and shoulders above most late-twentieth-century plays, I find them ultimately as his least successful ("Horrors! Albee is mad!"), for his craft was not fully under control yet. By *Krapp's Last Tape* and *Happy Days* it was, and with the later, short plays he reached an "essencing," a reduction to that needed least to accomplish the most, which renders these relatively brief works fuller than some of the earlier, larger ones.

Drama is literature—at its best at any rate; when it is less it is merely "writing"—and exists as completely on the page as it does on the stage. See and hear these plays as you read them. Read passages out loud for the music and the humanity.

What a wonderful book you have.

EDWARD ALBEE

WAITING FOR GODOT

Tragicomedy in 2 acts

Estragon
Vladimir
Lucky
Pozzo
a boy

ACT I

A country road. A tree.
Evening.

Estragon, sitting on a low mound, is trying to take off his boot. He pulls at it
with both hands, panting. He gives up, exhausted, rests, tries again. As before.
    Enter Vladimir.

ESTRAGON   [*giving up again*] Nothing to be done.

VLADIMIR   [*advancing with short, stiff strides, legs wide apart*] I'm beginning
                  to come round to that opinion. All my life I've tried to put it
                  from me, saying, Vladimir, be reasonable, you haven't yet tried
                  everything. And I resumed the struggle. [*He broods, musing*
                  on the struggle. Turning to Estragon.] So there you are again.

ESTRAGON   Am I?

VLADIMIR   I'm glad to see you back. I thought you were gone for ever.

ESTRAGON   Me too.

VLADIMIR   Together again at last! We'll have to celebrate this. But how?
                  [*He reflects.*] Get up till I embrace you.

ESTRAGON   [*irritably*] Not now, not now.

VLADIMIR   [*hurt, coldly*] May one enquire where His Highness spent the
                  night?

ESTRAGON   In a ditch.

VLADIMIR   [*admiringly*] A ditch! Where?

ESTRAGON   [without gesture] Over there.

VLADIMIR   And they didn't beat you?

ESTRAGON   Beat me? Certainly they beat me.

VLADIMIR   The same lot as usual?

ESTRAGON   The same? I don't know.

VLADIMIR   When I think of it . . . all these years . . . but for me . . . where would you be . . . [*Decisively.*] You'd be nothing more than a little heap of bones at the present minute, no doubt about it.

ESTRAGON   And what of it?

VLADIMIR   [*gloomily*] It's too much for one man. [*Pause. Cheerfully.*] On the other hand what's the good of losing heart now, that's what I say. We should have thought of it a million years ago, in the nineties.

ESTRAGON   Ah stop blathering and help me off with this bloody thing.

VLADIMIR   Hand in hand from the top of the Eiffel Tower, among the first. We were respectable in those days. Now it's too late. They wouldn't even let us up. [*Estragon tears at his boot.*] What are you doing?

ESTRAGON   Taking off my boot. Did that never happen to you?

VLADIMIR   Boots must be taken off every day, I'm tired telling you that. Why don't you listen to me?

ESTRAGON   [*feebly*] Help me!

VLADIMIR   It hurts?

ESTRAGON   [*angrily*] Hurts! He wants to know if it hurts!

VLADIMIR   [*angrily*] No one ever suffers but you. I don't count. I'd like to hear what you'd say if you had what I have.

ESTRAGON   It hurts?

VLADIMIR   [*angrily*] Hurts! He wants to know if it hurts!

ESTRAGON   [*pointing*] You might button it all the same.

VLADIMIR   [*stooping*] True. [*He buttons his fly.*] Never neglect the little things of life.

ESTRAGON   What do you expect, you always wait till the last moment.

VLADIMIR   [*musingly*] The last moment . . . [*He meditates.*] Hope deferred maketh the something sick, who said that?

ESTRAGON   Why don't you help me?

VLADIMIR   Sometimes I feel it coming all the same. Then I go all queer. [*He takes off his hat, peers inside it, feels about inside it, shakes it, puts it on again.*] How shall I say? Relieved and at the same time . . . [*he searches for the word*] . . . appalled. [*With emphasis.*] AP-PALLED. [*He takes off his hat again, peers inside it.*] Funny. [*He knocks on the crown as though to dislodge a foreign body, peers into it again, puts it on again.*] Nothing to be done. [*Estragon with a supreme effort succeeds in pulling off his boot. He peers inside it, feels about inside it, turns it upside down, shakes it, looks on the ground to see if anything has fallen out, finds nothing, feels inside it again, staring sightlessly before him.*] Well?

ESTRAGON   Nothing.

VLADIMIR   Show.

ESTRAGON   There's nothing to show.

VLADIMIR   Try and put it on again.

ESTRAGON   [*examining his foot*] I'll air it for a bit.

VLADIMIR   There's man all over for you, blaming on his boots the faults of his feet. [*He takes off his hat again, peers inside it, feels about inside it, knocks on the crown, blows into it, puts it on again.*] This is getting alarming. [*Silence. Vladimir deep in thought, Estragon pulling at his toes.*] One of the thieves was saved. [*Pause.*] It's a reasonable percentage. [*Pause.*] Gogo.

ESTRAGON   What?

VLADIMIR   Suppose we repented.

ESTRAGON   Repented what?

VLADIMIR   Oh . . . [*He reflects.*] We wouldn't have to go into the details.

ESTRAGON   Our being born?
            [*Vladimir breaks into a hearty laugh which he immediately stifles, his hand pressed to his pubis, his face contorted.*]

VLADIMIR   One daren't even laugh any more.

ESTRAGON   Dreadful privation.

VLADIMIR   Merely smile. [*He smiles suddenly from ear to ear, keeps smiling, ceases as suddenly.*] It's not the same thing. Nothing to be done. [*Pause.*] Gogo.

ESTRAGON   [*irritably*] What is it?

VLADIMIR   Did you ever read the Bible?

ESTRAGON   The Bible . . . [*He reflects.*] I must have taken a look at it.

VLADIMIR   Do you remember the Gospels?

ESTRAGON   I remember the maps of the Holy Land. Coloured they were. Very pretty. The Dead Sea was pale blue. The very look of it made me thirsty. That's where we'll go, I used to say, that's where we'll go for our honeymoon. We'll swim. We'll be happy.

VLADIMIR   You should have been a poet.

ESTRAGON   I was. [*Gesture towards his rags.*] Isn't that obvious? [*Silence.*]

VLADIMIR   Where was I . . . How's your foot?

ESTRAGON   Swelling visibly.

VLADIMIR   Ah yes, the two thieves. Do you remember the story?

ESTRAGON   No.

VLADIMIR   Shall I tell it to you?

ESTRAGON   No.

VLADIMIR   It'll pass the time. [*Pause.*] Two thieves, crucified at the same time as our Saviour. One—

ESTRAGON   Our what?

VLADIMIR   Our Saviour. Two thieves. One is supposed to have been saved and the other . . . [*He searches for the contrary of saved.*] . . . damned.

ESTRAGON   Saved from what?

VLADIMIR   Hell.

ESTRAGON   I'm going.
[*He does not move.*]

VLADIMIR   And yet . . . [*pause*] . . . how is it—this is not boring you I hope—how is it that of the four Evangelists only one speaks of a thief being saved. The four of them were there—or thereabouts—and only one speaks of a thief being saved. [*Pause.*] Come on, Gogo, return the ball, can't you, once in a way?

ESTRAGON   [*with exaggerated enthusiasm*] I find this really most extraordinarily interesting.

VLADIMIR   One out of four. Of the other three two don't mention any thieves at all and the third says that both of them abused him.

ESTRAGON   Who?

VLADIMIR   What?

ESTRAGON   What's all this about? Abused who?

VLADIMIR   The Saviour.

ESTRAGON   Why?

VLADIMIR   Because he wouldn't save them.

ESTRAGON   From hell?

VLADIMIR   Imbecile! From death.

ESTRAGON   I thought you said hell.

VLADIMIR   From death, from death.

ESTRAGON   Well what of it?

VLADIMIR   Then the two of them must have been damned.

ESTRAGON   And why not?

VLADIMIR   But one of the four says that one of the two was saved.

ESTRAGON   Well? They don't agree and that's all there is to it.

VLADIMIR   But all four were there. And only one speaks of a thief being saved. Why believe him rather than the others?

ESTRAGON   Who believes him?

VLADIMIR   Everybody. It's the only version they know.

ESTRAGON   People are bloody ignorant apes.
           [*He rises painfully, goes limping to extreme left, halts, gazes into distance off with his hand screening his eyes, turns, goes to extreme right, gazes into distance. Vladimir watches him, then goes and picks up the boot, peers into it, drops it hastily.*]

VLADIMIR   Pah!
           [*He spits. Estragon moves to center, halts with his back to auditorium.*]

ESTRAGON   Charming spot. [*He turns, advances to front, halts facing auditorium.*] Inspiring prospects. [*He turns to Vladimir.*] Let's go.

VLADIMIR   We can't.

ESTRAGON   Why not?

VLADIMIR   Were waiting for Godot.

ESTRAGON   [*despairingly*] Ah! [*Pause.*] You're sure it was here?

VLADIMIR   What?

ESTRAGON   That we were to wait.

VLADIMIR   He said by the tree. [*They look at the tree.*] Do you see any others.

ESTRAGON   What is it?

VLADIMIR   I don't know. A willow.

ESTRAGON   Where are the leaves?

VLADIMIR   It must be dead.

ESTRAGON   No more weeping.

VLADIMIR   Or perhaps it's not the season.

ESTRAGON   Looks to me more like a bush.

VLADIMIR   A shrub.

ESTRAGON   A bush.

VLADIMIR   A—. What are you insinuating? That we've come to the wrong place?

ESTRAGON   He should be here.

VLADIMIR   He didn't say for sure he'd come.

ESTRAGON   And if he doesn't come?

VLADIMIR   We'll come back tomorrow.

ESTRAGON   And then the day after tomorrow.

VLADIMIR   Possibly.

ESTRAGON   And so on.

VLADIMIR   The point is—

ESTRAGON   Until he comes.

VLADIMIR   You're merciless.

ESTRAGON   We came here yesterday.

VLADIMIR   Ah no, there you're mistaken.

ESTRAGON   What did we do yesterday?

VLADIMIR   What did we do yesterday?

ESTRAGON   Yes.

VLADIMIR   Why . . . [*Angrily.*] Nothing is certain when you're about.

ESTRAGON   In my opinion we were here.

VLADIMIR   [*looking round*] You recognize the place?

ESTRAGON   I didn't say that.

VLADIMIR   Well?

ESTRAGON   That makes no difference.

VLADIMIR   All the same . . . that tree . . . [*turning towards auditorium*] that bog . . .

ESTRAGON   You're sure it was this evening?

VLADIMIR   What?

ESTRAGON   That we were to wait.

VLADIMIR   He said Saturday. [*Pause.*] I think.

ESTRAGON   You think.

VLADIMIR   I must have made a note of it. [*He fumbles in his pockets, bursting with miscellaneous rubbish.*]

ESTRAGON   [*very insidious*] But what Saturday? And is it Saturday? Is it not rather Sunday? [*Pause.*] Or Monday? [*Pause.*] Or Friday?

VLADIMIR   [*looking wildly about him, as though the date was inscribed in the landscape*] It's not possible!

ESTRAGON   Or Thursday?

VLADIMIR   What'll we do?

ESTRAGON   If he came yesterday and we weren't here you may be sure he won't come again today.

VLADIMIR   But you say we were here yesterday.

ESTRAGON   I may be mistaken. [*Pause.*] Let's stop talking for a minute, do you mind?

VLADIMIR   [*feebly*] All right. [*Estragon sits down on the mound. Vladimir paces agitatedly to and fro, halting from time to time to gaze into distance off. Estragon falls asleep. Vladimir halts finally before Estragon.*] Gogo! . . . Gogo! . . . GOGO!
[*Estragon wakes with a start.*]

ESTRAGON   [*restored to the horror of his situation*] I was asleep! [*Despairingly.*]
            Why will you never let me sleep?

VLADIMIR   I felt lonely.

ESTRAGON   I had a dream.

VLADIMIR   Don't tell me!

ESTRAGON   I dreamt that—

VLADIMIR   DON'T TELL ME!

ESTRAGON   [*gesture towards the universe*] This one is enough for you?
            [*Silence.*] It's not nice of you, Didi. Who am I to tell my
            private nightmares to if I can't tell them to you?

VLADIMIR   Let them remain private. You know I can't bear that.

ESTRAGON   [*coldly*] There are times when I wonder if it wouldn't be better
            for us to part.

VLADIMIR   You wouldn't go far.

ESTRAGON   That would be too bad, really too bad. [*Pause.*] Wouldn't it,
            Didi, be really too bad? [*Pause.*] When you think of the
            beauty of the way. [*Pause.*] And the goodness of the
            wayfarers. [*Pause. Wheedling.*] Wouldn't it, Didi?

VLADIMIR   Calm yourself.

ESTRAGON   [*voluptuously*] Calm . . . calm . . . The English say cawm. [*Pause.*]
            You know the story of the Englishman in the brothel?

VLADIMIR   Yes.

ESTRAGON   Tell it to me.

VLADIMIR   Ah stop it!

ESTRAGON   An Englishman having drunk a little more than usual
            proceeds to a brothel. The bawd asks him if he wants a fair
            one, a dark one or a red-haired one. Go on.

VLADIMIR   STOP IT!
            [*Exit Vladimir hurriedly. Estragon gets up and follows him as far
            as the limit of the stage. Gestures of Estragon like those of a
            spectator encouraging a pugilist. Enter Vladimir. He brushes past
            Estragon, crosses the stage with bowed head. Estragon takes a step
            towards him, halts.*]

ESTRAGON   [*gently*] You wanted to speak to me? [*Silence. Estragon takes a step forward.*] You had something to say to me? [*Silence. Another step forward.*] Didi . . .

VLADIMIR [*without turning*] I've nothing to say to you.

ESTRAGON [*step forward*] You're angry? [*Silence. Step forward.*] Forgive me. [*Silence. Step forward. Estragon lays his hand on Vladimir's shoulder.*] Come, Didi. [*Silence.*] Give me your hand. [*Vladimir half turns.*] Embrace me! [*Vladimir stiffens.*] Don't be stubborn! [*Vladimir softens. They embrace. Estragon recoils.*] You stink of garlic!

VLADIMIR It's for the kidneys. [*Silence. Estragon looks attentively at the tree.*] What do we do now?

ESTRAGON Wait.

VLADIMIR Yes, but while waiting.

ESTRAGON What about hanging ourselves?

VLADIMIR Hmm. It'd give us an erection.

ESTRAGON [*highly excited*] An erection!

VLADIMIR With all that follows. Where it falls mandrakes grow. That's why they shriek when you pull them up. Did you not know that?

ESTRAGON Let's hang ourselves immediately!

VLADIMIR From a bough? [*They go towards the tree.*] I wouldn't trust it.

ESTRAGON We can always try.

VLADIMIR Go ahead.

ESTRAGON After you.

VLADIMIR No no, you first.

ESTRAGON Why me?

VLADIMIR You're lighter than I am.

ESTRAGON Just so!

VLADIMIR I don't understand.

ESTRAGON Use your intelligence, can't you?
[*Vladimir uses his intelligence.*]

VLADIMIR [*finally*] I remain in the dark.

ESTRAGON This is how it is. [*He reflects.*] The bough . . . the bough . . . [*Angrily.*] Use your head, can't you?

VLADIMIR You're my only hope.

ESTRAGON   [*with effort*] Gogo light—bough not break—Gogo dead. Didi heavy—bough break—Didi alone. Whereas—

VLADIMIR   I hadn't thought of that.

ESTRAGON   If it hangs you it'll hang anything.

VLADIMIR   But am I heavier than you?

ESTRAGON   So you tell me. I don't know. There's an even chance. Or nearly.

VLADIMIR   Well? What do we do?

ESTRAGON   Don't let's do anything. It's safer.

VLADIMIR   Let's wait and see what he says.

ESTRAGON   Who?

VLADIMIR   Godot.

ESTRAGON   Good idea.

VLADIMIR   Let's wait till we know exactly how we stand.

ESTRAGON   On the other hand it might be better to strike the iron before it freezes.

VLADIMIR   I'm curious to hear what he has to offer. Then we'll take it or leave it.

ESTRAGON   What exactly did we ask him for?

VLADIMIR   Were you not there?

ESTRAGON   I can't have been listening.

VLADIMIR   Oh . . . Nothing very definite.

ESTRAGON   A kind of prayer.

VLADIMIR   Precisely.

ESTRAGON   A vague supplication.

VLADIMIR   Exactly.

ESTRAGON   And what did he reply?

VLADIMIR   That he'd see.

ESTRAGON   That he couldn't promise anything.

VLADIMIR   That he'd have to think it over.

ESTRAGON   In the quiet of his home.

VLADIMIR   Consult his family.

ESTRAGON   His friends.

VLADIMIR   His agents.

ESTRAGON   His correspondents.

VLADIMIR	His books.
ESTRAGON	His bank account.
VLADIMIR	Before taking a decision.
ESTRAGON	It's the normal thing.
VLADIMIR	Is it not?
ESTRAGON	I think it is.
VLADIMIR	I think so too.
	[*Silence.*]
ESTRAGON	[*anxious*] And we?
VLADIMIR	I beg your pardon?
ESTRAGON	I said, And we?
VLADIMIR	I don't understand.
ESTRAGON	Where do we come in?
VLADIMIR	Come in?
ESTRAGON	Take your time.
VLADIMIR	Come in? On our hands and knees.
ESTRAGON	As bad as that?
VLADIMIR	Your Worship wishes to assert his prerogatives?
ESTRAGON	We've no rights any more?
	[*Laugh of Vladimir, stifled as before, less the smile.*]
VLADIMIR	You'd make me laugh if it wasn't prohibited.
ESTRAGON	We've lost our rights?
VLADIMIR	[*distinctly*] We got rid of them.
	[*Silence. They remain motionless, arms dangling, heads sunk, sagging at the knees.*]
ESTRAGON	[*feebly*] We're not tied? [*Pause.*] We're not—
VLADIMIR	Listen!
	[*They listen, grotesquely rigid.*]
ESTRAGON	I hear nothing.
VLADIMIR	Hsst! [*They listen. Estragon loses his balance, almost falls. He clutches the arm of Vladimir who totters. They listen, huddled together.*] Nor I.
	[*Sighs of relief. They relax and separate.*]
ESTRAGON	You gave me a fright.

VLADIMIR	I thought it was he.
ESTRAGON	Who?
VLADIMIR	Godot.
ESTRAGON	Pah! The wind in the reeds.
VLADIMIR	I could have sworn I heard shouts.
ESTRAGON	And why would he shout?
VLADIMIR	At his horse.
	[*Silence.*]
ESTRAGON	[*violently*] I'm hungry!
VLADIMIR	Do you want a carrot?
ESTRAGON	Is that all there is?
VLADIMIR	I might have some turnips.
ESTRAGON	Give me a carrot. [*Vladimir rummages in his pockets, takes out a turnip and gives it to Estragon who takes a bite out of it. Angrily.*] It's a turnip!
VLADIMIR	Oh pardon! I could have sworn it was a carrot. [*He rummages again in his pockets, finds nothing but turnips.*] All that's turnips. [*He rummages.*] You must have eaten the last. [*He rummages.*] Wait, I have it. [*He brings out a carrot and gives it to Estragon.*] There, dear fellow. [*Estragon wipes the carrot on his sleeve and begins to eat it.*] Make it last, that's the end of them.
ESTRAGON	[*chewing*] I asked you a question.
VLADIMIR	Ah.
ESTRAGON	Did you reply?
VLADIMIR	How's the carrot?
ESTRAGON	It's a carrot.
VLADIMIR	So much the better, so much the better. [*Pause.*] What was it you wanted to know?
ESTRAGON	I've forgotten. [*Chews.*] That's what annoys me. [*He looks at the carrot appreciatively, dangles it between finger and thumb.*] I'll never forget this carrot. [*He sucks the end of it meditatively.*] Ah yes, now I remember.
VLADIMIR	Well?

ESTRAGON   [*his mouth full, vacuously*] We're not tied?

VLADIMIR   I don't hear a word you're saying.

ESTRAGON   [*chews, swallows*] I'm asking you if we're tied.

VLADIMIR   Tied?

ESTRAGON   Ti-ed.

VLADIMIR   How do you mean tied?

ESTRAGON   Down.

VLADIMIR   But to whom? By whom?

ESTRAGON   To your man.

VLADIMIR   To Godot? Tied to Godot! What an idea! No question of it. [*Pause.*] For the moment.

ESTRAGON   His name is Godot?

VLADIMIR   I think so.

ESTRAGON   Fancy that. [*He raises what remains of the carrot by the stub of leaf, twirls it before his eyes.*] Funny, the more you eat the worse it gets.

VLADIMIR   With me it's just the opposite.

ESTRAGON   In other words?

VLADIMIR   I get used to the muck as I go along.

ESTRAGON   [*after prolonged reflection*] Is that the opposite?

VLADIMIR   Question of temperament.

ESTRAGON   Of character.

VLADIMIR   Nothing you can do about it.

ESTRAGON   No use struggling.

VLADIMIR   One is what one is.

ESTRAGON   No use wriggling.

VLADIMIR   The essential doesn't change.

ESTRAGON   Nothing to be done. [*He proffers the remains of the carrot to Vladimir.*] Like to finish it?
            [*A terrible cry, close at hand. Estragon drops the carrot. They remain motionless, then together make a sudden rush towards the wings. Estragon stops halfway, runs back, picks up the carrot, stuffs it in his pocket, runs to rejoin Vladimir who is waiting for him, stops again, runs back, picks up his boot, runs to rejoin*

Vladimir. Huddled together, shoulders hunched, cringing away from the menace, they wait.

Enter Pozzo and Lucky. Pozzo drives Lucky by means of a rope passed round his neck, so that Lucky is the first to enter, followed by the rope which is long enough to let him reach the middle of the stage before Pozzo appears. Lucky carries a heavy bag, a folding stool, a picnic basket and a greatcoat, Pozzo a whip.]

POZZO   [*off*] On! [*Crack of whip. Pozzo appears. They cross the stage. Lucky passes before Vladimir and Estragon and exit. Pozzo at the sight of Vladimir and Estragon stops short. The rope tautens. Pozzo jerks at it violently.*] Back!

[*Noise of Lucky falling with all his baggage. Vladimir and Estragon turn towards him, half wishing half fearing to go to his assistance. Vladimir takes a step towards Lucky, Estragon holds him back by the sleeve.*]

VLADIMIR   Let me go!

ESTRAGON   Stay where you are!

POZZO   Be careful! He's wicked. [*Vladimir and Estragon turn towards Pozzo.*] With strangers.

ESTRAGON   [*undertone*] Is that him?

VLADIMIR   Who?

ESTRAGON   [*trying to remember the name*] Er . . .

VLADIMIR   Godot?

ESTRAGON   Yes.

POZZO   I present myself: Pozzo.

VLADIMIR   [*to Estragon*] Not at all!

ESTRAGON   He said Godot.

VLADIMIR   Not at all!

ESTRAGON   [*timidly, to Pozzo*] You're not Mr. Godot, Sir?

POZZO   [*terrifying voice*] I am Pozzo! [*Silence.*] Pozzo! [*Silence.*] Does that name mean nothing to you? [*Silence.*] I say does that name mean nothing to you?

[*Vladimir and Estragon look at each other questioningly.*]

ESTRAGON   [*pretending to search*] Bozzo . . . Bozzo . . .

VLADIMIR	[*ditto*] Pozzo . . . Pozzo . . .
POZZO	PPPOZZZO!
ESTRAGON	Ah! Pozzo . . . let me see . . . Pozzo . . .
VLADIMIR	Is it Pozzo or Bozzo?
ESTRAGON	Pozzo . . . no . . . I'm afraid I . . . no . . . I don't seem to . . . [*Pozzo advances threateningly.*]
VLADIMIR	[*conciliating*] I once knew a family called Cozzo. The mother had the clap.
ESTRAGON	[*hastily*] We're not from these parts, Sir.
POZZO	[*halting*] You are human beings none the less. [*He puts on his glasses.*] As far as one can see. [*He takes off his glasses.*] Of the same species as myself. [*He bursts into an enormous laugh.*] Of the same species as Pozzo! Made in God's image!
VLADIMIR	Well you see—
POZZO	[*peremptory*] Who is Godot?
ESTRAGON	Godot?
POZZO	You took me for Godot.
VLADIMIR	Oh no, Sir, not for an instant, Sir.
POZZO	Who is he?
VLADIMIR	Oh he's a . . . he's a kind of acquaintance.
ESTRAGON	Nothing of the kind, we hardly know him.
VLADIMIR	True . . . we don't know him very well . . . but all the same . . .
ESTRAGON	Personally I wouldn't even know him if I saw him.
POZZO	You took me for him.
ESTRAGON	[*recoiling before Pozzo*] That's to say . . . you understand . . . the dusk . . . the strain . . . waiting . . . I confess . . . I imagined . . . for a second . . .
POZZO	Waiting? So you were waiting for him?
VLADIMIR	Well you see—
POZZO	Here? On my land?
VLADIMIR	We didn't intend any harm.
ESTRAGON	We meant well.
POZZO	The road is free to all.
VLADIMIR	That's how we looked at it.

POZZO   It's a disgrace. But there you are.

ESTRAGON   Nothing we can do about it.

POZZO   [*with magnanimous gesture*] Let's say no more about it. [*He jerks the rope.*] Up pig! [*Pause.*] Every time he drops he falls asleep. [*Jerks the rope.*] Up hog! [*Noise of Lucky getting up and picking up his baggage. Pozzo jerks the rope.*] Back! [*Enter Lucky backwards.*] Stop! [*Lucky stops.*] Turn! [*Lucky turns. To Vladimir and Estragon, affably.*] Gentlemen, I am happy to have met you. [*Before their incredulous expression.*] Yes yes, sincerely happy. [*He jerks the rope.*] Closer! [*Lucky advances.*] Stop! [*Lucky stops.*] Yes, the road seems long when one journeys all alone for . . . [*he consults his watch*] . . . yes . . . [*he calculates*] . . . yes, six hours, that's right, six hours on end, and never a soul in sight. [*To Lucky.*] Coat! [*Lucky puts down the bag, advances, gives the coat, goes back to his place, takes up the bag.*] Hold that! [*Pozzo holds out the whip. Lucky advances and, both his hands being occupied, takes the whip in his mouth, then goes back to his place. Pozzo begins to put on his coat, stops.*] Coat! [*Lucky puts down bag, basket and stool, advances, helps Pozzo on with his coat, goes back to his place and takes up bag, basket and stool.*] Touch of autumn in the air this evening. [*Pozzo finishes buttoning his coat, stoops, inspects himself, straightens up.*] Whip! [*Lucky advances, stoops, Pozzo snatches the whip from his mouth, Lucky goes back to his place.*] Yes, gentlemen, I cannot go for long without the society of my likes [*he puts on his glasses and looks at the two likes*] even when the likeness is an imperfect one. [*He takes off his glasses.*] Stool! [*Lucky puts down bag and basket, advances, opens stool, puts it down, goes back to his place, takes up bag and basket.*] Closer! [*Lucky puts down bag and basket, advances, moves stool, goes back to his place, takes up bag and basket. Pozzo sits down, places the butt of his whip against Lucky's chest and pushes.*] Back! [*Lucky takes a step back.*] Further! [*Lucky takes another step back.*] Stop! [*Lucky stops. To Vladimir and Estragon.*] That is why, with your

permission, I propose to dally with you a moment, before I
venture any further. Basket! [*Lucky advances, gives the basket,
goes back to his place.*] The fresh air stimulates the jaded
appetite. [*He opens the basket, takes out a piece of chicken and a
bottle of wine.*] Basket! [*Lucky advances, picks up the basket and
goes back to his place.*] Further! [*Lucky takes a step back.*] He
stinks. Happy days!

[*He drinks from the bottle, puts it down and begins to eat. Silence.
Vladimir and Estragon, cautiously at first, then more boldly, begin
to circle about Lucky, inspecting him up and down. Pozzo eats his
chicken voraciously, throwing away the bones after having sucked
them. Lucky sags slowly, until bag and basket touch the ground,
then straightens up with a start and begins to sag again. Rhythm
of one sleeping on his feet.*]

ESTRAGON What ails him?

VLADIMIR He looks tired.

ESTRAGON Why doesn't he put down his bags?

VLADIMIR How do I know? [*They close in on him.*] Careful!

ESTRAGON Say something to him.

VLADIMIR Look!

ESTRAGON What?

VLADIMIR [*pointing*] His neck!

ESTRAGON [*looking at the neck*] I see nothing.

VLADIMIR Here.

[*Estragon goes over beside Vladimir.*]

ESTRAGON Oh I say!

VLADIMIR A running sore!

ESTRAGON It's the rope.

VLADIMIR It's the rubbing.

ESTRAGON It's inevitable.

VLADIMIR It's the knot.

ESTRAGON It's the chafing.

[*They resume their inspection, dwell on the face.*]

VLADIMIR [*grudgingly*] He's not bad looking.

ESTRAGON   [*shrugging his shoulders, wry face*] Would you say so?

VLADIMIR   A trifle effeminate.

ESTRAGON   Look at the slobber.

VLADIMIR   It's inevitable.

ESTRAGON   Look at the slaver.

VLADIMIR   Perhaps he's a halfwit.

ESTRAGON   A cretin.

VLADIMIR   [*looking closer*] Looks like a goiter.

ESTRAGON   [*ditto*] It's not certain.

VLADIMIR   He's panting.

ESTRAGON   It's inevitable.

VLADIMIR   And his eyes!

ESTRAGON   What about them?

VLADIMIR   Goggling out of his head.

ESTRAGON   Looks at his last gasp to me.

VLADIMIR   It's not certain. [*Pause.*] Ask him a question.

ESTRAGON   Would that be a good thing?

VLADIMIR   What do we risk?

ESTRAGON   [*timidly*] Mister . . .

VLADIMIR   Louder.

ESTRAGON   [*louder*] Mister . . .

POZZO   Leave him in peace! [*They turn towards Pozzo who, having finished eating, wipes his mouth with the back of his hand.*] Can't you see he wants to rest? Basket! [*He strikes a match and begins to light his pipe. Estragon sees the chicken bones on the ground and stares at them greedily. As Lucky does not move Pozzo throws the match angrily away and jerks the rope.*] Basket! [*Lucky starts, almost falls, recovers his senses, advances, puts the bottle in the basket and goes back to his place. Estragon stares at the bones. Pozzo strikes another match and lights his pipe.*] What can you expect, it's not his job. [*He pulls at his pipe, stretches out his legs.*] Ah! That's better.

ESTRAGON   [*timidly*] Please Sir . . .

POZZO   What is it, my good man?

ESTRAGON Er ... you've finished with the ... er ... you don't need the ...
          er ... bones, Sir?

VLADIMIR [*scandalized*] You couldn't have waited?

POZZO   No no, he does well to ask. Do I need the bones? [*He turns
          them over with the end of his whip.*] No, personally I do not
          need them any more. [*Estragon takes a step towards the bones.*]
          But ... [*Estragon stops short*] ... but in theory the bones go to
          the carrier. He is therefore the one to ask. [*Estragon turns
          towards Lucky, hesitates.*] Go on, go on, don't be afraid, ask
          him, he'll tell you.
          [*Estragon goes towards Lucky, stops before him.*]

ESTRAGON Mister ... excuse me, Mister ...

POZZO   You're being spoken to, pig! Reply! [*To Estragon.*] Try him
          again.

ESTRAGON Excuse me, Mister, the bones, you won't be wanting the bones?
          [*Lucky looks long at Estragon.*]

POZZO   [*in raptures*] Mister! [*Lucky bows his head.*] Reply! Do you want
          them or don't you? [*Silence of Lucky. To Estragon.*] They're
          yours. [*Estragon makes a dart at the bones, picks them up and
          begins to gnaw them.*] I don't like it. I've never known him
          refuse a bone before. [*He looks anxiously at Lucky.*] Nice
          business it'd be if he fell sick on me! [*He puffs at his pipe.*]

VLADIMIR [*exploding*] It's a scandal!
          [*Silence. Flabbergasted, Estragon stops gnawing, looks at Pozzo
          and Vladimir in turn. Pozzo outwardly calm. Vladimir
          embarrassed.*]

POZZO   [*to Vladimir*] Are you alluding to anything in particular?

VLADIMIR [*stutteringly resolute*] To treat a man ... [*gesture towards
          Lucky*] ... like that ... I think that ... no ... a human
          being ... no ... it's a scandal!

ESTRAGON [*not to be outdone*] A disgrace! [*He resumes his gnawing.*]

POZZO   You are severe. [*To Vladimir.*] What age are you, if it's not a
          rude question? [*Silence.*] Sixty? Seventy? [*To Estragon.*] What
          age would you say he was?

ESTRAGON   Eleven.

POZZO   I am impertinent. [*He knocks out his pipe against the whip, gets up.*] I must be getting on. Thank you for your society. [*He reflects.*] Unless I smoke another pipe before I go. What do you say? [*They say nothing.*] Oh I'm only a small smoker, a very small smoker, I'm not in the habit of smoking two pipes one on top of the other, it makes [*hand to heart, sighing*] my heart go pit-a-pat. [*Silence.*] It's the nicotine, one absorbs it in spite of one's precautions. [*Sighs.*] You know how it is. [*Silence.*] But perhaps you don't smoke? Yes? No? It's of no importance. [*Silence.*] But how am I to sit down now, without affectation, now that I have risen? Without appearing to—how shall I say—without appearing to falter. [*To Vladimir.*] I beg your pardon? [*Silence.*] Perhaps you didn't speak? [*Silence.*] It's of no importance. Let me see . . . [*He reflects.*]

ESTRAGON   Ah! That's better. [*He puts the bones in his pocket.*]

VLADIMIR   Let's go.

ESTRAGON   So soon?

POZZO   One moment! [*He jerks the rope.*] Stool! [*He points with his whip. Lucky moves the stool.*] More! There! [*He sits down. Lucky goes back to his place.*] Done it! [*He fills his pipe.*]

VLADIMIR   [*vehemently*] Let's go!

POZZO   I hope I'm not driving you away. Wait a little longer, you'll never regret it.

ESTRAGON   [*scenting charity*] We're in no hurry.

POZZO   [*having lit his pipe*] The second is never so sweet . . . [*he takes the pipe out of his mouth, contemplates it*] . . . as the first I mean. [*He puts the pipe back in his mouth.*] But it's sweet just the same.

VLADIMIR   I'm going.

POZZO   He can no longer endure my presence. I am perhaps not particularly human, but who cares? [*To Vladimir.*] Think twice before you do anything rash. Suppose you go now while it is still day, for there is no denying it is still day.

[*They all look up at the sky.*] Good. [*They stop looking at the sky.*] What happens in that case—[*he takes the pipe out of his mouth, examines it*]—I'm out—[*he relights his pipe*]—in that case—[*puff*]—in that case—[*puff*]—what happens in that case to your appointment with this . . . Godet . . . Godot . . . Godin . . . anyhow you see who I mean, who has your future in his hands . . . [*pause*] . . . at least your immediate future?

VLADIMIR Who told you?

POZZO He speaks to me again! If this goes on much longer we'll soon be old friends.

ESTRAGON Why doesn't he put down his bags?

POZZO I too would be happy to meet him. The more people I meet the happier I become. From the meanest creature one departs wiser, richer, more conscious of one's blessings. Even you . . . [*he looks at them ostentatiously in turn to make it clear they are both meant*] . . . even you, who knows, will have added to my store.

ESTRAGON Why doesn't he put down his bags?

POZZO But that would surprise me.

VLADIMIR You're being asked a question.

POZZO [*delighted*] A question! Who? What? A moment ago you were calling me Sir, in fear and trembling. Now you're asking me questions. No good will come of this!

VLADIMIR [*to Estragon*] I think he's listening.

ESTRAGON [*circling about Lucky*] What?

VLADIMIR You can ask him now. He's on the alert.

ESTRAGON Ask him what?

VLADIMIR Why he doesn't put down his bags.

ESTRAGON I wonder.

VLADIMIR Ask him, can't you?

POZZO [*who has followed these exchanges with anxious attention, fearing lest the question get lost*] You want to know why he doesn't put down his bags, as you call them.

VLADIMIR	That's it.
POZZO	[*to Estragon*] You are sure you agree with that?
ESTRAGON	He's puffing like a grampus.
POZZO	The answer is this. [*To Estragon.*] But stay still, I beg of you, you're making me nervous!
VLADIMIR	Here.
ESTRAGON	What is it?
VLADIMIR	He's about to speak.
	[*Estragon goes over beside Vladimir. Motionless, side by side, they wait.*]
POZZO	Good. Is everybody ready? Is everybody looking at me? [*He looks at Lucky, jerks the rope. Lucky raises his head.*] Will you look at me, pig! [*Lucky looks at him.*] Good. [*He puts the pipe in his pocket, takes out a little vaporizer and sprays his throat, puts back the vaporizer in his pocket, clears his throat, spits, takes out the vaporizer again, sprays his throat again, puts back the vaporizer in his pocket.*] I am ready. Is everybody listening? Is everybody ready? [*He looks at them all in turn, jerks the rope.*] Hog! [*Lucky raises his head.*] I don't like talking in a vacuum. Good. Let me see. [*He reflects.*]
ESTRAGON	I'm going.
POZZO	What was it exactly you wanted to know?
VLADIMIR	Why he—
POZZO	[*angrily*] Don't interrupt me! [*Pause. Calmer.*] If we all speak at once we'll never get anywhere. [*Pause.*] What was I saying? [*Pause. Louder.*] What was I saying?
	[*Vladimir mimics one carrying a heavy burden. Pozzo looks at him, puzzled.*]
ESTRAGON	[*forcibly*] Bags. [*He points at Lucky.*] Why? Always hold. [*He sags, panting.*] Never put down. [*He opens his hands, straightens up with relief.*] Why?
POZZO	Ah! Why couldn't you say so before? Why he doesn't make himself comfortable? Let's try and get this clear. Has he not the right to? Certainly he has. It follows that he doesn't

want to. There's reasoning for you. And why doesn't he want to? [*Pause.*] Gentlemen, the reason is this.

VLADIMIR [*to Estragon*] Make a note of this.

POZZO He wants to impress me, so that I'll keep him.

ESTRAGON What?

POZZO Perhaps I haven't got it quite right. He wants to mollify me, so that I'll give up the idea of parting with him. No, that's not exactly it either.

VLADIMIR You want to get rid of him?

POZZO He wants to cod me, but he won't.

VLADIMIR You want to get rid of him?

POZZO He imagines that when I see how well he carries I'll be tempted to keep him on in that capacity.

ESTRAGON You've had enough of him?

POZZO In reality he carries like a pig. It's not his job.

VLADIMIR You want to get rid of him?

POZZO He imagines that when I see him indefatigable I'll regret my decision. Such is his miserable scheme. As though I were short of slaves! [*All three look at Lucky.*] Atlas, son of Jupiter! [*Silence.*] Well, that's that I think. Anything else? [*Vaporizer.*]

VLADIMIR You want to get rid of him?

POZZO Remark that I might just as well have been in his shoes and he in mine. If chance had not willed otherwise. To each one his due.

VLADIMIR You waagerrim?

POZZO I beg your pardon?

VLADIMIR You want to get rid of him?

POZZO I do. But instead of driving him away as I might have done, I mean instead of simply kicking him out on his arse, in the goodness of my heart I am bringing him to the fair, where I hope to get a good price for him. The truth is you can't drive such creatures away. The best thing would be to kill them. [*Lucky weeps.*]

ESTRAGON He's crying!

POZZO Old dogs have more dignity. [*He proffers his handkerchief to Estragon.*] Comfort him, since you pity him. [*Estragon hesitates.*] Come on. [*Estragon takes the handkerchief.*] Wipe away his tears, he'll feel less forsaken.
[*Estragon hesitates.*]

VLADIMIR Here, give it to me, I'll do it.
[*Estragon refuses to give the handkerchief. Childish gestures.*]

POZZO Make haste, before he stops. [*Estragon approaches Lucky and makes to wipe his eyes. Lucky kicks him violently in the shins. Estragon drops the handkerchief, recoils, staggers about the stage howling with pain.*] Hanky!
[*Lucky puts down bag and basket, picks up handkerchief and gives it to Pozzo, goes back to his place, picks up bag and basket.*]

ESTRAGON Oh the swine! [*He pulls up the leg of his trousers.*] He's crippled me!

POZZO I told you he didn't like strangers.

VLADIMIR [*to Estragon*] Show. [*Estragon shows his leg. To Pozzo, angrily.*] He's bleeding!

POZZO It's a good sign.

ESTRAGON [*on one leg*] I'll never walk again!

VLADIMIR [*tenderly*] I'll carry you. [*Pause.*] If necessary.

POZZO He's stopped crying. [*To Estragon.*] You have replaced him as it were. [*Lyrically.*] The tears of the world are a constant quantity. For each one who begins to weep somewhere else another stops. The same is true of the laugh. [*He laughs.*] Let us not then speak ill of our generation, it is not any unhappier than its predecessors. [*Pause.*] Let us not speak well of it either. [*Pause.*] Let us not speak of it at all. [*Pause. Judiciously.*] It is true the population has increased.

VLADIMIR Try and walk.
[*Estragon takes a few limping steps, stops before Lucky and spits on him, then goes and sits down on the mound.*]

POZZO Guess who taught me all these beautiful things. [*Pause. Pointing to Lucky.*] My Lucky!

VLADIMIR   [*looking at the sky*] Will night never come?

POZZO   But for him all my thoughts, all my feelings, would have been of common things. [*Pause. With extraordinary vehemence.*] Professional worries! [*Calmer.*] Beauty, grace, truth of the first water, I knew they were all beyond me. So I took a knook.

VLADIMIR   [*startled from his inspection of the sky*] A knook?

POZZO   That was nearly sixty years ago ... [*he consults his watch*] ... yes, nearly sixty. [*Drawing himself up proudly.*] You wouldn't think it to look at me, would you? Compared to him I look like a young man, no? [*Pause.*] Hat! [*Lucky puts down the basket and takes off his hat. His long white hair falls about his face. He puts his hat under his arm and picks up the basket.*] Now look. [*Pozzo takes off his hat.*[1] *He is completely bald. He puts on his hat again.*] Did you see?

VLADIMIR   And now you turn him away? Such an old and faithful servant!

ESTRAGON   Swine!

[*Pozzo more and more agitated.*]

VLADIMIR   After having sucked all the good out of him you chuck him away like a ... like a banana skin. Really ...

POZZO   [*groaning, clutching his head*] I can't bear it ... any longer ... the way he goes on ... you've no idea ... it's terrible ... he must go ... [*he waves his arms*] ... I'm going mad ... [*he collapses, his head in his hands*] ... I can't bear it ... any longer ...

[*Silence. All look at Pozzo.*]

VLADIMIR   He can't bear it.

ESTRAGON   Any longer.

VLADIMIR   He's going mad.

ESTRAGON   It's terrible.

VLADIMIR   [*to Lucky*] How dare you! It's abominable! Such a good master! Crucify him like that! After so many years! Really!

POZZO   [*sobbing*] He used to be so kind ... so helpful ... and

---

1. All four wear bowlers.

entertaining ... my good angel ... and now ... he's killing me.

ESTRAGON [*to Vladimir*] Does he want to replace him?

VLADIMIR What?

ESTRAGON Does he want someone to take his place or not?

VLADIMIR I don't think so.

ESTRAGON What?

VLADIMIR I don't know.

ESTRAGON Ask him.

POZZO [*calmer*] Gentlemen, I don't know what came over me. Forgive me. Forget all I said. [*More and more his old self.*] I don't remember exactly what it was, but you may be sure there wasn't a word of truth in it. [*Drawing himself up, striking his chest.*] Do I look like a man that can be made to suffer? Frankly? [*He rummages in his pockets.*] What have I done with my pipe?

VLADIMIR Charming evening we're having.

ESTRAGON Unforgettable.

VLADIMIR And it's not over.

ESTRAGON Apparently not.

VLADIMIR It's only beginning.

ESTRAGON It's awful.

VLADIMIR Worse than the pantomime.

ESTRAGON The circus.

VLADIMIR The music-hall.

ESTRAGON The circus.

POZZO What can I have done with that briar?

ESTRAGON He's a scream. He's lost his dudeen. [*Laughs noisily.*]

VLADIMIR I'll be back. [*He hastens towards the wings.*]

ESTRAGON End of the corridor, on the left.

VLADIMIR Keep my seat. [*Exit Vladimir.*]

POZZO [*on the point of tears*] I've lost my Kapp and Peterson!

ESTRAGON [*convulsed with merriment*] He'll be the death of me!

POZZO You didn't see by any chance—. [*He misses Vladimir.*] Oh! He's gone! Without saying goodbye! How could he! He might have waited!

ESTRAGON   He would have burst.

POZZO   Oh! [*Pause.*] Oh well then of course in that case ...

ESTRAGON   Come here.

POZZO   What for?

ESTRAGON   You'll see.

POZZO   You want me to get up?

ESTRAGON   Quick! [*Pozzo gets up and goes over beside Estragon. Estragon points off.*] Look!

POZZO   [*having put on his glasses*] Oh I say!

ESTRAGON   It's all over.

[*Enter Vladimir, somber. He shoulders Lucky out of his way, kicks over the stool, comes and goes agitatedly.*]

POZZO   He's not pleased.

ESTRAGON   [*to Vladimir*] You missed a treat. Pity.

[*Vladimir halts, straightens the stool, comes and goes, calmer.*]

POZZO   He subsides. [*Looking round.*] Indeed all subsides. A great calm descends. [*Raising his hand.*] Listen! Pan sleeps.

VLADIMIR   Will night never come?

[*All three look at the sky.*]

POZZO   You don't feel like going until it does?

ESTRAGON   Well you see—

POZZO   Why it's very natural, very natural. I myself in your situation, if I had an appointment with a Godin ... Godet ... Godot ... anyhow you see who I mean, I'd wait till it was black night before I gave up. [*He looks at the stool.*] I'd very much like to sit down, but I don't quite know how to go about it.

ESTRAGON   Could I be of any help?

POZZO   If you asked me perhaps.

ESTRAGON   What?

POZZO   If you asked me to sit down.

ESTRAGON   Would that be a help?

POZZO   I fancy so.

ESTRAGON   Here we go. Be seated, Sir, I beg of you.

POZZO   No no, I wouldn't think of it! [*Pause. Aside.*] Ask me again.

ESTRAGON   Come come, take a seat I beseech you, you'll get pneumonia.

POZZO   You really think so?

ESTRAGON   Why it's absolutely certain.

POZZO   No doubt you are right. [*He sits down.*] Done it again! [*Pause.*] Thank you, dear fellow. [*He consults his watch.*] But I must really be getting along, if I am to observe my schedule.

VLADIMIR   Time has stopped.

POZZO   [*cuddling his watch to his ear*] Don't you believe it, Sir, don't you believe it. [*He puts his watch back in his pocket.*] Whatever you like, but not that.

ESTRAGON   [*to Pozzo*] Everything seems black to him today.

POZZO   Except the firmament. [*He laughs, pleased with this witticism.*] But I see what it is, you are not from these parts, you don't know what our twilights can do. Shall I tell you? [*Silence. Estragon is fiddling with his boot again, Vladimir with his hat.*] I can't refuse you. [*Vaporizer.*] A little attention, if you please. [*Vladimir and Estragon continue their fiddling, Lucky is half asleep. Pozzo cracks his whip feebly.*] What's the matter with this whip? [*He gets up and cracks it more vigorously, finally with success. Lucky jumps. Vladimir's hat, Estragon's boot, Lucky's hat, fall to the ground. Pozzo throws down the whip.*] Worn out, this whip. [*He looks at Vladimir and Estragon.*] What was I saying?

VLADIMIR   Let's go.

ESTRAGON   But take the weight off your feet, I implore you, you'll catch your death.

POZZO   True. [*He sits down. To Estragon.*] What is your name?

ESTRAGON   Adam.

POZZO   [*who hasn't listened*] Ah yes! The night. [*He raises his head.*] But be a little more attentive, for pity's sake, otherwise we'll never get anywhere. [*He looks at the sky.*] Look! [*All look at the sky except Lucky who is dozing off again. Pozzo jerks the rope.*] Will you look at the sky, pig! [*Lucky looks at the sky.*] Good, that's enough. [*They stop looking at the sky.*] What is there so extraordinary about it? Qua sky. It is pale and luminous like any sky at this hour of the day. [*Pause.*] In these latitudes. [*Pause.*] When the weather is fine. [*Lyrical.*] An hour ago [*he looks at his watch, prosaic*] roughly [*lyrical*] after having poured forth even since [*he hesitates, prosaic*] say ten o'clock in the morning [*lyrical*] tirelessly torrents of red and white light it begins to lose its effulgence, to grow pale [*gesture of the two hands lapsing by stages*] pale, ever a little paler, a little paler until [*dramatic pause, ample gesture of the two hands flung wide apart*] pppfff! finished! it comes to rest. But—[*hand raised in admonition*]—but behind this veil of gentleness and peace night is charging [*vibrantly*] and will burst upon us [*snaps his fingers*] pop! like that! [*his inspiration leaves him*] just when we least expect it. [*Silence. Gloomily.*] That's how it is on this bitch of an earth.

[*Long silence.*]

ESTRAGON   So long as one knows.

VLADIMIR   One can bide one's time.

ESTRAGON   One knows what to expect.

VLADIMIR   No further need to worry.

ESTRAGON   Simply wait.

VLADIMIR   We're used to it. [*He picks up his hat, peers inside it, shakes it, puts it on.*]

POZZO   How did you find me? [*Vladimir and Estragon look at him blankly.*] Good? Fair? Middling? Poor? Positively bad?

VLADIMIR   [*first to understand*] Oh very good, very very good.

POZZO   [*to Estragon*] And you, Sir?

ESTRAGON   Oh tray bong, tray tray tray bong.

POZZO   [*fervently*] Bless you, gentlemen, bless you! [*Pause.*] I have such need of encouragement! [*Pause.*] I weakened a little towards the end, you didn't notice?

VLADIMIR   Oh perhaps just a teeny weeny little bit.

ESTRAGON   I thought it was intentional.

POZZO   You see my memory is defective.

          [*Silence.*]

ESTRAGON In the meantime nothing happens.

POZZO   You find it tedious?

ESTRAGON Somewhat.

POZZO   [*to Vladimir*] And you, Sir?

VLADIMIR I've been better entertained.

          [*Silence. Pozzo struggles inwardly.*]

POZZO   Gentlemen, you have been . . . civil to me.

ESTRAGON Not at all!

VLADIMIR What an idea!

POZZO   Yes yes, you have been correct. So that I ask myself is there anything I can do in my turn for these honest fellows who are having such a dull, dull time.

ESTRAGON Even ten francs would be a help.

VLADIMIR We are not beggars!

POZZO   Is there anything I can do, that's what I ask myself, to cheer them up? I have given them bones, I have talked to them about this and that, I have explained the twilight, admittedly. But is it enough, that's what tortures me, is it enough?

ESTRAGON Even five.

VLADIMIR [*to Estragon, indignantly*] That's enough!

ESTRAGON I couldn't accept less.

POZZO   Is it enough? No doubt. But I am liberal. It's my nature. This evening. So much the worse for me. [*He jerks the rope. Lucky looks at him.*] For I shall suffer, no doubt about that. [*He picks up the whip.*] What do you prefer? Shall we have him dance, or sing, or recite, or think, or—

ESTRAGON Who?

POZZO   Who! You know how to think, you two?

VLADIMIR He thinks?

POZZO   Certainly. Aloud. He even used to think very prettily once, I could listen to him for hours. Now . . . [*He shudders.*] So

much the worse for me. Well, would you like him to think
something for us?

ESTRAGON I'd rather he'd dance, it'd be more fun.

POZZO Not necessarily.

ESTRAGON Wouldn't it, Didi, be more fun?

VLADIMIR I'd like well to hear him think.

ESTRAGON Perhaps he could dance first and think afterwards, if it isn't
too much to ask him.

VLADIMIR [to Pozzo] Would that be possible?

POZZO By all means, nothing simpler. It's the natural order. [He
laughs briefly.]

VLADIMIR Then let him dance.
[Silence.]

POZZO Do you hear, hog?

ESTRAGON He never refuses?

POZZO He refused once. [Silence.] Dance, misery!
[Lucky puts down bag and basket, advances towards front, turns
to Pozzo. Lucky dances. He stops.]

ESTRAGON Is that all?

POZZO Encore!
[Lucky executes the same movements, stops.]

ESTRAGON Pooh! I'd do as well myself. [He imitates Lucky, almost falls.]
With a little practice.

POZZO He used to dance the farandole, the fling, the brawl, the jig,
the fandango and even the hornpipe. He capered. For joy.
Now that's the best he can do. Do you know what he calls it?

ESTRAGON The Scapegoat's Agony.

VLADIMIR The Hard Stool.

POZZO The Net. He thinks he's entangled in a net.

VLADIMIR [squirming like an aesthete] There's something about it . . .
[Lucky makes to return to his burdens.]

POZZO Woaa!
[Lucky stiffens.]

ESTRAGON Tell us about the time he refused.

POZZO With pleasure, with pleasure. [*He fumbles in his pockets.*] Wait. [*He fumbles.*] What have I done with my spray? [*He fumbles.*] Well now isn't that . . . [*He looks up, consternation on his features. Faintly.*] I can't find my pulverizer!

ESTRAGON [*faintly*] My left lung is very weak! [*He coughs feebly. In ringing tones.*] But my right lung is as sound as a bell!

POZZO [*normal voice*] No matter! What was I saying. [*He ponders.*] Wait. [*Ponders.*] Well now isn't that . . . [*He raises his head.*] Help me!

ESTRAGON Wait!

VLADIMIR Wait!

POZZO Wait!

[*All three take off their hats simultaneously, press their hands to their foreheads, concentrate.*]

ESTRAGON [*triumphantly*] Ah!

VLADIMIR He has it.

POZZO [*impatient*] Well?

ESTRAGON Why doesn't he put down his bags?

VLADIMIR Rubbish!

POZZO Are you sure?

VLADIMIR Damn it haven't you already told us?

POZZO I've already told you?

ESTRAGON He's already told us?

VLADIMIR Anyway he has put them down.

ESTRAGON [*glance at Lucky*] So he has. And what of it?

VLADIMIR Since he has put down his bags it is impossible we should have asked why he does not do so.

POZZO Stoutly reasoned!

ESTRAGON And why has he put them down?

POZZO Answer us that.

VLADIMIR In order to dance.

ESTRAGON True!

POZZO True!

[*Silence. They put on their hats.*]

ESTRAGON Nothing happens, nobody comes, nobody goes, it's awful!

VLADIMIR   [*to Pozzo*] Tell him to think.

POZZO   Give him his hat.

VLADIMIR   His hat?

POZZO   He can't think without his hat.

VLADIMIR   [*to Estragon*] Give him his hat.

ESTRAGON   Me! After what he did to me! Never!

VLADIMIR   I'll give it to him. [*He does not move.*]

ESTRAGON   [*to Pozzo*] Tell him to go and fetch it.

POZZO   It's better to give it to him.

VLADIMIR   I'll give it to him.
[*He picks up the hat and tenders it at arm's length to Lucky, who does not move.*]

POZZO   You must put it on his head.

ESTRAGON   [*to Pozzo*] Tell him to take it.

POZZO   It's better to put it on his head.

VLADIMIR   I'll put it on his head.
[*He goes round behind Lucky, approaches him cautiously, puts the hat on his head and recoils smartly. Lucky does not move. Silence.*]

ESTRAGON   What's he waiting for?

POZZO   Stand back! [*Vladimir and Estragon move away from Lucky. Pozzo jerks the rope. Lucky looks at Pozzo.*] Think, pig! [*Pause. Lucky begins to dance.*] Stop! [*Lucky stops.*] Forward! [*Lucky advances.*] Stop! [*Lucky stops.*] Think!
[*Silence.*]

LUCKY   On the other hand with regard to—

POZZO   Stop! [*Lucky stops.*] Back! [*Lucky moves back.*] Stop! [*Lucky stops.*] Turn! [*Lucky turns towards auditorium.*] Think!

LUCKY   Given the existence as uttered forth in the public works of Puncher and Wattmann of a personal God quaquaquaqua with white beard quaquaquaqua outside time without extension who from the heights of divine apathia divine athambia divine aphasia loves us dearly with some exceptions for reasons unknown but time will tell and

[*Vladimir* *and* *Estragon* *all* *attention,* *Pozzo* *dejected* *and* *disgusted.*] suffers like the divine Miranda with those who for reasons unknown but time will tell are plunged in torment plunged in fire whose fire flames if that continues and who can doubt it will fire the firmament that is to say blast hell to heaven so blue still and calm so calm with a calm which even though intermittent is better than nothing but not so fast and considering what is more that as a result of the labors left unfinished crowned by the Acacacacademy of Anthropopopometry of Essy-in-Possy of Testew and Cunard it is established beyond all doubt all other doubt [*Vladimir* *and* *Estragon* *begin to* *protest,* *Pozzo's* *sufferings* *increase.*] than that which clings to the labors of men that as a result of the labors unfinished of Testew and Cunard it is established as hereinafter but not so fast for reasons unknown that as a result of the public works of Puncher and Wattmann it is established beyond all doubt that in view of the labors of Fartov and Belcher left unfinished for reasons unknown of Testew and Cunard left unfinished it is established what many deny that man in Possy of Testew and Cunard that man in Essy that man in short that man in [*Vladimir* *and* *Estragon* *attentive* *again,* *Pozzo* *more and* *more* *agitated* *and* *groaning.*] brief in spite of the strides of alimentation and defecation wastes and pines wastes and pines and concurrently simultaneously what is more for reasons unknown in spite of the strides of physical culture the practice of sports such as tennis football running cycling swimming flying floating riding gliding conating camogie skating tennis of all kinds dying flying sports of all sorts autumn summer winter winter tennis of all kinds hockey of all sorts penicillin and succedanea in a word I resume flying gliding golf over nine and eighteen holes tennis of all sorts in a word for reasons unknown in Feckham Peckham Fulham Clapham namely concurrently simultaneously what is more for reasons unknown but time will tell fades away I resume Fulham Clapham in a word the dead loss per head since the death of Bishop Berkeley being to the tune of one inch four

[*Vladimir and Estragon protest violently. Pozzo jumps up, pulls on the rope. General outcry. Lucky pulls on the rope, staggers, shouts his text. All three throw themselves on Lucky who struggles and shouts his text.*] ounce per head approximately by and large more or less to the nearest decimal good measure round figures stark naked in the stockinged feet in Connemara in a word for reasons unknown no matter what matter the facts are there and considering what is more much more grave that in the light of the labors lost of Steinweg and Peterman it appears what is more much more grave that in the light the light the light of the labors lost of Steinweg and Peterman that in the plains in the mountains by the seas by the rivers running water running fire the air is the same and then the earth namely the air and then the earth in the great cold the great dark the air and the earth abode of stones in the great cold alas alas in the year of their Lord six hundred and something the air the earth the sea the earth abode of stones in the great deeps the great cold on sea on land and in the air I resume for reasons unknown in spite of the tennis the facts are there but time will tell I resume alas alas on on in short in fine on on abode of stones who can doubt it I resume but not so fast I resume the skull fading fading fading and concurrently simultaneously what is more for reasons unknown in spite of the tennis on on the beard the flames the tears the stones so blue so calm alas alas on on the skull the skull the skull the skull in Connemara in spite of the tennis the labors abandoned left unfinished graver still abode of stones in a word I resume alas alas abandoned unfinished the skull the skull in Connemara in spite of the tennis the skull alas the stones Cunard [*mêlée, final vociferations*] tennis . . . the stones . . . so calm . . . Cunard . . . unfinished . . .

POZZO His hat!

[*Vladimir seizes Lucky's hat. Silence of Lucky. He falls. Silence. Panting of the victors.*]

ESTRAGON Avenged!

[*Vladimir examines the hat, peers inside it.*]

POZZO   Give me that! [*He snatches the hat from Vladimir, throws it on the ground, tramples on it.*] There's an end to his thinking!

VLADIMIR   But will he be able to walk?

POZZO   Walk or crawl! [*He kicks Lucky.*] Up pig!

ESTRAGON   Perhaps he's dead.

VLADIMIR   You'll kill him.

POZZO   Up scum! [*He jerks the rope.*] Help me!

VLADIMIR   How?

POZZO   Raise him up!

[*Vladimir and Estragon hoist Lucky to his feet, support him an instant, then let him go. He falls.*]

ESTRAGON   He's doing it on purpose!

POZZO   You must hold him. [*Pause.*] Come on, come on, raise him up.

ESTRAGON   To hell with him!

VLADIMIR   Come on, once more.

ESTRAGON   What does he take us for?

[*They raise Lucky, hold him up.*]

POZZO   Don't let him go! [*Vladimir and Estragon totter.*] Don't move! [*Pozzo fetches bag and basket and brings them towards Lucky.*] Hold him tight! [*He puts the bag in Lucky's hand. Lucky drops it immediately.*] Don't let him go! [*He puts back the bag in Lucky's hand. Gradually, at the feel of the bag, Lucky recovers his senses and his fingers finally close round the handle.*] Hold him tight! [*As before with basket.*] Now! You can let him go. [*Vladimir and Estragon move away from Lucky who totters, reels, sags, but succeeds in remaining on his feet, bag and basket in his hands. Pozzo steps back, cracks his whip.*] Forward! [*Lucky totters forward.*] Back! [*Lucky totters back.*] Turn! [*Lucky turns.*] Done it! He can walk. [*Turning to Vladimir and Estragon.*] Thank you, gentlemen, and let me . . . [*he fumbles in his pockets*] . . . let me wish you . . . [*fumbles*] . . . wish you . . . [*fumbles*] . . . what have I done with my watch? [*Fumbles.*] A genuine half-hunter, gentlemen, with deadbeat escapement! [*Sobbing.*] Twas my granpa gave it to

	me! [*He searches on the ground, Vladimir and Estragon likewise. Pozzo turns over with his foot the remains of Lucky's hat.*] Well now isn't that just—
VLADIMIR	Perhaps it's in your fob.
POZZO	Wait! [*He doubles up in an attempt to apply his ear to his stomach, listens. Silence.*] I hear nothing. [*He beckons them to approach. Vladimir and Estragon go over to him, bend over his stomach.*] Surely one should hear the tick-tick.
VLADIMIR	Silence!
	[*All listen, bent double.*]
ESTRAGON	I hear something.
POZZO	Where?
VLADIMIR	It's the heart.
POZZO	[*disappointed*] Damnation!
VLADIMIR	Silence!
ESTRAGON	Perhaps it has stopped.
	[*They straighten up.*]
POZZO	Which of you smells so bad?
ESTRAGON	He has stinking breath and I have stinking feet.
POZZO	I must go.
ESTRAGON	And your half-hunter?
POZZO	I must have left it at the manor.
	[*Silence.*]
ESTRAGON	Then adieu.
POZZO	Adieu.
VLADIMIR	Adieu.
POZZO	Adieu.
	[*Silence. No one moves.*]
VLADIMIR	Adieu.
POZZO	Adieu.
ESTRAGON	Adieu.
	[*Silence.*]
POZZO	And thank you.
VLADIMIR	Thank *you*.

POZZO   Not at all.

ESTRAGON   Yes yes.

POZZO   No no.

VLADIMIR   Yes yes.

ESTRAGON   No no.

           [*Silence.*]

POZZO   I don't seem to be able . . . [*long hesitation*] . . . to depart.

ESTRAGON   Such is life.

           [*Pozzo turns, moves away from Lucky towards the wings, paying
           out the rope as he goes.*]

VLADIMIR   You're going the wrong way.

POZZO   I need a running start. [*Having come to the end of the rope, i.e. off
           stage, he stops, turns and cries.*] Stand back! [*Vladimir and
           Estragon stand back, look towards Pozzo. Crack of whip.*] On!
           On!

ESTRAGON   On!

VLADIMIR   On!

           [*Lucky moves off.*]

POZZO   Faster! [*He appears, crosses the stage preceded by Lucky. Vladimir
           and Estragon wave their hats. Exit Lucky.*] On! On! [*On the point
           of disappearing in his turn he stops and turns. The rope tautens.
           Noise of Lucky falling off.*] Stool! [*Vladimir fetches stool and gives
           it to Pozzo who throws it to Lucky.*] Adieu!

VLADIMIR ⎫
           ⎬ [*waving*] Adieu! Adieu!
ESTRAGON ⎭

POZZO   Up! Pig! [*Noise of Lucky getting up.*] On! [*Exit Pozzo.*] Faster! On!
           Adieu! Pig! Yip! Adieu!

           [*Long silence.*]

VLADIMIR   That passed the time.

ESTRAGON   It would have passed in any case.

VLADIMIR   Yes, but not so rapidly.

           [*Pause.*]

ESTRAGON   What do we do now?

VLADIMIR   I don't know.

ESTRAGON   Let's go.

VLADIMIR   We can't.

ESTRAGON   Why not?

VLADIMIR   We're waiting for Godot.

ESTRAGON   [*despairingly*] Ah!
           [*Pause.*]

VLADIMIR   How they've changed!

ESTRAGON   Who?

VLADIMIR   Those two.

ESTRAGON   That's the idea, let's make a little conversation.

VLADIMIR   Haven't they?

ESTRAGON   What?

VLADIMIR   Changed.

ESTRAGON   Very likely. They all change. Only we can't.

VLADIMIR   Likely! It's certain. Didn't you see them?

ESTRAGON   I suppose I did. But I don't know them.

VLADIMIR   Yes you do know them.

ESTRAGON   No I don't know them.

VLADIMIR   We know them, I tell you. You forget everything. [*Pause. To
           himself.*] Unless they're not the same . . .

ESTRAGON   Why didn't they recognize us then?

VLADIMIR   That means nothing. I too pretended not to recognize them.
           And then nobody ever recognizes us.

ESTRAGON   Forget it. What we need—ow! [*Vladimir does not react.*] Ow!

VLADIMIR   [*to himself*] Unless they're not the same . . .

ESTRAGON   Didi! It's the other foot! [*He goes hobbling towards the
           mound.*]

VLADIMIR   Unless they're not the same . . .

BOY   [*off*] Mister!
           [*Estragon halts. Both look towards the voice.*]

ESTRAGON   Off we go again.

VLADIMIR   Approach, my child.
           [*Enter Boy, timidly. He halts.*]

BOY   Mister Albert . . . ?

VLADIMIR	Yes.
ESTRAGON	What do you want?
VLADIMIR	Approach!
	[*The Boy does not move.*]
ESTRAGON	[*forcibly*] Approach when you're told, can't you?
	[*The Boy advances timidly, halts.*]
VLADIMIR	What is it?
BOY	Mr. Godot . . .
VLADIMIR	Obviously . . . [*Pause.*] Approach.
ESTRAGON	[*violently*] Will you approach! [*The Boy advances timidly.*] What kept you so late?
VLADIMIR	You have a message from Mr. Godot?
BOY	Yes Sir.
VLADIMIR	Well, what is it?
ESTRAGON	What kept you so late?
	[*The Boy looks at them in turn, not knowing to which he should reply.*]
VLADIMIR	[*to Estragon*] Let him alone.
ESTRAGON	[*violently*] You let me alone. [*Advancing, to the Boy.*] Do you know what time it is?
BOY	[*recoiling*] It's not my fault, Sir.
ESTRAGON	And whose is it? Mine?
BOY	I was afraid, Sir.
ESTRAGON	Afraid of what? Of us? [*Pause.*] Answer me!
VLADIMIR	I know what it is, he was afraid of the others.
ESTRAGON	How long have you been here?
BOY	A good while, Sir.
VLADIMIR	You were afraid of the whip?
BOY	Yes Sir.
VLADIMIR	The roars?
BOY	Yes Sir.
VLADIMIR	The two big men.
BOY	Yes Sir.
VLADIMIR	Do you know them?

BOY	No Sir.
VLADIMIR	Are you a native of these parts? [*Silence.*] Do you belong to these parts?
BOY	Yes Sir.
ESTRAGON	That's all a pack of lies. [*Shaking the Boy by the arm.*] Tell us the truth!
BOY	[*trembling*] But it is the truth, Sir!
VLADIMIR	Will you let him alone! What's the matter with you? [*Estragon releases the Boy, moves away, covering his face with his hands. Vladimir and the Boy observe him. Estragon drops his hands. His face is convulsed.*] What's the matter with you?
ESTRAGON	I'm unhappy.
VLADIMIR	Not really! Since when?
ESTRAGON	I'd forgotten.
VLADIMIR	Extraordinary the tricks that memory plays! [*Estragon tries to speak, renounces, limps to his place, sits down and begins to take off his boots. To Boy.*] Well?
BOY	Mr. Godot—
VLADIMIR	I've seen you before, haven't I?
BOY	I don't know, Sir.
VLADIMIR	You don't know me?
BOY	No Sir.
VLADIMIR	It wasn't you came yesterday?
BOY	No Sir.
VLADIMIR	This is your first time?
BOY	Yes Sir. [*Silence.*]
VLADIMIR	Words words. [*Pause.*] Speak.
BOY	[*in a rush*] Mr. Godot told me to tell you he won't come this evening but surely tomorrow. [*Silence.*]
VLADIMIR	Is that all?
BOY	Yes Sir. [*Silence.*]

VLADIMIR   You work for Mr. Godot?

BOY   Yes Sir.

VLADIMIR   What do you do?

BOY   I mind the goats, Sir.

VLADIMIR   Is he good to you?

BOY   Yes Sir.

VLADIMIR   He doesn't beat you?

BOY   No Sir, not me.

VLADIMIR   Whom does he beat?

BOY   He beats my brother, Sir.

VLADIMIR   Ah, you have a brother?

BOY   Yes Sir.

VLADIMIR   What does he do?

BOY   He minds the sheep, Sir.

VLADIMIR   And why doesn't he beat you?

BOY   I don't know, Sir.

VLADIMIR   He must be fond of you.

BOY   I don't know, Sir.
[*Silence.*]

VLADIMIR   Does he give you enough to eat? [*The Boy hesitates.*] Does he feed you well?

BOY   Fairly well, Sir.

VLADIMIR   You're not unhappy? [*The Boy hesitates.*] Do you hear me?

BOY   Yes Sir.

VLADIMIR   Well?

BOY   I don't know, Sir.

VLADIMIR   You don't know if you're unhappy or not?

BOY   No Sir.

VLADIMIR   You're as bad as myself. [*Silence.*] Where do you sleep?

BOY   In the loft, Sir.

VLADIMIR   With your brother?

BOY   Yes Sir.

VLADIMIR   In the hay?

BOY   Yes Sir.

[*Silence.*]

VLADIMIR   All right, you may go.

BOY   What am I to tell Mr. Godot, Sir?

VLADIMIR   Tell him . . . [*he hesitates*] . . . tell him you saw us. [*Pause.*] You did see us, didn't you?

BOY   Yes Sir.

[*He steps back, hesitates, turns and exit running. The light suddenly fails. In a moment it is night. The moon rises at back, mounts in the sky, stands still, shedding a pale light on the scene.*]

VLADIMIR   At last! [*Estragon gets up and goes towards Vladimir, a boot in each hand. He puts them down at edge of stage, straightens and contemplates the moon.*] What are you doing?

ESTRAGON   Pale for weariness.

VLADIMIR   Eh?

ESTRAGON   Of climbing heaven and gazing on the likes of us.

VLADIMIR   Your boots, what are you doing with your boots?

ESTRAGON   [*turning to look at the boots*] I'm leaving them there. [*Pause.*] Another will come, just as . . . as . . . as me, but with smaller feet, and they'll make him happy.

VLADIMIR   But you can't go barefoot!

ESTRAGON   Christ did.

VLADIMIR   Christ! What has Christ got to do with it? You're not going to compare yourself to Christ!

ESTRAGON   All my life I've compared myself to him.

VLADIMIR   But where he lived it was warm, it was dry!

ESTRAGON   Yes. And they crucified quick.

[*Silence.*]

VLADIMIR   We've nothing more to do here.

ESTRAGON   Nor anywhere else.

VLADIMIR   Ah Gogo, don't go on like that. Tomorrow everything will be better.

ESTRAGON   How do you make that out?

VLADIMIR   Did you not hear what the child said?

ESTRAGON   No.

VLADIMIR   He said that Godot was sure to come tomorrow. [*Pause.*] What
              do you say to that?

ESTRAGON   Then all we have to do is to wait on here.

VLADIMIR   Are you mad? We must take cover. [*He takes Estragon by the
              arm.*] Come on.
              [*He draws Estragon after him. Estragon yields, then resists. They
              halt.*]

ESTRAGON   [*looking at the tree*] Pity we haven't got a bit of rope.

VLADIMIR   Come on. It's cold.
              [*He draws Estragon after him. As before.*]

ESTRAGON   Remind me to bring a bit of rope tomorrow.

VLADIMIR   Yes. Come on.
              [*He draws him after him. As before.*]

ESTRAGON   How long have we been together all the time now?

VLADIMIR   I don't know. Fifty years maybe.

ESTRAGON   Do you remember the day I threw myself into the Rhône?

VLADIMIR   We were grape harvesting.

ESTRAGON   You fished me out.

VLADIMIR   That's all dead and buried.

ESTRAGON   My clothes dried in the sun.

VLADIMIR   There's no good harking back on that. Come on.
              [*He draws him after him. As before.*]

ESTRAGON   Wait!

VLADIMIR   I'm cold!

ESTRAGON   Wait! [*He moves away from Vladimir.*] I sometimes wonder if we
              wouldn't have been better off alone, each one for himself.
              [*He crosses the stage and sits down on the mound.*] We weren't
              made for the same road.

VLADIMIR   [*without anger*] It's not certain.

ESTRAGON   No, nothing is certain.
              [*Vladimir slowly crosses the stage and sits down beside Estragon.*]

VLADIMIR   We can still part, if you think it would be better.

ESTRAGON   It's not worth while now.

[*Silence.*]

VLADIMIR   No, it's not worth while now.

[*Silence.*]

ESTRAGON   Well, shall we go?

VLADIMIR   Yes, let's go.

[*They do not move.*]

Curtain

ACT II

Next day. Same time.
Same place.

Estragon's boots front center, heels together, toes splayed. Lucky's hat at same place.
The tree has four or five leaves.
    Enter Vladimir agitatedly. He halts and looks long at the tree, then suddenly
begins to move feverishly about the stage. He halts before the boots, picks one up,
examines it, sniffs it, manifests disgust, puts it back carefully. Comes and goes.
Halts extreme right and gazes into distance off, shading his eyes with his hand.
Comes and goes. Halts extreme left, as before. Comes and goes. Halts suddenly and
begins to sing loudly.

VLADIMIR A dog came in—

        [*Having begun too high he stops, clears his throat, resumes.*]
        A dog came in the kitchen
        And stole a crust of bread.
        Then cook up with a ladle
        And beat him till he was dead.

        Then all the dogs came running
        And dug the dog a tomb—

[*He stops, broods, resumes.*]
Then all the dogs came running
And dug the dog a tomb
And wrote upon the tombstone
For the eyes of dogs to come:

A dog came in the kitchen
And stole a crust of bread.
Then cook up with a ladle
And beat him till he was dead.

Then all the dogs came running
And dug the dog a tomb—

[*He stops, broods, resumes.*]

Then all the dogs came running
And dug the dog a tomb—

[*He stops, broods. Softly.*]
And dug the dog a tomb . . .

[*He remains a moment silent and motionless, then begins to move feverishly about the stage. He halts before the tree, comes and goes, before the boots, comes and goes, halts extreme right, gazes into distance, extreme left, gazes into distance. Enter Estragon right, barefoot, head bowed. He slowly crosses the stage. Vladimir turns and sees him.*]

VLADIMIR   You again! [*Estragon halts but does not raise his head. Vladimir goes towards him.*] Come here till I embrace you.

ESTRAGON   Don't touch me!
[*Vladimir holds back, pained.*]

VLADIMIR   Do you want me to go away? [*Pause.*] Gogo! [*Pause. Vladimir observes him attentively.*] Did they beat you? [*Pause.*] Gogo!

[*Estragon remains silent, head bowed.*] Where did you spend the night?

ESTRAGON   Don't touch me! Don't question me! Don't speak to me! Stay with me!

VLADIMIR   Did I ever leave you?

ESTRAGON   You let me go.

VLADIMIR   Look at me. [*Estragon does not raise his head. Violently.*] Will you look at me!

[*Estragon raises his head. They look long at each other, then suddenly embrace, clapping each other on the back. End of the embrace. Estragon, no longer supported, almost falls.*]

ESTRAGON   What a day!

VLADIMIR   Who beat you? Tell me.

ESTRAGON   Another day done with.

VLADIMIR   Not yet.

ESTRAGON   For me it's over and done with, no matter what happens. [*Silence.*] I heard you singing.

VLADIMIR   That's right, I remember.

ESTRAGON   That finished me. I said to myself, He's all alone, he thinks I'm gone for ever, and he sings.

VLADIMIR   One is not master of one's moods. All day I've felt in great form. [*Pause.*] I didn't get up in the night, not once!

ESTRAGON   [*sadly*] You see, you piss better when I'm not there.

VLADIMIR   I missed you . . . and at the same time I was happy. Isn't that a queer thing?

ESTRAGON   [*shocked*] Happy?

VLADIMIR   Perhaps it's not quite the right word.

ESTRAGON   And now?

VLADIMIR   Now? . . . [*Joyous.*] There you are again . . . [*Indifferent.*] There we are again . . . [*Gloomy.*] There I am again.

ESTRAGON   You see, you feel worse when I'm with you. I feel better alone too.

VLADIMIR   [*vexed*] Then why do you always come crawling back?

ESTRAGON   I don't know.

VLADIMIR   No, but I do. It's because you don't know how to defend
            yourself. I wouldn't have let them beat you.

ESTRAGON   You couldn't have stopped them.

VLADIMIR   Why not?

ESTRAGON   There was ten of them.

VLADIMIR   No, I mean before they beat you. I would have stopped you
            from doing whatever it was you were doing.

ESTRAGON   I wasn't doing anything.

VLADIMIR   Then why did they beat you?

ESTRAGON   I don't know.

VLADIMIR   Ah no, Gogo, the truth is there are things escape you that
            don't escape me, you must feel it yourself.

ESTRAGON   I tell you I wasn't doing anything.

VLADIMIR   Perhaps you weren't. But it's the way of doing it that counts,
            the way of doing it, if you want to go on living.

ESTRAGON   I wasn't doing anything.

VLADIMIR   You must be happy too, deep down, if you only knew it.

ESTRAGON   Happy about what?

VLADIMIR   To be back with me again.

ESTRAGON   Would you say so?

VLADIMIR   Say you are, even if it's not true.

ESTRAGON   What am I to say?

VLADIMIR   Say, I am happy.

ESTRAGON   I am happy.

VLADIMIR   So am I.

ESTRAGON   So am I.

VLADIMIR   We are happy.

ESTRAGON   We are happy. [*Silence.*] What do we do now, now that we are
            happy?

VLADIMIR   Wait for Godot. [*Estragon groans. Silence.*] Things have changed
            here since yesterday.

ESTRAGON   And if he doesn't come.

VLADIMIR   [*after a moment of bewilderment*] We'll see when the time comes.

	[*Pause.*] I was saying that things have changed here since yesterday.
ESTRAGON	Everything oozes.
VLADIMIR	Look at the tree.
ESTRAGON	It's never the same pus from one second to the next.
VLADIMIR	The tree, look at the tree.

[*Estragon looks at the tree.*]

ESTRAGON	Was it not there yesterday?
VLADIMIR	Yes of course it was there. Do you not remember? We nearly hanged ourselves from it. But you wouldn't. Do you not remember?
ESTRAGON	You dreamt it.
VLADIMIR	Is it possible you've forgotten already?
ESTRAGON	That's the way I am. Either I forget immediately or I never forget.
VLADIMIR	And Pozzo and Lucky, have you forgotten them too?
ESTRAGON	Pozzo and Lucky?
VLADIMIR	He's forgotten everything!
ESTRAGON	I remember a lunatic who kicked the shins off me. Then he played the fool.
VLADIMIR	That was Lucky.
ESTRAGON	I remember that. But when was it?
VLADIMIR	And his keeper, do you not remember him?
ESTRAGON	He gave me a bone.
VLADIMIR	That was Pozzo.
ESTRAGON	And all that was yesterday, you say?
VLADIMIR	Yes of course it was yesterday.
ESTRAGON	And here where we are now?
VLADIMIR	Where else do you think? Do you not recognize the place?
ESTRAGON	[*suddenly furious*] Recognize! What is there to recognize? All my lousy life I've crawled about in the mud! And you talk to me about scenery! [*Looking wildly about him.*] Look at this muckheap! I've never stirred from it!
VLADIMIR	Calm yourself, calm yourself.

ESTRAGON   You and your landscapes! Tell me about the worms!

VLADIMIR   All the same, you can't tell me that this [*gesture*] bears any
            resemblance to . . . [*he hesitates*] . . . to the Mâcon country for
            example. You can't deny there's a big difference.

ESTRAGON   The Mâcon country! Who's talking to you about the Mâcon
            country?

VLADIMIR   But you were there yourself, in the Mâcon country.

ESTRAGON   No I was never in the Mâcon country! I've puked my puke of a
            life away here, I tell you! Here! In the Cackon country!

VLADIMIR   But we were there together, I could swear to it! Picking grapes
            for a man called . . . [*he snaps his fingers*] . . . can't think of the
            name of the man, at a place called . . . [*snaps his fingers*] . . .
            can't think of the name of the place, do you not remember?

ESTRAGON   [*a little calmer*] It's possible. I didn't notice anything.

VLADIMIR   But down there everything is red!

ESTRAGON   [*exasperated*] I didn't notice anything, I tell you!
            [*Silence. Vladimir sighs deeply.*]

VLADIMIR   You're a hard man to get on with, Gogo.

ESTRAGON   It'd be better if we parted.

VLADIMIR   You always say that and you always come crawling back.

ESTRAGON   The best thing would be to kill me, like the other.

VLADIMIR   What other? [*Pause.*] What other?

ESTRAGON   Like billions of others.

VLADIMIR   [*sententious*] To every man his little cross. [*He sighs.*] Till he
            dies. [*Afterthought.*] And is forgotten.

ESTRAGON   In the meantime let us try and converse calmly, since we are
            incapable of keeping silent.

VLADIMIR   You're right, we're inexhaustible.

ESTRAGON   It's so we won't think.

VLADIMIR   We have that excuse.

ESTRAGON   It's so we won't hear.

VLADIMIR   We have our reasons.

ESTRAGON   All the dead voices.

VLADIMIR   They make a noise like wings.

ESTRAGON Like leaves.
VLADIMIR Like sand.
ESTRAGON Like leaves.
          [*Silence.*]
VLADIMIR They all speak at once.
ESTRAGON Each one to itself.
          [*Silence.*]
VLADIMIR Rather they whisper.
ESTRAGON They rustle.
VLADIMIR They murmur.
ESTRAGON They rustle.
          [*Silence.*]
VLADIMIR What do they say?
ESTRAGON They talk about their lives.
VLADIMIR To have lived is not enough for them.
ESTRAGON They have to talk about it.
VLADIMIR To be dead is not enough for them.
ESTRAGON It is not sufficient.
          [*Silence.*]
VLADIMIR They make a noise like feathers.
ESTRAGON Like leaves.
VLADIMIR Like ashes.
ESTRAGON Like leaves.
          [*Long silence.*]
VLADIMIR Say something!
ESTRAGON I'm trying.
          [*Long silence.*]
VLADIMIR [*in anguish*] Say anything at all!
ESTRAGON What do we do now?
VLADIMIR Wait for Godot.
ESTRAGON Ah!
          [*Silence.*]
VLADIMIR This is awful!
ESTRAGON Sing something.

VLADIMIR   No no! [*He reflects.*] We could start all over again perhaps.

ESTRAGON   That should be easy.

VLADIMIR   It's the start that's difficult.

ESTRAGON   You can start from anything.

VLADIMIR   Yes, but you have to decide.

ESTRAGON   True.

[*Silence.*]

VLADIMIR   Help me!

ESTRAGON   I'm trying.

[*Silence.*]

VLADIMIR   When you seek you hear.

ESTRAGON   You do.

VLADIMIR   That prevents you from finding.

ESTRAGON   It does.

VLADIMIR   That prevents you from thinking.

ESTRAGON   You think all the same.

VLADIMIR   No no, impossible.

ESTRAGON   That's the idea, let's contradict each other.

VLADIMIR   Impossible.

ESTRAGON   You think so?

VLADIMIR   We're in no danger of ever thinking any more.

ESTRAGON   Then what are we complaining about?

VLADIMIR   Thinking is not the worst.

ESTRAGON   Perhaps not. But at least there's that.

VLADIMIR   That what?

ESTRAGON   That's the idea, let's ask each other questions.

VLADIMIR   What do you mean, at least there's that?

ESTRAGON   That much less misery.

VLADIMIR   True.

ESTRAGON   Well? If we gave thanks for our mercies?

VLADIMIR   What is terrible is to *have* thought.

ESTRAGON   But did that ever happen to us?

VLADIMIR   Where are all these corpses from?

ESTRAGON   These skeletons.

VLADIMIR   Tell me that.

ESTRAGON   True.

VLADIMIR   We must have thought a little.

ESTRAGON   At the very beginning.

VLADIMIR   A charnel-house! A charnel-house!

ESTRAGON   You don't have to look.

VLADIMIR   You can't help looking.

ESTRAGON   True.

VLADIMIR   Try as one may.

ESTRAGON   I beg your pardon?

VLADIMIR   Try as one may.

ESTRAGON   We should turn resolutely towards Nature.

VLADIMIR   We've tried that.

ESTRAGON   True.

VLADIMIR   Oh it's not the worst, I know.

ESTRAGON   What?

VLADIMIR   To have thought.

ESTRAGON   Obviously.

VLADIMIR   But we could have done without it.

ESTRAGON   Que voulez-vous?

VLADIMIR   I beg your pardon?

ESTRAGON   Que voulez-vous.

VLADIMIR   Ah! que voulez-vous. Exactly.
           [*Silence.*]

ESTRAGON   That wasn't such a bad little canter.

VLADIMIR   Yes, but now we'll have to find something else.

ESTRAGON   Let me see. [*He takes off his hat, concentrates.*]

VLADIMIR   Let me see. [*He takes off his hat, concentrates. Long silence.*] Ah!
           [*They put on their hats, relax.*]

ESTRAGON   Well?

VLADIMIR   What was I saying, we could go on from there.

ESTRAGON   What were you saying when?

VLADIMIR   At the very beginning.

ESTRAGON   The very beginning of WHAT?

VLADIMIR   This evening . . . I was saying . . . I was saying . . .

ESTRAGON   I'm not a historian.

VLADIMIR   Wait . . . we embraced . . . we were happy . . . happy . . . what do
we do now that we're happy . . . go on waiting . . . waiting . . .
let me think . . . it's coming . . . go on waiting . . . now that
we're happy . . . let me see . . . ah! The tree!

ESTRAGON   The tree?

VLADIMIR   Do you not remember?

ESTRAGON   I'm tired.

VLADIMIR   Look at it.

[*They look at the tree.*]

ESTRAGON   I see nothing.

VLADIMIR   But yesterday evening it was all black and bare. And now it's
covered with leaves.

ESTRAGON   Leaves?

VLADIMIR   In a single night.

ESTRAGON   It must be the Spring.

VLADIMIR   But in a single night!

ESTRAGON   I tell you we weren't here yesterday. Another of your
nightmares.

VLADIMIR   And where were we yesterday evening according to you?

ESTRAGON   How would I know? In another compartment. There's no lack
of void.

VLADIMIR   [*sure of himself*] Good. We weren't here yesterday evening.
Now what did we do yesterday evening?

ESTRAGON   Do?

VLADIMIR   Try and remember.

ESTRAGON   Do . . . I suppose we blathered.

VLADIMIR   [*controlling himself*] About what?

ESTRAGON   Oh . . . this and that I suppose, nothing in particular. [*With
assurance.*] Yes, now I remember, yesterday evening we spent
blathering about nothing in particular. That's been going
on now for half a century.

VLADIMIR   You don't remember any fact, any circumstance?

ESTRAGON   [*weary*] Don't torment me, Didi.

VLADIMIR   The sun. The moon. Do you not remember?

ESTRAGON   They must have been there, as usual.

VLADIMIR   You didn't notice anything out of the ordinary?

ESTRAGON   Alas!

VLADIMIR   And Pozzo? And Lucky?

ESTRAGON   Pozzo?

VLADIMIR   The bones.

ESTRAGON   They were like fishbones.

VLADIMIR   It was Pozzo gave them to you.

ESTRAGON   I don't know.

VLADIMIR   And the kick.

ESTRAGON   That's right, someone gave me a kick.

VLADIMIR   It was Lucky gave it to you.

ESTRAGON   And all that was yesterday?

VLADIMIR   Show your leg.

ESTRAGON   Which?

VLADIMIR   Both. Pull up your trousers. [*Estragon gives a leg to Vladimir,
            staggers. Vladimir takes the leg. They stagger.*] Pull up your
            trousers.

ESTRAGON   I can't.
            [*Vladimir pulls up the trousers, looks at the leg, lets it go. Estragon
            almost falls.*]

VLADIMIR   The other. [*Estragon gives the same leg.*] The other, pig! [*Estragon
            gives the other leg. Triumphantly.*] There's the wound!
            Beginning to fester!

ESTRAGON   And what about it?

VLADIMIR   [*letting go the leg*] Where are your boots?

ESTRAGON   I must have thrown them away.

VLADIMIR   When?

ESTRAGON   I don't know.

VLADIMIR   Why?

ESTRAGON   [*exasperated*] I don't know why I don't know!

VLADIMIR   No, I mean why did you throw them away?

ESTRAGON   [*exasperated*] Because they were hurting me!

VLADIMIR   [*triumphantly, pointing to the boots*] There they are! [*Estragon
            looks at the boots.*] At the very spot where you left them
            yesterday!
            [*Estragon goes towards the boots, inspects them closely.*]

ESTRAGON   They're not mine.

VLADIMIR   [*stupefied*] Not yours!

ESTRAGON   Mine were black. These are brown.

VLADIMIR   You're sure yours were black?

ESTRAGON   Well they were a kind of grey.

VLADIMIR   And these are brown. Show.

ESTRAGON   [*picking up a boot*] Well they're a kind of green.

VLADIMIR   Show. [*Estragon hands him the boot. Vladimir inspects it, throws it
            down angrily.*] Well of all the—

ESTRAGON   You see, all that's a lot of bloody—

VLADIMIR   Ah! I see what it is. Yes, I see what's happened.

ESTRAGON   All that's a lot of bloody—

VLADIMIR   It's elementary. Someone came and took yours and left you
            his.

ESTRAGON   Why?

VLADIMIR   His were too tight for him, so he took yours.

ESTRAGON   But mine were too tight

VLADIMIR   For you. Not for him.

ESTRAGON   [*having tried in vain to work it out*] I'm tired! [*Pause.*] Let's go.

VLADIMIR   We can't.

ESTRAGON   Why not?

VLADIMIR   We're waiting for Godot.

ESTRAGON   Ah! [*Pause. Despairing.*] What'll we do, what'll we do!

VLADIMIR   There's nothing we can do.

ESTRAGON   But I can't go on like this!

VLADIMIR   Would you like a radish?

ESTRAGON   Is that all there is?

VLADIMIR   There are radishes and turnips.

ESTRAGON   Are there no carrots?

VLADIMIR   No. Anyway you overdo it with your carrots.

ESTRAGON   Then give me a radish. [*Vladimir fumbles in his pockets, finds nothing but turnips, finally brings out a radish and hands it to Estragon who examines it, sniffs it.*] It's black!

VLADIMIR   It's a radish.

ESTRAGON   I only like the pink ones, you know that!

VLADIMIR   Then you don't want it?

ESTRAGON   I only like the pink ones!

VLADIMIR   Then give it back to me. [*Estragon gives it back.*]

ESTRAGON   I'll go and get a carrot. [*He does not move.*]

VLADIMIR   This is becoming really insignificant.

ESTRAGON   Not enough.

            [*Silence.*]

VLADIMIR   What about trying them.

ESTRAGON   I've tried everything.

VLADIMIR   No, I mean the boots.

ESTRAGON   Would that be a good thing?

VLADIMIR   It'd pass the time. [*Estragon hesitates.*] I assure you, it'd be an occupation.

ESTRAGON   A relaxation.

VLADIMIR   A recreation.

ESTRAGON   A relaxation.

VLADIMIR   Try.

ESTRAGON   You'll help me?

VLADIMIR   I will of course.

ESTRAGON   We don't manage too badly, eh Didi, between the two of us?

VLADIMIR   Yes yes. Come on, we'll try the left first.

ESTRAGON   We always find something, eh Didi, to give us the impression we exist?

VLADIMIR   [*impatiently*] Yes yes, we're magicians. But let us persevere in what we have resolved, before we forget. [*He picks up a boot.*] Come on, give me your foot. [*Estragon raises his foot.*] The other, hog! [*Estragon raises the other foot.*] Higher!

[*Wreathed together they stagger about the stage. Vladimir succeeds finally in getting on the boot.*] Try and walk. [*Estragon walks.*] Well?

ESTRAGON   It fits.

VLADIMIR   [*taking string from his pocket*] We'll try and lace it.

ESTRAGON   [*vehemently*] No no, no laces, no laces!

VLADIMIR   You'll be sorry. Let's try the other. [*As before.*] Well?

ESTRAGON   [*grudgingly*] It fits too.

VLADIMIR   They don't hurt you?

ESTRAGON   Not yet.

VLADIMIR   Then you can keep them.

ESTRAGON   They're too big.

VLADIMIR   Perhaps you'll have socks some day.

ESTRAGON   True.

VLADIMIR   Then you'll keep them?

ESTRAGON   That's enough about these boots.

VLADIMIR   Yes, but—

ESTRAGON   [*violently*] Enough! [*Silence.*] I suppose I might as well sit down. [*He looks for a place to sit down, then goes and sits down on the mound.*]

VLADIMIR   That's where you were sitting yesterday evening.

ESTRAGON   If I could only sleep.

VLADIMIR   Yesterday you slept.

ESTRAGON   I'll try. [*He resumes his foetal posture, his head between his knees.*]

VLADIMIR   Wait. [*He goes over and sits down beside Estragon and begins to sing in a loud voice.*]
Bye bye bye bye
Bye bye—

ESTRAGON   [*looking up angrily*] Not so loud!

VLADIMIR   [*softly*] Bye bye bye bye
Bye bye bye bye
Bye bye bye bye
Bye bye . . .
[*Estragon sleeps. Vladimir gets up softly, takes off his coat and lays*

it across Estragon's shoulders, then starts walking up and down,
swinging his arms to keep himself warm. Estragon wakes with a
start, jumps up, casts about wildly. Vladimir returns to him, puts
his arms round him.] There . . . there . . . Didi is there . . .
don't be afraid . . .

ESTRAGON   Ah!

VLADIMIR   There . . . there . . . it's all over.

ESTRAGON   I was falling—

VLADIMIR   It's all over, it's all over.

ESTRAGON   I was on top of a—

VLADIMIR   Don't tell me! Come, we'll walk it off.
[*He takes Estragon by the arm and walks him up and down until*
Estragon refuses to go any further.]

ESTRAGON   That's enough. I'm tired.

VLADIMIR   You'd rather be stuck there doing nothing?

ESTRAGON   Yes.

VLADIMIR   Please yourself.
[*He releases Estragon, picks up his coat and puts it on.*]

ESTRAGON   Let's go.

VLADIMIR   We can't.

ESTRAGON   Why not?

VLADIMIR   We're waiting for Godot.

ESTRAGON   Ah! [*Vladimir walks up and down.*] Can you not stay still?

VLADIMIR   I'm cold.

ESTRAGON   We came too soon.

VLADIMIR   It's always at nightfall.

ESTRAGON   But night doesn't fall.

VLADIMIR   It'll fall all of a sudden, like yesterday.

ESTRAGON   Then it'll be night.

VLADIMIR   And we can go.

ESTRAGON   Then it'll be day again. [*Pause. Despairing.*] What'll we do,
what'll we do!

VLADIMIR   [*halting, violently*] Will you stop whining! I've had about my
bellyful of your lamentations!

ESTRAGON   I'm going.

VLADIMIR   [*seeing Lucky's hat*] Well!

ESTRAGON   Farewell.

VLADIMIR   Lucky's hat. [*He goes towards it.*] I've been here an hour and
never saw it. [*Very pleased.*] Fine!

ESTRAGON   You'll never see me again.

VLADIMIR   I knew it was the right place. Now our troubles are over. [*He
picks up the hat, contemplates it, straightens it.*] Must have been
a very fine hat. [*He puts it on in place of his own which he hands
to Estragon.*] Here.

ESTRAGON   What?

VLADIMIR   Hold that.

[*Estragon takes Vladimir's hat. Vladimir adjusts Lucky's hat on his
head. Estragon puts on Vladimir's hat in place of his own which he
hands to Vladimir. Vladimir takes Estragon's hat. Estragon adjusts
Vladimir's hat on his head. Vladimir puts on Estragon's hat in place
of Lucky's which he hands to Estragon. Estragon takes Lucky's hat.
Vladimir adjusts Estragon's hat on his head. Estragon puts on
Lucky's hat in place of Vladimir's which he hands to Vladimir.
Vladimir takes his hat. Estragon adjusts Lucky's hat on his head.
Vladimir puts on his hat in place of Estragon's which he hands to
Estragon. Estragon takes his hat. Vladimir adjusts his hat on his
head. Estragon puts on his hat in place of Lucky's which he hands to
Vladimir. Vladimir takes Lucky's hat. Estragon adjusts his hat on
his head. Vladimir puts on Lucky's hat in place of his own which he
hands to Estragon. Estragon takes Vladimir's hat. Vladimir adjusts
Lucky's hat on his head. Estragon hands Vladimir's hat back to
Vladimir who takes it and hands it back to Estragon who takes it
and hands it back to Vladimir who takes it and throws it down.*]
How does it fit me?

ESTRAGON   How would I know?

VLADIMIR   No, but how do I look in it? [*He turns his head coquettishly to and
fro, minces like a mannequin.*]

ESTRAGON   Hideous.

VLADIMIR   Yes, but not more so than usual?

ESTRAGON   Neither more nor less.

VLADIMIR   Then I can keep it. Mine irked me. [*Pause.*] How shall I say? [*Pause.*] It itched me. [*He takes off Lucky's hat, peers into it, shakes it, knocks on the crown, puts it on again.*]

ESTRAGON   I'm going.
            [*Silence.*]

VLADIMIR   Will you not play?

ESTRAGON   Play at what?

VLADIMIR   We could play at Pozzo and Lucky.

ESTRAGON   Never heard of it.

VLADIMIR   I'll do Lucky, you do Pozzo. [*He imitates Lucky sagging under the weight of his baggage. Estragon looks at him with stupefaction.*] Go on.

ESTRAGON   What am I to do?

VLADIMIR   Curse me!

ESTRAGON   [*after reflection*] Naughty!

VLADIMIR   Stronger!

ESTRAGON   Gonococcus! Spirochete!
            [*Vladimir sways back and forth, doubled in two.*]

VLADIMIR   Tell me to think.

ESTRAGON   What?

VLADIMIR   Say, Think, pig!

ESTRAGON   Think, pig!
            [*Silence.*]

VLADIMIR   I can't!

ESTRAGON   That's enough of that.

VLADIMIR   Tell me to dance.

ESTRAGON   I'm going.

VLADIMIR   Dance, hog! [*He writhes. Exit Estragon left, precipitately.*] I can't! [*He looks up, misses Estragon.*] Gogo! [*He moves wildly about the stage. Enter Estragon left, panting. He hastens towards Vladimir, falls into his arms.*] There you are again at last!

ESTRAGON   I'm accursed!

VLADIMIR	Where were you? I thought you were gone for ever.
ESTRAGON	They're coming!
VLADIMIR	Who?
ESTRAGON	I don't know.
VLADIMIR	How many?
ESTRAGON	I don't know.
VLADIMIR	[*triumphantly*] It's Godot! At last! Gogo! It's Godot! We're saved! Let's go and meet him! [*He drags Estragon towards the wings. Estragon resists, pulls himself free, exit right.*] Gogo! Come back! [*Vladimir runs to extreme left, scans the horizon. Enter Estragon right, he hastens towards Vladimir, falls into his arms.*] There you are again again!
ESTRAGON	I'm in hell!
VLADIMIR	Where were you?
ESTRAGON	They're coming there too!
VLADIMIR	We're surrounded! [*Estragon makes a rush towards back.*] Imbecile! There's no way out there. [*He takes Estragon by the arm and drags him towards front. Gesture towards front.*] There! Not a soul in sight! Off you go! Quick! [*He pushes Estragon towards auditorium. Estragon recoils in horror.*] You won't? [*He contemplates auditorium.*] Well I can understand that. Wait till I see. [*He reflects.*] Your only hope left is to disappear.
ESTRAGON	Where?
VLADIMIR	Behind the tree. [*Estragon hesitates.*] Quick! Behind the tree. [*Estragon goes and crouches behind the tree, realizes he is not hidden, comes out from behind the tree.*] Decidedly this tree will not have been the slightest use to us.
ESTRAGON	[*calmer*] I lost my head. Forgive me. It won't happen again. Tell me what to do.
VLADIMIR	There's nothing to do.
ESTRAGON	You go and stand there. [*He draws Vladimir to extreme right and places him with his back to the stage.*] There, don't move, and watch out. [*Vladimir scans horizon, screening his eyes with his*

hand. Estragon runs and takes up same position extreme left. They turn their heads and look at each other.] Back to back like in the good old days. [*They continue to look at each other for a moment, then resume their watch. Long silence.*] Do you see anything coming?

VLADIMIR [*turning his head.*] What?

ESTRAGON [*louder*] Do you see anything coming?

VLADIMIR No.

ESTRAGON Nor I.

[*They resume their watch. Silence.*]

VLADIMIR You must have had a vision.

ESTRAGON [*turning his head*] What?

VLADIMIR [*louder*] You must have had a vision.

ESTRAGON No need to shout!

[*They resume their watch. Silence.*]

VLADIMIR }
ESTRAGON } [*turning simultaneously*] Do you—

VLADIMIR Oh pardon!

ESTRAGON Carry on.

VLADIMIR No no, after you.

ESTRAGON No no, you first.

VLADIMIR I interrupted you.

ESTRAGON On the contrary.

[*They glare at each other angrily.*]

VLADIMIR Ceremonious ape!

ESTRAGON Punctilious pig!

VLADIMIR Finish your phrase, I tell you!

ESTRAGON Finish your own!

[*Silence. They draw closer, halt.*]

VLADIMIR Moron!

ESTRAGON That's the idea, let's abuse each other.

[*They turn, move apart, turn again and face each other.*]

VLADIMIR Moron!

ESTRAGON Vermin!

VLADIMIR Abortion!

ESTRAGON Morpion!

VLADIMIR Sewer-rat!

ESTRAGON Curate!

VLADIMIR Cretin!

ESTRAGON [*with finality*] Crritic!

VLADIMIR Oh! [*He wilts, vanquished, and turns away.*]

ESTRAGON Now let's make it up.

VLADIMIR Gogo!

ESTRAGON Didi!

VLADIMIR Your hand!

ESTRAGON Take it!

VLADIMIR Come to my arms!

ESTRAGON Your arms?

VLADIMIR My breast!

ESTRAGON Off we go!

[*They embrace. They separate. Silence.*]

VLADIMIR How time flies when one has fun!

[*Silence.*]

ESTRAGON What do we do now?

VLADIMIR While waiting.

ESTRAGON While waiting.

[*Silence.*]

VLADIMIR We could do our exercises.

ESTRAGON Our movements.

VLADIMIR Our elevations.

ESTRAGON Our relaxations.

VLADIMIR Our elongations.

ESTRAGON Our relaxations.

VLADIMIR To warm us up.

ESTRAGON To calm us down.

VLADIMIR Off we go.

[*Vladimir hops from one foot to the other. Estragon imitates him.*]

ESTRAGON [*stopping*] That's enough. I'm tired.

VLADIMIR [*stopping*] We're not in form. What about a little deep breathing?

ESTRAGON I'm tired breathing.

VLADIMIR You're right. [*Pause.*] Let's just do the tree, for the balance.

ESTRAGON The tree?

[*Vladimir does the tree, staggering about on one leg.*]

VLADIMIR [*stopping*] Your turn.

[*Estragon does the tree, staggers.*]

ESTRAGON Do you think God sees me?

VLADIMIR You must close your eyes.

[*Estragon closes his eyes, staggers worse.*]

ESTRAGON [*stopping, brandishing his fists, at the top of his voice*] God have pity on me!

VLADIMIR [*vexed*] And me?

ESTRAGON On me! On me! Pity! On me!

[*Enter Pozzo and Lucky. Pozzo is blind. Lucky burdened as before. Rope as before, but much shorter, so that Pozzo may follow more easily. Lucky wearing a different hat. At the sight of Vladimir and Estragon he stops short. Pozzo, continuing on his way, bumps into him.*]

VLADIMIR Gogo!

POZZO [*clutching on to Lucky who staggers*] What is it? Who is it?

[*Lucky falls, drops everything and brings down Pozzo with him. They lie helpless among the scattered baggage.*]

ESTRAGON Is it Godot?

VLADIMIR At last! [*He goes towards the heap.*] Reinforcements at last!

POZZO Help!

ESTRAGON Is it Godot?

VLADIMIR We were beginning to weaken. Now we're sure to see the evening out.

POZZO Help!

ESTRAGON Do you hear him?

VLADIMIR We are no longer alone, waiting for the night, waiting for Godot, waiting for . . . waiting. All evening we have

struggled, unassisted. Now it's over. It's already
tomorrow.

POZZO   Help!

VLADIMIR   Time flows again already. The sun will set, the moon rise,
and we away . . . from here.

POZZO   Pity!

VLADIMIR   Poor Pozzo!

ESTRAGON   I knew it was him.

VLADIMIR   Who?

ESTRAGON   Godot.

VLADIMIR   But it's not Godot.

ESTRAGON   It's not Godot?

VLADIMIR   It's not Godot.

ESTRAGON   Then who is it?

VLADIMIR   It's Pozzo.

POZZO   Here! Here! Help me up!

VLADIMIR   He can't get up.

ESTRAGON   Let's go.

VLADIMIR   We can't.

ESTRAGON   Why not?

VLADIMIR   We're waiting for Godot.

ESTRAGON   Ah!

VLADIMIR   Perhaps he has another bone for you.

ESTRAGON   Bone?

VLADIMIR   Chicken. Do you not remember?

ESTRAGON   It was him?

VLADIMIR   Yes.

ESTRAGON   Ask him.

VLADIMIR   Perhaps we should help him first.

ESTRAGON   To do what?

VLADIMIR   To get up.

ESTRAGON   He can't get up?

VLADIMIR   He wants to get up.

ESTRAGON   Then let him get up.

VLADIMIR	He can't.
ESTRAGON	Why not?
VLADIMIR	I don't know.
	[*Pozzo writhes, groans, beats the ground with his fists.*]
ESTRAGON	We should ask him for the bone first. Then if he refuses we'll leave him there.
VLADIMIR	You mean we have him at our mercy?
ESTRAGON	Yes.
VLADIMIR	And that we should subordinate our good offices to certain conditions?
ESTRAGON	What?
VLADIMIR	That seems intelligent all right. But there's one thing I'm afraid of.
POZZO	Help!
ESTRAGON	What?
VLADIMIR	That Lucky might get going all of a sudden. Then we'd be ballocksed.
ESTRAGON	Lucky?
VLADIMIR	The one that went for you yesterday.
ESTRAGON	I tell you there was ten of them.
VLADIMIR	No, before that, the one that kicked you.
ESTRAGON	Is he there?
VLADIMIR	As large as life. [*Gesture towards Lucky.*] For the moment he is inert. But he might run amuck any minute.
POZZO	Help!
ESTRAGON	And suppose we gave him a good beating the two of us?
VLADIMIR	You mean if we fell on him in his sleep?
ESTRAGON	Yes.
VLADIMIR	That seems a good idea all right. But could we do it? Is he really asleep? [*Pause.*] No, the best would be to take advantage of Pozzo's calling for help—
POZZO	Help!
VLADIMIR	To help him—
ESTRAGON	*We* help *him*?

VLADIMIR   In anticipation of some tangible return.

ESTRAGON   And suppose he—

VLADIMIR   Let us not waste our time in idle discourse! [*Pause. Vehemently.*]
Let us do something, while we have the chance! It is not
every day that we are needed. Not indeed that we personally
are needed. Others would meet the case equally well, if not
better. To all mankind they were addressed, those cries for
help still ringing in our ears! But at this place, at this
moment of time, all mankind is us, whether we like it or
not. Let us make the most of it, before it is too late! Let us
represent worthily for once the foul brood to which a cruel
fate consigned us! What do you say? [*Estragon says nothing.*]
It is true that when with folded arms we weigh the pros and
cons we are no less a credit to our species. The tiger bounds
to the help of his congeners without the least reflexion, or
else he slinks away into the depths of the thickets. But that
is not the question. What are we doing here, *that* is the
question. And we are blessed in this, that we happen to
know the answer. Yes, in this immense confusion one thing
alone is clear. We are waiting for Godot to come—

ESTRAGON   Ah!

POZZO   Help!

VLADIMIR   Or for night to fall. [*Pause.*] We have kept our appointment
and that's an end to that. We are not saints, but we have
kept our appointment. How many people can boast as
much?

ESTRAGON   Billions.

VLADIMIR   You think so?

ESTRAGON   I don't know.

VLADIMIR   You may be right.

POZZO   Help!

VLADIMIR   All I know is that the hours are long, under these conditions,
and constrain us to beguile them with proceedings
which—how shall I say—which may at first sight seem

reasonable, until they become a habit. You may say it is to
prevent our reason from foundering. No doubt. But has it
not long been straying in the night without end of the
abyssal depths? That's what I sometimes wonder. You follow
my reasoning?

ESTRAGON [*aphoristic for once*] We are all born mad. Some remain so.

POZZO Help! I'll pay you!

ESTRAGON How much?

POZZO One hundred francs!

ESTRAGON It's not enough.

VLADIMIR I wouldn't go so far as that.

ESTRAGON You think it's enough?

VLADIMIR No, I mean so far as to assert that I was weak in the head
when I came into the world. But that is not the question.

POZZO Two hundred!

VLADIMIR We wait. We are bored. [*He throws up his hand.*] No, don't
protest, we are bored to death, there's no denying it. Good.
A diversion comes along and what do we do? We let it go to
waste. Come, let's get to work! [*He advances towards the heap,
stops in his stride.*] In an instant all will vanish and we'll be
alone once more, in the midst of nothingness! [*He broods.*]

POZZO Two hundred!

VLADIMIR We're coming!
[*He tries to pull Pozzo to his feet, fails, tries again, stumbles, falls,
tries to get up, fails.*]

ESTRAGON What's the matter with you all?

VLADIMIR Help!

ESTRAGON I'm going.

VLADIMIR Don't leave me! They'll kill me!

POZZO Where am I?

VLADIMIR Gogo!

POZZO Help!

VLADIMIR Help!

ESTRAGON I'm going.

VLADIMIR   Help me up first, then we'll go together.

ESTRAGON   You promise?

VLADIMIR   I swear it!

ESTRAGON   And we'll never come back?

VLADIMIR   Never!

ESTRAGON   We'll go to the Pyrenees.

VLADIMIR   Wherever you like.

ESTRAGON   I've always wanted to wander in the Pyrenees.

VLADIMIR   You'll wander in them.

ESTRAGON   [*recalling*] Who farted?

VLADIMIR   Pozzo.

POZZO   Here! Here! Pity!

ESTRAGON   It's revolting!

VLADIMIR   Quick! Give me your hand!

ESTRAGON   I'm going. [*Pause. Louder.*] I'm going.

VLADIMIR   Well I suppose in the end I'll get up by myself. [*He tries, fails.*] In the fullness of time.

ESTRAGON   What's the matter with you?

VLADIMIR   Go to hell.

ESTRAGON   Are you staying there?

VLADIMIR   For the time being.

ESTRAGON   Come on, get up, you'll catch a chill.

VLADIMIR   Don't worry about me.

ESTRAGON   Come on, Didi, don't be pig-headed!
[*He stretches out his hand which Vladimir makes haste to seize.*]

VLADIMIR   Pull!
[*Estragon pulls, stumbles, falls. Long silence.*]

POZZO   Help!

VLADIMIR   We've arrived.

POZZO   Who are you?

VLADIMIR   We are men.
[*Silence.*]

ESTRAGON   Sweet mother earth!

VLADIMIR   Can you get up?

ESTRAGON   I don't know.

VLADIMIR   Try.

ESTRAGON   Not now, not now.

           [*Silence.*]

POZZO   What happened?

VLADIMIR   [*violently*] Will you stop it, you! Pest! He can think of nothing
           but himself!

ESTRAGON   What about a little snooze?

VLADIMIR   Did you hear him? He wants to know what happened!

ESTRAGON   Don't mind him. Sleep.

           [*Silence.*]

POZZO   Pity! Pity!

ESTRAGON   [*with a start*] What is it?

VLADIMIR   Were you asleep?

ESTRAGON   I must have been.

VLADIMIR   It's this bastard Pozzo at it again.

ESTRAGON   Make him stop it. Kick him in the crotch.

VLADIMIR   [*striking Pozzo*] Will you stop it! Crablouse! [*Pozzo extricates
           himself with cries of pain and crawls away. He stops, saws the air
           blindly, calling for help. Vladimir, propped on his elbow, observes
           his retreat.*] He's off! [*Pozzo collapses.*] He's down!

ESTRAGON   What do we do now?

VLADIMIR   Perhaps I could crawl to him.

ESTRAGON   Don't leave me!

VLADIMIR   Or I could call to him.

ESTRAGON   Yes, call to him.

VLADIMIR   Pozzo! [*Silence.*] Pozzo! [*Silence.*] No reply.

ESTRAGON   Together.

VLADIMIR ⎤
         ⎬ Pozzo! Pozzo!
ESTRAGON ⎦

VLADIMIR   He moved.

ESTRAGON   Are you sure his name is Pozzo?

VLADIMIR   [*alarmed*] Mr. Pozzo! Come back! We won't hurt you!

           [*Silence.*]

ESTRAGON   We might try him with other names.

VLADIMIR   I'm afraid he's dying.

ESTRAGON   It'd be amusing.

VLADIMIR   What'd be amusing?

ESTRAGON   To try him with other names, one after the other. It'd pass the time. And we'd be bound to hit on the right one sooner or later.

VLADIMIR   I tell you his name is Pozzo.

ESTRAGON   We'll soon see. [*He reflects.*] Abel! Abel!

POZZO   Help!

ESTRAGON   Got it in one!

VLADIMIR   I begin to weary of this motif.

ESTRAGON   Perhaps the other is called Cain. Cain! Cain!

POZZO   Help!

ESTRAGON   He's all humanity. [*Silence.*] Look at the little cloud.

VLADIMIR   [*raising his eyes*] Where?

ESTRAGON   There. In the zenith.

VLADIMIR   Well? [*Pause.*] What is there so wonderful about it? [*Silence.*]

ESTRAGON   Let's pass on now to something else, do you mind?

VLADIMIR   I was just going to suggest it.

ESTRAGON   But to what?

VLADIMIR   Ah! [*Silence.*]

ESTRAGON   Suppose we got up to begin with?

VLADIMIR   No harm trying. [*They get up.*]

ESTRAGON   Child's play.

VLADIMIR   Simple question of will-power.

ESTRAGON   And now?

POZZO   Help!

ESTRAGON   Let's go.

VLADIMIR   We can't.

ESTRAGON   Why not?

VLADIMIR	We're waiting for Godot.
ESTRAGON	Ah! [*Despairing.*] What'll we do, what'll we do!
POZZO	Help!
VLADIMIR	What about helping him?
ESTRAGON	What does he want?
VLADIMIR	He wants to get up.
ESTRAGON	Then why doesn't he?
VLADIMIR	He wants us to help him to get up.
ESTRAGON	Then why don't we? What are we waiting for? [*They help Pozzo to his feet, let him go. He falls.*]
VLADIMIR	We must hold him. [*They get him up again. Pozzo sags between them, his arms round their necks.*] Feeling better?
POZZO	Who are you?
VLADIMIR	Do you not recognize us?
POZZO	I am blind. [*Silence.*]
ESTRAGON	Perhaps he can see into the future.
VLADIMIR	Since when?
POZZO	I used to have wonderful sight—but are you friends?
ESTRAGON	[*laughing noisily*] He wants to know if we are friends!
VLADIMIR	No, he means friends of his.
ESTRAGON	Well?
VLADIMIR	We've proved we are, by helping him.
ESTRAGON	Exactly. Would we have helped him if we weren't his friends?
VLADIMIR	Possibly.
ESTRAGON	True.
VLADIMIR	Don't let's quibble about that now.
POZZO	You are not highwaymen?
ESTRAGON	Highwaymen! Do we look like highwaymen?
VLADIMIR	Damn it can't you see the man is blind!
ESTRAGON	Damn it so he is. [*Pause.*] So he says.
POZZO	Don't leave me!
VLADIMIR	No question of it.

ESTRAGON	For the moment.
POZZO	What time is it?
VLADIMIR	[*inspecting the sky*] Seven o'clock ... eight o'clock ...
ESTRAGON	That depends what time of year it is.
POZZO	Is it evening?

[*Silence. Vladimir and Estragon scrutinize the sunset.*]

ESTRAGON	It's rising.
VLADIMIR	Impossible.
ESTRAGON	Perhaps it's the dawn.
VLADIMIR	Don't be a fool. It's the west over there.
ESTRAGON	How do you know?
POZZO	[*anguished*] Is it evening?
VLADIMIR	Anyway it hasn't moved.
ESTRAGON	I tell you it's rising.
POZZO	Why don't you answer me?
ESTRAGON	Give us a chance.
VLADIMIR	[*reassuring*] It's evening, Sir, it's evening, night is drawing nigh. My friend here would have me doubt it and I must confess he shook me for a moment. But it is not for nothing I have lived through this long day and I can assure you it is very near the end of its repertory. [*Pause.*] How do you feel now?
ESTRAGON	How much longer are we to cart him around. [*They half release him, catch him again as he falls.*] We are not caryatids!
VLADIMIR	You were saying your sight used to be good, if I heard you right.
POZZO	Wonderful! Wonderful, wonderful sight!

[*Silence.*]

ESTRAGON	[*irritably*] Expand! Expand!
VLADIMIR	Let him alone. Can't you see he's thinking of the days when he was happy. [*Pause.*] *Memoria praeteritorum bonorum*—that must be unpleasant.
ESTRAGON	We wouldn't know.

VLADIMIR	And it came on you all of a sudden?
POZZO	Quite wonderful!
VLADIMIR	I'm asking you if it came on you all of a sudden.
POZZO	I woke up one fine day as blind as Fortune. [*Pause.*] Sometimes I wonder if I'm not still asleep.
VLADIMIR	And when was that?
POZZO	I don't know.
VLADIMIR	But no later than yesterday—
POZZO	[*violently*] Don't question me! The blind have no notion of time. The things of time are hidden from them too.
VLADIMIR	Well just fancy that! I could have sworn it was just the opposite.
ESTRAGON	I'm going.
POZZO	Where are we?
VLADIMIR	I couldn't tell you.
POZZO	It isn't by any chance the place known as the Board?
VLADIMIR	Never heard of it.
POZZO	What is it like?
VLADIMIR	[*looking round*] It's indescribable. It's like nothing. There's nothing. There's a tree.
POZZO	Then it's not the Board.
ESTRAGON	[*sagging*] Some diversion!
POZZO	Where is my menial?
VLADIMIR	He's about somewhere,
POZZO	Why doesn't he answer when I call?
VLADIMIR	I don't know. He seems to be sleeping. Perhaps he's dead.
POZZO	What happened exactly?
ESTRAGON	Exactly!
VLADIMIR	The two of you slipped. [*Pause.*] And fell.
POZZO	Go and see is he hurt.
VLADIMIR	We can't leave you.
POZZO	You needn't both go.
VLADIMIR	[*to Estragon*] You go.
ESTRAGON	After what he did to me? Never!

POZZO   Yes yes, let your friend go, he stinks so. [*Silence.*] What is he waiting for?

VLADIMIR   What you waiting for?

ESTRAGON   I'm waiting for Godot.
[*Silence.*]

VLADIMIR   What exactly should he do?

POZZO   Well to begin with he should pull on the rope, as hard as he likes so long as he doesn't strangle him. He usually responds to that. If not he should give him a taste of his boot, in the face and the privates as far as possible.

VLADIMIR   [*to Estragon*] You see, you've nothing to be afraid of. It's even an opportunity to revenge yourself.

ESTRAGON   And if he defends himself?

POZZO   No no, he never defends himself.

VLADIMIR   I'll come flying to the rescue.

ESTRAGON   Don't take your eyes off me. [*He goes towards Lucky.*]

VLADIMIR   Make sure he's alive before you start. No point in exerting yourself if he's dead.

ESTRAGON   [*bending over Lucky*] He's breathing.

VLADIMIR   Then let him have it.
[*With sudden fury Estragon starts kicking Lucky, hurling abuse at him as he does so. But he hurts his foot and moves away, limping and groaning. Lucky stirs.*]

ESTRAGON   Oh the brute!
[*He sits down on the mound and tries to take off his boot. But he soon desists and disposes himself for sleep, his arms on his knees and his head on his arms.*]

POZZO   What's gone wrong now?

VLADIMIR   My friend has hurt himself

POZZO   And Lucky?

VLADIMIR   So it is he?

POZZO   What?

VLADIMIR   It is Lucky?

POZZO   I don't understand.

VLADIMIR And you are Pozzo?

POZZO Certainly I am Pozzo.

VLADIMIR The same as yesterday?

POZZO Yesterday?

VLADIMIR We met yesterday. [*Silence.*] Do you not remember?

POZZO I don't remember having met anyone yesterday. But tomorrow I won't remember having met anyone today. So don't count on me to enlighten you.

VLADIMIR But—

POZZO Enough! Up pig!

VLADIMIR You were bringing him to the fair to sell him. You spoke to us. He danced. He thought. You had your sight.

POZZO As you please. Let me go! [*Vladimir moves away.*] Up! [*Lucky gets up, gathers up his burdens.*]

VLADIMIR Where do you go from here.

POZZO On. [*Lucky, laden down, takes his place before Pozzo.*] Whip! [*Lucky puts everything down, looks for whip, finds it, puts it into Pozzo's hand, takes up everything again.*] Rope! [*Lucky puts everything down, puts end of rope into Pozzo's hand, takes up everything again.*]

VLADIMIR What is there in the bag?

POZZO Sand. [*He jerks the rope.*] On!

VLADIMIR Don't go yet.

POZZO I'm going.

VLADIMIR What do you do when you fall far from help?

POZZO We wait till we can get up. Then we go on. On!

VLADIMIR Before you go tell him to sing.

POZZO Who?

VLADIMIR Lucky.

POZZO To sing?

VLADIMIR Yes. Or to think. Or to recite.

POZZO But he is dumb.

VLADIMIR Dumb!

POZZO Dumb. He can't even groan.

VLADIMIR   Dumb! Since when?

POZZO   [*suddenly furious*] Have you not done tormenting me with your accursed time! It's abominable! When! When! One day, is that not enough for you, one day he went dumb, one day I went blind, one day we'll go deaf, one day we were born, one day we shall die, the same day, the same second, is that not enough for you? [*Calmer.*] They give birth astride of a grave, the light gleams an instant, then it's night once more. [*He jerks the rope.*] On!

[*Exeunt Pozzo and Lucky. Vladimir follows them to the edge of the stage, looks after them. The noise of falling, reinforced by mimic of Vladimir, announces that they are down again. Silence. Vladimir goes towards Estragon, contemplates him a moment, then shakes him awake.*]

ESTRAGON   [*wild gestures, incoherent words. Finally.*] Why will you never let me sleep?

VLADIMIR   I felt lonely.

ESTRAGON   I was dreaming I was happy.

VLADIMIR   That passed the time.

ESTRAGON   I was dreaming that—

VLADIMIR   [*violently*] Don't tell me! [*Silence.*] I wonder is he really blind.

ESTRAGON   Blind? Who?

VLADIMIR   Pozzo.

ESTRAGON   Blind?

VLADIMIR   He told us he was blind.

ESTRAGON   Well what about it?

VLADIMIR   It seemed to me he saw us.

ESTRAGON   You dreamt it. [*Pause.*] Let's go. We can't. Ah! [*Pause.*] Are you sure it wasn't him?

VLADIMIR   Who?

ESTRAGON   Godot.

VLADIMIR   But who?

ESTRAGON   Pozzo.

VLADIMIR   Not at all! [*Less sure.*] Not at all! [*Still less sure.*] Not at all!

ESTRAGON   I suppose I might as well get up. [*He gets up painfully.*] Ow! Didi!

VLADIMIR   I don't know what to think any more.

ESTRAGON   My feet! [*He sits down again and tries to take off his boots.*] Help me!

VLADIMIR   Was I sleeping, while the others suffered? Am I sleeping now? Tomorrow, when I wake, or think I do, what shall I say of today? That with Estragon my friend, at this place, until the fall of night, I waited for Godot? That Pozzo passed, with his carrier, and that he spoke to us? Probably. But in all that what truth will there be? [*Estragon, having struggled with his boots in vain, is dozing off again. Vladimir looks at him.*] He'll know nothing. He'll tell me about the blows he received and I'll give him a carrot. [*Pause.*] Astride of a grave and a difficult birth. Down in the hole, lingeringly, the grave-digger puts on the forceps. We have time to grow old. The air is full of our cries. [*He listens.*] But habit is a great deadener. [*He looks again at Estragon.*] At me too someone is looking, of me too someone is saying, He is sleeping, he knows nothing, let him sleep on. [*Pause.*] I can't go on! [*Pause.*] What have I said?

[*He goes feverishly to and fro, halts finally at extreme left, broods. Enter Boy right. He halts. Silence.*]

BOY   Mister . . . [*Vladimir turns.*] Mister Albert . . .

VLADIMIR   Off we go again. [*Pause.*] Do you not recognize me?

BOY   No Sir.

VLADIMIR   It wasn't you came yesterday.

BOY   No Sir.

VLADIMIR   This is your first time.

BOY   Yes Sir.

[*Silence.*]

VLADIMIR   You have a message from Mr. Godot.

BOY   Yes Sir.

VLADIMIR   He won't come this evening.

BOY   No Sir.

VLADIMIR   But he'll come tomorrow.

BOY   Yes Sir.

VLADIMIR   Without fail.

BOY   Yes Sir.

           [*Silence.*]

VLADIMIR   Did you meet anyone?

BOY   No Sir.

VLADIMIR   Two other . . . [*he hesitates*] . . . men?

BOY   I didn't see anyone, Sir.

           [*Silence.*]

VLADIMIR   What does he do, Mr. Godot? [*Silence.*] Do you hear me?

BOY   Yes Sir.

VLADIMIR   Well?

BOY   He does nothing, Sir.

           [*Silence.*]

VLADIMIR   How is your brother?

BOY   He's sick, Sir.

VLADIMIR   Perhaps it was he came yesterday.

BOY   I don't know, Sir.

           [*Silence.*]

VLADIMIR   [*softly*] Has he a beard, Mr. Godot?

BOY   Yes Sir.

VLADIMIR   Fair or . . . [*he hesitates*] . . . or black?

BOY   I think it's white, Sir.

           [*Silence.*]

VLADIMIR   Christ have mercy on us!

           [*Silence.*]

BOY   What am I to tell Mr. Godot, Sir?

VLADIMIR   Tell him . . . [*he hesitates*] . . . tell him you saw me and that . . .
           [*he hesitates*] . . . that you saw me. [*Pause. Vladimir advances,
           the Boy recoils. Vladimir halts, the Boy halts. With sudden
           violence.*] You're sure you saw me, you won't come and tell
           me tomorrow that you never saw me!

[*Silence. Vladimir makes a sudden spring forward, the Boy avoids him and exit running. Silence. The sun sets, the moon rises. As in Act 1. Vladimir stands motionless and bowed. Estragon wakes, takes off his boots, gets up with one in each hand and goes and puts them down center front, then goes towards Vladimir.*]

ESTRAGON What's wrong with you?

VLADIMIR Nothing.

ESTRAGON I'm going.

VLADIMIR So am I.

ESTRAGON Was I long asleep?

VLADIMIR I don't know.

[*Silence.*]

ESTRAGON Where shall we go?

VLADIMIR Not far.

ESTRAGON Oh yes, let's go far away from here.

VLADIMIR We can't.

ESTRAGON Why not?

VLADIMIR We have to come back tomorrow.

ESTRAGON What for?

VLADIMIR To wait for Godot.

ESTRAGON Ah! [*Silence.*] He didn't come?

VLADIMIR No.

ESTRAGON And now it's too late.

VLADIMIR Yes, now it's night.

ESTRAGON And if we dropped him? [*Pause.*] If we dropped him?

VLADIMIR He'd punish us. [*Silence. He looks at the tree.*] Everything's dead but the tree.

ESTRAGON [*looking at the tree*] What is it?

VLADIMIR It's the tree.

ESTRAGON Yes, but what kind?

VLADIMIR I don't know. A willow.

[*Estragon draws Vladimir towards the tree. They stand motionless before it. Silence.*]

ESTRAGON Why don't we hang ourselves?

VLADIMIR   With what?

ESTRAGON   You haven't got a bit of rope?

VLADIMIR   No.

ESTRAGON   Then we can't.

[*Silence.*]

VLADIMIR   Let's go.

ESTRAGON   Wait, there's my belt.

VLADIMIR   It's too short.

ESTRAGON   You could hang on to my legs.

VLADIMIR   And who'd hang on to mine?

ESTRAGON   True.

VLADIMIR   Show all the same. [*Estragon loosens the cord that holds up his trousers which, much too big for him, fall about his ankles. They look at the cord.*] It might do at a pinch. But is it strong enough?

ESTRAGON   We'll soon see. Here.

[*They each take an end of the cord and pull. It breaks. They almost fall.*]

VLADIMIR   Not worth a curse.

[*Silence.*]

ESTRAGON   You say we have to come back tomorrow?

VLADIMIR   Yes.

ESTRAGON   Then we can bring a good bit of rope.

VLADIMIR   Yes.

[*Silence.*]

ESTRAGON   Didi.

VLADIMIR   Yes.

ESTRAGON   I can't go on like this.

VLADIMIR   That's what you think.

ESTRAGON   If we parted? That might be better for us.

VLADIMIR   We'll hang ourselves tomorrow. [*Pause.*] Unless Godot comes.

ESTRAGON   And if he comes?

VLADIMIR   We'll be saved.

[*Vladimir takes off his hat (Lucky's), peers inside it, feels about inside it, shakes it, knocks on the crown, puts it on again.*]

ESTRAGON   Well? Shall we go?

VLADIMIR   Pull on your trousers.

ESTRAGON   What?

VLADIMIR   Pull on your trousers.

ESTRAGON   You want me to pull off my trousers?

VLADIMIR   Pull ON your trousers.

ESTRAGON   [*realizing his trousers are down*] True. [*He pulls up his trousers.*]

VLADIMIR   Well? Shall we go?

ESTRAGON   Yes, let's go.

[*They do not move.*]

Curtain

ENDGAME

A play in one act

For Roger Blin

Nagg
Nell
Hamm
Clov

Bare interior.

Grey light.

Left and right back, high up, two small windows, curtains drawn.

Front right, a door. Hanging near door, its face to wall, a picture.

Front left, touching each other, covered with an old sheet, two ashbins.

Center, in an armchair on castors, covered with an old sheet, Hamm.

Motionless by the door, his eyes fixed on Hamm, Clov. Very red face.

Brief tableau.

Clov goes and stands under window left. Stiff, staggering walk. He looks up at window left. He turns and looks at window right. He goes and stands under window right. He looks up at window right. He turns and looks at window left. He goes out, comes back immediately with a small step-ladder, carries it over and sets it down under window left, gets up on it, draws back curtain. He gets down, takes six steps (for example) towards window right, goes back for ladder, carries it over and sets it down under window right, gets up on it, draws back curtain. He gets down, takes three steps towards window left, goes back for ladder, carries it over and sets it down under window left, gets up on it, looks out of window. Brief laugh. He gets down, takes one step towards window right, goes back for ladder, carries it over and sets it down under window right, gets up on it, looks out of window. Brief laugh. He gets down, goes with ladder towards ashbins, halts, turns, carries back ladder and sets it down under window right, goes to ashbins, removes sheet covering them, folds it over his arm. He raises one lid, stoops and looks into bin. Brief laugh. He closes lid. Same with other bin. He goes to Hamm, removes sheet covering him, folds it over his arm. In a dressing-gown, a stiff toque on his head, a large blood-stained handkerchief over his face, a whistle hanging from his neck, a rug over his knees, thick socks on his feet, Hamm seems to be asleep. Clov looks him over. Brief laugh. He goes to door, halts, turns towards auditorium.

CLOV [*fixed gaze, tonelessly*] Finished, it's finished, nearly finished, it must be nearly finished.
[*Pause.*]
Grain upon grain, one by one, and one day, suddenly, there's a heap, a little heap, the impossible heap.
[*Pause.*]
I can't be punished any more.
[*Pause.*]
I'll go now to my kitchen, ten feet by ten feet by ten feet, and wait for him to whistle me.
[*Pause.*]
Nice dimensions, nice proportions, I'll lean on the table, and look at the wall, and wait for him to whistle me.
[*He remains a moment motionless, then goes out. He comes back immediately, goes to window right, takes up the ladder and carries it out. Pause. Hamm stirs. He yawns under the handkerchief. He removes the handkerchief from his face. Very red face. Black glasses.*]

HAMM Me—
[*he yawns*]
—to play.
[*He holds the handkerchief spread out before him.*]
Old stancher!
[*He takes off his glasses, wipes his eyes, his face, the glasses, puts them on again, folds the handkerchief and puts it back neatly in the breast-pocket of his dressing-gown. He clears his throat, joins the tips of his fingers.*]
Can there be misery—
[*he yawns*]

—loftier than mine? No doubt. Formerly. But now?

[*Pause.*]

My father?

[*Pause.*]

My mother?

[*Pause.*]

My . . . dog?

[*Pause.*]

Oh I am willing to believe they suffer as much as such creatures can suffer. But does that mean their sufferings equal mine? No doubt.

[*Pause.*]

No, all is a—

[*he yawns*]

—bsolute,

[*proudly*]

the bigger a man is the fuller he is.

[*Pause. Gloomily.*]

And the emptier.

[*He sniffs.*]

Clov!

[*Pause.*]

No, alone.

[*Pause.*]

What dreams! Those forests!

[*Pause.*]

Enough, it's time it ended, in the shelter too.

[*Pause.*]

And yet I hesitate, I hesitate to . . . to end. Yes, there it is, it's time it ended and yet I hesitate to—

[*he yawns*]

—to end.

[*Yawns.*]

God, I'm tired, I'd be better off in bed.

[*He whistles. Enter Clov immediately. He halts beside the chair.*]

You pollute the air!

[*Pause.*]

Get me ready, I'm going to bed.

CLOV   I've just got you up.

HAMM   And what of it?

CLOV   I can't be getting you up and putting you to bed every five minutes, I have things to do.

[*Pause.*]

HAMM   Did you ever see my eyes?

CLOV   No.

HAMM   Did you never have the curiosity, while I was sleeping, to take off my glasses and look at my eyes?

CLOV   Pulling back the lids?

[*Pause.*]

No.

HAMM   One of these days I'll show them to you.

[*Pause.*]

It seems they've gone all white.

[*Pause.*]

What time is it?

CLOV   The same as usual.

HAMM   [*gesture towards window right*] Have you looked?

CLOV   Yes.

HAMM   Well?

CLOV   Zero.

HAMM   It'd need to rain.

CLOV   It won't rain.

[*Pause.*]

HAMM   Apart from that, how do you feel?

CLOV   I don't complain.

HAMM   You feel normal?

CLOV   [*irritably*] I tell you I don't complain.

HAMM   I feel a little queer.

[*Pause.*]

Clov!

CLOV   Yes.

HAMM   Have you not had enough?

CLOV   Yes!

[*Pause.*]

Of what?

HAMM   Of this ... this ... thing.

CLOV   I always had.

[*Pause.*]

Not you?

HAMM   [*gloomily*] Then there's no reason for it to change.

CLOV   It may end.

[*Pause.*]

All life long the same questions, the same answers.

HAMM   Get me ready.

[*Clov does not move.*]

Go and get the sheet.

[*Clov does not move.*]

Clov!

CLOV   Yes.

HAMM   I'll give you nothing more to eat.

CLOV   Then we'll die.

HAMM   I'll give you just enough to keep you from dying. You'll be
       hungry all the time.

CLOV   Then we won't die.

[*Pause.*]

I'll go and get the sheet.

[*He goes towards the door.*]

HAMM   No!

[*Clov halts.*]

I'll give you one biscuit per day.

[*Pause.*]

One and a half.

[*Pause.*]

Why do you stay with me?

CLOV   Why do you keep me?

HAMM   There's no one else.

CLOV   There's nowhere else.

[*Pause.*]

HAMM   You're leaving me all the same.

CLOV   I'm trying.

HAMM   You don't love me.

CLOV   No.

HAMM   You loved me once.

CLOV   Once!

HAMM   I've made you suffer too much.

[*Pause.*]

Haven't I?

CLOV   It's not that.

HAMM   [*shocked*] I haven't made you suffer too much?

CLOV   Yes!

HAMM   [*relieved*] Ah you gave me a fright!

[*Pause. Coldly.*]

Forgive me.

[*Pause. Louder.*]

I said, Forgive me.

CLOV   I heard you.

[*Pause.*]

Have you bled?

HAMM   Less.

[*Pause.*]

Is it not time for my pain-killer?

CLOV   No.

[*Pause.*]

HAMM   How are your eyes?

CLOV   Bad.

HAMM   How are your legs?

CLOV   Bad.

HAMM   But you can move.

CLOV   Yes.

HAMM   [*violently*] Then move!

[*Clov goes to back wall, leans against it with his forehead and hands.*]

Where are you?

CLOV   Here.

HAMM   Come back!

[*Clov returns to his place beside the chair.*]

Where are you?

CLOV   Here.

HAMM   Why don't you kill me?

CLOV   I don't know the combination of the cupboard.

[*Pause.*]

HAMM   Go and get two bicycle-wheels.

CLOV   There are no more bicycle-wheels.

HAMM   What have you done with your bicycle?

CLOV   I never had a bicycle.

HAMM   The thing is impossible.

CLOV   When there were still bicycles I wept to have one. I crawled at your feet. You told me to go to hell. Now there are none.

HAMM   And your rounds? When you inspected my paupers. Always on foot?

CLOV   Sometimes on horse.

[*The lid of one of the bins lifts and the hands of Nagg appear, gripping the rim. Then his head emerges. Nightcap. Very white face. Nagg yawns, then listens.*]

I'll leave you, I have things to do.

HAMM   In your kitchen?

CLOV   Yes.

HAMM   Outside of here it's death.

[*Pause.*]

All right, be off.

[*Exit Clov. Pause.*]

We're getting on.

NAGG   Me pap!

HAMM   Accursed progenitor!

NAGG   Me pap!

HAMM   The old folks at home! No decency left! Guzzle, guzzle, that's all they think of.

[*He whistles. Enter Clov. He halts beside the chair.*]

Well! I thought you were leaving me.

CLOV   Oh not just yet, not just yet.

NAGG   Me pap!

HAMM   Give him his pap.

CLOV   There's no more pap.

HAMM   [*to Nagg*] Do you hear that? There's no more pap. You'll never get any more pap.

NAGG   I want me pap!

HAMM   Give him a biscuit.

[*Exit Clov.*]

Accursed fornicator! How are your stumps?

NAGG   Never mind me stumps.

[*Enter Clov with biscuit.*]

CLOV   I'm back again, with the biscuit.

[*He gives biscuit to Nagg who fingers it, sniffs it.*]

NAGG   [*plaintively*] What is it?

CLOV   Spratt's medium.

NAGG   [*as before*] It's hard! I can't!

HAMM   Bottle him!

[*Clov pushes Nagg back into the bin, closes the lid.*]

CLOV   [*returning to his place beside the chair*] If age but knew!

HAMM   Sit on him!

CLOV   I can't sit.

HAMM   True. And I can't stand.

CLOV   So it is.

HAMM   Every man his speciality.

[*Pause.*]

No phone calls?

[*Pause.*]

Don't we laugh?

CLOV   [*after reflection*] I don't feel like it.

HAMM   [*after reflection*] Nor I.

[*Pause.*]

Clov!

CLOV   Yes.

HAMM   Nature has forgotten us.

CLOV   There's no more nature.

HAMM   No more nature! You exaggerate.

CLOV   In the vicinity.

HAMM   But we breathe, we change! We lose our hair, our teeth! Our bloom! Our ideals!

CLOV   Then she hasn't forgotten us.

HAMM   But you say there is none.

CLOV   [*sadly*] No one that ever lived ever thought so crooked as we.

HAMM   We do what we can.

CLOV   We shouldn't.

[*Pause.*]

HAMM   You're a bit of all right, aren't you?

CLOV   A smithereen.

[*Pause.*]

HAMM   This is slow work.

[*Pause.*]

Is it not time for my pain-killer?

CLOV   No.

[*Pause.*]

I'll leave you, I have things to do.

HAMM   In your kitchen?

CLOV   Yes.

HAMM   What, I'd like to know.

CLOV   I look at the wall.

HAMM   The wall! And what do you see on your wall? Mene, mene? Naked bodies?

CLOV   I see my light dying.

HAMM   Your light dying! Listen to that! Well, it can die just as well here, *your* light. Take a look at me and then come back and tell me what you think of *your* light.

               [*Pause.*]

CLOV   You shouldn't speak to me like that.

               [*Pause.*]

HAMM   [*coldly*] Forgive me.

               [*Pause. Louder.*]

               I said, Forgive me.

CLOV   I heard you.

               [*The lid of Nagg's bin lifts. His hands appear, gripping the rim. Then his head emerges. In his mouth the biscuit. He listens.*]

HAMM   Did your seeds come up?

CLOV   No.

HAMM   Did you scratch round them to see if they had sprouted?

CLOV   They haven't sprouted.

HAMM   Perhaps it's still too early.

CLOV   If they were going to sprout they would have sprouted.

               [*Violently.*]

               They'll never sprout!

               [*Pause. Nagg takes biscuit in his hand.*]

HAMM   This is not much fun.

               [*Pause.*]

               But that's always the way at the end of the day, isn't it, Clov?

CLOV   Always.

HAMM   It's the end of the day like any other day, isn't it, Clov?

CLOV   Looks like it.

               [*Pause.*]

HAMM   [*anguished*] What's happening, what's happening?

CLOV   Something is taking its course.

               [*Pause.*]

HAMM   All right, be off.

       [*He leans back in his chair, remains motionless. Clov does not move, heaves a great groaning sigh. Hamm sits up.*]

       I thought I told you to be off.

CLOV   I'm trying.

       [*He goes to door, halts.*]

       Ever since I was whelped.

       [*Exit Clov.*]

HAMM   We're getting on.

       [*He leans back in his chair, remains motionless. Nagg knocks on the lid of the other bin. Pause. He knocks harder. The lid lifts and the hands of Nell appear, gripping the rim. Then her head emerges. Lace cap. Very white face.*]

NELL   What is it, my pet?

       [*Pause.*]

       Time for love?

NAGG   Were you asleep?

NELL   Oh no!

NAGG   Kiss me.

NELL   We can't.

NAGG   Try.

       [*Their heads strain towards each other, fail to meet, fall apart again.*]

NELL   Why this farce, day after day?

       [*Pause.*]

NAGG   I've lost me tooth.

NELL   When?

NAGG   I had it yesterday.

NELL   [*elegiac*] Ah yesterday!

       [*They turn painfully towards each other.*]

NAGG   Can you see me?

NELL   Hardly. And you?

NAGG   What?

NELL   Can you see me?

NAGG   Hardly.

NELL   So much the better, so much the better.

NAGG   Don't say that.

[*Pause.*]

Our sight has failed.

NELL   Yes.

[*Pause. They turn away from each other.*]

NAGG   Can you hear me?

NELL   Yes. And you?

NAGG   Yes.

[*Pause.*]

Our hearing hasn't failed.

NELL   Our what?

NAGG   Our hearing.

NELL   No.

[*Pause.*]

Have you anything else to say to me?

NAGG   Do you remember—

NELL   No.

NAGG   When we crashed on our tandem and lost our shanks.

[*They laugh heartily.*]

NELL   It was in the Ardennes.

[*They laugh less heartily.*]

NAGG   On the road to Sedan.

[*They laugh still less heartily.*]

Are you cold?

NELL   Yes, perished. And you?

NAGG   [*Pause.*]

I'm freezing.

[*Pause.*]

Do you want to go in?

NELL   Yes.

NAGG   Then go in.

[*Nell does not move*]

Why don't you go in?

NELL   I don't know.

     [*Pause.*]

NAGG   Has he changed your sawdust?

NELL   It isn't sawdust.

     [*Pause. Wearily.*]

     Can you not be a little accurate, Nagg?

NAGG   Your sand then. It's not important.

NELL   It is important.

     [*Pause.*]

NAGG   It was sawdust once.

NELL   Once!

NAGG   And now it's sand.

     [*Pause.*]

     From the shore.

     [*Pause. Impatiently.*]

     Now it's sand he fetches from the shore.

NELL   Now it's sand.

NAGG   Has he changed yours?

NELL   No.

NAGG   Nor mine.

     [*Pause.*]

     I won't have it!

     [*Pause. Holding up the biscuit.*]

     Do you want a bit?

NELL   No.

     [*Pause.*]

     Of what?

NAGG   Biscuit. I've kept you half.

     [*He looks at the biscuit. Proudly.*]

     Three quarters. For you. Here.

     [*He proffers the biscuit.*]

     No?

     [*Pause.*]

     Do you not feel well?

HAMM [*wearily*] Quiet, quiet, you're keeping me awake.

[*Pause.*]

Talk softer.

[*Pause.*]

If I could sleep I might make love. I'd go into the woods. My eyes would see . . . the sky, the earth. I'd run, run, they wouldn't catch me.

[*Pause.*]

Nature!

[*Pause.*]

There's something dripping in my head.

[*Pause.*]

A heart, a heart in my head.

[*Pause.*]

NAGG [*soft*] Do you hear him? A heart in his head!

[*He chuckles cautiously.*]

NELL One mustn't laugh at those things, Nagg. Why must you always laugh at them?

NAGG Not so loud!

NELL [*without lowering her voice*] Nothing is funnier than unhappiness, I grant you that. But—

NAGG [*shocked*] Oh!

NELL Yes, yes, it's the most comical thing in the world. And we laugh, we laugh, with a will, in the beginning. But it's always the same thing. Yes, it's like the funny story we have heard too often, we still find it funny, but we don't laugh any more.

[*Pause.*]

Have you anything else to say to me?

NAGG No.

NELL Are you quite sure?

[*Pause.*]

Then I'll leave you.

NAGG Do you not want your biscuit?

[*Pause.*]

I'll keep it for you.

[*Pause.*]

I thought you were going to leave me.

NELL   I am going to leave you.

NAGG   Could you give me a scratch before you go?

NELL   No.

[*Pause.*]

Where?

NAGG   In the back.

NELL   No.

[*Pause.*]

Rub yourself against the rim.

NAGG   It's lower down. In the hollow.

NELL   What hollow?

NAGG   The hollow!

[*Pause.*]

Could you not?

[*Pause.*]

Yesterday you scratched me there.

NELL   [*elegiac*] Ah yesterday!

NAGG   Could you not?

[*Pause.*]

Would you like me to scratch you?

[*Pause.*]

Are you crying again?

NELL   I was trying.

[*Pause.*]

HAMM   Perhaps it's a little vein.

[*Pause.*]

NAGG   What was that he said?

NELL   Perhaps it's a little vein.

NAGG   What does that mean?

[*Pause.*]

That means nothing.

[*Pause.*]

Will I tell you the story of the tailor?

NELL   No.

[*Pause.*]

What for?

NAGG   To cheer you up.

NELL   It's not funny.

NAGG   It always made you laugh.

[*Pause.*]

The first time I thought you'd die.

NELL   It was on Lake Como.

[*Pause.*]

One April afternoon.

[*Pause.*]

Can you believe it?

NAGG   What?

NELL   That we once went out rowing on Lake Como.

[*Pause.*]

One April afternoon.

NAGG   We had got engaged the day before.

NELL   Engaged!

NAGG   You were in such fits that we capsized. By rights we should have been drowned.

NELL   It was because I felt happy.

NAGG   [*indignant*] It was not, it was not, it was my story and nothing else. Happy! Don't you laugh at it still? Every time I tell it. Happy!

NELL   It was deep, deep. And you could see down to the bottom. So white. So clean.

NAGG   Let me tell it again.

[*Raconteur's voice.*]

An Englishman, needing a pair of striped trousers in a hurry for the New Year festivities, goes to his tailor who takes his measurements.

[*Tailor's voice.*]

"That's the lot, come back in four days, I'll have it ready." Good.
Four days later.
[*Tailor's voice.*]
"So sorry, come back in a week, I've made a mess of the seat."
Good, that's all right, a neat seat can be very ticklish. A week
later.
[*Tailor's voice.*]
"Frightfully sorry, come back in ten days, I've made a hash of
the crotch." Good, can't be helped, a snug crotch is always a
teaser. Ten days later.
[*Tailor's voice.*]
"Dreadfully sorry, come back in a fortnight, I've made a balls of
the fly." Good, at a pinch, a smart fly is a stiff proposition.
[*Pause. Normal voice.*]
I never told it worse.
[*Pause. Gloomy.*]
I tell this story worse and worse.
[*Pause. Raconteur's voice.*]
Well, to make it short, the bluebells are blowing and he
ballockses the buttonholes.
[*Customer's voice.*]
"God damn you to hell, Sir, no, it's indecent, there are limits! In
six days, do you hear me, six days, God made the world. Yes Sir,
no less Sir, the WORLD! And you are not bloody well capable of
making me a pair of trousers in three months!"
[*Tailor's voice, scandalized.*]
"But my dear Sir, my dear Sir, look—
[*disdainful gesture, disgustedly*]
—at the world—
[*pause*]
and look—
[*loving gesture, proudly*]
—at my TROUSERS!"
[*Pause. He looks at Nell who has remained impassive, her eyes*]

unseeing, breaks into a high forced laugh, cuts it short, pokes his head towards Nell, launches his laugh again.]

HAMM   Silence!

[*Nagg starts, cuts short his laugh.*]

NELL   You could see down to the bottom.

HAMM   [*exasperated*] Have you not finished? Will you never finish?

[*With sudden fury.*]

Will this never finish?

[*Nagg disappears into his bin, closes the lid behind him. Nell does not move. Frenziedly.*]

My kingdom for a nightman!

[*He whistles. Enter Clov.*]

Clear away this muck! Chuck it in the sea!

[*Clov goes to bins, halts.*]

NELL   So white.

HAMM   What? What's she blathering about?

[*Clov stoops, takes Nell's hand, feels her pulse.*]

NELL   [*to Clov*] Desert!

[*Clov lets go her hand, pushes her back in the bin, closes the lid.*]

CLOV   [*returning to his place beside the chair*] She has no pulse.

HAMM   What was she drivelling about?

CLOV   She told me to go away, into the desert.

HAMM   Damn busybody! Is that all?

CLOV   No.

HAMM   What else?

CLOV   I didn't understand.

HAMM   Have you bottled her?

CLOV   Yes.

HAMM   Are they both bottled?

CLOV   Yes.

HAMM   Screw down the lids.

[*Clov goes towards door.*]

Time enough.

[*Clov halts.*]

My anger subsides, I'd like to pee.

CLOV [*with alacrity*] I'll go and get the catheter.

[*He goes towards door.*]

HAMM Time enough.

[*Clov halts.*]

Give me my pain-killer.

CLOV It's too soon.

[*Pause.*]

It's too soon on top of your tonic, it wouldn't act.

HAMM In the morning they brace you up and in the evening they
calm you down. Unless it's the other way round.

[*Pause.*]

That old doctor, he's dead naturally?

CLOV He wasn't old.

HAMM But he's dead?

CLOV Naturally.

[*Pause.*]

You ask *me* that?

[*Pause.*]

HAMM Take me for a little turn.

[*Clov goes behind the chair and pushes it forward.*]

Not too fast!

[*Clov pushes chair.*]

Right round the world!

[*Clov pushes chair.*]

Hug the walls, then back to the center again.

[*Clov pushes chair.*]

I was right in the center, wasn't I?

CLOV [*pushing*] Yes.

HAMM We'd need a proper wheel-chair. With big wheels. Bicycle-wheels!

[*Pause.*]

Are you hugging?

CLOV [*pushing*] Yes.

HAMM [*groping for wall*] It's a lie! Why do you lie to me?

CLOV [*bearing closer to wall*] There! There!

HAMM Stop!

[*Clov stops chair close to back wall. Hamm lays his hand against wall.*]

Old wall!

[*Pause.*]

Beyond is the . . . other hell.

[*Pause. Violently.*]

Closer! Closer! Up against!

CLOV Take away your hand.

[*Hamm withdraws his hand. Clov rams chair against wall.*]

There!

[*Hamm leans towards wall, applies his ear to it.*]

HAMM Do you hear?

[*He strikes the wall with his knuckles.*]

Do you hear? Hollow bricks!

[*He strikes again.*]

All that's hollow!

[*Pause. He straightens up. Violently.*]

That's enough. Back!

CLOV We haven't done the round.

HAMM Back to my place!

[*Clov pushes chair back to center.*]

Is that my place?

CLOV Yes, that's your place.

HAMM Am I right in the center?

CLOV I'll measure it.

HAMM More or less! More or less!

CLOV [*moving chair slightly*] There!

HAMM I'm more or less in the center?

CLOV I'd say so.

HAMM You'd say so! Put me right in the center!

CLOV I'll go and get the tape.

HAMM Roughly! Roughly!

[*Clov moves chair slightly.*]

Bang in the center!

CLOV There!

[*Pause.*]

HAMM I feel a little too far to the left.

[*Clov moves chair slightly.*]

Now I feel a little too far to the right.

[*Clov moves chair slightly.*]

I feel a little too far forward.

[*Clov moves chair slightly.*]

Now I feel a little too far back.

[*Clov moves chair slightly.*]

Don't stay there,

[*i.e. behind the chair*].

you give me the shivers.

[*Clov returns to his place beside the chair.*]

CLOV If I could kill him I'd die happy.

[*Pause.*]

HAMM What's the weather like?

CLOV As usual.

HAMM Look at the earth.

CLOV I've looked.

HAMM With the glass?

CLOV No need of the glass.

HAMM Look at it with the glass.

CLOV I'll go and get the glass.

[*Exit Clov.*]

HAMM No need of the glass!

[*Enter Clov with telescope.*]

CLOV I'm back again, with the glass.

[*He goes to window right, looks up at it.*]

I need the steps.

HAMM Why? Have you shrunk?

[*Exit Clov with telescope.*]

I don't like that, I don't like that.

[*Enter Clov with ladder, but without telescope.*]

CLOV I'm back again, with the steps.

[*He sets down ladder under window right, gets up on it, realizes he has not the telescope, gets down.*]

I need the glass.

[*He goes towards door.*]

HAMM [*violently*] But you have the glass!

CLOV [*halting, violently*] No, I haven't the glass!

[*Exit Clov.*]

HAMM This is deadly.

[*Enter Clov with telescope. He goes towards ladder.*]

CLOV Things are livening up.

[*He gets up on ladder, raises the telescope, lets it fall.*]

I did it on purpose.

[*He gets down, picks up the telescope, turns it on auditorium.*]

I see . . . a multitude . . . in transports . . . of joy.

[*Pause.*]

That's what I call a magnifier.

[*He lowers the telescope, turns towards Hamm.*]

Well? Don't we laugh?

HAMM [*after reflection*] I don't.

CLOV [*after reflection*] Nor I.

[*He gets up on ladder, turns the telescope on the without.*]

Let's see.

[*He looks, moving the telescope.*]

Zero . . .

[*he looks*]

. . . zero.

[*he looks*]

and zero.

HAMM Nothing stirs. All is—

CLOV Zer—

HAMM [*violently*] Wait till you're spoken to!

[*Normal voice.*]

All is . . . all is . . . all is what?

[*Violently.*]

All is what?

CLOV What all is? in a word? Is that what you want to know? Just a moment.

[*He turns the telescope on the without, looks, lowers the telescope, turns towards Hamm.*]

Corpsed.

[*Pause.*]

Well? Content?

HAMM Look at the sea.

CLOV It's the same.

HAMM Look at the ocean!

[*Clov gets down, takes a few steps towards window left, goes back for ladder, carries it over and sets it down under window left, gets up on it, turns the telescope on the without, looks at length. He starts, lowers the telescope, examines it, turns it again on the without.*]

CLOV Never seen anything like that!

HAMM [*anxious*] What? A sail? A fin? Smoke?

CLOV [*looking*] The light is sunk.

HAMM [*relieved*] Pah! We all knew that.

CLOV [*looking*] There was a bit left.

HAMM The base.

CLOV [*looking*] Yes.

HAMM And now?

CLOV [*looking*] All gone.

HAMM No gulls?

CLOV [*looking*] Gulls!

HAMM And the horizon? Nothing on the horizon?

CLOV [*lowering the telescope, turning towards Hamm, exasperated*] What in God's name could there be on the horizon?

[*Pause.*]

HAMM The waves, how are the waves?

CLOV The waves?

[*He turns the telescope on the waves.*]

Lead.

HAMM And the sun?

CLOV   [*looking*] Zero.

HAMM   But it should be sinking. Look again.

CLOV   [*looking*] Damn the sun.

HAMM   Is it night already then?

CLOV   [*looking*] No.

HAMM   Then what is it?

CLOV   [*looking*] Grey.

       [*Lowering the telescope, turning towards Hamm, louder.*]

       Grey!

       [*Pause. Still louder.*]

       GRREY!

       [*Pause. He gets down, approaches Hamm from behind, whispers in his ear.*]

HAMM   [*starting*] Grey! Did I hear you say grey?

CLOV   Light black. From pole to pole.

HAMM   You exaggerate.

       [*Pause.*]

       Don't stay there, you give me the shivers.

       [*Clov returns to his place beside the chair.*]

CLOV   Why this farce, day after day?

HAMM   Routine. One never knows.

       [*Pause.*]

       Last night I saw inside my breast. There was a big sore.

CLOV   Pah! You saw your heart.

HAMM   No, it was living.

       [*Pause. Anguished.*]

       Clov!

CLOV   Yes.

HAMM   What's happening?

CLOV   Something is taking its course.

       [*Pause.*]

HAMM   Clov!

CLOV   [*impatiently*] What is it?

HAMM   We're not beginning to . . . to . . . mean something?

CLOV   Mean something! You and I, mean something!
[*Brief laugh.*]
Ah that's a good one!

HAMM   I wonder.
[*Pause.*]
Imagine if a rational being came back to earth, wouldn't he be liable to get ideas into his head if he observed us long enough.
[*Voice of rational being.*]
Ah, good, now I see what it is, yes, now I understand what they're at!
[*Clov starts, drops the telescope and begins to scratch his belly with both hands. Normal voice.*]
And without going so far as that, we ourselves . . .
[*with emotion*]
we ourselves . . . at certain moments . . .
[*Vehemently.*]
To think perhaps it won't all have been for nothing!

CLOV   [*anguished, scratching himself*] I have a flea!

HAMM   A flea! Are there still fleas?

CLOV   On me there's one.
[*Scratching.*]
Unless it's a crablouse.

HAMM   [*very perturbed*] But humanity might start from there all over again! Catch him, for the love of God!

CLOV   I'll go and get the powder.
[*Exit Clov.*]

HAMM   A flea! This is awful! What a day!
[*Enter Clov with a sprinkling-tin.*]

CLOV   I'm back again, with the insecticide.

HAMM   Let him have it!
[*Clov loosens the top of his trousers, pulls it forward and shakes powder into the aperture. He stoops, looks, waits, starts, frenziedly shakes more powder, stoops, looks, waits.*]

CLOV   The bastard!

HAMM   Did you get him?

CLOV   Looks like it.

[*He drops the tin and adjusts his trousers.*]

Unless he's laying doggo.

HAMM   Laying! Lying you mean. Unless he's *lying* doggo.

CLOV   Ah? One says lying? One doesn't say laying?

HAMM   Use your head, can't you. If he was laying we'd be bitched.

CLOV   Ah.

[*Pause.*]

What about that pee?

HAMM   I'm having it.

CLOV   Ah that's the spirit, that's the spirit!

[*Pause.*]

HAMM   [*with ardour*] Let's go from here, the two of us! South! You can make a raft and the currents will carry us away, far away, to other . . . mammals!

CLOV   God forbid!

HAMM   Alone, I'll embark alone! Get working on that raft immediately. Tomorrow I'll be gone for ever.

CLOV   [*hastening towards door*] I'll start straight away.

HAMM   Wait!

[*Clov halts.*]

Will there be sharks, do you think?

CLOV   Sharks? I don't know. If there are there will be.

[*He goes towards door.*]

HAMM   Wait!

[*Clov halts.*]

Is it not yet time for my pain-killer?

CLOV   [*violently*] No!

[*He goes towards door.*]

HAMM   Wait!

[*Clov halts.*]

How are your eyes?

CLOV   Bad.

HAMM But you can see.

CLOV All I want.

HAMM How are your legs?

CLOV Bad.

HAMM But you can walk.

CLOV I come ... and go.

HAMM In my house.

[*Pause. With prophetic relish.*]

One day you'll be blind, like me. You'll be sitting there, a speck in the void, in the dark, for ever, like me.

[*Pause.*]

One day you'll say to yourself, I'm tired, I'll sit down, and you'll go and sit down. Then you'll say, I'm hungry, I'll get up and get something to eat. But you won't get up. You'll say, I shouldn't have sat down, but since I have I'll sit on a little longer, then I'll get up and get something to eat. But you won't get up and you won't get anything to eat.

[*Pause.*]

You'll look at the wall a while, then you'll say, I'll close my eyes, perhaps have a little sleep, after that I'll feel better, and you'll close them. And when you open them again there'll be no wall any more.

[*Pause.*]

Infinite emptiness will be all around you, all the resurrected dead of all the ages wouldn't fill it, and there you'll be like a little bit of grit in the middle of the steppe.

[*Pause.*]

Yes, one day you'll know what it is, you'll be like me, except that you won't have anyone with you, because you won't have had pity on anyone and because there won't be anyone left to have pity on.

[*Pause.*]

CLOV It's not certain.

[*Pause.*]

And there's one thing you forget.

HAMM Ah?

CLOV I can't sit down.

HAMM [*impatiently*] Well you'll lie down then, what the hell! Or you'll come to a standstill, simply stop and stand still, the way you are now. One day you'll say, I'm tired, I'll stop. What does the attitude matter?

[*Pause.*]

CLOV So you all want me to leave you.

HAMM Naturally.

CLOV Then I'll leave you.

HAMM You can't leave us.

CLOV Then I won't leave you.

[*Pause.*]

HAMM Why don't you finish us?

[*Pause.*]

I'll tell you the combination of the cupboard if you promise to finish me.

CLOV I couldn't finish you.

HAMM Then you won't finish me.

[*Pause.*]

CLOV I'll leave you, I have things to do.

HAMM Do you remember when you came here?

CLOV No. Too small, you told me.

HAMM Do you remember your father.

CLOV [*wearily*] Same answer.

[*Pause.*]

You've asked me these questions millions of times.

HAMM I love the old questions.

[*With fervour.*]

Ah the old questions, the old answers, there's nothing like them!

[*Pause.*]

It was I was a father to you.

CLOV Yes.

[*He looks at Hamm fixedly.*]

You were that to me.

HAMM   My house a home for you.

CLOV   Yes.

[*He looks about him.*]

This was that for me.

HAMM   [*proudly*] But for me [*gesture towards himself*],

no father. But for Hamm [*gesture towards surroundings*],

no home.

[*Pause.*]

CLOV   I'll leave you.

HAMM   Did you ever think of one thing?

CLOV   Never.

HAMM   That here we're down in a hole.

[*Pause.*]

But beyond the hills? Eh? Perhaps it's still green. Eh?

[*Pause.*]

Flora! Pomona!

[*Ecstatically.*]

Ceres!

[*Pause.*]

Perhaps you won't need to go very far.

CLOV   I can't go very far.

[*Pause.*]

I'll leave you.

HAMM   Is my dog ready?

CLOV   He lacks a leg.

HAMM   Is he silky?

CLOV   He's a kind of Pomeranian.

HAMM   Go and get him.

CLOV   He lacks a leg.

HAMM   Go and get him!

[*Exit Clov.*]

We're getting on.

[*Enter Clov holding by one of its three legs a black toy dog.*]

CLOV   Your dogs are here.

[*He hands the dog to Hamm who feels it, fondles it.*]

HAMM   He's white, isn't he?

CLOV   Nearly.

HAMM   What do you mean, nearly? Is he white or isn't he?

CLOV   He isn't.

[*Pause.*]

HAMM   You've forgotten the sex.

CLOV   [*vexed*] But he isn't finished. The sex goes on at the end.

[*Pause.*]

HAMM   You haven't put on his ribbon.

CLOV   [*angrily*] But he isn't finished, I tell you! First you finish your dog and then you put on his ribbon!

[*Pause.*]

HAMM   Can he stand?

CLOV   I don't know.

HAMM   Try.

[*He hands the dog to Clov who places it on the ground.*]

Well?

CLOV   Wait!

[*He squats down and tries to get the dog to stand on its three legs, fails, lets it go. The dog falls on its side.*]

HAMM   [*impatiently*] Well?

CLOV   He's standing.

HAMM   [*groping for the dog*] Where? Where is he?

[*Clov holds up the dog in a standing position.*]

CLOV   There.

[*He takes Hamm's hand and guides it towards the dog's head.*]

HAMM   [*his hand on the dog's head*] Is he gazing at me?

CLOV   Yes.

HAMM   [*proudly*] As if he were asking me to take him for a walk?

CLOV   If you like.

HAMM   [*as before*] Or as if he were begging me for a bone.

[*He withdraws his hand.*]

Leave him like that, standing there imploring me.

[*Clov straightens up. The dog falls on its side.*]

CLOV   I'll leave you.

HAMM   Have you had your visions?

CLOV   Less.

HAMM   Is Mother Pegg's light on?

CLOV   Light! How could anyone's light be on?

HAMM   Extinguished!

CLOV   Naturally it's extinguished. If it's not on it's extinguished.

HAMM   No, I mean Mother Pegg.

CLOV   But naturally she's extinguished!

[*Pause.*]

What's the matter with you today?

HAMM   I'm taking my course.

[*Pause.*]

Is she buried?

CLOV   Buried! Who would have buried her?

HAMM   You.

CLOV   Me! Haven't I enough to do without burying people?

HAMM   But you'll bury me.

CLOV   No I won't bury you.

[*Pause.*]

HAMM   She was bonny once, like a flower of the field.

[*With reminiscent leer.*]

And a great one for the men!

CLOV   We too were bonny—once. It's a rare thing not to have been bonny—once.

[*Pause.*]

HAMM   Go and get the gaff.

[*Clov goes to door, halts.*]

CLOV   Do this, do that, and I do it. I never refuse. Why?

HAMM   You're not able to.

CLOV   Soon I won't do it any more.

HAMM You won't be able to any more.
       [*Exit Clov.*]
       Ah the creatures, the creatures, everything has to be explained
       to them.
       [*Enter Clov with gaff.*]

CLOV Here's your gaff. Stick it up.
       [*He gives the gaff to Hamm who, wielding it like a puntpole, tries to
       move his chair.*]

HAMM Did I move?

CLOV No.
       [*Hamm throws down the gaff.*]

HAMM Go and get the oilcan.

CLOV What for?

HAMM To oil the castors.

CLOV I oiled them yesterday.

HAMM Yesterday! What does that mean? Yesterday!

CLOV [*violently*] That means that bloody awful day, long ago, before
       this bloody awful day. I use the words you taught me. If they
       don't mean anything any more, teach me others. Or let me be
       silent.
       [*Pause.*]

HAMM I once knew a madman who thought the end of the world had
       come. He was a painter—and engraver. I had a great fondness
       for him. I used to go and see him, in the asylum. I'd take him by
       the hand and drag him to the window. Look! There! All that
       rising corn! And there! Look! The sails of the herring fleet! All
       that loveliness!
       [*Pause.*]
       He'd snatch away his hand and go back into his corner.
       Appalled. All he had seen was ashes.
       [*Pause.*]
       He alone had been spared.
       [*Pause.*]
       Forgotten.

[*Pause.*]

It appears the case is . . . was not so . . . so unusual.

CLOV A madman? When was that?

HAMM Oh way back, way back, you weren't in the land of the living.

CLOV God be with the days!

[*Pause. Hamm raises his toque.*]

HAMM I had a great fondness for him.

[*Pause. He puts on his toque again.*]

He was a painter—and engraver.

CLOV There are so many terrible things.

HAMM No, no, there are not so many now.

[*Pause.*]

Clov!

CLOV Yes.

HAMM Do you not think this has gone on long enough?

CLOV Yes!

[*Pause.*]

What?

HAMM This . . . this . . . thing.

CLOV I've always thought so.

[*Pause.*]

You not?

HAMM [*gloomily*] Then it's a day like any other day.

CLOV As long as it lasts.

[*Pause.*]

All life long the same inanities.

HAMM I can't leave you.

CLOV I know. And you can't follow me.

[*Pause.*]

HAMM If you leave me how shall I know?

CLOV [*briskly*] Well you simply whistle me and if I don't come running it means I've left you.

[*Pause.*]

HAMM You won't come and kiss me goodbye?

CLOV   Oh I shouldn't think so.

[*Pause.*]

HAMM   But you might be merely dead in your kitchen.

CLOV   The result would be the same.

HAMM   Yes, but how would I know, if you were merely dead in your kitchen?

CLOV   Well . . . sooner or later I'd start to stink.

HAMM   You stink already. The whole place stinks of corpses.

CLOV   The whole universe.

HAMM   [*angrily*] To hell with the universe.

[*Pause.*]

Think of something.

CLOV   What?

HAMM   An idea, have an idea.

[*Angrily.*]

A bright idea!

CLOV   Ah good.

[*He starts pacing to and fro, his eyes fixed on the ground, his hands behind his back. He halts.*]

The pains in my legs! It's unbelievable! Soon I won't be able to think any more.

HAMM   You won't be able to leave me.

[*Clov resumes his pacing.*]

What are you doing?

CLOV   Having an idea.

[*He paces.*]

Ah!

[*He halts.*]

HAMM   What a brain!

[*Pause.*]

Well?

CLOV   Wait!

[*He meditates. Not very convinced.*]

Yes . . .

[*Pause. More convinced.*]

Yes!

[*He raises his head.*]

I have it! I set the alarm.

[*Pause.*]

HAMM This is perhaps not one of my bright days, but frankly—

CLOV You whistle me. I don't come. The alarm rings. I'm gone. It doesn't ring. I'm dead.

[*Pause.*]

HAMM Is it working?

[*Pause. Impatiently.*]

The alarm, is it working?

CLOV Why wouldn't it be working?

HAMM Because it's worked too much.

CLOV But it's hardly worked at all.

HAMM [*angrily*] Then because it's worked too little!

CLOV I'll go and see.

[*Exit Clov. Brief ring of alarm off. Enter Clov with alarm-clock. He holds it against Hamm's ear and releases alarm. They listen to it ringing to the end. Pause.*]

Fit to wake the dead! Did you hear it?

HAMM Vaguely.

CLOV The end is terrific!

HAMM I prefer the middle.

[*Pause.*]

Is it not time for my pain-killer?

CLOV No!

[*He goes to door, turns.*]

I'll leave you.

HAMM It's time for my story. Do you want to listen to my story.

CLOV No.

HAMM Ask my father if he wants to listen to my story.

[*Clov goes to bins, raises the lid of Nagg's, stoops, looks into it. Pause. He straightens up.*]

CLOV   He's asleep.

HAMM   Wake him.

[*Clov stoops, wakes Nagg with the alarm. Unintelligible words. Clov straightens up.*]

CLOV   He doesn't want to listen to your story.

HAMM   I'll give him a bon-bon.

[*Clov stoops. As before.*]

CLOV   He wants a sugar-plum.

HAMM   He'll get a sugar-plum.

[*Clov stoops. As before.*]

CLOV   It's a deal.

[*He goes towards door. Nagg's hands appear, gripping the rim. Then the head emerges. Clov reaches door, turns.*]

Do you believe in the life to come?

HAMM   Mine was always that.

[*Exit Clov.*]

Got him that time!

NAGG   I'm listening.

HAMM   Scoundrel! Why did you engender me?

NAGG   I didn't know.

HAMM   What? What didn't you know?

NAGG   That it'd be you.

[*Pause.*]

You'll give me a sugar-plum?

HAMM   After the audition.

NAGG   You swear?

HAMM   Yes.

NAGG   On what?

HAMM   My honor.

[*Pause. They laugh heartily.*]

NAGG   Two.

HAMM   One.

NAGG   One for me and one for—

HAMM   One! Silence!

[*Pause.*]

Where was I?

[*Pause. Gloomily.*]

It's finished, we're finished.

[*Pause.*]

Nearly finished.

[*Pause.*]

There'll be no more speech.

[*Pause.*]

Something dripping in my head, ever since the fontanelles.

[*Stifled hilarity of Nagg.*]

Splash, splash, always on the same spot.

[*Pause.*]

Perhaps it's a little vein.

[*Pause.*]

A little artery.

[*Pause. More animated.*]

Enough of that, it's story time, where was I?

[*Pause. Narrative tone.*]

The man came crawling towards me, on his belly. Pale, wonderfully pale and thin, he seemed on the point of—

[*Pause. Normal tone.*]

No, I've done that bit.

[*Pause. Narrative tone.*]

I calmly filled my pipe—the meerschaum, lit it with . . . let us say a vesta, drew a few puffs. Aah!

[*Pause.*]

Well, what is it *you* want?

[*Pause.*]

It was an extra-ordinarily bitter day, I remember, zero by the thermometer. But considering it was Christmas Eve there was nothing . . . extra-ordinary about that. Seasonable weather, for once in a way.

[*Pause.*]

Well, what ill wind blows you my way? He raised his face to me, black with mingled dirt and tears.

[*Pause. Normal tone.*]

That should do it.

[*Narrative tone.*]

No no, don't look at me, don't look at me. He dropped his eyes and mumbled something, apologies I presume.

[*Pause.*]

I'm a busy man, you know, the final touches, before the festivities, you know what it is.

[*Pause. Forcibly.*]

Come on now, what is the object of this invasion?

[*Pause.*]

It was a glorious bright day, I remember, fifty by the heliometer, but already the sun was sinking down into the . . . down among the dead.

[*Normal tone.*]

Nicely put, that.

[*Narrative tone.*]

Come on now, come on, present your petition and let me resume my labours.

[*Pause. Normal tone.*]

There's English for you. Ah well . . .

[*Narrative tone.*]

It was then he took the plunge. It's my little one, he said. Tsstss, a little one, that's bad. My little boy, he said, as if the sex mattered. Where did he come from? He named the hole. A good half-day, on horse. What are you insinuating? That the place is still inhabited? No no, not a soul, except himself and the child—assuming he existed. Good. I enquired about the situation at Kov, beyond the gulf. Not a sinner. Good. And you expect me to believe you have left your little one back there, all alone, and alive into the bargain? Come now!

[*Pause.*]

It was a howling wild day, I remember, a hundred by the anenometer. The wind was tearing up the dead pines and sweeping them . . . away.

[*Pause. Normal tone.*]

A bit feeble, that.

[*Narrative tone.*]

Come on, man, speak up, what is it you want from me, I have to put up my holly.

[*Pause.*]

Well to make it short it finally transpired that what he wanted from me was . . . bread for his brat? Bread? But I have no bread, it doesn't agree with me. Good. Then perhaps a little corn?

[*Pause. Normal tone.*]

That should do it.

[*Narrative tone.*]

Corn, yes, I have corn, it's true, in my granaries. But use your head. I give you some corn, a pound, a pound and a half, you bring it back to your child and you make him—if he's still alive—a nice pot of porridge,

[*Nagg reacts*]

a nice pot and a half of porridge, full of nourishment. Good. The colours come back into his little cheeks—perhaps. And then?

[*Pause.*]

I lost patience.

[*Violently.*]

Use your head, can't you, use your head, you're on earth, there's no cure for that!

[*Pause.*]

It was an exceedingly dry day, I remember, zero by the hygrometer. Ideal weather, for my lumbago.

[*Pause. Violently.*]

But what in God's name do you imagine? That the earth will awake in spring? That the rivers and seas will run with fish

again? That there's manna in heaven still for imbeciles like
you?

[*Pause.*]

Gradually I cooled down, sufficiently at least to ask him how
long he had taken on the way. Three whole days. Good. In what
condition he had left the child. Deep in sleep.

[*Forcibly.*]

But deep in what sleep, deep in what sleep already?

[*Pause.*]

Well to make it short I finally offered to take him into my
service. He had touched a chord. And then I imagined already
that I wasn't much longer for this world.

[*He laughs. Pause.*]

Well?

[*Pause.*]

Well? Here if you were careful you might die a nice natural
death, in peace and comfort.

[*Pause.*]

Well?

[*Pause.*]

In the end he asked me would I consent to take in the child as
well—if he were still alive.

[*Pause.*]

It was the moment I was waiting for.

[*Pause.*]

Would I consent to take in the child . . .

[*Pause.*]

I can see him still, down on his knees, his hands flat on the
ground, glaring at me with his mad eyes, in defiance of my
wishes.

[*Pause. Normal tone.*]

I'll soon have finished with this story.

[*Pause.*]

Unless I bring in other characters.

[*Pause.*]

But where would I find them?

[*Pause.*]

Where would I look for them?

[*Pause. He whistles. Enter Clov.*]

Let us pray to God.

NAGG   Me sugar-plum!

CLOV   There's a rat in the kitchen!

HAMM   A rat! Are there still rats?

CLOV   In the kitchen there's one.

HAMM   And you haven't exterminated him?

CLOV   Half. You disturbed us.

HAMM   He can't get away?

CLOV   No.

HAMM   You'll finish him later. Let us pray to God.

CLOV   Again!

NAGG   Me sugar-plum!

HAMM   God first!

[*Pause.*]

Are you right?

CLOV   [*resigned*] Off we go.

HAMM   [*to Nagg*] And you?

NAGG   [*clasping his hands, closing his eyes, in a gabble*] Our Father which art—

HAMM   Silence! In silence! Where are your manners?

[*Pause.*]

Off we go.

[*Attitudes of prayer. Silence. Abandoning his attitude, discouraged.*]

Well?

CLOV   [*abandoning his attitude*] What a hope! And you?

HAMM   Sweet damn all!

[*To Nagg.*]

And you?

NAGG   Wait!

[*Pause. Abandoning his attitude.*]

Nothing doing!

HAMM   The bastard! He doesn't exist!

CLOV   Not yet.

NAGG   Me sugar-plum!

HAMM   There are no more sugar-plums!

[*Pause.*]

NAGG   It's natural. After all I'm your father. It's true if it hadn't been me
it would have been someone else. But that's no excuse.

[*Pause.*]

Turkish Delight, for example, which no longer exists, we all
know that, there is nothing in the world I love more. And one
day I'll ask you for some, in return for a kindness, and you'll
promise it to me. One must live with the times.

[*Pause.*]

Whom did you call when you were a tiny boy, and were
frightened, in the dark? Your mother? No. Me. We let you cry.
Then we moved you out of earshot, so that we might sleep in
peace.

[*Pause.*]

I was asleep, as happy as a king, and you woke me up to have me
listen to you. It wasn't indispensable, you didn't really need to
have me listen to you. Besides I didn't listen to you.

[*Pause.*]

I hope the day will come when you'll really need to have me
listen to you, and need to hear my voice, any voice.

[*Pause.*]

Yes, I hope I'll live till then, to hear you calling me like when
you were a tiny boy, and were frightened, in the dark, and I was
your only hope.

[*Pause. Nagg knocks on lid of Nell's bin. Pause.*]

Nell!

[*Pause. He knocks louder. Pause. Louder.*]

Nell!

[*Pause. Nagg sinks back into his bin, closes the lid behind him. Pause.*]

HAMM   Our revels now are ended.

[*He gropes for the dog.*]

The dog's gone.

CLOV   He's not a real dog, he can't go.

HAMM   [*groping*] He's not there.

CLOV   He's lain down.

HAMM   Give him up to me.

[*Clov picks up the dog and gives it to Hamm. Hamm holds it in his arms. Pause. Hamm throws away the dog.*]

Dirty brute!

[*Clov begins to pick up the objects lying on the ground.*]

What are you doing?

CLOV   Putting things in order.

[*He straightens up. Fervently.*]

I'm going to clear everything away!

[*He starts picking up again.*]

HAMM   Order!

CLOV   [*straightening up*] I love order. It's my dream. A world where all would be silent and still and each thing in its last place, under the last dust.

[*He starts picking up again.*]

HAMM   [*exasperated*] What in God's name do you think you are doing?

CLOV   [*straightening up*] I'm doing my best to create a little order.

HAMM   Drop it!

[*Clov drops the objects he has picked up.*]

CLOV   After all, there or elsewhere.

[*He goes towards door.*]

HAMM   [*irritably*] What's wrong with your feet?

CLOV   My feet?

HAMM   Tramp! Tramp!

CLOV   I must have put on my boots.

HAMM   Your slippers were hurting you?

[*Pause.*]

CLOV   I'll leave you.

HAMM   No!

CLOV   What is there to keep me here?

HAMM   The dialogue.

[*Pause.*]

I've got on with my story.

[*Pause.*]

I've got on with it well.

[*Pause. Irritably.*]

Ask me where I've got to.

CLOV   Oh, by the way, your story?

HAMM   [*surprised*] What story?

CLOV   The one you've been telling yourself all your days.

HAMM   Ah you mean my chronicle?

CLOV   That's the one.

[*Pause.*]

HAMM   [*angrily*] Keep going, can't you, keep going!

CLOV   You've got on with it, I hope.

HAMM   [*modestly*] Oh not very far, not very far.

[*He sighs.*]

There are days like that, one isn't inspired.

[*Pause.*]

Nothing you can do about it, just wait for it to come.

[*Pause.*]

No forcing, no forcing, it's fatal.

[*Pause.*]

I've got on with it a little all the same.

[*Pause.*]

Technique, you know.

[*Pause. Irritably.*]

I say I've got on with it a little all the same.

CLOV   [*admiringly*] Well I never! In spite of everything you were able to get on with it!

HAMM [*modestly*] Oh not very far, you know, not very far, but nevertheless, better than nothing.

CLOV Better than nothing! Is it possible?

HAMM I'll tell you how it goes. He comes crawling on his belly—

CLOV Who?

HAMM What?

CLOV Who do you mean, he?

HAMM Who do I mean! Yet another.

CLOV Ah him! I wasn't sure.

HAMM Crawling on his belly, whining for bread for his brat. He's offered a job as gardener. Before—

[*Clov bursts out laughing.*]

What is there so funny about that?

CLOV A job as gardener!

HAMM Is that what tickles you?

CLOV It must be that.

HAMM It wouldn't be the bread?

CLOV Or the brat.

[*Pause.*]

HAMM The whole thing is comical, I grant you that. What about having a good guffaw the two of us together?

CLOV [*after reflection*] I couldn't guffaw again today.

HAMM [*after reflection*] Nor I.

[*Pause.*]

I continue then. Before accepting with gratitude he asks if he may have his little boy with him.

CLOV What age?

HAMM Oh tiny.

CLOV He would have climbed the trees.

HAMM All the little odd jobs.

CLOV And then he would have grown up.

HAMM Very likely.

[*Pause.*]

CLOV Keep going, can't you, keep going!

HAMM That's all. I stopped there.

[*Pause.*]

CLOV Do you see how it goes on.

HAMM More or less.

CLOV Will it not soon be the end?

HAMM I'm afraid it will.

CLOV Pah! You'll make up another.

HAMM I don't know.

[*Pause.*]

I feel rather drained.

[*Pause.*]

The prolonged creative effort.

[*Pause.*]

If I could drag myself down to the sea! I'd make a pillow of sand for my head and the tide would come.

CLOV There's no more tide.

[*Pause.*]

HAMM Go and see is she dead.

[*Clov goes to bins, raises the lid of Nell's, stoops, looks into it. Pause.*]

CLOV Looks like it.

[*He closes the lid, straightens up. Hamm raises his toque. Pause. He puts it on again.*]

HAMM [*with his hand to his toque*] And Nagg?

[*Clov raises lid of Nagg's bin, stoops, looks into it. Pause.*]

CLOV Doesn't look like it.

[*He closes the lid, straightens up.*]

HAMM [*letting go his toque*] What's he doing?

[*Clov raises lid of Nagg's bin, stoops, looks into it. Pause.*]

CLOV He's crying.

[*He closes lid, straightens up.*]

HAMM Then he's living.

[*Pause.*]

Did you ever have an instant of happiness?

CLOV   Not to my knowledge.

[*Pause.*]

HAMM   Bring me under the window.

[*Clov goes towards chair.*]

I want to feel the light on my face.

[*Clov pushes chair.*]

Do you remember, in the beginning, when you took me for a turn? You used to hold the chair too high. At every step you nearly tipped me out.

[*With senile quaver.*]

Ah great fun, we had, the two of us, great fun.

[*Gloomily.*]

And then we got into the way of it.

[*Clov stops the chair under window right.*]

There already?

[*Pause. He tilts back his head.*]

Is it light?

CLOV   It isn't dark.

HAMM   [*angrily*] I'm asking you is it light.

CLOV   Yes.

[*Pause.*]

HAMM   The curtain isn't closed?

CLOV   No.

HAMM   What window is it?

CLOV   The earth.

HAMM   I knew it!

[*Angrily.*]

But there's no light there! The other!

[*Clov pushes chair towards window left.*]

The earth!

[*Clov stops the chair under window left. Hamm tilts back his head.*]

That's what I call light!

[*Pause.*]

Feels like a ray of sunshine.

[*Pause.*]

No?

CLOV   No.

HAMM   It isn't a ray of sunshine I feel on my face?

CLOV   No.

[*Pause.*]

HAMM   Am I very white?

[*Pause. Angrily.*]

I'm asking you am I very white!

CLOV   Not more so than usual.

[*Pause.*]

HAMM   Open the window.

CLOV   What for?

HAMM   I want to hear the sea.

CLOV   You wouldn't hear it.

HAMM   Even if you opened the window?

CLOV   No.

HAMM   Then it's not worth while opening it?

CLOV   No.

HAMM   [*violently*] Then open it!

[*Clov gets up on the ladder, opens the window. Pause.*]

Have you opened it?

CLOV   Yes.

[*Pause.*]

HAMM   You swear you've opened it?

CLOV   Yes.

[*Pause.*]

HAMM   Well . . . !

[*Pause.*]

It must be very calm.

[*Pause. Violently.*]

I'm asking you is it very calm!

CLOV   Yes.

HAMM   It's because there are no more navigators.

[*Pause.*]

You haven't much conversation all of a sudden. Do you not feel well?

CLOV I'm cold.

HAMM What month are we?

[*Pause.*]

Close the window, we're going back.

[*Clov closes the window, gets down, pushes the chair back to its place, remains standing behind it, head bowed.*]

Don't stay there, you give me the shivers!

[*Clov returns to his place beside the chair.*]

Father!

[*Pause. Louder.*]

Father!

[*Pause.*]

Go and see did he hear me.

[*Clov goes to Nagg's bin, raises the lid, stoops. Unintelligible words. Clov straightens up.*]

CLOV Yes.

HAMM Both times?

[*Clov stoops. As before.*]

CLOV Once only.

HAMM The first time or the second?

[*Clov stoops. As before.*]

CLOV He doesn't know.

HAMM It must have been the second.

CLOV We'll never know.

[*He closes lid.*]

HAMM Is he still crying?

CLOV No.

HAMM The dead go fast.

[*Pause.*]

What's he doing?

CLOV Sucking his biscuit.

HAMM   Life goes on.
        [*Clov returns to his place beside the chair.*]
        Give me a rug, I'm freezing.

CLOV   There are no more rugs.
        [*Pause.*]

HAMM   Kiss me.
        [*Pause.*]
        Will you not kiss me?

CLOV   No.

HAMM   On the forehead.

CLOV   I won't kiss you anywhere.
        [*Pause.*]

HAMM   [*holding out his hand*] Give me your hand at least.
        [*Pause.*]
        Will you not give me your hand?

CLOV   I won't touch you.
        [*Pause.*]

HAMM   Give me the dog.
        [*Clov looks round for the dog.*]
        No!

CLOV   Do you not want your dog?

HAMM   No.

CLOV   Then I'll leave you.

HAMM   [*head bowed, absently*] That's right.
        [*Clov goes to door, turns.*]

CLOV   If I don't kill that rat he'll die.

HAMM   [*as before*] That's right.
        [*Exit Clov. Pause.*]
        Me to play.
        [*He takes out his handkerchief, unfolds it, holds it spread out before him.*]
        We're getting on.
        [*Pause.*]
        You weep, and weep, for nothing, so as not to laugh, and little
        by little ... you begin to grieve.

[*He folds the handkerchief, puts it back in his pocket, raises his head.*]
All those I might have helped.
[*Pause.*]
Helped!
[*Pause.*]
Saved.
[*Pause.*]
Saved!
[*Pause.*]
The place was crawling with them!
[*Pause. Violently.*]
Use your head, can't you, use your head, you're on earth, there's
no cure for that!
[*Pause.*]
Get out of here and love one another! Lick your neighbor as
yourself!
[*Pause. Calmer.*]
When it wasn't bread they wanted it was crumpets.
[*Pause. Violently.*]
Out of my sight and back to your petting parties!
[*Pause.*]
All that, all that!
[*Pause.*]
Not even a real dog!
[*Calmer.*]
The end is in the beginning and yet you go on.
[*Pause.*]
Perhaps I could go on with my story, end it and begin another.
[*Pause.*]
Perhaps I could throw myself out on the floor.
[*He pushes himself painfully off his seat, falls back again.*]
Dig my nails into the cracks and drag myself forward with my
fingers.
[*Pause.*]

It will be the end and there I'll be, wondering what can have brought it on and wondering what can have . . .

[*he hesitates*]

. . . why it was so long coming.

[*Pause.*]

There I'll be, in the old shelter, alone against the silence and . . .

[*he hesitates*]

. . . the stillness. If I can hold my peace, and sit quiet, it will be all over with sound, and motion, all over and done with.

[*Pause.*]

I'll have called my father and I'll have called my . . .

[*he hesitates*]

. . . my son. And even twice, or three times, in case they shouldn't have heard me, the first time, or the second.

[*Pause.*]

I'll say to myself, He'll come back.

[*Pause.*]

And then?

[*Pause.*]

And then?

[*Pause.*]

He couldn't, he has gone too far.

[*Pause.*]

And then?

[*Pause. Very agitated.*]

All kinds of fantasies! That I'm being watched! A rat! Steps! Breath held and then . . .

[*He breathes out.*]

Then babble, babble, words, like the solitary child who turns himself into children, two, three, so as to be together, and whisper together, in the dark.

[*Pause.*]

Moment upon moment, pattering down, like the millet grains of . . .

[*he hesitates*]

. . . that old Greek, and all life long you wait for that to mount up to a life.

[*Pause. He opens his mouth to continue, renounces.*]

Ah let's get it over!

[*He whistles. Enter Clov with alarm-clock. He halts beside the chair.*]

What? Neither gone nor dead?

CLOV In spirit only.

HAMM Which?

CLOV Both.

HAMM Gone from me you'd be dead.

CLOV And vice versa.

HAMM Outside of here it's death!

[*Pause.*]

And the rat?

CLOV He's got away.

HAMM He can't go far.

[*Pause. Anxious.*]

Eh?

CLOV He doesn't need to go far.

[*Pause.*]

HAMM Is it not time for my pain-killer?

CLOV Yes.

HAMM Ah! At last! Give it to me! Quick!

[*Pause.*]

CLOV There's no more pain-killer.

[*Pause.*]

HAMM [*appalled*] Good . . . !

[*Pause.*]

No more pain-killer!

CLOV No more pain-killer. You'll never get any more pain-killer.

[*Pause.*]

HAMM But the little round box. It was full!

CLOV Yes. But now it's empty.

[*Pause. Clov starts to move about the room. He is looking for a place to put down the alarm-clock.*]

HAMM [*soft*] What'll I do?

[*Pause. In a scream.*]

What'll I do?

[*Clov sees the picture, takes it down, stands it on the floor with its face to the wall, hangs up the alarm-clock in its place.*]

What are you doing?

CLOV Winding up.

HAMM Look at the earth.

CLOV Again!

HAMM Since it's calling to you.

CLOV Is your throat sore?

[*Pause.*]

Would you like a lozenge?

[*Pause.*]

No.

[*Pause.*]

Pity.

[*Clov goes, humming, towards window right, halts before it, looks up at it.*]

HAMM Don't sing.

CLOV [*turning towards Hamm*] One hasn't the right to sing any more?

HAMM No.

CLOV Then how can it end?

HAMM You want it to end?

CLOV I want to sing.

HAMM I can't prevent you.

[*Pause. Clov turns towards window right.*]

CLOV What did I do with that steps?

[*He looks around for ladder.*]

You didn't see that steps?

[*He sees it.*]

Ah, about time.

[*He goes towards window left.*]

Sometimes I wonder if I'm in my right mind. Then it passes over and I'm as lucid as before.

[*He gets up on ladder, looks out of window.*]

Christ, she's under water!

[*He looks.*]

How can that be?

[*He pokes forward his head, his hand above his eyes.*]

It hasn't rained.

[*He wipes the pane, looks. Pause.*]

Ah what a fool I am! I'm on the wrong side!

[*He gets down, takes a few steps towards window right.*]

Under water!

[*He goes back for ladder.*]

What a fool I am!

[*He carries ladder towards window right.*]

Sometimes I wonder if I'm in my right senses. Then it passes off and I'm as intelligent as ever.

[*He sets down ladder under window right, gets up on it, looks out of window. He turns towards Hamm.*]

Any particular sector you fancy? Or merely the whole thing?

HAMM   Whole thing.

CLOV   The general effect? Just a moment.

[*He looks out of window. Pause.*]

HAMM   Clov.

CLOV   [*absorbed*] Mmm.

HAMM   Do you know what it is?

CLOV   [*as before*] Mmm.

HAMM   I was never there.

[*Pause.*]

Clov!

CLOV   [*turning towards Hamm, exasperated*] What is it?

HAMM   I was never there.

CLOV   Lucky for you.

[*He looks out of window.*]

HAMM Absent, always. It all happened without me. I don't know what's happened.

[*Pause.*]

Do you know what's happened?

[*Pause.*]

Clov!

CLOV [*turning towards Hamm, exasperated*] Do you want me to look at this muckheap, yes or no?

HAMM Answer me first.

CLOV What?

HAMM Do you know what's happened?

CLOV When? Where?

HAMM [*violently*] When! What's happened? Use your head, can't you! What has happened?

CLOV What for Christ's sake does it matter?

[*He looks out of window.*]

HAMM I don't know.

[*Pause. Clov turns towards Hamm.*]

CLOV [*harshly*] When old Mother Pegg asked you for oil for her lamp and you told her to get out to hell, you knew what was happening then, no?

[*Pause.*]

You know what she died of, Mother Pegg? Of darkness.

HAMM [*feebly*] I hadn't any.

CLOV [*as before*] Yes, you had.

[*Pause.*]

HAMM Have you the glass?

CLOV No, it's clear enough as it is.

HAMM Go and get it.

[*Pause. Clov casts up his eyes, brandishes his fists. He loses balance, clutches on to the ladder. He starts to get down, halts.*]

CLOV There's one thing I'll never understand.

[*He gets down.*]

Why I always obey you. Can you explain that to me?

HAMM   No. . . . Perhaps it's compassion.

[*Pause.*]

A kind of great compassion.

[*Pause.*]

Oh you won't find it easy, you won't find it easy.

[*Pause. Clov begins to move about the room in search of the telescope.*]

CLOV   I'm tired of our goings on, very tired.

[*He searches.*]

You're not sitting on it?

[*He moves the chair, looks at the place where it stood, resumes his search.*]

HAMM   [*anguished*] Don't leave me there!

[*Angrily Clov restores the chair to its place.*]

Am I right in the center?

CLOV   You'd need a microscope to find this—

[*He sees the telescope.*]

Ah, about time.

[*He picks up the telescope, gets up on the ladder, turns the telescope on the without.*]

HAMM   Give me the dog.

CLOV   [*looking*] Quiet!

HAMM   [*angrily*] Give me the dog!

[*Clov drops the telescope, clasps his hands to his head. Pause. He gets down precipitately, looks for the dog, sees it, picks it up, hastens towards Hamm and strikes him violently on the head with the dog.*]

CLOV   There's your dog for you!

[*The dog falls to the ground. Pause.*]

HAMM   He hit me!

CLOV   You drive me mad, I'm mad!

HAMM   If you must hit me, hit me with the axe.

[*Pause.*]

Or with the gaff, hit me with the gaff. Not with the dog. With the gaff. Or with the axe.

[*Clov picks up the dog and gives it to Hamm who takes it in his arms.*]

CLOV [*imploringly*] Let's stop playing!

HAMM Never!

[*Pause.*]

Put me in my coffin.

CLOV There are no more coffins.

HAMM Then let it end!

[*Clov goes towards ladder.*]

With a bang!

[*Clov gets up on ladder, gets down again, looks for telescope, sees it, picks it up, gets up ladder, raises telescope.*]

Of darkness! And me? Did anyone ever have pity on me?

CLOV [*lowering the telescope, turning towards Hamm*] What?

[*Pause.*]

Is it me you're referring to?

HAMM [*angrily*] An aside, ape! Did you never hear an aside before?

[*Pause.*]

I'm warming up for my last soliloquy.

CLOV I warn you. I'm going to look at this filth since it's an order. But it's the last time.

[*He turns the telescope on the without.*]

Let's see.

[*He moves the telescope.*]

Nothing . . . nothing . . . good . . . good . . . nothing . . . goo—

[*He starts, lowers the telescope, examines it, turns it again on the without. Pause.*]

Bad luck to it!

HAMM More complications!

[*Clov gets down.*]

Not an underplot, I trust.

[*Clov moves ladder nearer window, gets up on it, turns telescope on the without.*]

CLOV [*dismayed*] Looks like a small boy!

HAMM [*sarcastic*] A small . . . boy!

CLOV I'll go and see.

[*He gets down, drops the telescope, goes towards door, turns.*]
I'll take the gaff.

[*He looks for the gaff, sees it, picks it up, hastens towards door.*]

HAMM No!

[*Clov halts.*]

CLOV No? A potential procreator?

HAMM If he exists he'll die there or he'll come here. And if he doesn't . . .

[*Pause.*]

CLOV You don't believe me? You think I'm inventing?

[*Pause.*]

HAMM It's the end, Clov, we've come to the end. I don't need you any more.

[*Pause.*]

CLOV Lucky for you.

[*He goes towards door.*]

HAMM Leave me the gaff.

[*Clov gives him the gaff, goes towards door, halts, looks at alarm-clock, takes it down, looks round for a better place to put it, goes to bins, puts it on lid of Nagg's bin. Pause.*]

CLOV I'll leave you.

[*He goes towards door.*]

HAMM Before you go . . .

[*Clov halts near door.*]

. . . say something.

CLOV There is nothing to say.

HAMM A few words . . . to ponder . . . in my heart.

CLOV Your heart!

HAMM Yes.

[*Pause. Forcibly.*]

Yes!

[*Pause.*]

With the rest, in the end, the shadows, the murmurs, all the trouble, to end up with.

[*Pause.*]

Clov. . . . He never spoke to me. Then, in the end, before he went, without my having asked him, he spoke to me. He said . . .

CLOV [*despairingly*] Ah . . . !

HAMM Something . . . from your heart.

CLOV My heart!

HAMM A few words . . . from your heart.

[*Pause.*]

CLOV [*fixed gaze, tonelessly, towards auditorium*] They said to me, That's love, yes, yes, not a doubt, now you see how—

HAMM Articulate!

CLOV [*as before*] How easy it is. They said to me, That's friendship, yes, yes, no question, you've found it. They said to me, Here's the place, stop, raise your head and look at all that beauty. That order! They said to me, Come now, you're not a brute beast, think upon these things and you'll see how all becomes clear. And simple! They said to me, What skilled attention they get, all these dying of their wounds.

HAMM Enough!

CLOV [*as before*] I say to myself—sometimes, Clov, you must learn to suffer better than that if you want them to weary of punishing you—one day. I say to myself—sometimes, Clov, you must be there better than that if you want them to let you go—one day. But I feel too old, and too far, to form new habits. Good, it'll never end, I'll never go.

[*Pause.*]

Then one day, suddenly, it ends, it changes, I don't understand, it dies, or it's me, I don't understand, that either. I ask the words that remain—sleeping, waking, morning, evening. They have nothing to say.

[*Pause.*]

I open the door of the cell and go. I am so bowed I only see my feet, if I open my eyes, and between my legs a little trail of black dust. I say to myself that the earth is extinguished, though I never saw it lit.

[*Pause.*]

It's easy going.

[*Pause.*]

When I fall I'll weep for happiness.

[*Pause. He goes towards door.*]

HAMM   Clov!

[*Clov halts, without turning.*]

Nothing.

[*Clov moves on.*]

Clov!

[*Clov halts, without turning.*]

CLOV   This is what we call making an exit.

HAMM   I'm obliged to you, Clov. For your services.

CLOV   [*turning, sharply*] Ah pardon, it's I am obliged to you.

HAMM   It's we are obliged to each other.

[*Pause. Clov goes towards door.*]

One thing more.

[*Clov halts.*]

A last favor.

[*Exit Clov.*]

Cover me with the sheet.

[*Long pause.*]

No? Good.

[*Pause.*]

Me to play.

[*Pause. Wearily.*]

Old endgame lost of old, play and lose and have done with losing.

[*Pause. More animated.*]

Let me see.

[*Pause.*]

Ah yes!

[*He tries to move the chair, using the gaff as before. Enter Clov, dressed for the road. Panama hat, tweed coat, raincoat over his arm, umbrella, bag. He halts by the door and stands there, impassive and motionless, his eyes fixed on Hamm, till the end. Hamm gives up.*]

Good.

[*Pause.*]

Discard.

[*He throws away the gaff, makes to throw away the dog, thinks better of it.*]

Take it easy.

[*Pause.*]

And now?

[*Pause.*]

Raise hat.

[*He raises his toque.*]

Peace to our . . . arses.

[*Pause.*]

And put on again.

[*He puts on his toque.*]

Deuce.

[*Pause. He takes off his glasses.*]

Wipe.

[*He takes out his handkerchief and, without unfolding it, wipes his glasses.*]

And put on again.

[*He puts on his glasses, puts back the handkerchief in his pocket.*]

We're coming. A few more squirms like that and I'll call.

[*Pause.*]

A little poetry.

[*Pause.*]

You prayed—

[*Pause. He corrects himself.*]

You CRIED for night; it comes—

[*Pause. He corrects himself.*]

It FALLS: now cry in darkness.

[*He repeats, chanting.*]

You cried for night; it falls: now cry in darkness.

[*Pause.*]

Nicely put, that.

[*Pause.*]

And now?

[*Pause.*]

Moments for nothing, now as always, time was never and time is over, reckoning closed and story ended.

[*Pause. Narrative tone.*]

If he could have his child with him. . . .

[*Pause.*]

It was the moment I was waiting for.

[*Pause.*]

You don't want to abandon him? You want him to bloom while you are withering? Be there to solace your last million last moments?

[*Pause.*]

He doesn't realize, all he knows is hunger, and cold, and death to crown it all. But you! You ought to know what the earth is like, nowadays. Oh I put him before his responsibilities!

[*Pause. Normal tone.*]

Well, there we are, there I am, that's enough.

[*He raises the whistle to his lips, hesitates, drops it. Pause.*]

Yes, truly!

[*He whistles. Pause. Louder. Pause.*]

Good.

[*Pause.*]

Father!

[*Pause. Louder.*]

Father!

[*Pause.*]

Good.

[*Pause.*]

We're coming.

[*Pause.*]

And to end up with?

[*Pause.*]

Discard.

[*He throws away the dog. He tears the whistle from his neck.*]

With my compliments.

[*He throws whistle towards auditorium. Pause. He sniffs. Soft.*]

Clov!

[*Long pause.*]

No? Good.

[*He takes out the handkerchief.*]

Since that's the way we're playing it . . .

[*he unfolds handkerchief*]

. . . let's play it that way . . .

[*he unfolds*]

. . . and speak no more about it . . .

[*he finishes unfolding*]

. . . speak no more.

[*He holds handkerchief spread out before him.*]

Old stancher!

[*Pause.*]

You . . . remain.

[*Pause. He covers his face with handkerchief, lowers his arms to armrests, remains motionless.*]

[*Brief tableau.*]

Curtain

ALL THAT FALL

A play for radio

Mrs. Rooney (Maddy), a lady in her seventies
Christy, a carter
Mr. Tyler, a retired bill-broker
Mr. Slocum, Clerk of the Racecourse
Tommy, a porter
Mr. Barrell, a station-master
Miss Fitt, a lady in her thirties
A Female Voice
Dolly, a small girl
Mr. Rooney (Dan), husband of Mrs. Rooney, blind
Jerry, a small boy

Rural sounds. Sheep, bird, cow, cock, severally, then together.

Silence.

Mrs. Rooney advances along country road towards railway station. Sound of her dragging feet.

Music faint from house by way. "Death and the Maiden."

The steps slow down, stop.

MRS. ROONEY   Poor woman. All alone in that ruinous old house. [*Music louder. Silence but for music playing. The steps resume. Music dies. Mrs. Rooney murmurs, melody. Her murmur dies.*

Sound of approaching cartwheels. The cart stops.

The steps slow down, stop.] Is that you, Christy?

CHRISTY   It is, Ma'am.

MRS. ROONEY   I thought the hinny was familiar. How is your poor wife?

CHRISTY   No better, Ma'am.

MRS. ROONEY   Your daughter then?

CHRISTY   No worse, Ma'am.

[*Silence.*]

MRS. ROONEY   Why do you halt? [*Pause.*] But why do I halt? [*Silence.*]

CHRISTY   Nice day for the races, Ma'am.

MRS. ROONEY   No doubt it is. [*Pause.*] But will it hold up? [*Pause. With emotion.*] Will it hold up?

[*Silence.*]

CHRISTY   I suppose you wouldn't—

MRS. ROONEY   Hist! [*Pause.*] Surely to goodness that cannot be the up mail I hear already.

[*Silence. The hinny neighs. Silence.*]

CHRISTY   Damn the mail.

MRS. ROONEY   Oh thank God for that! I could have sworn I heard it, thundering up the track in the far distance. [*Pause.*] So hinnies whinny. Well, it is not surprising.

CHRISTY   I suppose you wouldn't be in need of a small load of dung?

MRS. ROONEY   Dung? What class of dung?

CHRISTY   Stydung.

MRS. ROONEY   Stydung . . . I like your frankness, Christy. [*Pause.*] I'll ask the master. [*Pause.*] Christy.

CHRISTY   Yes, Ma'am.

MRS. ROONEY   Do you find anything . . . bizarre about my way of speaking? [*Pause.*] I do not mean the voice. [*Pause.*] No, I mean the words. [*Pause. More to herself.*] I use none but the simplest words, I hope, and yet I sometimes find my way of speaking very . . . bizarre. [*Pause.*] Mercy! What was that?

CHRISTY   Never mind her, Ma'am, she's very fresh in herself today.

[*Silence.*]

MRS. ROONEY   Dung? What would we want with dung, at our time of life? [*Pause.*] Why are you on your feet down on the road? Why do you not climb up on the crest of your manure and let yourself be carried along? Is it that you have no head for heights?

[*Silence.*]

CHRISTY   [*to the hinny*] Yep! [*Pause. Louder.*] Yep wiyya to hell owwa that!

[*Silence.*]

MRS. ROONEY   She does not move a muscle. [*Pause.*] I too should be getting along, if I do not wish to arrive late at the station. [*Pause.*] But a moment ago she neighed and pawed the ground. And now she refuses to advance. Give her a good welt on the rump. [*Sound of welt. Pause.*] Harder! [*Sound of welt. Pause.*] Well! If someone were to do that for me I should not dally. [*Pause.*] How she gazes at me to be sure, with her great moist cleg-tormented eyes! Perhaps if I were to move on, down the road, out of her field of vision. . . . [*Sound of welt.*] No, no, enough! Take her by the snaffle and pull her eyes away from me. Oh this is awful! [*She moves on. Sound of her dragging feet.*] What have I done to deserve all this, what, what? [*Dragging feet.*] So long ago. . . . No! No! [*Dragging feet. Quotes.*] "Sigh out a something something tale of things, Done long ago and ill done." [*She halts.*] How can I go on, I cannot. Oh let me just flop down flat on the road like a big fat jelly out of a bowl and never move again! A great big slop thick with grit and dust and flies, they would have to scoop me up with a shovel. [*Pause.*] Heavens, there is that up mail again, what will become of me! [*The dragging steps resume.*] Oh I am just a hysterical old hag I know, destroyed with sorrow and pining and gentility and church-going and fat and rheumatism and childlessness. [*Pause. Brokenly.*] Minnie! Little Minnie! [*Pause.*] Love, that is all I asked, a little love, daily, twice daily, fifty years of twice daily love like a Paris horse-butcher's regular, what normal woman wants affection? A peck on the jaw at morning, near the ear, and another at evening, peck, peck, till you grow whiskers on you. There is that lovely laburnum again. [*Dragging feet. Sound of bicycle-bell. It is old Mr. Tyler*

coming up behind her on his bicycle, on his way to the
station. Squeak of brakes. He slows down and rides abreast
of her.]

MR. TYLER   Mrs. Rooney! Pardon me if I do not doff my cap, I'd fall
off. Divine day for the meeting.

MRS. ROONEY   Oh, Mr. Tyler, you startled the life out of me stealing up
behind me like that like a deer-stalker! Oh!

MR. TYLER   [*playfully*] I rang my bell, Mrs. Rooney, the moment I
sighted you I started tinkling my bell, now don't you
deny it.

MRS. ROONEY   Your bell is one thing, Mr. Tyler, and you are another.
What news of your poor daughter?

MR. TYLER   Fair, fair. They removed everything, you know, the
whole . . . er . . . bag of tricks. Now I am
grandchildless.
[*Dragging feet.*]

MRS. ROONEY   Gracious how you wobble! Dismount, for mercy's sake,
or ride on.

MR. TYLER   Perhaps if I were to lay my hand lightly on your
shoulder, Mrs. Rooney, how would that be?
[*Pause.*] Would you permit that?

MRS. ROONEY   No, Mr. Rooney, Mr. Tyler I mean, I am tired of light old
hands on my shoulders and other senseless places,
sick and tired of them. Heavens, here comes
Connolly's van! [*She halts. Sound of motor-van. It*
approaches, passes with thunderous rattles, recedes.] Are
you all right, Mr. Tyler? [*Pause.*] Where is he? [*Pause.*]
Ah there you are! [*The dragging steps resume.*] That was a
narrow squeak.

MR. TYLER   I alit in the nick of time.

MRS. ROONEY   It is suicide to be abroad. But what is it to be at home,
Mr. Tyler, what is it to be at home? A lingering
dissolution. Now we are white with dust from head to
foot. I beg your pardon?

MR. TYLER   Nothing, Mrs. Rooney, nothing, I was merely cursing, under my breath, God and man, under my breath, and the wet Saturday afternoon of my conception. My back tyre has gone down again. I pumped it hard as iron before I set out. And now I am on the rim.

MRS. ROONEY   Oh what a shame!

MR. TYLER   Now if it were the front I should not so much mind. But the back. The back! The chain! The oil! The grease! The hub! The brakes! The gear! No! It is too much!
[*Dragging steps.*]

MRS. ROONEY   Are we very late, Mr. Tyler? I have not the courage to look at my watch.

MR. TYLER   [*bitterly*] Late! I on my bicycle as I bowled along was already late. Now therefore we are doubly late, trebly, quadrupedly late. Would I had shot by you, without a word.
[*Dragging feet.*]

MRS. ROONEY   Whom are you meeting, Mr. Tyler?

MR. TYLER   Hardy. [*Pause.*] We used to climb together. [*Pause.*] I saved his life once. [*Pause.*] I have not forgotten it.
[*Dragging feet. They stop.*]

MRS. ROONEY   Let us halt a moment and let this vile dust fall back upon the viler worms.
[*Silence. Rural sounds.*]

MR. TYLER   What sky! What light! Ah in spite of all it is a blessed thing to be alive in such weather, and out of hospital.

MRS. ROONEY   Alive?

MR. TYLER   Well half alive shall we say?

MRS. ROONEY   Speak for yourself, Mr. Tyler. I am not half alive nor anything approaching it. [*Pause.*] What are we standing here for? This dust will not settle in our time. And when it does some great roaring machine will come and whirl it all skyhigh again.

MR. TYLER   Well, shall we be getting along in that case?

MRS. ROONEY   No.

MR. TYLER   Come, Mrs. Rooney—

MRS. ROONEY   Go, Mr. Tyler, go on and leave me, listening to the cooing of the ringdoves. [*Cooing.*] If you see my poor blind Dan tell him I was on my way to meet him when it all came over me again, like a flood. Say to him, Your poor wife, she told me to tell you it all came flooding over her again and . . . [*the voice breaks*] . . . she simply went back home . . . straight back home. . . .

MR. TYLER   Come, Mrs. Rooney, come, the mail has not yet gone up, just take my free arm and we'll be there with time and to spare.

MRS. ROONEY   [*sobbing*] What? What's all this now? [*Calmer.*] Can't you see I'm in trouble? [*With anger.*] Have you no respect for misery? [*Sobbing.*] Minnie! Little Minnie!

MR. TYLER   Come, Mrs. Rooney, come, the mail has not yet gone up, just take my free arm and we'll be there with time and to spare.

MRS. ROONEY   [*brokenly*] In her forties now she'd be, I don't know, fifty, girding up her lovely little loins, getting ready for the change. . . .

MR. TYLER   Come, Mrs. Rooney, come, the mail—

MRS. ROONEY   [*exploding*] Will you get along with you, Mr. Rooney, Mr. Tyler I mean, will you get along with you now and cease molesting me? What kind of a country is this where a woman can't weep her heart out on the highways and byways without being tormented by retired bill-brokers! [*Mr. Tyler prepares to mount his bicycle.*] Heavens you're not going to ride her flat! [*Mr. Tyler mounts.*] You'll tear your tube to ribbons! [*Mr. Tyler rides off. Receding sound of bumping bicycle. Silence. Cooing.*] Venus birds! Billing in the woods all the long summer long. [*Pause.*] Oh cursed corset! If I could let it out, without indecent exposure. Mr. Tyler! Mr. Tyler! Come back and unlace me behind the hedge! [*She laughs wildly, ceases.*] What's wrong with me, what's wrong with me, never tranquil, seething out of my dirty old pelt, out of my skull, oh to be in atoms, in atoms! [*Frenziedly.*] ATOMS! [*Silence. Cooing. Faintly.*] Jesus! [*Pause.*] Jesus! [*Sound of car coming up behind her. It slows down and draws up beside her, engine running. It is Mr. Slocum, the Clerk of the Racecourse.*]

MR. SLOCUM   Is anything wrong, Mrs. Rooney? You are bent all double. Have you a pain in the stomach?
[*Silence. Mrs. Rooney laughs wildly. Finally.*]

MRS. ROONEY   Well if it isn't my old admirer the Clerk of the Course, in his limousine.

MR. SLOCUM   May I offer you a lift, Mrs. Rooney? Are you going in my direction?

MRS. ROONEY   I am, Mr. Slocum, we all are. [*Pause.*] How is your poor mother?

MR. SLOCUM   Thank you, she is fairly comfortable. We manage to keep her out of pain. That is the great thing, Mrs. Rooney, is it not?

MRS. ROONEY   Yes, indeed, Mr. Slocum, that is the great thing, I don't know how you do it. [*Pause. She slaps her cheek violently.*] Ah these wasps!

MR. SLOCUM   [*coolly*] May I then offer you a seat, Madam?

MRS. ROONEY   [*with exaggerated enthusiasm*] Oh that would be heavenly, Mr. Slocum, just simply heavenly. [*Dubiously.*] But would I ever get in, you look very high off the ground today, these new balloon tyres I presume. [*Sound of door opening and Mrs. Rooney trying to get in.*] Does this roof never come off? No? [*Efforts of Mrs. Rooney.*] No. . . . I'll never do it . . . you'll have to get down, Mr. Slocum, and help me from the rear. [*Pause.*] What was that? [*Pause. Aggrieved.*] This is all your suggestion, Mr. Slocum, not mine. Drive on, Sir, drive on.

MR. SLOCUM   [*switching off engine*] I'm coming, Mrs. Rooney, I'm coming, give me time, I'm as stiff as yourself. [*Sound of Mr. Slocum extracting himself from driver's seat.*]

MRS. ROONEY   Stiff! Well I like that! And me heaving all over back and front. [*To herself.*] The dry old reprobate!

MR. SLOCUM   [*in position behind her*] Now, Mrs. Rooney, how shall we do this?

MRS. ROONEY   As if I were a bale, Mr. Slocum, don't be afraid. [*Pause. Sounds of effort.*] That's the way! [*Effort.*] Lower! [*Effort.*] Wait! [*Pause.*] No, don't let go! [*Pause.*] Suppose I do get up, will I ever get down?

MR. SLOCUM   [*breathing hard*] You'll get down, Mrs. Rooney, you'll get down. We may not get you up, but I warrant you we'll get you down.

[*He resumes his efforts. Sound of these.*]

MRS. ROONEY   Oh! . . . Lower! . . . Don't be afraid! . . . We're past the age when . . . There! . . . Now! . . . Get your shoulder under it. . . . Oh! . . . [*Giggles.*] Oh glory! . . . Up! Up! . . . Ah! . . . I'm in! [*Panting of Mr. Slocum. He slams the door. In a scream.*] My frock! You've nipped my frock! [*Mr. Slocum opens the door. Mrs. Rooney frees her frock. Mr. Slocum slams the door. His violent unintelligible muttering as he walks round to the other door. Tearfully.*] My nice frock! Look what you've done to my nice frock! [*Mr. Slocum gets into his seat, slams driver's door, presses starter. The engine does not start. He releases starter.*] What will Dan say when he sees me?

MR. SLOCUM   Has he then recovered his sight?

MRS. ROONEY   No, I mean when he knows, what will he say when he feels the hole? [*Mr. Slocum presses starter. As before. Silence.*] What are you doing, Mr. Slocum?

MR. SLOCUM   Gazing straight before me, Mrs. Rooney, through the windscreen, into the void.

MRS. ROONEY   Start her up, I beseech you, and let us be off. This is awful!

MR. SLOCUM   [*dreamily*] All morning she went like a dream and now she is dead. That is what you get for a good deed. [*Pause. Hopefully.*] Perhaps if I were to choke her. [*He does so, presses the starter. The engine roars. Roaring to make himself heard.*] She was getting too much air! [*He throttles down, grinds in his first gear, moves off, changes up in a grinding of gears.*]

MRS. ROONEY   [*in anguish*] Mind the hen! [*Scream of brakes. Squawk of hen.*] Oh, mother, you have squashed her, drive on, drive on! [*The car accelerates. Pause.*] What a death! One minute picking happy at the dung, on the road, in the sun, with now and then a dust bath, and then— bang!—all her troubles over. [*Pause.*] All the laying and the hatching. [*Pause.*] Just one great squawk and then ... peace. [*Pause.*] They would have slit her weasand in any case. [*Pause.*] Here we are, let me down. [*The car slows down, stops, engine running. Mr. Slocum blows his horn. Pause. Louder. Pause.*] What are you up to now, Mr. Slocum? We are at a standstill, all danger is past and you blow your horn. Now if instead of blowing it now you had blown it at that unfortunate— [*Horn violently. Tommy the porter appears at top of station steps.*]

MR. SLOCUM   [*calling*] Will you come down, Tommy, and help this lady out, she's stuck. [*Tommy descends the steps.*] Open the door, Tommy, and ease her out. [*Tommy opens the door.*]

TOMMY   Certainly, Sir. Nice day for the races, sir. What would you fancy for—

MRS. ROONEY   Don't mind me. Don't take any notice of me. I do not
exist. The fact is well known.

MR. SLOCUM   Do as you're asked, Tommy, for the love of God.

TOMMY   Yessir. Now, Mrs. Rooney.
[*He starts pulling her out.*]

MRS. ROONEY   Wait, Tommy, wait now, don't bustle me, just let me
wheel round and get my feet to the ground. [*Her efforts
to achieve this.*] Now.

TOMMY   [*pulling her out*] Mind your feather, Ma'am. [*Sounds of
effort.*] Easy now, easy.

MRS. ROONEY   Wait, for God's sake, you'll have me beheaded.

TOMMY   Crouch down, Mrs. Rooney, crouch down, and get your
head in the open.

MRS. ROONEY   Crouch down! At my time of life! This is lunacy!

TOMMY   Press her down, sir. [*Sounds of combined efforts.*]

MRS. ROONEY   Pity!

TOMMY   Now! She's coming! Straighten up, Ma'am! There!
[*Mr. Slocum slams the door.*]

MRS. ROONEY   Am I out?
[*The voice of Mr. Barrell, the station-master, raised in anger.*]

MR. BARRELL   Tommy! Tommy! Where the hell is he? [*Mr. Slocum grinds
in his gear.*]

TOMMY   [*hurriedly*] You wouldn't have something for the Ladies
Plate, sir? I was given Flash Harry.

MR. SLOCUM   [*scornfully*] Flash Harry! That carthorse!

MR. BARRELL   [*at top of steps, roaring*] Tommy! Blast your bleeding
bloody— [*He sees Mrs. Rooney.*] Oh, Mrs. Rooney. . . .
[*Mr. Slocum drives away in a grinding of gears.*] Who's
that crucifying his gearbox, Tommy?

TOMMY   Old Cissy Slocum.

MRS. ROONEY   Cissy Slocum! That's a nice way to refer to your betters.
Cissy Slocum! And you an orphan!

MR. BARRELL   [*angrily to Tommy*] What are you doing stravaging down
here on the public road? This is no place for you at

all! Nip up there on the platform now and whip out the truck! Won't the twelve thirty be on top of us before we can turn round?

TOMMY   [*bitterly*] And that's the thanks you get for a Christian act.

MR. BARRELL   [*violently*] Get on with you now before I report you! [*Slow feet of Tommy climbing steps.*] Do you want me to come down to you with the shovel? [*The feet quicken, recede, cease.*] Ah God forgive me, it's a hard life. [*Pause.*] Well, Mrs. Rooney, it's nice to see you up and about again. You were laid up there a long time.

MRS. ROONEY   Not long enough, Mr. Barrell. [*Pause.*] Would I were still in bed, Mr. Barrell. [*Pause.*] Would I were lying stretched out in my comfortable bed, Mr. Barrell, just wasting slowly, painlessly away, keeping up my strength with arrowroot and calves-foot jelly, till in the end you wouldn't see me under the blankets any more than a board. [*Pause.*] Oh no coughing or spitting or bleeding or vomiting, just drifting gently down into the higher life, and remembering, remembering . . . [*the voice breaks*] . . . all the silly unhappiness . . . as though . . . it had never happened. . . . What did I do with that handkerchief? [*Sound of handkerchief loudly applied.*] How long have you been master of this station now, Mr. Barrell?

MR. BARRELL   Don't ask me, Mrs. Rooney, don't ask me.

MRS. ROONEY   You stepped into your father's shoes, I believe, when he took them off.

MR. BARRELL   Poor Pappy! [*Reverent pause.*] He didn't live long to enjoy his ease.

MRS. ROONEY   I remember him clearly. A small ferrety purple-faced widower, deaf as a doornail, very testy and snappy. [*Pause.*] I suppose you'll be retiring soon yourself, Mr. Barrell, and growing your roses. [*Pause.*] Did I understand you to say the twelve thirty would soon be upon us?

MR. BARRELL   Those were my words.

MRS. ROONEY   But according to my watch which is more or less right—
or was—by the eight o'clock news the time is now
coming up to twelve ... [*pause as she consults her
watch*] ... thirty-six. [*Pause.*] And yet upon the other
hand the up mail has not yet gone through. [*Pause.*] Or
has it sped by unbeknown to me? [*Pause.*] For there
was a moment there, I remember now, I was so
plunged in sorrow I wouldn't have heard a steam
roller go over me. [*Pause. Mr. Barrell turns to go.*] Don't
go, Mr. Barrell! [*Mr. Barrell goes. Loud.*] Mr. Barrell!
[*Pause. Louder.*] Mr. Barrell! [*Mr. Barrell comes back.*]

MR. BARRELL   [*testily*] What is it, Mrs. Rooney, I have my work to do.
[*Silence. Sound of wind.*]

MRS. ROONEY   The wind is getting up. [*Pause. Wind.*] The best of the day
is over. [*Pause. Wind. Dreamily.*] Soon the rain will
begin to fall and go on falling, all afternoon.
[*Mr. Barrell goes.*] Then at evening the clouds will part,
the setting sun will shine an instant, then sink,
behind the hills. [*She realizes Mr. Barrell has gone.*]
Mr. Barrell! Mr. Barrell! [*Silence.*] I estrange them all.
They come towards me, uninvited, bygones bygones,
full of kindness, anxious to help ... [*the voice breaks*] ...
genuinely pleased ... to see me again ... looking so
well. ... [*Handkerchief.*] A few simple words ... from
my heart ... and I am all alone ... once more. ...
[*Handkerchief. Vehemently.*] I should not be out at all! I
should never leave the grounds! [*Pause.*] Oh there is
that Fitt woman, I wonder will she bow to me. [*Sound
of Miss Fitt approaching, humming a hymn. She starts
climbing the steps.*] Miss Fitt! [*Miss Fitt halts, stops
humming.*] Am I then invisible, Miss Fitt? Is this
cretonne so becoming to me that I merge into the
masonry? [*Miss Fitt descends a step.*] That is right,

Miss Fitt, look closely and you will finally distinguish a once female shape.

MISS FITT   Mrs. Rooney! I saw you, but I did not know you.

MRS. ROONEY   Last Sunday we worshipped together. We knelt side by side at the same altar. We drank from the same chalice. Have I so changed since then?

MISS FITT   [shocked] Oh but in church, Mrs. Rooney, in church I am alone with my Maker. Are not you? [Pause.] Why even the sexton himself, you know, when he takes up the collection, knows it is useless to pause before me. I simply do not see the plate, or bag, whatever it is they use, how could I? [Pause.] Why even when all is over and I go out into the sweet fresh air, why even then for the first furlong or so I stumble in a kind of daze as you might say, oblivious to my co-religionists. And they are very kind I must admit—the vast majority—very kind and understanding. They know me now and take no umbrage. There she goes, they say, there goes the dark Miss Fitt, alone with her Maker, take no notice of her. And they step down off the path to avoid my running into them. [Pause.] Ah yes, I am distray, very distray, even on week-days. Ask Mother, if you do not believe me. Hetty, she says, when I start eating my doily instead of the thin bread and butter, Hetty, how can you be so distray? [Sighs.] I suppose the truth is I am not there, Mrs. Rooney, just not really there at all. I see, hear, smell, and so on, I go through the usual motions, but my heart is not in it, Mrs. Rooney, my heart is in none of it. Left to myself, with no one to check me, I would soon be flown . . . home. [Pause.] So if you think I cut you just now, Mrs. Rooney, you do me an injustice. All I saw was a big pale blur, just another big pale blur. [Pause.] Is anything amiss, Mrs. Rooney, you do not look normal somehow. So bowed and bent.

MRS. ROONEY   [*ruefully*] Maddy Rooney, née Dunne, the big pale blur. [*Pause.*] You have piercing sight, Miss Fitt, if you only knew it, literally piercing. [*Pause.*]

MISS FITT   Well . . . is there anything I can do, now that I am here?

MRS. ROONEY   If you would help me up the face of this cliff, Miss Fitt, I have little doubt your Maker would requite you, if no one else.

MISS FITT   Now, now, Mrs. Rooney, don't put your teeth in me. Requite! I make these sacrifices for nothing—or not at all. [*Pause. Sound of her descending steps.*] I take it you want to lean on me, Mrs. Rooney.

MRS. ROONEY   I asked Mr. Barrell to give me his arm, just give me his arm. [*Pause.*] He turned on his heel and strode away.

MISS FITT   Is it my arm you want then? [*Pause. Impatiently.*] Is it my arm you want, Mrs. Rooney, or what is it?

MRS. ROONEY   [*exploding*] Your arm! Any arm! A helping hand! For five seconds! Christ what a planet!

MISS FITT   Really. . . . Do you know what it is, Mrs. Rooney, I do not think it is wise of you to be going about at all.

MRS. ROONEY   [*violently*] Come down here, Miss Fitt, and give me your arm, before I scream down the parish! [*Pause. Wind. Sound of Miss Fitt descending last steps.*]

MISS FITT   [*resignedly*] Well, I suppose it is the Protestant thing to do.

MRS. ROONEY   Pismires do it for one another. [*Pause.*] I have seen slugs do it. [*Miss Fitt proffers her arm.*] No, the other side, my dear, if it's all the same to you, I'm left-handed on top of everything else. [*She takes Miss Fitt's right arm.*] Heavens, child, you're just a bag of bones, you need building up. [*Sound of her toiling up steps on Miss Fitt's arm.*] This is worse than the Matterhorn, were you ever up the Matterhorn, Miss Fitt, great honeymoon resort. [*Sound of toiling.*] Why don't they have a handrail? [*Panting.*] Wait till I get some air. [*Pause.*]

	Don't let me go! [*Miss Fitt hums her hymn. After a moment Mrs. Rooney joins in with the words.*] . . . the encircling gloo-oom . . . [*Miss Fitt stops humming.*] . . . tum tum me on. [*Forte.*] The night is dark and I am far from ho-ome, tum tum—
MISS FITT	[*hysterically*] Stop it, Mrs. Rooney, stop it, or I'll drop you!
MRS. ROONEY	Wasn't it that they sung on the *Lusitania?* Or Rock of Ages? Most touching it must have been. Or was it the *Titanic?* [*Attracted by the noise a group, including Mr. Tyler, Mr. Barrell and Tommy, gathers at top of steps.*]
MR. BARRELL	What the— [*Silence.*]
MR. TYLER	Lovely day for the fixture. [*Loud titter from Tommy cut short by Mr. Barrell with backhanded blow in the stomach. Appropriate noise from Tommy.*]
A FEMALE VOICE	[*shrill*] Oh look, Dolly, look!
DOLLY	What, Mamma?
A FEMALE VOICE	They are stuck! [*Cackling laugh.*] They are stuck!
MRS. ROONEY	Now we are the laughing-stock of the twenty-six counties. Or is it thirty-six?
MR. TYLER	That is a nice way to treat your defenceless subordinates, Mr. Barrell, hitting them without warning in the pit of the stomach.
MISS FITT	Has anyone seen my mother?
MR. BARRELL	Who is that?
TOMMY	The dark Miss Fitt.
MR. BARRELL	Where is her face?
MRS. ROONEY	Now, deary, I am ready if you are. [*They toil up remaining steps.*] Stand back, you cads! [*Shuffle of feet.*]
A FEMALE VOICE	Mind yourself, Dolly!
MRS. ROONEY	Thank you, Miss Fitt, thank you, that will do, just prop me up against the wall like a roll of tarpaulin and that will be all, for the moment. [*Pause.*] I am sorry for all

	this ramdam, Miss Fitt, had I known you were looking for your mother I should not have importuned you, I know what it is.
MISS FITT	[*in marvelling aside*] Ramdam!
A FEMALE VOICE	Come, Dolly darling, let us take up our stand before the first class smokers. Give me your hand and hold me tight, one can be sucked under.
MR. TYLER	You have lost your mother, Miss Fitt?
MISS FITT	Good morning, Mr. Tyler.
MR. TYLER	Good morning, Miss Fitt.
MR. BARRELL	Good morning, Miss Fitt.
MISS FITT	Good morning, Mr. Barrell.
MR. TYLER	You have lost your mother, Miss Fitt?
MISS FITT	She said she would be on the last train.
MRS. ROONEY	Do not imagine, because I am silent, that I am not present, and alive, to all that is going on.
MR. TYLER	[*to Miss Fitt*] When you say the last train—
MRS. ROONEY	Do not flatter yourselves for one moment, because I hold aloof, that my sufferings have ceased. No. The entire scene, the hills, the plain, the racecourse with its miles and miles of white rails and three red stands, the pretty little wayside station, even you yourselves, yes, I mean it, and over all the clouding blue, I see it all, I stand here and see it all with eyes . . . [*the voice breaks*] . . . through eyes . . . oh if you had my eyes . . . you would understand . . . the things they have seen . . . and not looked away . . . this is nothing . . . nothing . . . what did I do with that handkerchief? [*Pause.*]
MR. TYLER	[*to Miss Fitt*] When you say the last train— [*Mrs. Rooney blows her nose violently and long.*] —when you say the last train, Miss Fitt, I take it you mean the twelve thirty.
MISS FITT	What else could I mean, Mr. Tyler, what else could I *conceivably* mean?

MR. TYLER   Then you have no cause for anxiety, Miss Fitt, for the twelve thirty has not yet arrived. Look. [*Miss Fitt looks.*] No, up the line. [*Miss Fitt looks. Patiently.*] No, Miss Fitt, follow the direction of my index. [*Miss Fitt looks.*] There. You see now. The signal. At the bawdy hour of nine. [*In rueful afterthought.*] Or three alas! [*Mr. Barrell stifles a guffaw.*] Thank you, Mr. Barrell.

MISS FITT   But the time is now getting on for—

MR. TYLER   [*patiently*] We all know, Miss Fitt, we all know only too well what the time is now getting on for, and yet the cruel fact remains that the twelve thirty has not yet arrived.

MISS FITT   Not an accident, I trust! [*Pause.*] Do not tell me she has left the track! [*Pause.*] Oh darling mother! With the fresh sole for lunch!

[*Loud titter from Tommy, checked as before by Mr. Barrell.*]

MR. BARRELL   That's enough old guff out of you. Nip up to the box now and see has Mr. Case anything for me.

[*Tommy goes.*]

MRS. ROONEY   Poor Dan!

MISS FITT   [*in anguish*] What terrible thing has happened?

MR. TYLER   Now now, Miss Fitt, do not—

MRS. ROONEY   [*with vehement sadness*] Poor Dan!

MR. TYLER   Now now, Miss Fitt, do not give way . . . to despair, all will come right . . . in the end. [*Aside to Mr. Barrell.*] What *is* the situation, Mr. Barrell? Not a collision surely?

MRS. ROONEY   [*enthusiastically*] A collision! Oh that would be wonderful!

MISS FITT   [*horrified*] A collision! I knew it!

MR. TYLER   Come, Miss Fitt, let us move a little up the platform.

MRS. ROONEY   Yes, let us all do that. [*Pause.*] No? [*Pause.*] You have changed your mind? [*Pause.*] I quite agree, we are better here, in the shadow of the waiting-room.

MR. BARRELL   Excuse me a moment.

MRS. ROONEY   Before you slink away, Mr. Barrell, please, a statement of some kind, I insist. Even the slowest train on this brief line is not ten minutes and more behind its scheduled time without good cause, one imagines. [*Pause.*] We all know your station is the best kept of the entire network, but there are times when that is not enough, just not enough. [*Pause.*] Now, Mr. Barrell, leave off chewing your whiskers, we are waiting to hear from you—we the unfortunate ticket-holders' nearest if not dearest. [*Pause.*]

MR. TYLER   [*reasonably*] I do think we are owed some kind of explanation, Mr. Barrell, if only to set our minds at rest.

MR. BARRELL   I know nothing. All I know is there has been a hitch. All traffic is retarded.

MRS. ROONEY   [*derisively*] Retarded! A hitch! Ah these celibates! Here we are eating our hearts out with anxiety for our loved ones and he calls that a hitch! Those of us like myself with heart and kidney trouble may collapse at any moment and he calls that a hitch! In our ovens the Saturday roast is burning to a shrivel and he calls that—

MR. TYLER   Here comes Tommy, running! I am glad I have been spared to see this.

TOMMY   [*excitedly, in the distance*] She's coming. [*Pause. Nearer.*] She's at the level-crossing!

[*Immediately exaggerated station sounds. Falling signals. Bells. Whistles. Crescendo of train whistle approaching. Sound of train rushing through station.*]

MRS. ROONEY   [*above rush of train*] The up mail! The up mail! [*The up mail recedes, the down train approaches, enters the station, pulls up with great hissing of steam and clashing of couplings. Noise of passengers descending, doors banging, Mr. Barrell shouting "Boghill! Boghill!," etc. Piercingly.*]

Dan! . . . Are you all right? . . . Where is he? . . . Dan! Did you see my husband? . . . Dan! . . . [*Noise of station emptying. Guard's whistle. Train departing, receding. Silence.*] He isn't on it! The misery I have endured to get here, and he isn't on it! . . . Mr. Barrell! . . . Was he not on it? [*Pause.*] Is anything the matter, you look as if you had seen a ghost. [*Pause.*] Tommy! . . . Did you see the master?

TOMMY   He'll be along, Ma'am, Jerry is minding him.
[*Mr. Rooney suddenly appears on platform, advancing on small boy Jerry's arm. He is blind, thumps the ground with his stick and pants incessantly.*]

MRS. ROONEY   Oh, Dan! There you are! [*Her dragging feet as she hastens towards him. She reaches him. They halt.*] Where in the world were you?

MR. ROONEY   [*coolly*] Maddy.

MRS. ROONEY   Where were you all this time?

MR. ROONEY   In the men's.

MRS. ROONEY   Kiss me!

MR. ROONEY   Kiss you? In public? On the platform? Before the boy? Have you taken leave of your senses?

MRS. ROONEY   Jerry wouldn't mind. Would you, Jerry?

JERRY   No, Ma'am.

MRS. ROONEY   How is your poor father?

JERRY   They took him away, Ma'am.

MRS. ROONEY   Then you are all alone?

JERRY   Yes, Ma'am.

MR. ROONEY   Why are you here? You did not notify me.

MRS. ROONEY   I wanted to give you a surprise. For your birthday.

MR. ROONEY   My birthday?

MRS. ROONEY   Don't you remember? I wished you your happy returns in the bathroom.

MR. ROONEY   I did not hear you.

MRS. ROONEY   But I gave you a tie! You have it on!

[*Pause.*]

MR. ROONEY   How old am I now?

MRS. ROONEY   Now never mind about that. Come.

MR. ROONEY   Why did you not cancel the boy? Now we shall have to give him a penny.

MRS. ROONEY   [*miserably*] I forgot! I had such a time getting here! Such horrid nasty people! [*Pause. Pleading.*] Be nice to me, Dan, be nice to me today!

MR. ROONEY   Give the boy a penny.

MRS. ROONEY   Here are two halfpennies, Jerry. Run along now and buy yourself a nice gobstopper.

JERRY   Yes, Ma'am.

MR. ROONEY   Come for me on Monday, if I am still alive.

JERRY   Yessir.

[*He runs off.*]

MR. ROONEY   We could have saved sixpence. We have saved fivepence. [*Pause.*] But at what cost?

[*They move off along platform arm in arm. Dragging feet, panting, thudding stick.*]

MRS. ROONEY   Are you not well?

[*They halt, on Mr. Rooney's initiative.*]

MR. ROONEY   Once and for all, do not ask me to speak and move at the same time. I shall not say this in this life again.

[*They move off. Dragging feet, etc. They halt at top of steps.*]

MRS. ROONEY   Are you not—

MR. ROONEY   Let us get this precipice over.

MRS. ROONEY   Put your arm around me.

MR. ROONEY   Have you been drinking again? [*Pause.*] You are quivering like a blancmange. [*Pause.*] Are you in a condition to lead me? [*Pause.*] We shall fall into the ditch.

MRS. ROONEY   Oh, Dan! It will be like old times!

MR. ROONEY   Pull yourself together or I shall send Tommy for the cab. Then instead of having saved sixpence, no, fivepence,

we shall have lost . . . [*calculating mumble*] . . . two and
three less six one and no plus one one and no plus
three one and nine and one ten and three two and
one . . . [*normal voice*] two and one, we shall be the
poorer to the tune of two and one. [*Pause.*] Curse that
sun, it has gone in. What is the day doing?
[*Wind.*]

MRS. ROONEY   Shrouding, shrouding, the best of it is past. [*Pause.*] Soon
the first great drops will fall splashing in the dust.

MR. ROONEY   And yet the glass was firm. [*Pause.*] Let us hasten home
and sit before the fire. We shall draw the blinds. You
will read to me. I think Effie is going to commit
adultery with the Major. [*Brief drag of feet.*] Wait! [*Feet
cease. Stick tapping at steps.*] I have been up and down
these steps five thousand times and still I do not
know how many there are. When I think there are six
there are four or five or seven or eight and when I
remember there are five there three or four or six or
seven and when finally I realize there are seven there
are five or six or eight or nine. Sometimes I wonder if
they do not change them in the night. [*Pause. Irritably.*]
Well? How many do you make them today?

MRS. ROONEY   Do not ask me to count, Dan, not now.

MR. ROONEY   Not count! One of the few satisfactions in life!

MRS. ROONEY   Not steps, Dan, please, I always get them wrong. Then
you might fall on your wound and I would have that
on my manure-heap on top of everything else. No,
just cling to me and all will be well.
[*Confused noise of their descent. Panting, stumbling,
ejaculations, curses. Silence.*]

MR. ROONEY   Well! That is what you call well!

MRS. ROONEY   We are down. And little the worse. [*Silence. A donkey brays.
Silence.*] That was a true donkey. Its father and mother
were donkeys.

[*Silence.*]

MR. ROONEY   Do you know what it is, I think I shall retire.

MRS. ROONEY   [*appalled*] Retire! And live at home? On your grant!

MR. ROONEY   Never tread these cursed steps again. Trudge this hellish road for the last time. Sit at home on the remnants of my bottom counting the hours—till the next meal. [*Pause.*] The very thought puts life in me! Forward, before it dies!

[*They move on. Dragging feet, panting, thudding stick.*]

MRS. ROONEY   Now mind, here is the path. . . . Up! . . . Well done! Now we are in safety and a straight run home.

MR. ROONEY   [*without halting, between gasps*] A straight . . . run! . . . She calls that . . . a straight . . . run! . . .

MRS. ROONEY   Hush! Do not speak as you go along, you know it is not good for your coronary. [*Dragging steps, etc.*] Just concentrate on putting one foot before the next or whatever the expression is. [*Dragging feet, etc.*] That is the way, now we are doing nicely. [*Dragging feet, etc. They suddenly halt, on Mrs. Rooney's initiative.*] Heavens! I knew there was something! With all the excitement! I forgot!

MR. ROONEY   [*quietly*] Good God!

MRS. ROONEY   But you must know, Dan, of course, you were on it. Whatever happened? Tell me!

MR. ROONEY   I have never known anything to happen.

MRS. ROONEY   But you must—

MR. ROONEY   [*violently*] All this stopping and starting again is devilish, devilish! I get a little way on me and begin to be carried along when suddenly you stop dead! Two hundred pounds of unhealthy fat! What possessed you to come out at all? Let go of me!

MRS. ROONEY   [*in great agitation*] No, I must know, we won't stir from here till you tell me. Fifteen minutes late! On a thirty minute run! It's unheard of!

MR. ROONEY   I know nothing. Let go of me before I shake you off.

MRS. ROONEY   But you must know! You were on it! Was it at the terminus? Did you leave on time? Or was it on the line? [*Pause.*] Did something happen on the line? [*Pause.*] Dan! [*Brokenly.*] Why won't you tell me! [*Silence. They move off. Dragging feet, etc. They halt. Pause.*]

MR. ROONEY   Poor Maddy! [*Pause. Children's cries.*] What was that? [*Pause for Mrs. Rooney to ascertain.*]

MRS. ROONEY   The Lynch twins jeering at us. [*Cries.*]

MR. ROONEY   Will they pelt us with mud today, do you suppose? [*Cries.*]

MRS. ROONEY   Let us turn and face them. [*Cries. They turn. Silence.*] Threaten them with your stick. [*Silence.*] They have run away.
[*Pause.*]

MR. ROONEY   Did you ever wish to kill a child? [*Pause.*] Nip some young doom in the bud. [*Pause.*] Many a time at night, in winter, on the black road home, I nearly attacked the boy. [*Pause.*] Poor Jerry! [*Pause.*] What restrained me then? [*Pause.*] Not fear of man. [*Pause.*] Shall we go on backwards now a little?

MRS. ROONEY   Backwards?

MR. ROONEY   Yes. Or you forwards and I backwards. The perfect pair. Like Dante's damned, with their faces arsy-versy. Our tears will water our bottoms.

MRS. ROONEY   What is the matter, Dan? Are you not well?

MR. ROONEY   Well! Did you ever know me to be well? The day you met me I should have been in bed. The day you proposed to me the doctors gave me up. You knew that, did you not? The night you married me they came for me with an ambulance. You have not forgotten that, I suppose? [*Pause.*] No, I cannot be said to be well. But I am no worse. Indeed I am better than I was. The loss of my sight was a great fillip. If I could go deaf and dumb I think I might pant on to be a hundred. Or have I done so? [*Pause.*] Was I a hundred today? [*Pause.*] Am I a hundred, Maddy?

[*Silence.*]

MRS. ROONEY   All is still. No living soul in sight. There is no one to ask. The world is feeding. The wind—[*brief wind*]—scarcely stirs the leaves and the birds—[*brief chirp*]—are tired singing. The cows— [*brief moo*]—and sheep—[*brief baa*]—ruminate in silence. The dogs—[*brief bark*]—are hushed and the hens—[*brief cackle*]—sprawl torpid in the dust. We are alone. There is no one to ask.

[*Silence*]

MR. ROONEY   [*clearing his throat, narrative tone*] We drew out on the tick of time, I can vouch for that. I was—

MRS. ROONEY   How can you vouch for it?

MR. ROONEY   [*normal tone, angrily*] I can vouch for it, I tell you! Do you want my relation or don't you? [*Pause. Narrative tone.*] On the tick of time. I had the compartment to myself, as usual. At least I hope so, for I made no attempt to restrain myself. My mind— [*Normal tone.*] But why do we not sit down somewhere? Are we afraid we should never rise again?

MRS. ROONEY   Sit down on what?

MR. ROONEY   On a bench, for example.

MRS. ROONEY   There is no bench.

MR. ROONEY   Then on a bank, let us sink down upon a bank.

MRS. ROONEY   There is no bank.

MR. ROONEY   Then we cannot. [*Pause.*] I dream of other roads, in other lands. Of another home, another— [*He hesitates.*] —another home. [*Pause.*] What was I trying to say?

MRS. ROONEY   Something about your mind.

MR. ROONEY   [*startled*] My mind? Are you sure? [*Pause. Incredulous.*] My mind? . . . [*Pause.*] Ah yes. [*Narrative tone.*] Alone in the compartment my mind began to work, as so often after office hours, on the way home, in the train, to the lilt of the bogeys. Your season-ticket, I said, costs you twelve pounds a year and you earn, on an average, seven and six a day, that is to say barely enough to keep you alive and twitching with the help of food, drink, tobacco and periodicals until you finally reach home and fall into bed. Add to this—or subtract from it—rent, stationery, various subscriptions, tramfares to and fro, light and heat, permits and licences, hairtrims and shaves, tips to escorts, upkeep of premises and appearances, and a thousand unspecifiable sundries, and it is clear that by lying at home in bed, day and night, winter and summer, with a change of pyjamas once a fortnight, you would add very considerably to your income. Business, I said— [*A cry. Pause. Again. Normal tone.*] Did I hear a cry?

MRS. ROONEY   Mrs. Tully I fancy. Her poor husband is in constant pain and beats her unmercifully.
[*Silence.*]

MR. ROONEY   That was a short knock. [*Pause.*] What was I trying to get at?

MRS. ROONEY   Business.

MR. ROONEY   Ah yes, business. [*Narrative tone.*] Business, old man, I said, retire from business, it has retired from you. [*Normal tone.*] One has these moments of lucidity.

MRS. ROONEY   I feel very cold and weak.

MR. ROONEY   [*narrative tone*] On the other hand, I said, there are the horrors of home life, the dusting, sweeping, airing, scrubbing, waxing, waning, washing, mangling, drying, mowing, clipping, raking, rolling, scuffling, shovelling, grinding, tearing, pounding, banging and slamming. And the brats, the happy little healthy little howling neighbours' brats. Of all this and much more the week-end, the Saturday intermission and then the

day of rest, have given you some idea. But what must
it be like on a working-day? A Wednesday? A Friday?
What must it be like on a Friday! And I fell to
thinking of my silent, backstreet, basement office,
with its obliterated plate, rest-couch and velvet
hangings, and what it means to be buried there alive,
if only from ten to five, with convenient to the one
hand a bottle of light pale ale and to the other a long
ice-cold fillet of hake. Nothing, I said, not even fully
certified death, can ever take the place of that. It was
then I noticed that we were at a standstill. [*Pause.
Normal tone. Irritably.*] Why are you hanging out of me
like that? Have you swooned away?

MRS. ROONEY   I feel very cold and faint. The wind—[*whistling wind*]—is
whistling through my summer frock as if I had
nothing on over my bloomers. I have had no solid
food since my elevenses.

MR. ROONEY   You have ceased to care. I speak—and you listen to the
wind.

MRS. ROONEY   No, no, I am agog, tell me all, then we shall press on and
never pause, never pause, till we come safe to haven.
[*Pause.*]

MR. ROONEY   Never pause . . . safe to haven. . . . Do you know, Maddy,
sometimes one would think you were struggling with
a dead language.

MRS. ROONEY   Yes indeed, Dan, I know full well what you mean, I often
have that feeling, it is unspeakably excruciating.

MR. ROONEY   I confess I have it sometimes myself, when I happen to
overhear what I am saying.

MRS. ROONEY   Well, you know, it will be dead in time, just like our own
poor dear Gaelic, there is that to be said. [*Urgent baa.*]

MR. ROONEY   [*startled*] Good God!

MRS. ROONEY   Oh the pretty little woolly lamb, crying to suck its
mother! Theirs has not changed, since Arcady.

[*Pause.*]

MR. ROONEY   Where was I in my composition?

MRS. ROONEY   At a standstill.

MR. ROONEY   Ah yes. [*Clears his throat. Narrative tone.*] I concluded naturally that we had entered a station and would soon be on our way again, and I sat on, without misgiving. Not a sound. Things are very dull today, I said, nobody getting down, nobody getting on. Then as time flew by and nothing happened I realized my error. We had not entered a station.

MRS. ROONEY   Did you not spring up and poke your head out of the window?

MR. ROONEY   What good would that have done me?

MRS. ROONEY   Why to call out to be told what was amiss.

MR. ROONEY   I did not care what was amiss. No, I just sat on, saying, If this train were never to move again I should not greatly mind. Then gradually a—how shall I say—a growing desire to—er—you know—welled up within me. Nervous probably. In fact now I am sure. You know, the feeling of being confined.

MRS. ROONEY   Yes yes, I have been through that.

MR. ROONEY   If we sit here much longer, I said, I really do not know what I shall do. I got up and paced to and fro between the seats, like a caged beast.

MRS. ROONEY   That is a help sometimes.

MR. ROONEY   After what seemed an eternity we simply moved off. And the next thing was Barrell bawling the abhorred name. I got down and Jerry led me to the men's, or Fir as they call it now, from Vir Viris I suppose, the V becoming F, in accordance with Grimm's Law. [*Pause.*] The rest you know. [*Pause.*] You say nothing? [*Pause.*] Say something. Maddy. Say you believe me.

MRS. ROONEY   I remember once attending a lecture by one of these new mind doctors. I forget what you call them. He spoke—

MR. ROONEY   A lunatic specialist?

MRS. ROONEY   No no, just the troubled mind. I was hoping he might shed a little light on my lifelong preoccupation with horses' buttocks.

MR. ROONEY   A neurologist.

MRS. ROONEY   No no, just mental distress, the name will come back to me in the night. I remember his telling us the story of a little girl, very strange and unhappy in her ways, and how he treated her unsuccessfully over a period of years and was finally obliged to give up the case. He could find nothing wrong with her, he said. The only thing wrong with her as far as he could see was that she was dying. And she did in fact die, shortly after he had washed his hands of her.

MR. ROONEY   Well? What is there so wonderful about that?

MRS. ROONEY   No, it was just something he said, and the way he said it, that have haunted me ever since.

MR. ROONEY   You lie awake at night, tossing to and fro and brooding on it.

MRS. ROONEY   On it and other . . . wretchedness. [*Pause.*] When he had done with the little girl he stood there motionless for some time, quite two minutes I should say, looking down at his table. Then he suddenly raised his head and exclaimed, as if he had had a revelation, The trouble with her was she had never really been born! [*Pause.*] He spoke throughout without notes. [*Pause.*] I left before the end.

MR. ROONEY   Nothing about your buttocks? [*Mrs. Rooney weeps. In affectionate remonstrance.*] Maddy!

MRS. ROONEY   There is nothing to be done for those people!

MR. ROONEY   For which is there? [*Pause.*] That does not sound right somehow. [*Pause.*] What way am I facing?

MRS. ROONEY   What?

MR. ROONEY   I have forgotten what way I am facing.

MRS. ROONEY   You have turned aside and are bowed down over the ditch.

MR. ROONEY   There is a dead dog down there.

MRS. ROONEY   No no, just the rotting leaves.

MR. ROONEY   In June? Rotting leaves in June?

MRS. ROONEY   Yes, dear, from last year, and from the year before last, and from the year before that again. [*Silence. Rainy wind. They move on. Dragging steps, etc.*] There is that lovely laburnum again. Poor thing, it is losing all its tassels. [*Dragging steps, etc.*] There are the first drops. [*Rain. Dragging steps, etc.*] Golden drizzle. [*Dragging steps, etc.*] Do not mind me, dear, I am just talking to myself. [*Rain heavier. Dragging steps, etc.*] Can hinnies procreate, I wonder? [*They halt.*]

MR. ROONEY   Say that again.

MRS. ROONEY   Come on, dear, don't mind me, we are getting drenched.

MR. ROONEY   [*forcibly*] Can what what?

MRS. ROONEY   Hinnies procreate. [*Silence.*] You know, hinnies, or jinnies, aren't they barren, or sterile, or whatever it is? [*Pause.*] It wasn't an ass's colt at all, you know, I asked the Regius Professor.
                [*Pause.*]

MR. ROONEY   He should know.

MRS. ROONEY   Yes, it was a hinny, he rode into Jerusalem or wherever it was on a hinny. [*Pause.*] That must mean something. [*Pause.*] It's like the sparrows, than many of which we are of more value, they weren't sparrows at all.

MR. ROONEY   Than many of which! . . . You exaggerate, Maddy.

MRS. ROONEY   [*with emotion*] They weren't sparrows at all!

MR. ROONEY   Does that put our price up?
                [*Silence. They move on. Wind and rain. Dragging feet, etc. They halt.*]

MRS. ROONEY   Do you want some dung? [*Silence. They move on. Wind and rain, etc. They halt.*] Why do you stop? Do you want to say something?

MR. ROONEY   No.

MRS. ROONEY   Then why do you stop?

MR. ROONEY   It is easier.

MRS. ROONEY   Are you very wet?

MR. ROONEY   To the buff.

MRS. ROONEY   The buff?

MR. ROONEY   The buff. From buffalo.

MRS. ROONEY   We shall hang up all our things in the hot-cupboard and
get into our dressing-gowns. [*Pause.*] Put your arm
round me. [*Pause.*] Be nice to me! [*Pause. Gratefully.*]
Ah, Dan! [*They move on. Wind and rain. Dragging feet, etc.
Faintly same music as before. They halt. Music clearer.
Silence but for music playing. Music dies.*] All day the same
old record. All alone in that great empty house. She
must be a very old woman now.

MR. ROONEY   [*indistinctly*] Death and the Maiden. [*Silence.*]

MRS. ROONEY   You are crying. [*Pause.*] Are you crying?

MR. ROONEY   [*violently*] Yes! [*They move on. Wind and rain. Dragging feet,
etc. They halt. They move on. Wind and rain. Dragging feet,
etc. They halt.*] Who is the preacher tomorrow? The
incumbent?

MRS. ROONEY   No.

MR. ROONEY   Thank God for that. Who?

MRS. ROONEY   Hardy.

MR. ROONEY   "How to be Happy though Married"?

MRS. ROONEY   No no, he died, you remember. No connexion.

MR. ROONEY   Has he announced his text?

MRS. ROONEY   "The Lord upholdeth all that fall and raiseth up all
those that be bowed down." [*Silence. They join in wild
laughter. They move on. Wind and rain. Dragging feet, etc.*]
Hold me tighter, Dan! [*Pause.*] Oh yes!
[*They halt.*]

MR. ROONEY   I hear something behind us.
[*Pause.*]

MRS. ROONEY   It looks like Jerry. [*Pause.*] It is Jerry.
               [*Sound of Jerry's running steps approaching. He halts beside them, panting.*]

JERRY   [*panting*] You dropped—

MRS. ROONEY   Take your time, my little man, you will burst a blood-vessel.

JERRY   [*panting*] You dropped something, sir. Mr. Barrell told me to run after you.

MRS. ROONEY   Show. [*She takes the object.*] What is it? [*She examines it.*] What is this thing, Dan?

MR. ROONEY   Perhaps it is not mine at all.

JERRY   Mr. Barrell said it was, sir.

MRS. ROONEY   It looks like a kind of ball. And yet it is not a ball.

MR. ROONEY   Give it to me.

MRS. ROONEY   [*giving it*] What *is* it, Dan?

MR. ROONEY   It is a thing I carry about with me.

MRS. ROONEY   Yes, but what—

MR. ROONEY   [*violently*] It is a thing I carry about with me!
               [*Silence. Mrs. Rooney looks for a penny.*]

MRS. ROONEY   I have no small money. Have you?

MR. ROONEY   I have none of any kind.

MRS. ROONEY   We are out of change, Jerry. Remind Mr. Rooney on Monday and he will give you a penny for your pains.

JERRY   Yes, Ma'am.

MR. ROONEY   If I am alive.

JERRY   Yessir.
               [*Jerry starts running back towards the station.*]

MRS. ROONEY   Jerry! [*Jerry halts.*] Did you hear what the hitch was? [*Pause.*] Did you hear what kept the train so late?

MR. ROONEY   How would he have heard? Come on.

MRS. ROONEY   What was it, Jerry?

JERRY   It was a—

MR. ROONEY   Leave the boy alone, he knows nothing! Come on!

MRS. ROONEY   What was it, Jerry?

JERRY   It was a little child, Ma'am.

[*Mr. Rooney groans.*]

MRS. ROONEY   What do you mean, it was a little child?

JERRY   It was a little child fell out of the carriage, Ma'am. [*Pause.*] On to the line, Ma'am. [*Pause.*] Under the wheels, Ma'am.

[*Silence. Jerry runs off. His steps die away. Tempest of wind and rain. It abates. They move on. Dragging steps, etc. They halt. Tempest of wind and rain.*]

End

ACT WITHOUT WORDS I

A mime for one player

Desert. Dazzling light.

The man is flung backwards on stage from right wing. He falls, gets up immediately, dusts himself, turns aside, reflects.

Whistle from right wing.

He reflects, goes out right.

Immediately flung back on stage he falls, gets up immediately, dusts himself, turns aside, reflects.

Whistle from left wing.

He reflects, goes out left.

Immediately flung back on stage he falls, gets up immediately, dusts himself, turns aside, reflects.

Whistle from left wing.

He reflects, goes towards left wing, hesitates, thinks better of it, halts, turns aside, reflects.

A little tree descends from flies, lands. It has a single bough some three yards from ground and at its summit a meagre tuft of palms casting at its foot a circle of shadow.

He continues to reflect.

Whistle from above.

He turns, sees tree, reflects, goes to it, sits down in its shadow, looks at his hands.

A pair of tailor's scissors descends from flies, comes to rest before tree, a yard from ground.

He continues to look at his hands.

Whistle from above.

He looks up, sees scissors, takes them and starts to trim his nails.

The palms close like a parasol, the shadow disappears.

He drops scissors, reflects.

A tiny carafe, to which is attached a huge label inscribed WATER, descends from flies, comes to rest some three yards from ground.

He continues to reflect.

Whistle from above.

He looks up, sees carafe, reflects, gets up, goes and stands under it, tries in vain to reach it, renounces, turns aside, reflects.

A big cube descends from flies, lands.

He continues to reflect.

Whistle from above.

He turns, sees cube, looks at it, at carafe, reflects, goes to cube, takes it up, carries it over and sets it down under carafe, tests its stability, gets up on it, tries in vain to reach carafe, renounces, gets down, carries cube back to its place, turns aside, reflects.

A second smaller cube descends from flies, lands.

He continues to reflect.

Whistle from above.

He turns, sees second cube, looks at it, at carafe, goes to second cube, takes it up, carries it over and sets it down under carafe, tests its stability, gets up on it, tries in vain to reach carafe, renounces, gets down, takes up second cube to carry it back to its place, hesitates, thinks better of it, sets it down, goes to big cube, takes it up, carries it over and puts it on small one, tests their stability, gets up on them, the cubes collapse, he falls, gets up immediately, brushes himself, reflects.

He takes up small cube, puts it on big one, tests their stability, gets up on them and is about to reach carafe when it is pulled up a little way and comes to rest beyond his reach.

He gets down, reflects, carries cubes back to their place, one by one, turns aside, reflects.

A third still smaller cube descends from flies, lands.

He continues to reflect.

Whistle from above.

He turns, sees third cube, looks at it, reflects, turns aside, reflects.

The third cube is pulled up and disappears in flies.

Beside carafe a rope descends from flies, with knots to facilitate ascent.

He continues to reflect.

Whistle from above.

He turns, sees rope, reflects, goes to it, climbs up it and is about to reach carafe when rope is let out and deposits him back on ground.

He reflects, looks around for scissors, sees them, goes and picks them up, returns to rope and starts to cut it with scissors.

The rope is pulled up, lifts him off ground, he hangs on, succeeds in cutting rope, falls back on ground, drops scissors, gets up again immediately, brushes himself, reflects.

The rope is pulled up quickly and disappears in flies.

With length of rope in his possession he makes a lasso with which he tries to lasso the carafe.

The carafe is pulled up quickly and disappears in flies.

He turns aside, reflects.

He goes with lasso in his hand to tree, looks at bough, turns and looks at cubes, looks again at bough, drops lasso, goes to cubes, takes up small one, carries it over and sets it down under bough, goes back for big one, takes it up and carries it over under bough, makes to put it on small one, hesitates, thinks better of it, sets it down, takes up small one and puts it on big one, tests their stability, turns aside and stoops to pick up lasso.

The bough folds down against trunk.

He straightens up with lasso in his hand, turns and sees what has happened.

He drops lasso, turns aside, reflects.

He carries back cubes to their place, one by one, goes back for lasso, carries it over to the cubes and lays it in a neat coil on small one.

He turns aside, reflects.

Whistle from right wing.

He reflects, goes out right.

Immediately flung back on stage he falls, gets up immediately, brushes himself, turns aside, reflects.

Whistle from left wing.

He does not move.

He looks at his hands, looks round for scissors, sees them, goes and picks them up, starts to trim his nails, stops, reflects, runs his finger along blade of scissors, goes and lays them on small cube, turns aside, opens his collar, frees his neck and fingers it.

The small cube is pulled up and disappears in flies, carrying away rope and scissors.

He turns to take scissors, sees what has happened.

He turns aside, reflects.

He goes and sits down on big cube.

The big cube is pulled from under him. He falls. The big cube is pulled up and disappears in flies.

He remains lying on his side, his face towards auditorium, staring before him.

The carafe descends from flies and comes to rest a few feet from his body.

He does not move.

Whistle from above.

He does not move.

The carafe descends further, dangles and plays about his face.

He does not move.

The carafe is pulled up and disappears in flies.

The bough returns to horizontal, the palms open, the shadow returns.

Whistle from above.

He does not move.

The tree is pulled up and disappears in flies.

He looks at his hands.

Curtain

EMBERS

A piece for radio

Sea scarcely audible.

   Henry's boots on shingle. He halts.

   Sea a little louder.

HENRY   On. [*Sea. Voice louder.*] On! [*He moves on. Boots on shingle. As he goes.*] Stop. [*Boots on shingle. As he goes, louder.*] Stop! [*He halts. Sea a little louder.*] Down. [*Sea. Voice louder.*] Down! [*Slither of shingle as he sits. Sea, still faint, audible throughout what follows whenever pause indicated.*] Who is beside me now? [*Pause.*] An old man, blind and foolish. [*Pause.*] My father, back from the dead, to be with me. [*Pause.*] As if he hadn't died. [*Pause.*] No, simply back from the dead, to be with me, in this strange place. [*Pause.*] Can he hear me? [*Pause.*] Yes, he must hear me. [*Pause.*] To answer me? [*Pause.*] No, he doesn't answer me. [*Pause.*] Just be with me. [*Pause.*] That sound you hear is the sea. [*Pause. Louder.*] I say that sound you hear is the sea, we are sitting on the strand. [*Pause.*] I mention it because the sound is so strange, so unlike the sound of the sea, that if you didn't see what it was you wouldn't know what it was. [*Pause.*] Hooves! [*Pause. Louder.*] Hooves! [*Sound of hooves walking on hard road.

They die rapidly away. Pause.] Again! [*Hooves as before. Pause. Excitedly.*] Train it to mark time! Shoe it with steel and tie it up in the yard, have it stamp all day! [*Pause.*] A ten-ton mammoth back from the dead, shoe it with steel and have it tramp the world down! Listen to it! [*Pause.*] Listen to the light now, you always loved light, not long past noon and all the shore in shadow and the sea out as far as the island. [*Pause.*] You would never live this side of the bay, you wanted the sun on the water for that evening bathe you took once too often. But when I got your money I moved across, as perhaps you may know. [*Pause.*] We never found your body, you know, that held up probate an unconscionable time, they said there was nothing to prove you hadn't run away from us all and alive and well under a false name in the Argentine for example, that grieved mother greatly. [*Pause.*] I'm like you in that, can't stay away from it, but I never go in, no, I think the last time I went in was with you. [*Pause.*] Just be near it. [*Pause.*] Today it's calm, but I often hear it above in the house and walking the roads and start talking, oh just loud enough to drown it, nobody notices. [*Pause.*] But I'd be talking now no matter where I was, I once went to Switzerland to get away from the cursed thing and never stopped all the time I was there. [*Pause.*] I usen't to need anyone, just to myself, stories, there was a great one about an old fellow called Bolton, I never finished it, I never finished any of them, I never finished anything, everything always went on for ever. [*Pause.*] Bolton. [*Pause. Louder.*] Bolton! [*Pause.*] There before the fire. [*Pause.*] Before the fire with all the shutters . . . no, hangings, hangings, all the hangings drawn and the light, no light, only the light of the fire, sitting there in the . . . no, standing, standing there on the hearthrug in

the dark before the fire with his arms on the chimney-
piece and his head on his arms, standing there waiting
in the dark before the fire in his old red dressing-gown
and no sound in the house of any kind, only the sound
of the fire. [*Pause.*] Standing there in his old red
dressing-gown might go on fire any minute like when
he was a child, no, that was his pyjamas, standing there
waiting in the dark, no light, only the light of the fire,
and no sound of any kind, only the fire, an old man in
great trouble. [*Pause.*] Ring then at the door and over he
goes to the window and looks out between the
hangings, fine old chap, very big and strong, bright
winter's night, snow everywhere, bitter cold, white
world, cedar boughs bending under load and then as
the arm goes up to ring again recognizes . . .
Holloway . . . [*long pause*] . . . yes, Holloway, recognizes
Holloway, goes down and opens. [*Pause.*] Outside all
still, not a sound, dog's chain maybe or a bough
groaning if you stood there listening long enough,
white world, Holloway with his little black bag, not a
sound, bitter cold, full moon small and white, crooked
trail of Holloway's galoshes, Vega in the Lyre very
green. [*Pause.*] Vega in the Lyre very green. [*Pause.*]
Following conversation then on the step, no, in the
room, back in the room, following conversation then
back in the room, Holloway: "My dear Bolton, it is now
past midnight, if you would be good enough—," gets
no further, Bolton: "Please! PLEASE!" Dead silence
then, not a sound, only the fire, all coal, burning down
now, Holloway on the hearthrug trying to toast his arse,
Bolton, where's Bolton, no light, only the fire, Bolton at
the window his back to the hangings, holding them a
little apart with his hand looking out, white world, even
the spire, white to the vane, most unusual, silence in

the house, not a sound, only the fire, no flames now, embers. [*Pause.*] Embers. [*Pause.*] Shifting, lapsing, furtive like, dreadful sound, Holloway on the rug, fine old chap, six foot, burly, legs apart, hands behind his back holding up the tails of his old macfarlane, Bolton at the window, grand old figure in his old red dressing-gown, back against the hangings, hand stretched out widening the chink, looking out, white world great trouble, not a sound, only the embers, sound of dying, dying glow, Holloway, Bolton, Bolton, Holloway, old men, great trouble, white world, not a sound. [*Pause.*] Listen to it! [*Pause.*] Close your eyes and listen to it, what would you think it was? [*Pause. Vehement.*] A drip! A drip! [*Sound of drip, rapidly amplified, suddenly cut off.*] Again! [*Drip again. Amplification begins.*] No! [*Drip cut off. Pause.*] Father! [*Pause. Agitated.*] Stories, stories, years and years of stories, till the need came on me, for someone, to be with me, anyone, a stranger, to talk to, imagine he hears me, years of that, and then, now, for someone who . . . knew me, in the old days, anyone, to be with me, imagine he hears me, what I am, now. [*Pause.*] No good either. [*Pause.*] Not there either. [*Pause.*] Try again. [*Pause.*] White world, not a sound. [*Pause.*] Holloway. [*Pause.*] Holloway says he'll go, damned if he'll sit up all night before a black grate, doesn't understand, call a man out, an old friend, in the cold and dark, an old friend, urgent need, bring the bag, then not a word, no explanation no heat, no light, Bolton: "Please! PLEASE!" Holloway, no refreshment, no welcome, chilled to the medulla, catch his death, can't understand, strange treatment, old friend, says he'll go, doesn't move, not a sound, fire dying, white beam from window, ghastly scene, wishes to God he hadn't come, no good, fire out, bitter cold, great trouble,

white world, not a sound, no good. [*Pause.*] No good.
[*Pause.*] Can't do it. [*Pause.*] Listen to it! [*Pause.*] Father!
[*Pause.*] You wouldn't know me now, you'd be sorry you
ever had me, but you were that already, a washout, that's
the last I heard from you, a washout. [*Pause. Imitating
father's voice.*] "Are you coming for a dip?" "No." "Come
on, come on." "No." Glare, stump to door, turn, glare. "A
washout, that's all you are, a washout!" [*Violent slam of
door. Pause.*] Again! [*Slam. Pause.*] Slam life shut like that!
[*Pause.*] Washout. [*Pause.*] Wish to Christ she had.
[*Pause.*] Never met Ada, did you, or did you, I can't
remember, no matter, no one'd know her now. [*Pause.*]
What turned her against me do you think, the child I
suppose, horrid little creature, wish to God we'd never
had her, I use to walk with her in the fields, Jesus that
was awful, she wouldn't let go my hand and I mad to
talk. "Run along now, Addie, and look at the lambs."
[*imitating Addie's voice.*] "No papa." "Go on now, go on."
[*Plaintive.*] "No papa." [*Violent.*] "Go on with you when
you're told and look at the lambs!" [*Addie's loud wail.
Pause.*] Ada too, conversation with her, that was
something, that's what hell will be like, small chat to
the babbling of Lethe about the good old days when we
wished we were dead. [*Pause.*] Price of margarine fifty
years ago. [*Pause.*] And now. [*Pause. With solemn
indignation.*] Price of blueband now! [*Pause.*] Father!
[*Pause.*] Tired of talking to you. [*Pause.*] That was always
the way, walk all over the mountains with you talking
and talking and then suddenly mum and home in
misery and not a word to a soul for weeks, sulky little
bastard, better off dead. [*Long pause.*] Ada. [*Pause.
Louder.*] Ada!

ADA   [*low remote voice throughout*] Yes.

HENRY   Have you been there long?

ADA   Some little time. [*Pause.*] Why do you stop, don't mind me. [*Pause.*] Do you want me to go away? [*Pause.*] Where is Addie?

[*Pause.*]

HENRY   With her music master. [*Pause.*] Are you going to answer me today?

ADA   You shouldn't be sitting on the cold stones, they're bad for your growths. Raise yourself up till I slip my shawl under you. [*Pause.*] Is that better?

HENRY   No comparison, no comparison. [*Pause.*] Are you going to sit down beside me?

ADA   Yes. [*No sound as she sits.*] Like that? [*Pause.*] Or do you prefer like that? [*Pause.*] You don't care. [*Pause.*] Chilly enough I imagine, I hope you put on your jaegers. [*Pause.*] Did you put on your jaegers, Henry?

HENRY   What happened was this, I put them on and then I took them off again and then I put them on again and then I took them off again and then I took them on again and then I—

ADA   Have you them on now?

HENRY   I don't know. [*Pause.*] Hooves! [*Pause. Louder.*] Hooves! [*Sound of hooves walking on hard road. They die rapidly away.*] Again!

[*Hooves as before. Pause.*]

ADA   Did you hear them?

HENRY   Not well.

ADA   Galloping?

HENRY   No. [*Pause.*] Could a horse mark time?

[*Pause.*]

ADA   I'm not sure that I know what you mean.

HENRY   [*irritably*] Could a horse be trained to stand still and mark time with its four legs?

ADA   Oh. [*Pause.*] The ones I used to fancy all did. [*She laughs. Pause.*] Laugh, Henry, it's not every day I crack a joke. [*Pause.*] Laugh, Henry do that for me.

HENRY You wish *me* to laugh?

ADA You laughed so charmingly once, I think that's what first attracted me to you. That and your smile. [*Pause.*] Come on, it will be like old times.

[*Pause. He tries to laugh, fails.*]

HENRY Perhaps I should begin with the smile. [*Pause for smile.*] Did that attract you? [*Pause.*] Now I'll try again. [*Long horrible laugh.*] Any of the old charm there?

ADA Oh Henry!

[*Pause.*]

HENRY Listen to it! [*Pause.*] Lips and claws! [*Pause.*] Get away from it! Where it couldn't get at me! The Pampas! What?

ADA Calm yourself.

HENRY And I live on the brink of it! Why? Professional obligations? [*Brief laugh.*] Reasons of health? [*Brief laugh.*] Family ties? [*Brief laugh.*] A woman? [*Laugh in which she joins.*] Some old grave I cannot tear myself away from? [*Pause.*] Listen to it! What is it like?

ADA It is like an old sound I used to hear. [*Pause.*] It is like another time, in the same place. [*Pause.*] It was rough, the spray came flying over us. [*Pause.*] Strange it should have been rough then. [*Pause.*] And calm now. [*Pause.*]

HENRY Let us get up and go.

ADA Go? Where? And Addie? She would be very distressed if she came and found you had gone without her. [*Pause.*] What do you suppose is keeping her?

[*Smart blow of cylindrical ruler on piano case. Unsteadily, ascending and descending, Addie plays scale of A Flat Major, hands first together, then reversed. Pause.*]

MUSIC MASTER [*Italian accent*] Santa Cecilia!

[*Pause.*]

ADDIE Will I play my piece now please?

[*Pause. Music Master beats two bars of waltz time with ruler on piano case. Addie plays opening bars of Chopin's 5th Waltz in A Flat Major, Music Master beating time lightly with ruler as she plays. In first chord of bass, bar 5, she plays E instead of F. Resounding blow of ruler on piano case. Addie stops playing.*]

MUSIC MASTER   [*violently*] Fa!

ADDIE   [*tearfully*] What?

MUSIC MASTER   [*violently*] Eff! Eff!

ADDIE   [*tearfully*] Where?

MUSIC MASTER   [*violently*] Qua! [*He thumps note.*] Fa!
[*Pause. Addie begins again, Music Master beating time lightly with ruler. When she comes to bar 5 she makes same mistake. Tremendous blow of ruler on piano case. Addie stops playing, begins to wail.*]

MUSIC MASTER   [*frenziedly*] Eff! Eff! [*He hammers note.*] Eff! [*He hammers note.*] Eff!
[*Hammered note, "Eff!" and Addie's wail amplified to paroxysm, then suddenly cut off. Pause.*]

ADA   You are silent today.

HENRY   It was not enough to drag her into the world, now she must play the piano.

ADA   She must learn. She shall learn. That—and riding.
[*Hooves walking.*]

RIDING MASTER   Now Miss! Elbows in Miss! Hands down Miss!
[*Hooves trotting.*] Now Miss! Back straight Miss! Knees in Miss! [*Hooves cantering.*] Now Miss! Tummy in Miss! Chin up Miss! [*Hooves galloping.*] Now Miss! Eyes front Miss! [*Addie begins to wail.*] Now Miss! Now Miss!
[*Galloping hooves, "Now Miss!" and Addie's wail amplified to paroxysm, then suddenly cut off. Pause.*]

ADA   What are you thinking of? [*Pause.*] I was never taught, until it was too late. All my life I regretted it.

HENRY   What was your strong point, I forget.

ADA   Oh . . . geometry I suppose, plane and solid. [*Pause.*] First plane, then solid. [*Shingle as he gets up.*] Why do you get up?

HENRY   I thought I might try and get as far as the water's edge.
         [*Pause. With a sigh.*] And back. [*Pause.*] Stretch my old
         bones.
         [*Pause.*]

ADA   Well, why don't you? [*Pause.*] Don't stand there thinking
         about it. [*Pause.*] Don't stand there staring. [*Pause. He
         goes towards sea. Boots on shingle, say ten steps. He halts at
         water's edge. Pause. Sea a little louder. Distant.*] Don't wet
         your good boots.
         [*Pause.*]

HENRY   Don't! don't. . . .
         [*Sea suddenly rough.*]

ADA   [*twenty years earlier, imploring*] Don't! Don't!

HENRY   [*ditto, urgent*] Darling!

ADA   [*ditto, more feebly*] Don't!

HENRY   [*ditto, exultantly*] Darling!
         [*Rough sea. Ada cries out. Cry and sea amplified, cut off. End
         of evocation. Pause. Sea calm. He goes back up deeply
         shelving beach. Boots laborious on shingle. He halts. Pause.
         He moves on. He halts. Pause. Sea calm and faint.*]

ADA   Don't stand there gaping. Sit down. [*Pause. Shingle as he
         sits.*] On the shawl. [*Pause.*] Are you afraid we might
         touch? [*Pause.*] Henry.

HENRY   Yes.

ADA   You should see a doctor about your talking, it's worse,
         what must it be like for Addie? [*Pause.*] Do you know
         what she said to me once, when she was still quite
         small, she said, Mummy, why does Daddy keep on
         talking all the time? She heard you in the lavatory. I
         didn't know what to answer.

HENRY   Daddy! Addie! [*Pause.*] I told you to tell her I was praying.
         [*Pause.*] Roaring prayers at God and his saints.

ADA   It's very bad for the child. [*Pause.*] It's silly to say it keeps
         you from hearing it, it doesn't keep you from hearing it

and even if it does you shouldn't be hearing it, there must be something wrong with your brain. [*Pause.*]

HENRY   That! I shouldn't be hearing that!

ADA   I don't think you are hearing it. And if you are what's wrong with it, it's a lovely peaceful gentle soothing sound, why do you hate it? [*Pause.*] And if you hate it why don't you keep away from it? Why are you always coming down here? [*Pause.*] There's something wrong with your brain, you ought to see Holloway, he's alive still, isn't he? [*Pause.*]

HENRY   [*wildly*] Thuds, I want thuds! Like this! [*He fumbles in the shingle, catches up two big stones and starts dashing them together.*] Stone! [*Clash.*] Stone! [*Clash. "Stone!" and clash amplified, cut off. Pause. He throws one stone away. Sound of its fall.*] That's life! [*He throws the other stone away. Sound of its fall.*] Not this . . . [*pause*] . . . sucking!

ADA   And why life? [*Pause.*] Why life, Henry? [*Pause.*] Is there anyone about?

HENRY   Not a living soul.

ADA   I thought as much. [*Pause.*] When we longed to have it to ourselves there was always someone. Now that it does not matter the place is deserted.

HENRY   Yes, you were always very sensitive to being seen in gallant conversation. The least feather of smoke on the horizon and you adjusted your dress and became immersed in the *Manchester Guardian.* [*Pause.*] The hole is still there, after all these years. [*Pause. Louder.*] The hole is still there.

ADA   What hole? The earth is full of holes.

HENRY   Where we did it at last for the first time.

ADA   Ah yes, I think I remember. [*Pause.*] The place has not changed.

HENRY   Oh yes it has, *I* can see it. [*Confidentially.*] There is a levelling going on! [*Pause.*] What age is she now?

ADA   I have lost count of time.

HENRY Twelve? Thirteen? [*Pause.*] Fourteen?

ADA   I really could not tell you, Henry.

HENRY It took us a long time to have her. [*Pause.*] Years we kept
       hammering away at it. [*Pause.*] But we did it in the end.
       [*Pause. Sigh.*] We had her in the end. [*Pause.*] Listen to it!
       [*Pause.*] It's not so bad when you get out on it. [*Pause.*]
       Perhaps I should have gone into the merchant navy.

ADA   It's only on the surface, you know. Underneath all is as
       quiet as the grave. Not a sound. All day, all night, not a
       sound. [*Pause.*]

HENRY Now I walk about with the gramophone. But I forgot it
       today.

ADA   There is no sense in that. [*Pause.*] There is no sense in
       trying to drown it. [*Pause.*] See Holloway.
       [*Pause.*]

HENRY Let us go for a row.

ADA   A row? And Addie? She would be very distressed if she
       came and found you had gone for a row without her.
       [*Pause.*] Who were you with just now? [*Pause.*] Before
       you spoke to me.

HENRY I was trying to be with my father.

ADA   Oh. [*Pause.*] No difficulty about that.

HENRY I mean I was trying to get him to be with me. [*Pause.*]
       You seem a little cruder than usual today, Ada. [*Pause.*]
       I was asking him if he had ever met you, I couldn't
       remember.

ADA   Well?

HENRY He doesn't answer any more.

ADA   I suppose you have worn him out. [*Pause.*] You wore him
       out living and now you are wearing him out dead. [*Pause.*]
       The time comes when one cannot speak to you any more.
       [*Pause.*] The time will come when no one will speak to
       you at all, not even complete strangers. [*Pause.*] You will

be quite alone with your voice, there will be no other voice in the world but yours. [*Pause.*] Do you hear me? [*Pause.*]

HENRY   I can't remember if he met you.

ADA   You know he met me.

HENRY   No, Ada, I don't know, I'm sorry, I have forgotten almost everything connected with you.

ADA   You weren't there. Just your mother and sister. I had called to fetch you, as arranged. We were to go bathing together. [*Pause.*]

HENRY   [*irritably*] Drive on, drive on! Why do people always stop in the middle of what they are saying?

ADA   None of them knew where you were. Your bed had not been slept in. They were all shouting at one another. Your sister said she would throw herself off the cliff. Your father got up and went out, slamming the door. I left soon afterwards and passed him on the road. He did not see me. He was sitting on a rock looking out to sea. I never forgot his posture. And yet it was a common one. You used to have it sometimes. Perhaps just the stillness, as if he had been turned to stone. I could never make it out. [*Pause.*]

HENRY   Keep on, keep on! [*Imploringly.*] Keep it going, Ada, every syllable is a second gained.

ADA   That's all, I'm afraid. [*Pause.*] Go on now with your father or your stories or whatever you were doing, don't mind me any more.

HENRY   I can't! [*Pause.*] I can't do it any more!

ADA   You were doing it a moment ago, before you spoke to me.

HENRY   [*angrily*] I can't do it any more now! [*Pause.*] Christ! [*Pause.*]

ADA   Yes, you know what I mean, there are attitudes remain in one's mind for reasons that are clear, the carriage of a head for example, bowed when one would have thought it should be lifted, and vice versa, or a hand suspended in mid-air, as if unowned. That kind of thing. But with your father sitting on the rock that day nothing of the kind, no detail you could put your finger on and say, How very peculiar! No, I could never make it out. Perhaps, as I said, just the great stillness of the whole body, as if all the breath had left it. [*Pause.*] Is this rubbish a help to you, Henry? [*Pause.*] I can try and go on a little if you wish. [*Pause.*] No? [*Pause.*] Then I think I'll be getting back.

HENRY   Not yet! You needn't speak. Just listen. Not even. Be with me. [*Pause.*] Ada! [*Pause. Louder.*] Ada! [*Pause.*] Christ! [*Pause.*] Hooves! [*Pause. Louder.*] Hooves! [*Pause.*] Christ! [*Long pause.*] Left soon afterwards, passed you on the road, didn't see her, looking out to. . . . [*Pause.*] Can't have been looking out to *sea*. [*Pause.*] Unless you had gone round the other side. [*Pause.*] Had you gone round the cliff side? [*Pause.*] Father! [*Pause.*] Must have I suppose. [*Pause.*] Stands watching you a moment, then on down path to tram, up on open top and sits down in front. [*Pause.*] Sits down in front. [*Pause.*] Suddenly feels uneasy and gets down again, conductor: "Changed your mind, Miss?," goes back up path, no sign of you. [*Pause.*] Very unhappy and uneasy, hangs round a bit, not a soul about, cold wind coming in off sea, goes back down path and takes tram home. [*Pause.*] Takes tram home. [*Pause.*] Christ! [*Pause.*] "My dear Bolton. . . ." [*Pause.*] "If it's an injection you want, Bolton, let down your trousers and I'll give you one, I have a panhysterectomy at nine," meaning of course the anaesthetic. [*Pause.*] Fire out, bitter cold, white world, great trouble, not a sound. [*Pause.*] Bolton starts playing with the curtain, no, hanging, difficult to describe, draws it back no, kind of gathers it towards him and the moon comes flooding in, then lets it fall back, heavy velvet affair, and pitch black in the room, then towards him again, white, black, white, black, Holloway: "Stop that for the love of God, Bolton, do you want to finish me?" [*Pause.*] Black, white, black, white, maddening thing. [*Pause.*] Then he suddenly strikes a match, Bolton does, lights a candle, catches it up above his head, walks over and looks Holloway full in the eye. [*Pause.*] Not a word, just the look, the old blue eye, very glassy, lids worn thin, lashes gone, whole thing swimming, and the candle shaking over his head. [*Pause.*] Tears? [*Pause. Long laugh.*] Good God no! [*Pause.*] Not a word, just the look, the old blue eye, Holloway: "If you want a shot say so and let me get to hell out of here." [*Pause.*] "We've had this before, Bolton, don't ask me to go through it again." [*Pause.*] Bolton: "Please!" [*Pause.*] "Please!" [*Pause.*] "Please, Holloway!" [*Pause.*] Candle shaking and guttering all over the place, lower now, old arm tired takes it in the other hand and holds it high again, that's it, that was always it, night, and the embers cold, and the glim shaking in your old fist, saying, Please! Please! [*Pause.*] Begging. [*Pause.*] Of the poor. [*Pause.*] Ada! [*Pause.*] Father! [*Pause.*] Christ! [*Pause.*] Holds it high again, naughty world, fixes Holloway, eyes drowned, won't ask again, just the look, Holloway covers his face, not a sound, white world, bitter cold, ghastly scene, old men, great trouble, no good. [*Pause.*] No good. [*Pause.*] Christ! [*Pause. Shingle as he gets up. He goes towards sea. Boots on shingle. He halts. Pause. Sea a little louder.*] On. [*Pause. He moves on. Boots on shingle. He halts at water's edge. Pause. Sea a little louder.*] Little book. [*Pause.*] This evening. . . . [*Pause.*] Nothing this evening. [*Pause.*] Tomorrow . . . tomorrow . . . plumber at nine, then nothing. [*Pause.*

Puzzled.] Plumber at nine? [*Pause.*] Ah yes, the waste.
[*Pause.*] Words. [*Pause.*] Saturday . . . nothing. Sunday . . .
Sunday . . . nothing all day. [*Pause.*] Nothing, all day
nothing. [*Pause.*] All day all night nothing. [*Pause.*] Not a
sound.

ACT WITHOUT WORDS II

A mime for two players

NOTE

This mime should be played on a low and narrow platform at back of stage, violently lit in its entire length, the rest of the stage being in darkness. Frieze effect.

A is slow, awkward (gags dressing and undressing), absent. B brisk, rapid, precise. The two actions therefore, though B has more to do than A, should have approximately the same duration.

ARGUMENT

Beside each other on ground, two yards from right wing, two sacks, A's and B's, A's being to right (as seen from auditorium) of B's, i.e. nearer right wing. On ground beside sack B a little pile of clothes (C) neatly folded (coat and trousers surmounted by boots and hat).

Enter goad right, strictly horizontal. The point stops a foot short of sack A. Pause. The point draws back, pauses, darts forward into sack, withdraws, recoils to a foot short of sack. Pause. The sack does not move. The point draws back again, a little further than before, pauses, darts forward again into sack, withdraws, recoils to a foot short of sack. Pause. The sack moves. Exit goad.

A, wearing shirt, crawls out of sack, halts, broods, prays, broods, gets to his feet, broods, takes a little bottle of pills from his shirt pocket, broods, swallows a pill, puts bottle back, broods, goes to clothes, broods, puts on clothes, broods, takes a large partly eaten carrot from coat pocket, bites off a piece, chews an instant, spits it out with disgust, puts carrot back, broods, picks up two sacks, carries them bowed and staggering halfway to left wing, sets them down, broods, takes off clothes (except shirt), lets them fall in an untidy heap, broods, takes another pill, broods, kneels, prays, crawls into sack and lies still, sack A being now to left of sack B.

Pause.

Enter goad right on wheeled support (one wheel). The point stops a foot short of sack B. Pause. The point draws back, pauses, darts forward into sack, withdraws, recoils to a foot short of sack. Pause. The sack moves. Exit goad.

B, wearing shirt, crawls out of sack, gets to his feet, takes from shirt pocket and consults a large watch, puts watch back, does exercises, consults watch, takes a tooth brush from shirt pocket and brushes teeth vigorously, puts brush back, rubs scalp vigorously, takes a comb from shirt pocket and combs hair, puts comb back, consults watch, goes to clothes, puts them on, consults watch, takes a brush from coat pocket and brushes clothes vigorously, brushes hair vigorously, puts brush back, takes a little mirror from coat pocket and inspects appearance, puts mirror back, takes carrot from coat pocket, bites off a piece, chews and swallows with appetite, puts carrot back, consults watch, takes a map from coat pocket and consults it, puts map back, consults watch, takes a compass from coat pocket and consults it, puts compass back, consults watch, picks up two sacks and carries them bowed and staggering to two yards short of left wing, sets them down, consults watch, takes off clothes (except shirt), folds them in a neat pile, consults watch, does exercises, consults watch, rubs scalp, combs hair, brushes teeth, consults and winds watch, crawls into sack and lies still, sack B being now to left of sack A as originally.

Pause.

Enter goad right on wheeled support (two wheels). The point stops a foot short of sack A. Pause. The point draws back, pauses, darts forward into sack, withdraws, recoils to a foot short of sack. Pause. The sack does not move. The point draws back again, a little further than before, pauses, darts forward again into sack, withdraws, recoils to a foot short of sack. Pause. The sack moves. Exit goad.

A crawls out of sack, halts, broods, prays.

Curtain

POSITION I

CBA ←

POSITION II

CAB ←
⊙

POSITION III

CBA ←
⊙   ⊙

STAGE FRONT

KRAPP'S LAST TAPE

A late evening in the future.

    Krapp's den.

    Front centre a small table, the two drawers of which open towards the audience.

    Sitting at the table, facing front, i.e. across from the drawers, a wearish old man: Krapp.

    Rusty black narrow trousers too short for him. Rusty black sleeveless waist-coat, four capacious pockets. Heavy silver watch and chain. Grimy white shirt open at neck, no collar. Surprising pair of dirty white boots, size ten at least, very narrow and pointed.

    White face. Purple nose. Disordered grey hair. Unshaven.

    Very near-sighted (but unspectacled). Hard of hearing.

    Cracked voice. Distinctive intonation.

    Laborious walk.

    On the table a tape-recorder with microphone and a number of cardboard boxes containing reels of recorded tapes.

    Table and immediately adjacent area in strong white light. Rest of stage in darkness.

    Krapp remains a moment motionless, heaves a great sigh, looks at his watch, fumbles in his pockets, takes out an envelope, puts it back, fumbles, takes out a small bunch of keys, raises it to his eyes, chooses a key, gets up and moves to front of table. He stoops, unlocks first drawer, peers into it, feels about inside it, takes out a reel of tape, peers at it, puts it back, locks drawer, unlocks second

drawer, peers into it, feels about inside it, takes out a large banana, peers at it,
locks drawer, puts keys back in his pocket. He turns, advances to edge of stage,
halts, strokes banana, peels it, drops skin at his feet, puts end of banana in his
mouth and remains motionless, staring vacuously before him. Finally he bites
off the end, turns aside and begins pacing to and fro at edge of stage, in the light,
i.e. not more than four or five paces either way, meditatively eating banana.
He treads on skin, slips, nearly falls, recovers himself, stoops and peers at skin
and finally pushes it, still stooping, with his foot over edge of stage into pit.
He resumes his pacing, finishes banana, returns to table, sits down, remains a
moment motionless, heaves a great sigh, takes keys from his pockets, raises them
to his eyes, chooses key, gets up and moves to front of table, unlocks
second drawer, takes out a second large banana, peers at it, locks drawer, puts
back keys in his pocket, turns, advances to edge of stage, halts, strokes banana,
peels it, tosses skin into pit, puts end of banana in his mouth and remains
motionless, staring vacuously before him. Finally he has an idea, puts banana in
his waistcoat pocket, the end emerging, and goes with all the speed he can mus-
ter backstage into darkness. Ten seconds. Loud pop of cork. Fifteen seconds. He
comes back into light carrying an old ledger and sits down at table. He lays led-
ger on table, wipes his mouth, wipes his hands on the front of his waistcoat,
brings them smartly together and rubs them.

KRAPP   [*briskly*] Ah! [*He bends over ledger, turns the pages, finds the entry he*
         wants, reads.] Box . . . thrree . . . spool five. [*He raises his head and*
         stares front. With relish.] Spool! [*Pause.*] Spooool! [*Happy smile.*
         Pause. He bends over table, starts peering and poking at the boxes.]
         Box . . . thrree . . . thrree . . . four . . . two . . . [*with surprise*] nine!
         good God! . . . seven . . . ah! the little rascal! [*He takes up box, peers*
         at it.] Box thrree. [*He lays it on table, opens it and peers at spools*
         inside.] Spool . . . [*he peers at ledger*] . . . five . . . [*he peers at*
         spools] . . . five . . . five . . . ah! the little scoundrel! [*He takes out a*
         spool, peers at it.] Spool five. [*He lays it on table, closes box three, puts*
         it back with the others, takes up the spool.] Box thrree, spool five. [*He*
         bends over the machine, looks up. With relish.] Spooool! [*Happy smile.*
         He bends, loads spool on machine, rubs his hands.] Ah! [*He peers at*

ledger, reads entry at foot of page.] Mother at rest at last. . . . Hm. . . . The black ball. . . . [*He raises his head, stares blankly front. Puzzled.*] Black ball? . . . [*He peers again at ledger, reads.*] The dark nurse. . . . [*He raises his head, broods, peers again at ledger, reads.*] Slight improvement in bowel condition. . . . Hm. . . . Memorable . . . what? [*He peers closer.*] Equinox, memorable equinox. [*He raises his head, stares blankly front. Puzzled.*] Memorable equinox? . . . [*Pause. He shrugs his shoulders, peers again at ledger, reads.*] Farewell to—[*he turns page*]—love.
[*He raises his head, broods, bends over machine, switches on and assumes listening posture, i.e. leaning forward, elbows on table, hand cupping ear towards machine, face front.*]

TAPE [*strong voice, rather pompous, clearly Krapp's at a much earlier time*] Thirty-nine today, sound as a— [*Settling himself more comfortably he knocks one of the boxes off the table, curses, switches off, sweeps boxes and ledger violently to the ground, winds tape back to beginning, switches on, resumes posture.*] Thirty-nine today, sound as a bell, apart from my old weakness, and intellectually I have now every reason to suspect at the . . . [*hesitates*] . . . crest of the wave—or thereabouts. Celebrated the awful occasion, as in recent years, quietly at the Winehouse. Not a soul. Sat before the fire with closed eyes, separating the grain from the husks. Jotted down a few notes, on the back of an envelope. Good to be back in my den, in my old rags. Have just eaten I regret to say three bananas and only with difficulty refrained from a fourth. Fatal things for a man with my condition. [*Vehemently.*] Cut'em out! [*Pause.*] The new light above my table is a great improvement. With all this darkness round me I feel less alone. [*Pause.*] In a way. [*Pause.*] I love to get up and move about in it, then back here to [*hesitates*] . . . me. [*Pause.*] Krapp.
[*Pause.*]
The grain, now what I wonder do I mean by that, I mean . . . [*hesitates*] . . . I suppose I mean those things worth having when

all the dust has—when all *my* dust has settled. I close my eyes
and try and imagine them.
[*Pause. Krapp closes his eyes briefly.*]
Extraordinary silence this evening, I strain my ears and do not
hear a sound. Old Miss McGlome always sings at this hour. But
not tonight. Songs of her girlhood, she says. Hard to think of
her as a girl. Wonderful woman though. Connaught, I fancy.
[*Pause.*] Shall I sing when I am her age, if I ever am? No. [*Pause.*]
Did I sing as a boy? No. [*Pause.*] Did I ever sing? No.
[*Pause.*]
Just been listening to an old year, passages at random. I did not
check in the book, but it must be at least ten or twelve years ago.
At that time I think I was still living on and off with Bianca in
Kedar Street. Well out of that, Jesus yes! Hopeless business.
[*Pause.*] Not much about her, apart from a tribute to her eyes.
Very warm. I suddenly saw them again. [*Pause.*] Incomparable!
[*Pause.*] Ah well. . . . [*Pause.*] These old P.M.s are gruesome, but I
often find them—[*Krapp switches off, broods, switches on*]—a help
before embarking on a new . . . [*hesitates*] . . . retrospect. Hard to
believe I was ever that young whelp. The voice! Jesus! And the
aspirations! [*Brief laugh in which Krapp joins.*] And the
resolutions! [*Brief laugh in which Krapp joins.*] To drink less, in
particular. [*Brief laugh of Krapp alone.*] Statistics. Seventeen
hundred hours, out of the preceding eight thousand odd,
consumed on licensed premises alone. More than 20 per cent,
say 40 per cent of his waking life. [*Pause.*] Plans for a less . . .
[*hesitates*] engrossing sexual life. Last illness of his father.
Flagging pursuit of happiness. Unattainable laxation. Sneers at
what he calls his youth and thanks to God that it's over. [*Pause.*]
False ring there. [*Pause.*] Shadows of the opus . . . magnum.
Closing with a—[*brief laugh*]—yelp to Providence. [*Prolonged
laugh in which Krapp joins.*] What remains of all that misery? A
girl in a shabby green coat, on a railway-station platform? No?
[*Pause.*]

When I look—

[*Krapp switches off, broods, looks at his watch, gets up, goes backstage into darkness. Ten seconds. Pop of cork. Ten seconds. Second cork. Ten seconds. Third cork. Ten seconds. Brief burst of quavering song.*]

KRAPP   [*sings*] Now the day is over,

          Night is drawing nigh-igh,

          Shadows—

[*Fit of coughing. He comes back into light, sits down, wipes his mouth, switches on, resumes his listening posture.*]

TAPE   —back on the year that is gone, with what I hope is perhaps a glint of the old eye to come, there is of course the house on the canal where mother lay a-dying, in the late autumn, after her long viduity [*Krapp gives a start*] and the—[*Krapp switches off, winds back tape a little, bends his ear closer to machine, switches on*]— a-dying, in the late autumn, after her long viduity, and the— [*Krapp switches off, raises his head, stares blankly before him. His lips move in the syllables of "viduity." No sound. He gets up, goes backstage into darkness, comes back with an enormous dictionary, lays it on table, sits down and looks up the word.*]

KRAPP   [*reading from dictionary*] State—or condition—of being—or remaining—a widow—or widower. [*Looks up. Puzzled.*] Being— or remaining? . . . [*Pause. He peers again at dictionary. Reading.*] "Deep weeds of viduity." . . . Also of an animal, especially a bird . . . the vidua or weaver-bird. . . . Black plumage of male. . . . [*He looks up. With relish.*] The vidua-bird!

[*Pause. He closes dictionary, switches on, resumes listening posture.*]

TAPE   —bench by the weir from where I could see her window. There I sat, in the biting wind, wishing she were gone. [*Pause.*] Hardly a soul, just a few regulars, nursemaids, infants, old men, dogs. I got to know them quite well—oh by appearance of course I mean! One dark young beauty I recollect particularly, all white and starch, incomparable bosom, with a big black hooded perambulator, most funereal thing. Whenever I looked in her direction she had her eyes on me. And yet when I was bold enough to speak to her—not having been introduced—she threatened to call a policeman. As if I had designs on her virtue! [*Laugh. Pause.*] The face she had! The eyes! Like ... [*hesitates*] ... chrysolite! [*Pause.*] Ah well. ... [*Pause.*] I was there when—[*Krapp switches off, broods, switches on again*]—the blind went down, one of those dirty brown roller affairs, throwing a ball for a little white dog as chance would have it. I happened to look up and there it was. All over and done with, at last. I sat on for a few moments with the ball in my hand and the dog yelping and pawing at me. [*Pause.*] Moments. Her moments, my moments. [*Pause.*] The dog's moments. [*Pause.*] In the end I held it out to him and he took it in his mouth, gently, gently. A small, old, black, hard, solid rubber ball. [*Pause.*] I shall feel it, in my hand, until my dying day. [*Pause.*] I might have kept it. [*Pause.*] But I gave it to the dog.

[*Pause.*]

Ah well. ...

[*Pause.*]

Spiritually a year of profound gloom and indigence until that memorable night in March, at the end of the jetty, in the howling wind, never to be forgotten, when suddenly I saw the whole thing. The vision at last. This I fancy is what I have chiefly to record this evening, against the day when my work will be done and perhaps no place left in my memory, warm or cold, for the miracle that ... [*hesitates*] ... for the fire that set it alight. What I suddenly saw then was this, that the belief I had been going on all my life, namely—[*Krapp switches off impatiently, winds tape forward, switches on again*]—great granite rocks the foam flying up in the light of the lighthouse and the wind-gauge spinning like a propeller, clear to me at last that the dark I have always struggled to keep under is in reality my most—[*Krapp curses, switches off, winds tape forward, switches on again*]—unshatterable association until my dissolution of storm and night with the light of the understanding and the fire—[*Krapp*

curses louder, switches off, winds tape forward, switches on again]—
my face in her breasts and my hand on her. We lay there without
moving. But under us all moved, and moved us, gently, up and
down, and from side to side.
[*Pause.*]
Past midnight. Never knew such silence. The earth might be
uninhabited.
[*Pause.*] Here I end—
[*Krapp switches off, winds tape back, switches on again.*]
—upper lake, with the punt, bathed off the bank, then pushed
out into the stream and drifted. She lay stretched out on the
floorboards with her hands under her head and her eyes closed.
Sun blazing down, bit of a breeze, water nice and lively. I
noticed a scratch on her thigh and asked her how she came by
it. Picking gooseberries, she said. I said again I thought it was
hopeless and no good going on and she agreed, without
opening her eyes. [*Pause.*] I asked her to look at me and after a
few moments—[*pause*]—after a few moments she did, but the
eyes just slits, because of the glare. I bent over her to get them
in the shadow and they opened. [*Pause. Low.*] Let me in. [*Pause.*]
We drifted in among the flags and stuck. The way they went
down, sighing, before the stem! [*Pause.*] I lay down across her
with my face in her breasts and my hand on her. We lay there
without moving. But under us all moved, and moved us, gently,
up and down, and from side to side.
[*Pause.*]
Past midnight. Never knew—
[*Krapp switches off, broods. Finally he fumbles in his pockets,
encounters the banana, takes it out, peers at it, puts it back, fumbles,
brings out envelope, fumbles, puts back envelope, looks at his watch,
gets up and goes backstage into darkness. Ten seconds. Sound of bottle
against glass, then brief siphon. Ten seconds. Bottle against glass alone.
Ten seconds. He comes back a little unsteadily into light, goes to front
of table, takes out keys, raises them to his eyes, chooses key, unlocks first*

drawer, peers into it, feels about inside, takes out reel, peers at it, locks drawer, puts keys back in his pocket, goes and sits down, takes reel off machine, lays it on dictionary, loads virgin reel on machine, takes envelope from his pocket, consults back of it, lays it on table, switches on, clears his throat and begins to record.]

KRAPP   Just been listening to that stupid bastard I took myself for thirty years ago, hard to believe I was ever as bad as that. Thank God that's all done with anyway. [*Pause.*] The eyes she had! [*Broods, realizes he is recording silence, switches off, broods. Finally.*] Everything there, everything, all the— [*Realizes this is not being recorded, switches on.*] Everything there, everything on this old muckball, all the light and dark and famine and feasting of . . . [*hesitates*] . . . the ages! [*In a shout.*] Yes! [*Pause.*] Let that go! Jesus! Take his mind off his homework! Jesus! [*Pause. Weary.*] Ah well, maybe he was right. [*Pause.*] Maybe he was right. [*Broods. Realizes. Switches off. Consults envelope.*] Pah! [*Crumples it and throws it away. Broods. Switches on.*] Nothing to say, not a squeak. What's a year now? The sour cud and the iron stool. [*Pause.*] Revelled in the word spool. [*With relish.*] Spooool! Happiest moment of the past half million. [*Pause.*] Seventeen copies sold, of which eleven at trade price to free circulating libraries beyond the seas. Getting known. [*Pause.*] One pound six and something, eight I have little doubt. [*Pause.*] Crawled out once or twice, before the summer was cold. Sat shivering in the park, drowned in dreams and burning to be gone. Not a soul. [*Pause.*] Last fancies. [*Vehemently.*] Keep 'em under! [*Pause.*] Scalded the eyes out of me reading *Effie* again, a page a day, with tears again. Effie. . . . [*Pause.*] Could have been happy with her, up there on the Baltic, and the pines, and the dunes. [*Pause.*] Could I? [*Pause.*] And she? [*Pause.*] Pah! [*Pause.*] Fanny came in a couple of times. Bony old ghost of a whore. Couldn't do much, but I suppose better than a kick in the crutch. The last time wasn't so bad. How do you manage it, she said, at your age? I told her I'd been

saving up for her all my life. [*Pause.*] Went to Vespers once, like
when I was in short trousers. [*Pause. Sings.*]

    Now the day is over,

    Night is drawing nigh-igh,

    Shadows—[*coughing, then almost inaudible*]—of the evening

    Steal across the sky.

[*Gasping.*] Went to sleep and fell off the pew. [*Pause.*] Sometimes
wondered in the night if a last effort mightn't— [*Pause.*] Ah
finish your booze now and get to your bed. Go on with this
drivel in the morning. Or leave it at that. [*Pause.*] Leave it at that.
[*Pause.*] Lie propped up in the dark—and wander. Be again in
the dingle on a Christmas Eve, gathering holly, the red-berried.
[*Pause.*] Be again on Croghan on a Sunday morning, in the haze,
with the bitch, stop and listen to the bells. [*Pause.*] And so on.
[*Pause.*] Be again, be again. [*Pause.*] All that old misery. [*Pause.*]
Once wasn't enough for you. [*Pause.*] Lie down across her.
[*Long pause. He suddenly bends over machine, switches off, wrenches
off tape, throws it away, puts on the other, winds it forward to the
passage he wants, switches on, listens staring front.*]

TAPE   —gooseberries, she said. I said again I thought it was hopeless
and no good going on and she agreed, without opening her
eyes. [*Pause.*] I asked her to look at me and after a few
moments—[*pause*]—after a few moments she did, but the eyes
just slits, because of the glare. I bent over to get them in the
shadow and they opened. [*Pause. Low.*] Let me in. [*Pause.*] We
drifted in among the flags and stuck. The way they went down,
sighing, before the stem! [*Pause.*] I lay down across her with my
face in her breasts and my hand on her. We lay there without
moving. But under us all moved, and moved us, gently, up and
down, and from side to side.

[*Pause. Krapp's lips move. No sound.*]

Past midnight. Never knew such silence. The earth might be
uninhabited.

[*Pause.*]

Here I end this reel. Box—[*pause*]—three, spool—[*pause*]—five. [*Pause.*] Perhaps my best years are gone. When there was a chance of happiness. But I wouldn't want them back. Not with the fire in me now. No, I wouldn't want them back.

[*Krapp motionless staring before him. The tape runs on in silence.*]

Curtain

ROUGH FOR THEATRE I

Street corner. Ruins.

A, blind, sitting on a folding-stool, scrapes his fiddle. Beside him the case, half open, upended, surmounted by alms bowl. He stops playing, turns his head audience right, listens. Pause.

A A penny for a poor old man, a penny for a poor old man. [*Silence. He resumes playing, stops again, turns his head right, listens. Enter B right, in a wheelchair which he propels by means of a pole. He halts. Irritated.*] A penny for a poor old man!
   [*Pause.*]
B Music! [*Pause.*] So it is not a dream. At last! Nor a vision, they are mute and I am mute before them. [*He advances, halts, looks into bowl. Without emotion.*] Poor wretch. [*Pause.*] Now I may go back, the mystery is over. [*He pushes himself backwards, halts.*] Unless we join together, and live together, till death ensue. [*Pause.*] What would you say to that, Billy, may I call you Billy, like my son? [*Pause.*] Do you like company, Billy? [*Pause.*] Do you like tinned food, Billy?
A What tinned food?
B Corned beef, Billy, just corned beef. Enough to keep body and soul together, till summer, with care. [*Pause.*] No? [*Pause.*] A few potatoes too, a few pounds of potatoes too. [*Pause.*] Do you like potatoes, Billy? [*Pause.*] We might even let them sprout and then, when the time

came, put them in the ground, we might even try that. [*Pause.*] I
would choose the place and you would put them in the ground.
[*Pause.*] No? [*Pause.*]

A   How are the trees doing?

B   Hard to say. It's winter, you know.
[*Pause.*]

A   Is it day or night?

B   Oh . . . [*he looks at the sky*] . . . day, if you like. No sun of course,
otherwise you wouldn't have asked. [*Pause.*] Do you follow my
reasoning? [*Pause.*] Have you your wits about you, Billy, have you still
some of your wits about you?

A   But light?

B   Yes. [*Looks at sky.*] Yes, light, there is no other word for it. [*Pause.*] Shall I
describe it to you? [*Pause.*] Shall I try to give you an idea of this light?

A   It seems to me sometimes I spend the night here, playing and
listening. I used to feel twilight gather and make myself ready. I put
away fiddle and bowl and had only to get to my feet, when she took
me by the hand.
[*Pause.*]

B   She?

A   My woman. [*Pause.*] A woman. [*Pause.*] But now . . .
[*Pause.*]

B   Now?

A   When I set out I don't know, and when I get here I don't know, and
while I am here I don't know, whether it is day or night.

B   You were not always as you are. What befell you? Women? Gambling?
God?

A   I was always as I am.

B   Come!

A   [*violently*] I was always as I am, crouched in the dark, scratching an old
jangle to the four winds!

B   [*violently*] We had our women, hadn't we? You yours to lead you by the
hand and I mine to get me out of the chair in the evening and back
into it again in the morning and to push me as far as the corner
when I went out of my mind.

A   Cripple? [*Without emotion.*] Poor wretch.

B   Only one problem: the about-turn. I often felt, as I struggled, that it would be quicker to go on, right round the world. Till the day I realized I could go home backwards. [*Pause.*] For example, I am at A. [*He pushes himself forward a little, halts.*] I push on to B. [*He pushes himself back a little, halts.*] And I return to A. [*With élan.*] The straight line! The vacant space! [*Pause.*] Do I begin to move you?

A   Sometimes I hear steps. Voices. I say to myself, They are coming back, some are coming back, to try and settle again, or to look for something they had left behind, or to look for someone they had left behind.

B   Come back! [*Pause.*] Who would want to come back here? [*Pause.*] And you never called out? [*Pause.*] Cried out? [*Pause.*] No?

A   Have you observed nothing?

B   Oh me you know, observe . . . I sit there, in my lair, in my chair, in the dark, twenty-three hours out of the twenty-four. [*Violently.*] What would you have me observe? [*Pause.*] Do you think we would make a match, now you are getting to know me?

A   Corned beef, did you say?

B   Apropos, what have you been living on, all this time? You must be famished.

A   There are things lying around.

B   Edible?

A   Sometimes.

B   Why don't you let yourself die?

A   On the whole I have been lucky. The other day I tripped over a sack of nuts.

B   No!

A   A little sack, full of nuts, in the middle of the road.

B   Yes, all right, but why don't you let yourself die?

A   I have thought of it.

B   [*irritated*] But you don't do it!

A   I'm not unhappy enough. [*Pause.*] That was always my unhap, unhappy, but not unhappy enough.

B   But you must be every day a little more so.

A [*violently*] I am not unhappy enough!
   [*Pause.*]
B If you ask me we were made for each other.
A [*comprehensive gesture*] What does it all look like now?
B Oh me you know . . . I never go far, just a little up and down before my
   door. I never yet pushed on to here till now.
A But you look about you?
B No no.
A After all those hours of darkness you don't—
B [*violently*] No! [*Pause.*] Of course if you wish me to look about me I
   shall. And if you care to push me about I shall try to describe the
   scene, as we go along.
A You mean you would guide me? I wouldn't get lost any more?
B Exactly. I would say, Easy, Billy, we're heading for a great muckheap,
   turn back and wheel left when I give you the word.
A You'd do that!
B [*pressing his advantage*] Easy, Billy, easy, I see a round tin over there in
   the gutter, perhaps it's soup, or baked beans.
A Baked beans!
   [*Pause.*]
B Are you beginning to like me? [*Pause.*] Or is it only my imagination?
A Baked beans! [*He gets up, puts down fiddle and bowl on the stool and gropes
   towards B.*] Where are you?
B Here, dear fellow. [*A lays hold of the chair and starts pushing it blindly.*] Stop!
A [*pushing the chair*] It's a gift! A gift!
B Stop! [*He strikes behind him with the pole. A lets go the chair, recoils. Pause. A
   gropes towards his stool, halts, lost.*] Forgive me! [*Pause.*] Forgive me, Billy!
A Where am I? [*Pause.*] Where was I?
B Now I've lost him. He was beginning to like me and I struck him. He'll
   leave me and I'll never see him again. I'll never see anyone again.
   We'll never hear the human voice again.
A Have you not heard it enough? The same old moans and groans from
   the cradle to the grave.
B [*groaning*] Do something for me, before you go!

A   There! Do you hear it? [*Pause. Groaning.*] I can't go! [*Pause.*] Do you hear it?

B   You can't go?

A   I can't go without my things.

B   What good are they to you?

A   None.

B   And you can't go without them?

A   No. [*He starts groping again, halts.*] I'll find them in the end. [*Pause.*] Or leave them for ever behind me.
[*He starts groping again.*]

B   Straighten my rug, I feel the cold air on my foot. [*A halts.*] I'd do it myself, but it would take too long. [*Pause.*] Do that for me, Billy. Then I may go back, settle in the old nook again and say, I have seen man for the last time, I struck him and he succoured me. [*Pause.*] Find a few rags of love in my heart and die reconciled, with my species. [*Pause.*] What has you gaping at me like that? [*Pause.*] Have I said something I shouldn't have? [*Pause.*] What does my soul look like?
[*A gropes towards him.*]

A   Make a sound.
[*B makes one. A gropes towards it, halts.*]

B   Have you no sense of smell either?

A   It's the same stink everywhere. [*He stretches out his hand.*] Am I within reach of your hand?
[*He stands motionless with outstretched hand.*]

B   Wait, you're not going to do me a service for nothing? [*Pause.*] I mean unconditionally? [*Pause.*] Good God!
[*Pause. He takes A's hand and draws it towards him.*]

A   Your foot.

B   What?

A   You said your foot.

B   Had I but known! [*Pause.*] Yes, my foot, tuck it in. [*A stoops, groping.*] On your knees, on your knees, you'll be more at your ease. [*He helps him to kneel at the right place.*] There.

A   [*irritated*] Let go my hand! You want me to help you and you hold my hand! [*B lets go his hand. A fumbles in the rug.*] Have you only one leg?

B   Just the one.

A   And the other?

B   It went bad and was removed.

[*A tucks in the foot.*]

A   Will that do?

B   A little tighter. [*A tucks in tighter.*] What hands you have!

[*Pause.*]

A   [*groping towards B's torso*] Is all the rest there?

B   You may stand up now and ask me a favour.

A   Is all the rest there?

B   Nothing else has been removed, if that is what you mean.

[*A's hand, groping higher, reaches the face, stays.*]

A   Is that your face?

B   I confess it is. [*Pause.*] What else could it be? [*A's fingers stray, stay.*] That?

My wen.

A   Red?

B   Purple. [*A withdraws his hand, remains kneeling.*] What hands you have!

[*Pause.*]

A   Is it still day?

B   Day? [*Looks at sky.*] If you like. [*Looks.*] There is no other word for it.

A   Will it not soon be evening?

[*B stoops to A, shakes him.*]

B   Come, Billy, get up, you're beginning to incommode me.

A   Will it not soon be night?

[*B looks at sky.*]

B   Day . . . night . . . [*Looks.*] It seems to me sometimes the earth must have

got stuck, one sunless day, in the heart of winter, in the grey of

evening. [*Stoops to A, shakes him.*] Come on, Billy, up, you're beginning

to embarrass me.

A   Is there grass anywhere?

B   I see none.

A   [*vehement*] Is there no green anywhere?

B   There's a little moss. [*Pause. A clasps his hands on the rug and rests his head

on them.*] Good God! Don't tell me you're going to pray?

A   No.

B   Or weep?

A   No. [*Pause.*] I could stay like that for ever, with my head on an old man's knees.

B   Knee. [*Shaking him roughly.*] Get up, can't you!

A   [*settling himself more comfortably*] What peace! [*B pushes him roughly away, A falls to his hands and knees.*] Dora used to say, the days I hadn't earned enough, You and your harp! You'd do better crawling on all fours, with your father's medals pinned to your arse and a money box round your neck. You and your harp! Who do you think you are? And she made me sleep on the floor. [*Pause.*] Who I thought I was . . . [*Pause.*] Ah that . . . I never could . . . [*Pause. He gets up.*] Never could . . . [*He starts groping again for his stool, halts, listens.*] If I listened long enough I'd hear it, a string would give.

B   Your harp? [*Pause.*] What's all this about a harp?

A   I once had a little harp. Be still and let me listen.
    [*Pause.*]

B   How long are you going to stay like that?

A   I can stay for hours listening to all the sounds.
    [*They listen.*]

B   What sounds?

A   I don't know what they are.
    [*They listen.*]

B   I can see it. [*Pause.*] I can—

A   [*imploring*] Will you not be still?

B   No! [*A takes his head in his hands.*] I can see it clearly, over there on the stool. [*Pause.*] What if I took it, Billy, and made off with it? [*Pause.*] Eh Billy, what would you say to that? [*Pause.*] There might be another old man, some day, would come out of his hole and find you playing the mouth-organ. And you'd tell him of the little fiddle you once had. [*Pause.*] Eh Billy? [*Pause.*] Or singing. [*Pause.*] Eh Billy, what would you say to that? [*Pause.*] There croaking to the winter wind [*rime with unkind*], having lost his little mouth-organ. [*He pokes him in the back with the pole.*] Eh Billy? [*A whirls round, seizes the end of the pole and wrenches it from B's grasp.*]

ROUGH FOR THEATRE II

Upstage centre high double window open on bright night sky. Moon invisible.

Downstage audience left, equidistant from wall and axis of window, small table and chair. On table an extinguished reading-lamp and a briefcase crammed with documents.

Downstage right, forming symmetry, identical table and chair. Extinguished lamp only.

Downstage left door.

Standing motionless before left half of window with his back to stage, C. Long pause.

Enter A. He closes door, goes to table on right and sits with his back to right wall. Pause. He switches on lamp, takes out his watch, consults it and lays it on the table. Pause. He switches off. Long pause.

Enter B. He closes door, goes to table on left and sits with his back to left wall. Pause. He switches on lamp, opens briefcase and empties contents on table. He looks round, sees A.

B   Well!

A   Hsst! Switch off. [*B switches off. Long pause. Low.*] What a night! [*Long pause. Musing.*] I still don't understand. [*Pause.*] Why he needs our services. [*Pause.*] A man like him. [*Pause.*] And why we give them free. [*Pause.*] Men like us. [*Pause.*] Mystery. [*Pause.*] Ah well . . . [*Pause. He switches on.*] Shall we go? [*B switches on, rummages in his papers.*]

The crux. [*B rummages.*] We sum up and clear out. [*B rummages.*] Set to go?

B   Rearing.

A   We attend.

B   Let him jump.

A   When?

B   Now.

A   From where?

B   From here will do. Three to three and a half metres per floor, say twenty-five in all.
[*Pause.*]

A   I could have sworn we were only on the sixth. [*Pause.*] He runs no risk?

B   He has only to land on his arse, the way he lived. The spine snaps and the tripes explode.
[*Pause. A gets up, goes to the window, leans out, looks down. He straightens up, looks at the sky. Pause. He goes back to his seat.*]

A   Full moon.

B   Not quite. Tomorrow.
[*A takes a little diary from his pocket.*]

A   What's the date?

B   Twenty-fourth. Twenty-fifth tomorrow.

A   [*turning pages*] Nineteen ... twenty-two ... twenty-four. [*Reads.*] "Our Lady of Succour. Full moon." [*He puts back the diary in his pocket.*] We were saying then ... what was it ... let him jump. Our conclusion. Right?

B   Work, family, third fatherland, cunt, finances, art and nature, heart and conscience, health, housing conditions, God and man, so many disasters.
[*Pause.*]

A   [*meditative*] Does it follow? [*Pause.*] Does it follow? [*Pause.*] And his sense of humour? Of proportion?

B   Swamped.
[*Pause.*]

A   May we not be mistaken?

B   [*indignant*] We have been to the best sources. All weighed and weighed
     again, checked and verified. Not a word here [*brandishing sheaf of
     papers*] that is not cast iron. Tied together like a cathedral. [*He flings
     down the papers on the table. They scatter on the floor.*] Shit!
     [*He picks them up. A raises his lamp and shines it about him.*]

A   Seen worse dumps. [*Turning towards window.*] Worse outlooks. [*Pause.*] Is
     that Jupiter we see?
     [*Pause.*]

B   Where?

A   Switch off. [*They switch off.*] It must be.

B   [*irritated*] Where?

A   [*irritated*] There. [*B cranes.*] There, on the right, in the corner.
     [*Pause.*]

B   No. It twinkles.

A   What is it then?

B   [*indifferent*] No idea. Sirius. [*He switches on.*] Well? Do we work or play?
     [*A switches on.*] You forget this is not his home. He's only here to take
     care of the cat. At the end of the month shoosh back to the barge.
     [*Pause. Louder.*] You forget this is not his home.

A   [*irritated*] I forget, I forget! And he, does he not forget? [*With passion.*]
     But that's what saves us!

B   [*searching through his papers*] Memory . . . memory . . . [*He takes up a
     sheet.*] I quote: "An elephant's for the eating cares, a sparrow's for the
     Lydian airs." Testimony of Mr. Swell, organist at Seaton Sluice and
     lifelong friend.
     [*Pause.*]

A   [*glum*] Tsstss!

B   I quote: "Questioned on this occasion"—open brackets—"(judicial
     separation)"—close brackets—"regarding the deterioration of our
     relations, all he could adduce was the five or six miscarriages which
     clouded"—open brackets—"(oh through no act of mine!)"—close
     brackets—"the early days of our union and the veto which in
     consequence I had finally to oppose"—open brackets—"(oh not for
     want of inclination!)"—close brackets—"to anything remotely

resembling the work of love. But on the subject of our happiness"—
open brackets— "(for it too came our way, unavoidably, and here my
mind goes back to the first vows exchanged at Wootton Bassett
under the bastard acacias, or again to the first fifteen minutes of our
wedding night at Littlestone-on-Sea, or yet again to those first long
studious evenings in our nest on Commercial Road East)"—close
brackets—"on the subject of our happiness not a word, Sir, not one
word." Testimony of Mrs. Aspasia Budd-Croker, button designer in
residence, Commercial Road East.

A [*glum*] Tsstss!

B I quote again: "Of our national epos he remembered only the
calamities, which did not prevent him from winning a minor
scholarship in the subject." Testimony of Mr. Peaberry, market
gardener in the Deeping Fens and lifelong friend. [*Pause.*] "Not a tear
was known to fall in our family, and God knows they did in torrents,
that was not caught up and piously preserved in that inexhaustible
reservoir of sorrow, with the date, the hour and the occasion, and
not a joy, fortunately they were few, that was not on the contrary
irrevocably dissolved, as by a corrosive. In that he took after me."
Testimony of the late Mrs. Darcy-Croker, woman of letters. [*Pause.*]
Care for more?

A Enough.

B I quote: "To hear him talk about his life, after a glass or two, you would
have thought he had never set foot outside hell. He had us in
stitches. I worked it up into a skit that went down well." Testimony
of Mr. Moore, light comedian, c/o Widow Merryweather-Moore, All
Saints on the Wash, and lifelong friend.
[*Pause.*]

A [*stricken*] Tsstss! [*Pause.*] Tsstsstss!

B You see. [*Emphatic.*] This is not his home and he knows it full well.
[*Pause.*]

A Now let's have the positive elements.

B Positive? You mean of a nature to make him think . . . [*hesitates, then
with sudden violence*] . . . that some day things might change? Is that
what you want? [*Pause. Calmer.*] There are none.

A [*wearily*] Oh yes there are, that's the beauty of it.
[*Pause. B rummages in his papers.*]

B [*looking up*] Forgive me, Bertrand. [*Pause. Rummages. Looks up.*] I don't
know what came over me. [*Pause. Rummages. Looks up.*] A moment of
consternation. [*Pause. Rummages.*] There is that incident of the
lottery . . . possibly. Remember?

A No.

B [*reading*] "Two hundred lots . . . winner receives high class watch . . .
solid gold, hallmark nineteen carats, marvel of accuracy, showing
year, month, date, day, hour, minute and second, super chic,
unbreakable hair spring, chrono escapement nineteen rubies, anti-
shock, anti-magnetic, airtight, waterproof, stainless, self-winding,
centre seconds hand, Swiss parts, de luxe lizard band."

A What did I tell you? However unhopefully. The mere fact of chancing
his luck. I knew he had a spark left in him.

B The trouble is he didn't procure it himself. It was a gift. That you
forget.

A [*irritated*] I forget, I forget! And he, does he not— [*Pause.*] At least he
kept it.

B If you can call it that.

A At least he accepted it. [*Pause.*] At least he didn't refuse it.

B I quote: "The last time I laid eyes on him I was on my way to the Post
Office to cash an order for back-pay. The area before the building is
shut off by a row of bollards with chains hung between them. He
was seated on one of these with his back to the Thompson works. To
all appearances down and out. He sat doubled in two, his hands on
his knees, his legs astraddle, his head sunk. For a moment I
wondered if he was not vomiting. But on drawing nearer I could see
he was merely scrutinizing, between his feet, a lump of dogshit. I
moved it slightly with the tip of my umbrella and observed how his
gaze followed the movement and fastened on the object in its new
position. This at three o'clock in the afternoon if you please! I
confess I had not the heart to bid him the time of day, I was overcome. I simply slipped into his hip pocket a lottery ticket I had no
use for, while silently wishing him the best of luck. When two hours

later I emerged from the Post Office, having cashed my order, he was
at the same place and in the same attitude. I sometimes wonder if he
is still alive." Testimony of Mr. Feckman, certified accountant and
friend for better and for worse.
[*Pause.*]

A   Dated when?

B   Recent.

A   It has such a bygone ring. [*Pause.*] Nothing else?

B   Oh . . . bits and scraps . . . good graces of an heirless aunt . . .
unfinished—

A   Hairless aunt?

B   . . . heirless aunt . . . unfinished game of chess with a correspondent in
Tasmania . . . hope not dead of living to see the extermination of the
species . . . literary aspirations incompletely stifled . . . bottom of a
dairy-woman in Waterloo Lane . . . you see the kind of thing.
[*Pause.*]

A   We pack up this evening, right?

B   Without fail. Tomorrow we're at Bury St. Edmunds.

A   [*sadly*] We'll leave him none the wiser. We'll leave him now, never to
meet again, having added nothing to what he knew already.

B   All these testimonies were new to him. They will have finished him off.

A   Not necessarily. [*Pause.*] Any light on that? [*Papers.*] This is vital. [*Papers.*]
Something . . . I seem to remember . . . something . . . he said
himself.

B   [*papers*] Under "Confidences" then. [*Brief laugh.*] Slim file. [*Papers.*]
Confidences . . . confidences . . . ah!

A   [*impatient*] Well?

B   [*reading*] ". . . sick headaches . . . eye trouble . . . irrational fear of
vipers . . . ear trouble . . ."—nothing for us there—". . . fibroid
tumours . . . pathological horror of songbirds . . . throat trouble . . .
need of affection . . ."—we're coming to it—". . . inner void . . .
congenital timidity . . . nose trouble . . ."—ah! listen to this!—
" . . . morbidly sensitive to the opinion of others . . ." [*Looks up.*] What
did I tell you?

A   [*glum*] Tsstss!

B   I'll read the whole passage: "... morbidly sensitive to the opinion of others—" [*His lamp goes out.*] Well! The bulb has blown! [*The lamp goes on again.*] No, it hasn't! Must be a faulty connexion. [*Examines lamp, straightens flex.*] The flex was twisted, now all is well. [*Reading.*] "... morbidly sensitive—" [*The lamp goes out.*] Bugger and shit!

A   Try giving her a shake. [*B shakes the lamp. It goes on again.*] See! I picked up that wrinkle in the Band of Hope. [*Pause.*]

B ⎫
   ⎬ [*together*]
A ⎭
           "... morbidly sensitive—"
           Keep your hands off the table.

B   What?

A   Keep your hands off the table. If it's a connexion the least jog can do it.

B   [*having pulled back his chair a little way*] "... morbidly sensitive—" [*The lamp goes out. B bangs on the table with his fist. The lamp goes on again. Pause.*]

A   Mysterious affair, electricity.

B   [*hurriedly*] "... morbidly sensitive to the opinion of others at the time, I mean as often and for as long as they entered my awareness—" What kind of Chinese is that?

A   [*nervously*] Keep going, keep going!

B   "... for as long as they entered my awareness, and that in either case, I mean whether such on the one hand as to give me pleasure or on the contrary on the other to cause me pain, and truth to tell—" Shit! Where's the verb?

A   What verb?

B   The main!

A   I give up.

B   Hold on till I find the verb and to hell with all this drivel in the middle. [*Reading.*] "... were I but ... could I but ..." —Jesus!— "... though it be ... be it but ..."—Christ!—ah! I have it—"... I was unfortunately incapable ..." Done it!

A   How does it run now?

B   [*solemnly*] "... morbidly sensitive to the opinion of others at the
    time ..."—drivel drivel drivel—"... I was unfortunately incapable—"
    [*The lamp goes out. Long pause.*]

A   Would you care to change seats? [*Pause.*] You see what I mean? [*Pause.*]
    That you come over here with your papers and I go over there.
    [*Pause.*] Don't whinge, Morvan, that will get us nowhere.

B   It's my nerves. [*Pause.*] Ah if I were only twenty years younger I'd put an
    end to my sufferings!

A   Fie! Never say such horrid things! Even to a well-wisher!

B   May I come to you? [*Pause.*] I need animal warmth.
    [*Pause.*]

A   [*coldly*] As you like. [*B gets up and goes towards A.*] With your files if you
    don't mind. [*B goes back for papers and briefcase, returns towards A, puts
    them on A's table, remains standing. Pause.*] Do you want me to take you
    on my knees?
    [*Pause. B goes back for his chair, returns towards A, stops before A's table
    with the chair in his arms. Pause.*]

B   [*shyly*] May I sit beside you? [*They look at each other.*] No? [*Pause.*] Then
    opposite. [*He sits down opposite A, looks at him. Pause.*] Do we continue?

A   [*forcibly*] Let's get it over and go to bed.
    [*B rummages in his papers.*]

B   I'll take the lamp. [*He draws it towards him.*] Please God it holds out.
    What would we do in the dark the pair of us? [*Pause.*] Have you
    matches?

A   Never without. [*Pause.*] What we would do? Go and stand by the
    window in the starlight. [*B's lamp goes on again.*] That is to say you
    would.

B   [*fervently*] Oh no not alone I wouldn't!

A   Pass me a sheet. [*B passes him a sheet.*] Switch off. [*B switches off.*] Oh
    lord, yours is on again.

B   This gag has gone on long enough for me.

A   Just so. Go and switch it off.
    [*B goes to his table, switches off his lamp. Pause.*]

B   What am I to do now? Switch it on again?

A Come back.

B Switch on then till I see where I'm going.

[*A switches on. B goes back and sits down opposite A. A switches off, goes to window with sheet, halts, contemplates the sky.*]

A And to think all that is nuclear combustion! All that faerie! [*He stoops over sheet and reads haltingly.*] "Aged ten, runs away from home first time, brought back next day, admonished, forgiven." [*Pause.*] "Aged fifteen, runs away from home second time, dragged back a week later, thrashed, forgiven." [*Pause.*] "Aged seventeen, runs away from home third time, slinks back six months later with his tail between his legs, locked up, forgiven." [*Pause.*] "Aged seventeen runs away from home last time, crawls back a year later on his hands and knees, kicked out, forgiven."

[*Pause. He moves up against window to inspect C's face, to do which he has to lean out a little way, with his back to the void.*]

B Careful!

[*Long pause, all three dead still.*]

A [*sadly*] Tsstss! [*He resumes his equilibrium.*] Switch on. [*B switches on. A goes back to his table, sits, returns the sheet to B.*] It's heavy going, but we're nearly home.

B How does he look?

A Not at his best.

B Has he still got that little smile on his face?

A Probably.

B What do you mean, probably, haven't you just been looking at him?

A He didn't have it then.

B [*with satisfaction*] Ah! [*Pause.*] Could never make out what he thought he was doing with that smile on his face. And his eyes? Still goggling?

A Shut.

B Shut!

A Oh it was only so as not to see me. He must have opened them again since. [*Pause. Violently.*] You'd need to stare them in the face day and night! Never take your eyes off them for a week on end! Unbeknownst to them!

[*Pause.*]

B Looks to me we have him.

A [*impatiently*] Come on, we're getting nowhere, get on with it.

[*B rummages in his papers, finds the sheet.*]

B [*reading at top speed*] ". . . morbidly sensitive to the opinion of others at the time . . ." —drivel drivel drivel— ". . . I was unfortunately incapable of retaining it for more than ten or fifteen minutes at the most, that is to say the time required to take it in. From then on it might as well never have been uttered." [*Pause.*] Tsstss!

A [*with satisfaction*] You see. [*Pause.*] Where does that come in?

B In a letter presumably never posted to an anonymous admiratrix.

A An admiratrix? He had admiratrixes?

B It begins: "Dear friend and admiratrix . . ." That's all we know.

A Come, Morvan, calm yourself, letters to admiratrixes, we all know what they're worth. No need to take everything literally.

B [*violently, slapping down his hand on the pile of papers*] There's the record, closed and final. That's what we're going on. Too late now to start saying that [*slapping to his left*] is right and that [*slapping to his right*] wrong. You're a pain in the arse.

[*Pause.*]

A Good. Let us sum up.

B We do nothing else.

A A black future, an unpardonable past—so far as he can remember, inducements to linger on all equally preposterous and the best advice dead letter. Agreed?

B An heirless aunt preposterous?

A [*warmly*] He's not the interested type. [*Sternly.*] One has to consider the client's temperament. To accumulate documents is not enough.

B [*vexed, slapping on his papers*] Here, as far as I'm concerned the client is here and nowhere else.

A All right. Is there a single reference there to personal gain? That old aunt, was he ever as much as commonly civil to her? And that dairy-woman, come to that, in all the years he's been going to her for his bit of cheddar, was he ever once wanting in respect? [*Pause.*] No, Morvan, look you—

[*Feeble miaow. Pause. Second miaow, louder.*]

B   That must be the cat.

A   Sounds like it. [*Long pause.*] So, agreed? Black future, unpardonable—

B   As you wish. [*He starts to tidy back the papers in the briefcase. Wearily.*] Let
    him jump.

A   No further exhibit?

B   Let him jump, let him jump. [*He finishes tidying, gets up with the briefcase
    in his hand.*] Let's go.
    [*A consults his watch.*]

A   It is now . . . ten . . . twenty-five. We have no train before eleven twenty.
    Let us kill the time here, talking of this and that.

B   What do you mean, eleven twenty? Ten fifty.
    [*A takes a time-table from his pocket, opens it at relevant page and hands it
    to B.*]

A   Where it's marked with a cross. [*B consults the time-table, hands it back to
    A and sits down again. Long pause. A clears his throat. Pause.
    Impassionately.*] How many unfortunates would be so still today if
    they had known in time to what extent they were so? [*Pause.*]
    Remember Smith?

B   Smith? [*Pause.*] Never knew anyone of that name.

A   Yes you did! A big fat redhair. Always to be seen hanging round World's
    End. Hadn't done a hand's turn for years. Reputed to have lost his
    genitals in a shooting accident. His own double-barrel that went off
    between his legs in a moment of abstraction, just as he was getting
    set to let fly at a quail.

B   Stranger to me.

A   Well to make a long story short he had his head in the oven when they
    came to tell him his wife had gone under an ambulance. Hell, says
    he, I can't miss that, and now he has a steady job in Marks and
    Spencer's. [*Pause.*] How is Mildred?

B   [*disgustedly*] Oh you know— [*Brief burst of birdsong. Pause.*] Good God!

A   Philomel!

B   Oh that put the heart across me!

A   Hsst! [*Low.*] Hark hark! [*Pause. Second brief burst, louder. Pause.*] It's in the
    room! [*He gets up, moves away on tiptoe.*] Come on, let's have a look.

B I'm scared!
[*He gets up none the less and follows cautiously in the wake of A.
A advances on tiptoe upstage right, B tiptoes after.*]

A [*turning*] Hsst! [*They advance, halt in the corner. A strikes a match, holds it above his head. Pause. Low.*] She's not here. [*He drops the match and crosses the stage on tiptoe followed on tiptoe by B. They pass before the window, halt in the corner upstage left. Match as before. Pause.*] Here she is!

B [*recoiling*] Where?
[*A squats. Pause.*]

A Lend me a hand.

B Let her be! [*A straightens up painfully, clutching to his belly a large birdcage covered with a green silk cloth fringed with beads. He starts to stagger with it towards the table.*] Give it here.
[*B helps to carry the cage. Holding it between them they advance warily towards A's table.*]

A [*breathing hard*] Hold on a second. [*They halt. Pause.*] Let's go. [*They move on, set down cage gently on the table. A lifts cautiously the cloth on the side away from the audience, peers. Pause.*] Show a light.
[*B takes up the lamp and shines it inside the cage. They peer, stooped. Long pause.*]

B There's one dead.
[*They peer.*]

A Have you a pencil? [*B hands him a long pencil. A pokes it between the bars of the cage. Pause.*] Yes. [*He withdraws the pencil, puts it in his pocket.*]

B Hi!
[*A gives him back his pencil. They peer. A takes B's hand and changes its position.*]

A There.
[*They peer.*]

B Is it the cock or the hen?

A The hen. See how drab she is.

B [*revolted*] And he goes on singing! [*Pause.*] There's lovebirds for you!

A Lovebirds! [*Guffaw.*] Ah Morvan, you'd be the death of me if I were sufficiently alive! Lovebirds! [*Guffaw.*] Finches, pinhead! Look at that lovely little green rump! And the blue cap! And the white bars! And the gold breast! [*Didactic.*] Note moreover the characteristic warble, there can be no mistaking it. [*Pause.*] Oh you pretty little pet, oh you bonny wee birdie! [*Pause. Glum.*] And to think all that is organic waste! All that splendour!

[*They peer.*]

B   They have no seed. [*Pause.*] No water. [*Pointing.*] What's that there?

A   That? [*Pause. Slow, toneless.*] An old cuttle-bone.

B   Cuttle-bone?

A   Cuttle-bone.

[*He lets the cloth fall back. Pause.*]

B   Come, Bertrand, don't, there is nothing we can do. [*A takes up the cage and goes with it upstage left. B puts down the lamp and hastens after him.*] Give it here.

A   Leave it, leave it! [*He advances to the corner, followed by B, and puts down the cage where he found it. He straightens up and moves back towards his table, still followed by B. A stops short.*] Will you have done dogging me! Do you want me to jump too? [*Pause. B goes to A's table, takes up briefcase and chair, goes to his table and sits with back to window. He switches on his lamp, switches it off again immediately.*] How end? [*Long pause. A goes to window; strikes a match, holds it high and inspects C's face. The match burns out, he throws it out of window.*] Hi! Take a look at this! [*B does not move. A strikes another match, holds it high and inspects C's face.*] Come on! Quick! [*B does not move. The match burns out, A lets it fall.*] Well I'll be ... !

[*A takes out his handkerchief and raises it timidly towards C's face.*]

Curtain

THE OLD TUNE

An adaptation

Background of street noises, in the foreground a barrel-organ playing an old tune. 20 seconds. The mechanism jams. Thumps on the box to set it off again. No result.

GORMAN   [*old man's cracked voice, frequent pauses for breath even in the middle of a word, speech indistinct for want of front teeth, whistling sibilants*] There we go, bust again. [*Sound of lid raised. Scraping inside box.*] Cursed bloody music! [*Scraping. Creaking of handle. Thumps on box. The mechanism starts off again.*] Ah about time! [*Tune resumes. 10 seconds. Sound of faltering steps approaching.*]

CREAM   [*old man's cracked voice, stumbling speech, pauses in the middle of sentences, whistling sibilants due to ill-fitting denture*] Well, if it isn't—[*the tune stops*]—Gorman my old friend Gorman, do you recognize me Cream father of the judge, Cream you remember Cream.

GORMAN   Mr. Cream! Well, I'll be! Mr. Cream! [*Pause.*] Sit you down, sit you down, here, there. [*Pause.*] Great weather for the time of day Mr. Cream, eh.

CREAM   My old friend Gorman, it's a sight to see you again after all these years, all these years.

GORMAN   Yes indeed, Mr. Cream, yes indeed, that's the way it is. [*Pause.*] And you, tell me.

CREAM   I was living with my daughter and she died, then I came here to live with the other.

GORMAN   Miss Miss what?

CREAM   Bertha. You know she got married, yes, Moody the nurseryman, two children.

GORMAN   Grand match, Mr. Cream, grand match, more power to you. But tell me then the poor soul she was taken then was she.

CREAM   Malignant, tried everything, lingered three years, that's how it goes, the young pop off and the old hang on.

GORMAN   Ah dear oh dear Mr. Cream, dear oh dear.
    [*Pause.*]

CREAM   And you your wife?

GORMAN   Still in it, still in it, but for how long.

CREAM   Poor Daisy yes.

GORMAN   Had she children?

CREAM   Three, three children, Johnny, the eldest, then Ronnie, then a baby girl, Queenie, my favourite, Queenie, a baby girl.

GORMAN   Darling name.

CREAM   She's so quick for her years you wouldn't believe it, do you know what she came out with to me the other day ah only the other day poor Daisy.

GORMAN   And your son-in-law?

CREAM   Eh?

GORMAN   Ah dear oh dear, Mr. Cream, dear oh dear. [*Pause.*] Ah yes children that's the way it is. [*Roar of motor engine.*] They'd tear you to flitters with their flaming machines.

CREAM   Shocking crossing, sudden death.

GORMAN   As soon as look at you, tear you to flitters.

CREAM   Ah in our time Gorman this was the outskirts, you remember, peace and quiet.

GORMAN   Do I remember, fields it was, fields, bluebells, over there, on the bank, bluebells. When you think. . . . [*Suddenly complete silence. 10 seconds. The tune resumes, falters, stops. Silence. The street noises resume.*] Ah the horses, the carriages, and the

barouches, ah the barouches, all that's the dim distant past,
Mr. Cream.

CREAM   And the broughams, remember the broughams, there was style
for you, the broughams.
[*Pause.*]

GORMAN   The first car I remember I saw it here, here, on the corner, a
Pic-Pic she was.

CREAM   Not a Pic-Pic, Gorman, not a Pic-Pic, a Dee Dyan Button.

GORMAN   A Pic-Pic, a Pic-Pic, don't I remember it well, just as I was
coming out of Swan's the bookseller's beyond there on the
corner, Swan's the bookseller's that was, just as I was coming
out with a rise of fourpence ah there wasn't much money in
it in those days.

CREAM   A Dee Dyan, a Dee Dyan.

GORMAN   You had to work for your living in those days, it wasn't at six
you knocked off, nor at seven neither, eight it was, eight
o'clock, yes by God. [*Pause.*] Where was I? [*Pause.*] Ah yes eight
o'clock as I was coming out of Swan's there was the crowd
gathered and the car wheeling round the bend.

CREAM   A Dee Dyan Gorman, a Dee Dyan, I can remember the man
himself from Wougham he was the vintner what's this his
name was.

GORMAN   Bush, Seymour Bush.

CREAM   Bush that's the man.

GORMAN   One way or t'other, Mr. Cream, one way or t'other no matter it
wasn't the likes of nowadays, their flaming machines they'd
tear you to shreds.

CREAM   My dear Gorman do you know what it is I'm going to tell you,
all this speed do you know what it is has the whole place
ruinated, no living with it any more, the whole place
ruinated, even the weather. [*Roar of engine.*] Ah when you
think of the springs in our time remember the springs we
had, the heat there was in them, and the summers remember
the summers would destroy you with the heat.

GORMAN   Do I remember, there was one year back there seems like yesterday must have been round 95 when we were still out at Cruddy, didn't we water the roof of the house every evening with the rubber jet to have a bit of cool in the night, yes summer 95.

CREAM   That would surprise me Gorman, remember in those days the rubber hose was a great luxury a great luxury, wasn't till after the war the rubber hose.

GORMAN   You may be right.

CREAM   No may be about it. I tell you the first we ever had round here was in Drummond's place, old Da Drummond, that was after the war 1920 maybe, still very exorbitant it was at the time, don't you remember watering out of the can you must with that bit of garden you had didn't you, wasn't it your father owned that patch out on the Marston Road.

GORMAN   The Sheen Road Mr. Cream but true for you the watering you're right there, me and me hose how are you when we had no running water at the time or had we.

CREAM   The Sheen Road, that's the one out beyond Shackleton's sawpit.

GORMAN   We didn't get it in till 1925 now it comes back to me the wash-hand basin and jug.
[*Roar of engine.*]

CREAM   The Sheen Road you saw what they've done to that I was out on it yesterday with the son-in-law, you saw what they've done our little gardens and the grand sloe hedges.

GORMAN   Yes all those gazebos springing up like thistles there's trash for you if you like, collapse if you look at them am I right.

CREAM   Collapse is the word, when you think of the good stone made the cathedrals nothing to come up to it.

GORMAN   And on top of all no foundations, no cellars, no nothing, how are you going to live without cellars I ask you, on piles if you don't mind, piles, like in the lake age, there's progress for you.

CREAM   Ah Gorman you haven't changed a hair, just the same old wag he always was. Getting on for seventy-five is it?

GORMAN Seventy-three, seventy-three, soon due for the knock.

CREAM Now Gorman none of that, none of that, and me turning seventy-six, you're a young man Gorman.

GORMAN Ah Mr. Cream, always a great one for a crack.

CREAM Here Gorman while we're at it have a fag, here. [*Pause.*] The daughter must have whipped them again, doesn't want me to be smoking, mind her own damn business. [*Pause.*] Ah I have them, here, have one.

GORMAN I wouldn't leave you short.

CREAM Short for God's sake, here, have one.
[*Pause.*]

GORMAN They're packed so tight they won't come out.

CREAM Take hold of the packet. [*Pause.*] Ah what ails me all bloody thumbs. Can you pick it up.
[*Pause.*]

GORMAN Here we are. [*Pause.*] Ah yes a nice puff now and again but it's not what it was their gaspers now not worth a fiddler's, remember in the forces the shag remember the black shag that was tobacco for you.

CREAM Ah the black shag my dear Gorman the black shag, fit for royalty the black shag fit for royalty. [*Pause.*] Have you a light on you.

GORMAN Well then I haven't, the wife doesn't like me to be smoking.
[*Pause.*]

CREAM Must have whipped my lighter too the bitch, my old tinder jizzer.

GORMAN Well no matter I'll keep it and have a draw later on.

CREAM The bitch sure as a gun she must have whipped it too that's going beyond the beyonds, beyond the beyonds, nothing you can call your own. [*Pause.*] Perhaps we might ask this gentleman. [*Footsteps approach.*] Beg your pardon Sir trouble you for a light.
[*Footsteps recede.*]

GORMAN Ah the young nowadays Mr. Cream very wrapped up they are the young nowadays, no thought for the old. When you think, when you think. . . . [*Suddenly complete silence. 10 seconds. The tune resumes, falters, stops. Silence. The street noises resume.*] Where were we? [*Pause.*] Ah yes the forces, you went in in 1900, 1900, 1902, am I right?

CREAM   1903, 1903, and you 1906 was it?

GORMAN   1906 yes at Chatham.

CREAM   The Gunners?

GORMAN   The Foot, the Foot.

CREAM   But the Foot wasn't Chatham don't you remember, there it was the Gunners, you must have been at Caterham, Caterham, the Foot.

GORMAN   Chatham I tell you, isn't it like yesterday, Morrison's pub on the corner.

CREAM   Harrison's. Harrison's Oak Lounge, do you think I don't know Chatham. I used to go there on holiday with Mrs. Cream, I know Chatham backwards Gorman, inside and out, Harrison's Oak Lounge on the corner of what was the name of the street, on a rise it was, it'll come back to me, do you think I don't know Harrison's Oak Lounge there on the corner of dammit I'll forget my own name next and the square it'll come back to me.

GORMAN   Morrison or Harrison we were at Chatham.

CREAM   That would surprise me greatly, the Gunners were Chatham do you not remember that?

GORMAN   I was in the Foot, at Chatham, in the Foot.

CREAM   The Foot, that's right the Foot at Chatham.

GORMAN   That's what I'm telling you, Chatham the Foot.

CREAM   That would surprise me greatly, you must have it mucked up with the war, the mobilization.

GORMAN   The mobilization have a heart it's as clear in my mind as yesterday the mobilization, we were shifted straight away to Chesham, was it, no, Chester, that's the place, Chester, there was Morrison's pub on the corner and a chamber-maid what was her name, Joan, Jean, Jane, the very start of the war when we still didn't believe it, Chester, ah those are happy memories.

CREAM   Happy memories, happy memories, I wouldn't go so far as that.

GORMAN   I mean the start up, the start up at Chatham, we still didn't believe it, and that chamber-maid what was her name it'll come back to me. [*Pause.*] And your son by the same token. [*Roar of engine.*]

CREAM   Eh?

GORMAN   Your son the judge.

CREAM   He has rheumatism.

GORMAN   Ah rheumatism, rheumatism runs in the blood Mr. Cream.

CREAM   What are you talking about, I never had rheumatism.

GORMAN   When I think of my poor old mother, only sixty and couldn't move a muscle. [*Roar of engine.*] Rheumatism they never found the remedy for it yet, atom rockets is all they care about, I can thank my lucky stars touch wood. [*Pause.*] Your son yes he's in the papers the Carton affair, the way he managed that case he can be a proud man, the wife read it again in this morning's *Lark*.

CREAM   What do you mean the Barton affair.

GORMAN   The Carton affair Mr. Cream, the sex fiend, on the Assizes.

CREAM   That's not him, he's not the Assizes my boy isn't, he's the County Courts, you mean Judge . . . Judge . . . what's this his name was in the Barton affair.

GORMAN   Ah I thought it was him.

CREAM   Certainly not I tell you, the County Courts my boy, not the Assizes, the County Courts.

GORMAN   Oh you know the Courts and the Assizes it was always all six of one to me.

CREAM   Ah but there's a big difference Mr. Gorman, a power of differ-ence, a civil case and a criminal one, quite another how d'you do, what would a civil case be doing in the *Lark* now I ask you.

GORMAN   All that machinery you know I never got the swing of it and now it's all six of one to me.

CREAM   Were you never in the Courts?

GORMAN   I was once all right when my niece got her divorce that was
            when was it now thirty years ago yes thirty years, I was greatly
            put about I can tell you the poor little thing divorced after two
            years of married life, my sister was never the same after it.

CREAM   Divorce is the curse of society you can take it from me, the
            curse of society, ask my boy if you don't believe me.

GORMAN   Ah there I'm with you the curse of society look at what it leads
            up to, when you think my niece had a little girl as good as
            never knew her father.

CREAM   Did she get alimony.

GORMAN   She was put out to board and wasted away to a shadow, that's a
            nice thing for you.

CREAM   Did the mother get alimony.

GORMAN   Divil the money. [*Pause.*] So that's your son ladling out the
            divorces.

CREAM   As a judge he must, as a father it goes to his heart.

GORMAN   Has he children.

CREAM   Well in a way he had one, little Herbert, lived to be four months
            then passed away, how long is it now, how long is it now.

GORMAN   Ah dear oh dear, Mr. Cream, dear oh dear and did they never
            have another?
            [*Roar of engine.*]

CREAM   Eh?

GORMAN   Other children.

CREAM   Didn't I tell you, I have my daughters' children, my two
            daughters. [*Pause.*] Talking of that your man there Barton the
            sex boyo isn't that nice carryings on for you showing himself
            off like that without a stitch on him to little children might just
            as well have been ours Gorman, our own little grandchildren.
            [*Roar of engine.*]

GORMAN   Mrs. Cream must be a proud woman too to be a grandmother.

CREAM   Mrs. Cream is in her coffin these twenty years Mr. Gorman.

GORMAN   Oh God forgive me what am I talking about, I'm getting you wouldn't know what I'd be talking about, that's right you were saying you were with Miss Daisy.

CREAM With my daughter Bertha, Mr. Gorman, my daughter Bertha, Mrs. Rupert Moody.

GORMAN Your daughter Bertha that's right so she married Moody, gallous garage they have there near the slaughter-house.

CREAM Not him, his brother the nurseryman.

GORMAN Grand match, more power to you, have they children?
[Roar of engine.]

CREAM Eh?

GORMAN Children.

CREAM Two dotey little boys, little Johnny I mean Hubert and the other, the other.

GORMAN But tell me your daughter poor soul she was taken then was she. [Pause.] That cigarette while we're at it might try this gentleman. [Footsteps approach.] Beg your pardon Sir trouble you for a light. [Footsteps recede.] Ah the young are very wrapped up Mr. Cream.

CREAM Little Hubert and the other, the other, what's this his name is. [Pause.] And Mrs. Gorman.

GORMAN Still in it.

CREAM Ah you're the lucky jim Gorman, you're the lucky jim, Mrs. Gorman by gad, fine figure of a woman Mrs. Gorman, fine handsome woman.

GORMAN Handsome, all right, but you know, age. We have our health thanks be to God touch wood. [Pause.] You know what it is Mr. Cream, that'd be the way to pop off chatting away like this of a sunny morning.

CREAM None of that now Gorman, who's talking of popping off with the health you have as strong as an ox and a comfortable wife, ah I'd give ten years of mine to have her back do you hear me, living with strangers isn't the same.

GORMAN Miss Bertha's so sweet and good you're on the pig's back for God's sake, on the pig's back.

CREAM   It's not the same you can take it from me, can't call your soul your own, look at the cigarettes, the lighter.

GORMAN   Miss Bertha so sweet and good.

CREAM   Sweet and good, all right, but dammit if she doesn't take me for a doddering old drivelling dotard. [*Pause.*] What did I do with those cigarettes?

GORMAN   And tell me your poor dear daughter-in-law what am I saying your daughter-in-law.

CREAM   My daughter-in-law, my daughter-in-law, what about my daughter-in-law.

GORMAN   She had private means, it was said she had private means.

CREAM   Private means ah they were the queer private means, all swallied up in the war every ha'penny do you hear me, all in the bank the private means not as much land as you'd tether a goat. [*Pause.*] Land Gorman there's no security like land but that woman you might as well have been talking to the bedpost, a mule she was that woman was.

GORMAN   Ah well it's only human nature, you can't always pierce into the future.

CREAM   Now now Gorman don't be telling me, land wouldn't you live all your life off a bit of land damn it now wouldn't you any fool knows that unless they take the fantasy to go and build on the moon the way they say, ah that's all fantasy Gorman you can take it from me all fantasy and delusion, they'll smart for it one of these days by God they will.

GORMAN   You don't believe in the moon what they're experimenting at.

CREAM   My dear Gorman the moon is the moon and cheese is cheese what do they take us for, didn't it always exist the moon wasn't it always there as large as life and what did it ever mean only fantasy and delusion Gorman, fantasy and delusion. [*Pause.*] Or is it our forefathers were a lot of old bags maybe now is that on the cards I ask you, Bacon, Wellington, Washington, for them the moon was always in their opinion damn it I ask you you'd think to hear them talk no one ever bothered his arse with the moon before, make a cat swallow his whiskers they think they've discovered the moon as if as if. [*Pause.*] What was I driving at?

[*Roar of engine.*]

GORMAN   So you're against progress are you.

CREAM   Progress, progress, progress is all very fine and grand, there's such a thing I grant you, but it's scientific, progress, scientific, the moon's not progress, lunacy, lunacy.

GORMAN   Ah there I'm with you progress is scientific and the moon, the moon, that's the way it is.

CREAM   The wisdom of the ancients that's the trouble they don't give a rap or a snap for it any more, and the world going to rack and ruin, wouldn't it be better now to go back to the old maxims and not be gallivanting off killing one another in China over the moon, ah when I think of my poor father.

GORMAN   Your father that reminds me I knew your father well. [*Roar of engine.*] There was a man for you old Mr. Cream, what he had to say he lashed out with it straight from the shoulder and no humming and hawing, now it comes back to me one year there on the town council my father told me must have been wait now till I see 95, 95 or 6, a short while before he resigned, 95 that's it the year of the great frost.

CREAM   Ah I beg your pardon, the great frost was 93 I'd just turned ten, 93 Gorman the great frost.

[*Roar of engine.*]

GORMAN   My father used to tell the story how Mr. Cream went hell for leather for the mayor who was he in those days, must have been Overend, yes Overend.

CREAM   Ah there you're mistaken my dear Gorman, my father went on the council with Overend in 97, January 97.

GORMAN   That may be, that may be, but it must have been 95 or 6 just the same seeing as how my father went off in 96, April 96, there was a set against him and he had to give in his resignation.

CREAM   Well then your father was off when it happened, all I know is mine went on with Overend in 97 the year Marrable was burnt out.

GORMAN   Ah Marrable it wasn't five hundred yards from the door five hundred yards Mr. Cream, I can still hear my poor mother saying to us ah poor dear Maria she was saying to me again only last night, January 96 that's right.

CREAM   97 I tell you, 97, the year my father was voted on.

GORMAN   That may be but just the same the clout he gave Overend that's right now I have it.

CREAM   The clout was Oscar Bliss the butcher in Pollox Street.

GORMAN   The butcher in Pollox Street, there's a memory from the dim distant past for you, didn't he have a daughter do you remember.

CREAM   Helen, Helen Bliss, pretty girl, she'd be my age, 83 saw the light of day.

GORMAN   And Rosie Plumpton bonny Rosie staring up at the lid these thirty years she must be now and Molly Berry and Eva what was her name Eva Hart that's right Eva Hart didn't she marry a Crumplin.

CREAM   Her brother, her brother Alfred married Gertie Crumplin great one for the lads she was you remember, Gertie great one for the lads.

GORMAN   Do I remember, Gertie Crumplin great bit of skirt by God, hee hee hee great bit of skirt.

CREAM   You old dog you!
[Roar of engine.]

GORMAN   And Nelly Crowther there's one came to a nasty end.

CREAM   Simon's daughter that's right, the parents were greatly to blame you can take it from me.

GORMAN   They reared her well then just the same bled themselves white for her so they did, poor Mary used to tell us all we were very close in those days lived on the same landing you know, poor Mary yes she used to say what a drain it was having the child boarding out at Saint Theresa's can you imagine, very classy, daughters of the gentry Mr. Cream, even taught French they were the young ladies.

CREAM   Isn't that what I'm telling you, reared her like a princess of the blood they did, French now I ask you, French.

GORMAN   Would you blame them Mr. Cream, the best of parents, you can't deny it, education.

CREAM   French, French, isn't that what I'm saying.
[*Roar of engine.*]

GORMAN   They denied themselves everything, take the bits out of their mouths they would for their Nelly.

CREAM   Don't be telling me they had her on a string all the same the said young lady, remember that Holy Week 1912 was it or 13.
[*Roar of engine.*]

GORMAN   Eh?

CREAM   When you think of Simon the man he was don't be telling me that. [*Pause.*] Holy Week 1913 now it all comes back to me is that like as if they had her on a string what she did then.

GORMAN   Peace to her ashes Mr. Cream.

CREAM   Principles, Gorman, principles without principles I ask you. [*Roar of engine.*] Wasn't there an army man in it.

GORMAN   Eh?

CREAM   Wasn't there an army man in it?

GORMAN   In the car?

CREAM   Eh?

GORMAN   An army man in the car?

CREAM   In the Crowther blow-up.
[*Roar of engine.*]

GORMAN   You mean the Lootnant St. John Fitzball.

CREAM   St. John Fitzball that's the man, wasn't he mixed up in it?

GORMAN   They were keeping company all right. [*Pause.*] He died in 14. Wounds.

CREAM   And his aunt Miss Hester.

GORMAN   Dead then these how many years is it now how many.

CREAM   She was a great old one, a little on the high and mighty side perhaps you might say.

GORMAN   Take fire like gunpowder but a heart of gold if you only knew. [*Roar of engine.*] Her niece has a chip of the old block wouldn't you say.

CREAM   Her niece? No recollection.

GORMAN   No recollection, Miss Victoria, come on now, she was to have married an American and she's in the Turrets yet.

CREAM   I thought they'd sold.

GORMAN   Sell the Turrets is it they'll never sell, the family seat three centuries and maybe more, three centuries Mr. Cream.

CREAM   You might be their historiographer Gorman to hear you talk, what you don't know about those people.

GORMAN   Histryographer no Mr. Cream I wouldn't go so far as that but Miss Victoria right enough I know her through and through we stop and have a gas like when her aunt was still in it, ah yes nothing hoity-toity about Miss Victoria you can take my word she has a great chip of the old block.

CREAM   Hadn't she a brother.

GORMAN   The Lootnant yes, died in 14. Wounds.
          [*Deafening roar of engine.*]

CREAM   The bloody cars such a thing as a quiet chat I ask you. [*Pause.*] Well I'll be slipping along I'm holding you back from your work.

GORMAN   Slipping along what would you want slipping along and we only after meeting for once in a blue moon.

CREAM   Well then just a minute and smoke a quick one. [*Pause.*] What did I do with those cigarettes? [*Pause.*] You fire ahead don't mind me.

GORMAN   When you think, when you think. . . .
          [*Suddenly complete silence. 10 seconds. The tune resumes. The street noises resume and submerge tune a moment. Street noises and tune together crescendo. Tune finally rises above them triumphant.*]

HAPPY DAYS

Winnie, *a woman about fifty*
Willie, *a man about sixty*

ACT I

Expanse of scorched grass rising centre to low mound. Gentle slopes down to
front and either side of stage. Back an abrupter fall to stage level. Maximum of
simplicity and symmetry.

Blazing light.

Very pompier trompe-l'oeil backcloth to represent unbroken plain and sky
receding to meet in far distance.

Imbedded up to above her waist in exact centre of mound, Winnie. About
fifty, well preserved, blond for preference, plump, arms and shoulders bare, low
bodice, big bosom, pearl necklet. She is discovered sleeping, her arms on the
ground before her, her head on her arms. Beside her on ground to her left a capa-
cious black bag, shopping variety, and to her right a collapsible collapsed parasol,
beak of handle emerging from sheath.

To her right and rear, lying asleep on ground, hidden by mound, Willie.

Long pause. A bell rings piercingly, say ten seconds, stops. She does not move.
Pause. Bell more piercingly, say five seconds. She wakes. Bell stops. She raises her
head, gazes front. Long pause. She straightens up, lays her hands flat on ground,
throws back her head and gazes at zenith. Long pause.

WINNIE   [*gazing at zenith*] Another heavenly day. [*Pause. Head back level,*
            eyes front, pause. She clasps hands to breast, closes eyes. Lips move in
            inaudible prayer, say ten seconds. Lips still. Hands remain clasped.

Low.] For Jesus Christ sake Amen. [*Eyes open, hands unclasp, return to mound. Pause. She clasps hands to breast again, closes eyes, lips move again in inaudible addendum, say five seconds. Low.*] World without end Amen. [*Eyes open, hands unclasp, return to mound. Pause.*] Begin, Winnie. [*Pause.*] Begin your day, Winnie. [*Pause. She turns to bag, rummages in it without moving it from its place, brings out toothbrush, rummages again, brings out flat tube of toothpaste, turns back front, unscrews cap of tube, lays cap on ground, squeezes with difficulty small blob of paste on brush, holds tube in one hand and brushes teeth with other. She turns modestly aside and back to her right to spit out behind mound. In this position her eyes rest on Willie. She spits out. She cranes a little further back and down. Loud.*] Hoo-oo! [*Pause. Louder.*] Hoo-oo! [*Pause. Tender smile as she turns back front, lays down brush.*] Poor Willie— [*examines tube, smile off*]—running out—[*looks for cap*]—ah well—[*finds cap*]—can't be helped—[*screws on cap*]—just one of those old things—[*lays down tube*]—another of those old things—[*turns towards bag*]—just can't be cured—[*rummages in bag*]—cannot be cured—[*brings out small mirror, turns back front*]—ah yes—[*inspects teeth in mirror*]—poor dear Willie— [*testing upper front teeth with thumb, indistinctly*]—good Lord!— [*pulling back upper lip to inspect gums, do*]—good God!—[*pulling back corner of mouth, mouth open, do*]—ah well—[*other corner, do*]—no worse—[*abandons inspection, normal speech*]—no better, no worse—[*lays down mirror*]—no change—[*wipes fingers on grass*]—no pain—[*looks for toothbrush*]—hardly any—[*takes up toothbrush*]—great thing that—[*examines handle of brush*]— nothing like it—[*examines handle, reads*]—pure . . . what?— [*pause*]—what?—[*lays down brush*]—ah yes—[*turns towards bag*]—poor Willie—[*rummages in bag*]—no zest— [*rummages*]—for anything—[*brings out spectacles in case*]—no interest—[*turns back front*]—in life—[*takes spectacles from case*]—poor dear Willie—[*lays down case*]—sleep for ever— [*opens spectacles*]—marvellous gift—[*puts on spectacles*]—

nothing to touch it—[*looks for toothbrush*]—in my
opinion—[*takes up toothbrush*]—always said so—[*examines
handle of brush*]—wish I had it—[*examines handle, reads*]—
genuine . . . pure . . . what?—[*lays down brush*]—blind next—
[*takes off spectacles*]—ah well—[*lays down spectacles*]—seen
enough—[*feels in bodice for handkerchief*]—I suppose—[*takes
out folded handkerchief*]—by now—[*shakes out handkerchief*]—
what are those wonderful lines—[*wipes one eye*]—woe woe is
me—[*wipes the other*]—to see what I see—[*looks for spectacles*]—
ah yes—[*takes up spectacles*]—wouldn't miss it—[*starts polishing
spectacles, breathing on lenses*]—or would I?—[*polishes*]—holy
light—[*polishes*]—bob up out of dark—[*polishes*]—blaze of
hellish light. [*Stops polishing, raises face to sky, pause, head back
level, resumes polishing, stops polishing, cranes back to her right and
down.*] Hoo-oo! [*Pause. Tender smile as she turns back front and
resumes polishing. Smile off.*] Marvellous gift—[*stops polishing,
lays down spectacles*]—wish I had it—[*folds handkerchief*]—ah
well—[*puts handkerchief back in bodice*]—can't complain—
[*looks for spectacles*]—no no—[*takes up spectacles*]—mustn't
complain—[*holds up spectacles, looks through lens*]—so much to
be thankful for—[*looks through other lens*]—no pain—[*puts on
spectacles*]—hardly any—[*looks for toothbrush*]—wonderful
thing that—[*takes up toothbrush*]—nothing like it—[*examines
handle of brush*]—slight headache sometimes—[*examines
handle, reads*]—guaranteed . . . genuine . . . pure . . . what?—
[*looks closer*]—genuine pure . . . —[*takes handkerchief from
bodice*]—ah yes—[*shakes out handkerchief*]—occasional mild
migraine—[*starts wiping handle of brush*]—it comes—[*wipes*]—
then goes—[*wiping mechanically*]—ah yes—[*wiping*]—many
mercies—[*wiping*]—great mercies—[*stops wiping, fixed lost gaze,
brokenly*]—prayers perhaps not for naught—[*pause, do*]—first
thing—[*pause, do*]—last thing—[*head down, resumes wiping,
stops wiping, head up, calmed, wipes eyes, folds handkerchief, puts it
back in bodice, examines handle of brush, reads*]—fully

guaranteed . . . genuine pure . . . —[*looks closer*]—genuine pure . . . [*Takes off spectacles, lays them and brush down, gazes before her.*] Old things. [*Pause.*] Old eyes. [*Long pause.*] On, Winnie. [*She casts about her, sees parasol, considers it at length, takes it up and develops from sheath a handle of surprising length. Holding butt of parasol in right hand she cranes back and down to her right to hang over Willie.*] Hoo-oo! [*Pause.*] Willie! [*Pause.*] Wonderful gift. [*She strikes down at him with beak of parasol.*] Wish I had it. [*She strikes again. The parasol slips from her grasp and falls behind mound. It is immediately restored to her by Willie's invisible hand.*] Thank you, dear. [*She transfers parasol to left hand, turns back front and examines right palm.*] Damp. [*Returns parasol to right hand, examines left palm.*] Ah well, no worse. [*Head up, cheerfully.*] No better, no worse, no change. [*Pause. Do.*] No pain. [*Cranes back to look down at Willie, holding parasol by butt as before.*] Don't go off on me again now dear will you please, I may need you. [*Pause.*] No hurry, no hurry, just don't curl up on me again. [*Turns back front, lays down parasol, examines palms together, wipes them on grass.*] Perhaps a shade off colour just the same. [*Turns to bag, rummages in it, brings out revolver, holds it up, kisses it rapidly, puts it back, rummages, brings out almost empty bottle of red medicine, turns back front, looks for spectacles, puts them on, reads label.*] Loss of spirits . . . lack of keenness . . . want of appetite . . . infants . . . children . . . adults . . . six level . . . tablespoonfuls daily—[*head up, smile*]—the old style!—[*smile off, head down, reads*]—daily . . . before and after . . . meals . . . instantaneous . . . [*looks closer*] . . . improvement. [*Takes off spectacles, lays them down, holds up bottle at arm's length to see level, unscrews cap, swigs it off head well back, tosses cap and bottle away in Willie's direction. Sound of breaking glass.*] Ah that's better! [*Turns to bag, rummages in it, brings out lipstick, turns back front, examines lipstick.*] Running out. [*Looks for spectacles.*] Ah well. [*Puts on spectacles, looks for mirror.*] Musn't complain. [*Takes up mirror, starts doing lips.*] What is that wonderful line? [*Lips.*] Oh fleeting joys—[*lips*]—oh something lasting woe. [*Lips. She is interrupted by disturbance from Willie. He is sitting up. She lowers lipstick and mirror and cranes back and down to look at him. Pause. Top back of Willie's bald head, trickling blood, rises to view above slope, comes to rest. Winnie pushes up her spectacles. Pause. His hand appears with handkerchief, spreads it on skull, disappears. Pause. The hand appears with boater, club ribbon, settles it on head, rakish angle, disappears. Pause. Winnie cranes a little further back and down.*] Slip on your drawers, dear, before you get singed. [*Pause.*] No? [*Pause.*] Oh I see, you still have some of that stuff left. [*Pause.*] Work it well in, dear. [*Pause.*] Now the other. [*Pause. She turns back front, gazes before her. Happy expression.*] Oh this is going to be another happy day! [*Pause. Happy expression off. She pulls down spectacles and resumes lips. Willie opens newspaper, hands invisible. Tops of yellow sheets appear on either side of his head. Winnie finishes lips, inspects them in mirror held a little further away.*] Ensign crimson. [*Willie turns page. Winnie lays down lipstick and mirror, turns towards bag.*] Pale flag. [*Willie turns page. Winnie rummages in bag, brings out small ornate brimless hat with crumpled feather, turns back front, straightens hat, smooths feather, raises it towards head, arrests gesture as Willie reads.*]

WILLIE His Grace and Most Reverend Father in God Dr. Carolus Hunter dead in tub.

[*Pause.*]

WINNIE [*gazing front, hat in hand, tone of fervent reminiscence*] Charlie Hunter! [*Pause.*] I close my eyes—[*she takes off spectacles and does so, hat in one hand, spectacles in other, Willie turns page*]—and am sitting on his knees again, in the back garden at Borough Green, under the horse-beech. [*Pause. She opens eyes, puts on spectacles, fiddles with hat.*] Oh the happy memories!

[*Pause. She raises hat towards head, arrests gesture as Willie reads.*]

WILLIE Opening for smart youth.

[*Pause. She raises hat towards head, arrests gesture, takes off spectacles, gazes front, hat in one hand, spectacles in other.*]

WINNIE   My first ball! [*Long pause.*] My second ball! [*Long pause. Closes eyes.*]
My first kiss! [*Pause. Willie turns page. Winnie opens eyes.*] A
Mr. Johnson, or Johnston, or perhaps I should say John*stone.*
Very bushy moustache, very tawny. [*Reverently.*] Almost ginger!
[*Pause.*] Within a toolshed, though whose I cannot conceive.
We had no toolshed and he most certainly had no toolshed.
[*Closes eyes.*] I see the piles of pots. [*Pause.*] The tangles of bast.
[*Pause.*] The shadows deepening among the rafters.
[*Pause. She opens eyes, puts on spectacles, raises hat towards head,
arrests gesture as Willie reads.*]

WILLIE   Wanted bright boy.
[*Pause. Winnie puts on hat hurriedly, looks for mirror. Willie turns
page. Winnie takes up mirror, inspects hat, lays down mirror, turns
towards bag. Paper disappears. Winnie rummages in bag, brings out
magnifying-glass, turns back front, looks for toothbrush. Paper
reappears, folded, and begins to fan Willie's face, hand invisible.
Winnie takes up toothbrush and examines handle through glass.*]

WINNIE   Fully guaranteed . . . [*Willie stops fanning*] . . . genuine pure . . .
[*Pause. Willie resumes fanning. Winnie looks closer, reads.*] Fully
guaranteed . . . [*Willie stops fanning*] . . . genuine pure . . . [*Pause.
Willie resumes fanning. Winnie lays down glass and brush, takes
handkerchief from bodice, takes off and polishes spectacles, puts on
spectacles, looks for glass, takes up and polishes glass, lays down
glass, looks for brush, takes up brush and wipes handle, lays down
brush, puts handkerchief back in bodice, looks for glass, takes up
glass, looks for brush, takes up brush and examines handle through
glass.*] Fully guaranteed . . . [*Willie stops fanning*] . . . genuine
pure . . . [*pause, Willie resumes fanning*] . . . hog's [*Willie stops
fanning, pause*] . . . setae. [*Pause. Winnie lays down glass and brush,
paper disappears, Winnie takes off spectacles, lays them down, gazes
front.*] Hog's setae. [*Pause.*] That is what I find so wonderful,
that not a day goes by—[*smile*]—to speak in the old style—
[*smile off*]—hardly a day, without some addition to one's
knowledge however trifling, the addition I mean, provided

one takes the pains. [*Willie's hand reappears with a postcard which he examines close to eyes.*] And if for some strange reason no further pains are possible, why then just close the eyes—[*she does so*]—and wait for the day to come—[*opens eyes*]—the happy day to come when flesh melts at so many degrees and the night of the moon has so many hundred hours. [*Pause.*] That is what I find so comforting when I lose heart and envy the brute beast. [*Turning towards Willie.*] I hope you are taking in— [*She sees postcard, bends lower.*] What is that you have there, Willie, may I see? [*She reaches down with hand and Willie hands her card. The hairy forearm appears above slope, raised in gesture of giving, the hand open to take back, and remains in this position till card is returned. Winnie turns back front and examines card.*] Heavens what are they up to! [*She looks for spectacles, puts them on and examines card.*] No but this is just genuine pure filth! [*Examines card.*] Make any nice-minded person want to vomit! [*Impatience of Willie's fingers. She looks for glass, takes it up and examines card through glass. Long pause.*] What does that creature in the background think he's doing? [*Looks closer.*] Oh no really! [*Impatience of fingers. Last long look. She lays down glass, takes edge of card between right forefinger and thumb, averts head, takes nose between left forefinger and thumb.*] Pah! [*Drops card.*] Take it away! [*Willie's arm disappears. His hand reappears immediately, holding card. Winnie takes off spectacles, lays them down, gazes before her. During what follows Willie continues to relish card, varying angles and distance from his eyes.*] Hog's setae. [*Puzzled expression.*] What exactly is a hog? [*Pause. Do.*] A sow of course I know, but a hog . . . [*Puzzled expression off.*] Oh well what does it matter, that is what I always say, it will come back, that is what I find so wonderful, all comes back. [*Pause.*] All? [*Pause.*] No, not all. [*Smile.*] No no. [*Smile off.*] Not quite. [*Pause.*] A part. [*Pause.*] Floats up, one fine day, out of the blue. [*Pause.*] That is what I find so wonderful. [*Pause. She turns towards bag. Hand and card disappear. She makes to rummage in bag, arrests*

gesture.] No. [*She turns back front. Smile.*] No no. [*Smile off.*] Gently
Winnie. [*She gazes front. Willie's hand reappears, takes off hat,
disappears with hat.*] What then? [*Hand reappears, takes
handkerchief from skull, disappears with handkerchief. Sharply, as to
one not paying attention.*] Winnie! [*Willie bows head out of sight.*]
What *is* the alternative? [*Pause.*] What is the al— [*Willie blows
nose loud and long, head and hands invisible. She turns to look at
him. Pause. Head reappears. Pause. Hand reappears with
handkerchief, spreads it on skull, disappears. Pause. Hand reappears
with boater, settles it on head, rakish angle, disappears. Pause.*]
Would I had let you sleep on. [*She turns back front. Intermittent
plucking at grass, head up and down, to animate following.*] Ah yes,
if only I could bear to be alone, I mean prattle away with not a
soul to hear. [*Pause.*] Not that I flatter myself you hear much,
no Willie, God forbid. [*Pause.*] Days perhaps when you hear
nothing. [*Pause.*] But days too when you answer. [*Pause.*] So that
I may say at all times, even when you do not answer and
perhaps hear nothing, Something of this is being heard, I am
not merely talking to myself, that is in the wilderness, a thing
I could never bear to do—for any length of time. [*Pause.*] That
is what enables me to go on, go on talking that is. [*Pause.*]
Whereas if you were to die—[*smile*]—to speak in the old
style—[*smile off*]—or go away and leave me, then what would I
do, what *could* I do, all day long, I mean between the bell for
waking and the bell for sleep? [*Pause.*] Simply gaze before me
with compressed lips. [*Long pause while she does so. No more
plucking.*] Not another word as long as I drew breath, nothing
to break the silence of this place. [*Pause.*] Save possibly, now
and then, every now and then, a sigh into my looking-glass.
[*Pause.*] Or a brief . . . gale of laughter, should I happen to see
the old joke again. [*Pause. Smile appears, broadens and seems
about to culminate in laugh when suddenly replaced by expression of
anxiety.*] My hair! [*Pause.*] Did I brush and comb my hair?
[*Pause.*] I may have done. [*Pause.*] Normally I do. [*Pause.*] There

is so little one *can* do. [*Pause.*] One does it all. [*Pause.*] All one
can. [*Pause.*] Tis only human. [*Pause.*] Human nature. [*She
begins to inspect mound, looks up.*] Human weakness. [*She resumes
inspection of mound, looks up.*] Natural weakness. [*She resumes
inspection of mound.*] I see no comb. [*Inspects.*] Nor any
hairbrush. [*Looks up. Puzzled expression. She turns to bag,
rummages in it.*] The comb is here. [*Back front. Puzzled expression.
Back to bag. Rummages.*] The brush is here. [*Back front. Puzzled
expression.*] Perhaps I put them back, after use. [*Pause. Do.*] But
normally I do not put things back, after use, no, I leave them
lying about and put them back all together, at the end of the
day. [*Smile.*] To speak in the old style. [*Pause.*] The sweet old
style. [*Smile off.*] And yet . . . I seem . . . to remember . . .
[*Suddenly careless.*] Oh well, what does it matter, that is what I
always say, I shall simply brush and comb them later on,
purely and simply, I have the whole— [*Pause. Puzzled.*] Them?
[*Pause.*] Or it? [*Pause.*] *Brush and comb it?* [*Pause.*] Sounds
improper somehow. [*Pause. Turning a little towards Willie.*] What
would you say, Willie? [*Pause. Turning a little further.*] What
would you say, Willie, speaking of your hair, them or it?
[*Pause.*] The hair on your head, I mean. [*Pause. Turning a little
further.*] The hair on your head, Willie, what would you say
speaking of the hair on your head, them or it?
[*Long pause.*]

WILLIE   It.

WINNIE   [*turning back front, joyful*] Oh you are going to talk to me today,
this is going to be a happy day! [*Pause. Joy off.*] Another happy
day. [*Pause.*] Ah well, where was I, my hair, yes, later on, I shall
be thankful for it later on. [*Pause.*] I have my—[*raises hands to
hat*]—yes, on, my hat on—[*lowers hands*]—I cannot take it off
now. [*Pause.*] To think there are times one cannot take off
one's hat, not if one's life were at stake. Times one cannot put
it on, times one cannot take it off. [*Pause.*] How often I have
said, Put on your hat now, Winnie, there is nothing else for it,

take off your hat now, Winnie, like a good girl, it will do you good, and did not. [*Pause.*] Could not. [*Pause. She raises hand, frees a strand of hair from under hat, draws it towards eye, squints at it, lets it go, hand down.*] Golden you called it, that day, when the last guest was gone—[*hand up in gesture of raising a glass*]—to your golden . . . may it never . . . [*voice breaks*] . . . may it never . . . [*Hand down. Head down. Pause. Low.*] That day. [*Pause. Do.*] What day? [*Pause. Head up. Normal voice.*] What now? [*Pause.*] Words fail, there are times when even they fail. [*Turning a little towards Willie.*] Is that not so, Willie? [*Pause. Turning a little further.*] Is not that so, Willie, that even words fail, at times? [*Pause. Back front.*] What is one to do then, until they come again? Brush and comb the hair, if it has not been done, or if there is some doubt, trim the nails if they are in need of trimming, these things tide one over. [*Pause.*] That is what I mean. [*Pause.*] That is all I mean. [*Pause.*] That is what I find so wonderful, that not a day goes by—[*smile*]—to speak in the old style—[*smile off*]—without some blessing—[*Willie collapses behind slope, his head disappears, Winnie turns towards event*]—in disguise. [*She cranes back and down.*] Go back into your hole now, Willie, you've exposed yourself enough. [*Pause.*] Do as I say, Willie, don't lie sprawling there in this hellish sun, go back into your hole. [*Pause.*] Go on now, Willie. [*Willie invisible starts crawling left towards hole.*] That's the man. [*She follows his progress with her eyes.*] Not head first, stupid, how are you going to turn? [*Pause.*] That's it . . . right round . . . now . . . back in. [*Pause.*] Oh I know it is not easy, dear, crawling backwards, but it is rewarding in the end. [*Pause.*] You have left your vaseline behind. [*She watches as he crawls back for vaseline.*] The lid! [*She watches as he crawls back towards hole. Irritated.*] Not head first, I tell you! [*Pause.*] More to the right. [*Pause.*] The right, I said. [*Pause. Irritated.*] Keep your tail down, can't you! [*Pause.*] Now. [*Pause.*] There! [*All these directions loud. Now in her normal voice, still turned towards him.*] Can you hear me? [*Pause.*]

I beseech you, Willie, just yes or no, can you hear me, just yes
or nothing.

[*Pause.*]

WILLIE   Yes.

WINNIE   [*turning front, same voice*] And now?

WILLIE   [*irritated*] Yes.

WINNIE   [*less loud*] And now?

WILLIE   [*more irritated*] Yes.

WINNIE   [*still less loud*] And now? [*A little louder.*] And now?

WILLIE   [*violently*] Yes!

WINNIE   [*same voice*] Fear no more the heat o' the sun. [*Pause.*] Did you
hear that?

WILLIE   [*irritated*] Yes.

WINNIE   [*same voice*] What? [*Pause.*] What?

WILLIE   [*more irritated*] Fear no more.

[*Pause.*]

WINNIE   [*same voice*] No more what? [*Pause.*] Fear no more what?

WILLIE   [*violently*] Fear no more!

WINNIE   [*normal voice, gabbled*] Bless you Willie I do appreciate your
goodness I know what an effort it costs you, now you may
relax I shall not trouble you again unless I am obliged to, by
that I mean unless I come to the end of my own resources
which is most unlikely, just to know that in theory you can
hear me even though in fact you don't is all I need, just to feel
you there within earshot and conceivably on the qui vive is all
I ask, not to say anything I would not wish you to hear or
liable to cause you pain, not to be just babbling away on trust
as it is were not knowing and something gnawing at me.
[*Pause for breath.*] Doubt. [*Places index and second finger on heart
area, moves them about, brings them to rest.*] Here. [*Moves them
slightly.*] Abouts. [*Hand away.*] Oh no doubt the time will come
when before I can utter a word I must make sure you heard
the one that went before and then no doubt another come
another time when I must learn to talk to myself a thing I

could never bear to do such wilderness. [*Pause.*] Or gaze before me with compressed lips. [*She does so.*] All day long. [*Gaze and lips again.*] No. [*Smile.*] No no. [*Smile off.*] There is of course the bag. [*Turns towards it.*] There will always be the bag. [*Back front.*] Yes, I suppose so. [*Pause.*] Even when you are gone, Willie. [*She turns a little towards him.*] You *are* going, Willie, aren't you? [*Pause. Louder.*] You *will* be going soon, Willie, won't you? [*Pause. Louder.*] Willie! [*Pause. She cranes back and down to look at him.*] So you have taken off your straw, that is wise. [*Pause.*] You do look snug, I must say, with your chin on your hands and the old blue eyes like saucers in the shadows. [*Pause.*] Can you see me from there I wonder, I still wonder. [*Pause.*] No? [*Back front.*] Oh I know it does not follow when two are gathered together—[*faltering*]—in this way—[*normal*]—that because one sees the other the other sees the one, life has taught me that . . . too. [*Pause.*] Yes, life I suppose, there is no other word. [*She turns a little towards him.*] Could you see me, Willie, do you think, from where you are, if you were to raise your eyes in my direction? [*Turns a little further.*] Lift up your eyes to me, Willie, and tell me can you see me, do that for me, I'll lean back as far as I can. [*Does so. Pause.*] No? [*Pause.*] Well never mind. [*Turns back painfully front.*] The earth is very tight today, can it be I have put on flesh, I trust not. [*Pause. Absently, eyes lowered.*] The great heat possibly. [*Starts to pat and stroke ground.*] All things expanding, some more than others. [*Pause. Patting and stroking.*] Some less. [*Pause. Do.*] Oh I can well imagine what is passing through your mind, it is not enough to have to listen to the woman, now I must look at her as well. [*Pause. Do.*] Well it is very understandable. [*Pause. Do.*] Most understandable. [*Pause. Do.*] One does not appear to be asking a great deal, indeed at times it would seem hardly possible—[*voice breaks, falls to a murmur*]—to ask less—of a fellow-creature—to put it mildly—whereas actually—when you think about it—look into your heart—see the other—what he needs—peace—to

be left in peace—then perhaps the moon—all this time—
asking for the moon. [*Pause. Stroking hand suddenly still. Lively.*]
Oh I say, what have we here? [*Bending head to ground,
incredulous.*] Looks like life of some kind! [*Looks for spectacles,
puts them on, bends closer. Pause.*] An emmet! [*Recoils. Shrill.*]
Willie, an emmet, a live emmet! [*Seizes magnifying-glass, bends
to ground again, inspects through glass.*] Where's it gone? [*Inspects.*]
Ah! [*Follows its progress through grass.*] Has like a little white ball
in its arms. [*Follows progress. Hand still. Pause.*] It's gone in.
[*Continues a moment to gaze at spot through glass, then slowly
straightens up, lays down glass, takes off spectacles and gazes before
her, spectacles in hand. Finally.*] Like a little white ball.
[*Long pause. Gesture to lay down spectacles.*]

WILLIE   Eggs.

WINNIE   [*arresting gesture*] What?
[*Pause.*]

WILLIE   Eggs. [*Pause. Gesture to lay down glasses.*] Formication.

WINNIE   [*arresting gesture*] What?
[*Pause.*]

WILLIE   Formication.
[*Pause. She lays down spectacles, gazes before her. Finally.*]

WINNIE   [*murmur*] God. [*Pause. Willie laughs quietly. After a moment she joins
in. They laugh quietly together. Willie stops. She laughs on a moment
alone. Willie joins in. They laugh together. She stops. Willie laughs on
a moment alone. He stops. Pause. Normal voice.*] Ah well what a joy
in any case to hear you laugh again, Willie, I was convinced I
never would, you never would. [*Pause.*] I suppose some people
might think us a trifle irreverent, but I doubt it. [*Pause.*] How
can one better magnify the Almighty than by sniggering with
him at his little jokes, particularly the poorer ones? [*Pause.*] I
think you would back me up there, Willie. [*Pause.*] Or were we
perhaps diverted by two quite different things? [*Pause.*] Oh
well, what does it matter, that is what I always say, so long as
one . . . you know . . . what is that wonderful line . . . laughing

wild . . . something something laughing wild amid severest woe. [*Pause.*] And now? [*Long pause.*] Was I lovable once, Willie? [*Pause.*] Was I ever lovable? [*Pause.*] Do not misunderstand my question, I am not asking you if you loved me, we know all about that, I am asking you if you found me lovable—at one stage. [*Pause.*] No? [*Pause.*] You can't? [*Pause.*] Well I admit it is a teaser. And you have done more than your bit already, for the time being, just lie back now and relax, I shall not trouble you again unless I am compelled to, just to know you are there within hearing and conceivably on the semi-alert is . . . er . . . paradise enow. [*Pause.*] The day is now well advanced. [*Smile.*] To speak in the old style. [*Smile off.*] And yet it is perhaps a little soon for my song. [*Pause.*] To sing too soon is a great mistake, I find. [*Turning towards bag.*] There is of course the bag. [*Looking at bag.*] The bag. [*Back front.*] Could I enumerate its contents? [*Pause.*] No. [*Pause.*] Could I, if some kind person were to come along and ask, What all have you got in that big black bag, Winnie? give an exhaustive answer? [*Pause.*] No. [*Pause.*] The depths in particular, who knows what treasures. [*Pause.*] What comforts. [*Turns to look at bag.*] Yes, there is the bag. [*Back front.*] But something tells me, Do not overdo the bag, Winnie, make use of it of course, let it help you . . . along, when stuck, by all means, but cast your mind forward, something tells me, cast your mind forward, Winnie, to the time when words must fail—[*she closes eyes, pause, opens eyes*]— and do not overdo the bag. [*Pause. She turns to look at bag.*] Perhaps just one quick dip. [*She turns back front, closes eyes, throws out left arm, plunges hand in bag and brings out revolver. Disgusted.*] You again! [*She opens eyes, brings revolver front and contemplates it. She weighs it in her palm.*] You'd think the weight of this thing would bring it down among the . . . last rounds. But no. It doesn't. Ever uppermost, like Browning. [*Pause.*] Brownie . . . [*Turning a little towards Willie.*] Remember Brownie, Willie? [*Pause.*] Remember how you used to keep on at me to take it away from you? Take it away, Winnie, take it away, before I put myself out of my misery. [*Back front. Derisive.*] Your misery! [*To revolver.*] Oh I suppose it's a comfort to know you're there, but I'm tired of you. [*Pause.*] I'll leave you out, that's what I'll do. [*She lays revolver on ground to her right.*] There, that's your home from this day out. [*Smile.*] The old style! [*Smile off.*] And now? [*Long pause.*] Is gravity what it was, Willie, I fancy not. [*Pause.*] Yes, the feeling more and more that if I were not held—[*gesture*]—in this way, I would simply float up into the blue. [*Pause.*] And that perhaps some day the earth will yield and let me go, the pull is so great, yes, crack all round me and let me out. [*Pause.*] Don't you ever have that feeling, Willie, of being sucked up? [*Pause.*] Don't you have to cling on sometimes, Willie? [*Pause. She turns a little towards him.*] Willie. [*Pause.*]

WILLIE   *Sucked* up?

WINNIE   Yes love, up into the blue, like gossamer. [*Pause.*] No? [*Pause.*] You don't? [*Pause.*] Ah well, natural laws, natural laws, I suppose it's like everything else, it all depends on the creature you happen to be. All I can say is for my part is that for me they are not what they were when I was young and . . . foolish and . . . [*faltering, head down*] . . . beautiful . . . possibly . . . lovely . . . in a way . . . to look at. [*Pause. Head up.*] Forgive me, Willie, sorrow keeps breaking in. [*Normal voice.*] Ah well what a joy in any case to know you are there, as usual, and perhaps awake, and perhaps taking all this in, some of all this, what a happy day for me . . . it will have been. [*Pause.*] So far. [*Pause.*] What a blessing nothing grows, imagine if all this stuff were to start growing. [*Pause.*] Imagine. [*Pause.*] Ah yes, great mercies. [*Long pause.*] I can say no more. [*Pause.*] For the moment. [*Pause. Turns to look at bag. Back front. Smile.*] No no. [*Smile off. Looks at parasol.*] I suppose I might—[*takes up parasol*]—yes, I suppose I might . . . hoist this thing now. [*Begins to unfurl it. Following punctuated by mechanical difficulties overcome.*] One keeps putting off—putting up—for fear of putting up—too soon—and the day goes by—quite by—without one's having put up—at all. [*Parasol now fully open. Turned to her right she twirls it idly this way and that.*] Ah yes, so little to say, so little to do, and the fear so great, certain days, of finding oneself . . . left, with hours still to run, before the bell for sleep, and nothing more to say, nothing more to do, that the days go by, certain days go by, quite by, the bell goes, and little or nothing said, little or nothing done. [*Raising parasol.*] That is the danger. [*Turning front.*] To be guarded against. [*She gazes front, holding up parasol with right hand. Maximum pause.*] I used to perspire freely. [*Pause.*] Now hardly at all. [*Pause.*] The heat is much greater. [*Pause.*] The perspiration much less. [*Pause.*] That is what I find so wonderful. [*Pause.*] The way man adapts himself. [*Pause.*] To changing conditions. [*She transfers parasol to left hand. Long pause.*] Holding up wearies the arm. [*Pause.*] Not if one is going along. [*Pause.*] Only if one is at rest. [*Pause.*] That is a curious observation. [*Pause.*] I hope you heard that, Willie, I should be grieved to think you had not heard that. [*She takes parasol in both hands. Long pause.*] I am weary, holding it up, and I cannot put it down. [*Pause.*] I am worse off with it up than with it down, and I cannot put it down. [*Pause.*] Reason says, Put it down, Winnie, it is not helping you, put the thing down and get on with something else. [*Pause.*] I cannot. [*Pause.*] I cannot move. [*Pause.*] No, something must happen, in the world, take place, some change, I cannot, if I am to move again. [*Pause.*] Willie. [*Mildly.*] Help. [*Pause.*] No? [*Pause.*] Bid me put this thing down, Willie, I would obey you instantly, as I have always done, honoured and obeyed. [*Pause.*] Please, Willie. [*Mildly.*] For pity's sake. [*Pause.*] No? [*Pause.*] You can't? [*Pause.*] Well I don't blame you, no, it would ill become me, who cannot move, to blame my Willie because he cannot speak. [*Pause.*] Fortunately I am in tongue again. [*Pause.*] That is what I find so wonderful, my two lamps, when one goes out the other burns brighter. [*Pause.*] Oh yes, great mercies. [*Maximum pause. The parasol goes on fire. Smoke, flames if feasible. She sniffs, looks up, throws parasol to her right behind mound, cranes back to watch it burning. Pause.*] Ah earth you old extinguisher. [*Back front.*] I presume this has occurred before, though I cannot recall it. [*Pause.*] Can you, Willie? [*Turns a little towards him.*] Can you recall this having occurred before? [*Pause. Cranes back to look at him.*] Do you know what has occurred, Willie? [*Pause.*] Have you gone off on me again? [*Pause.*] I do not ask if you are alive to all that is going on, I merely ask if you have not gone off on me again. [*Pause.*] Your eyes appear to be closed, but that has no particular significance we know. [*Pause.*] Raise a finger, dear, will you please, if you are not quite senseless. [*Pause.*] Do that for me, Willie please, just the little finger, if you are still conscious. [*Pause. Joyful.*] Oh all five, you are a darling today, now I may continue with an easy mind. [*Back front.*] Yes, what ever occurred that did not occur before and yet . . . I wonder, yes, I confess I wonder. [*Pause.*] With the sun blazing so much fiercer down, and hourly fiercer, is it not natural things should go on fire never known to do so, in this way I mean, spontaneous like. [*Pause.*] Shall I myself not melt perhaps in the end, or burn, oh I do not mean necessarily burst into flames, no, just little by little be charred to a black cinder, all this—[*ample gesture of arms*]—visible flesh. [*Pause.*] On the other hand, did I ever know a temperate time? [*Pause.*] No. [*Pause.*] I speak of temperate times and torrid times, they are empty words. [*Pause.*] I speak of when I was not yet caught—in this way—and had my legs and had the use of my legs, and could seek out a shady place, like you, when I was tired of the sun, or a sunny place when I was tired of the shade, like you, and they are all empty words. [*Pause.*] It is no hotter today than yesterday, it will be no hotter tomorrow than today, how could it, and so on back into the far past, forward into the far future. [*Pause.*] And should one day the earth cover my breasts, then I shall never have seen my breasts, no one ever seen my breasts. [*Pause.*] I hope you caught something of that, Willie, I should be sorry to think you had caught nothing of all that, it is not every day I rise to such heights. [*Pause.*] Yes, something seems to have occurred, something has seemed to occur, and nothing has occurred, nothing at all, you are quite right, Willie. [*Pause.*] The sunshade will be there again tomorrow, beside me on this mound, to help me through the day. [*Pause. She takes up mirror.*] I take up this little glass, I shiver it on a stone—[*does so*]—I throw it away—[*does so far behind her*]—it will be in the bag again tomorrow, without a scratch, to help me through the day. [*Pause.*] No, one can do nothing. [*Pause.*] That is what I find so wonderful, the way things . . . [*voice breaks, head down*] . . . things . . . so wonderful. [*Long pause, head down. Finally turns, still bowed, to bag, brings out unidentifiable odds and ends, stuffs them back, fumbles deeper, brings out finally musical-box, winds it up, turns it on, listens for a moment holding it in both hands, huddled over it, turns back front, straightens up and listens to tune, holding box to breast with both hands. It plays the Waltz Duet "I love you so" from* The Merry Widow. *Gradually happy expression. She sways to the rhythm. Music stops. Pause. Brief burst of hoarse song without words—musical-box tune—from Willie. Increase of happy expression. She lays down box.*] Oh this will have been a happy day! [*She claps hands.*] Again, Willie, again! [*Claps.*] Encore, Willie, please! [*Pause. Happy expression off.*] No? You won't do that for me? [*Pause.*] Well it is very understandable, very understandable. One cannot sing just to please someone, however much one loves them, no, song must come from the heart, that is what I always say, pour out from the inmost, like a thrush. [*Pause.*] How often I have said, in evil hours, Sing now, Winnie, sing your song, there is nothing else for it, and did not. [*Pause.*] Could not. [*Pause.*] No, like the thrush, or the bird of dawning, with no thought of benefit, to oneself or

anyone else. [*Pause.*] And now? [*Long pause. Low.*] Strange
feeling. [*Pause. Do.*] Strange feeling that someone is looking at
me. I am clear, then dim, then gone, then dim again, then
clear again, and so on, back and forth, in and out of someone's
eye. [*Pause. Do.*] Strange? [*Pause. Do.*] No, here all is strange.
[*Pause. Normal voice.*] Something says, Stop talking now,
Winnie, for a minute, don't squander all your words for the
day, stop talking and do something for a change, will you? [*She
raises hands and holds them open before her eyes. Apostrophic.*] Do
something! [*She closes hands.*] What claws! [*She turns to bag,
rummages in it, brings out finally a nailfile, turns back front and
begins to file nails. Files for a time in silence, then the following
punctuated by filing.*] There floats up—into my thoughts—a
Mr. Shower—a Mr. and perhaps a Mrs. Shower—no—they are
holding hands—his fiancée then more likely—or just some—
loved one. [*Looks closer at nails.*] Very brittle today. [*Resumes
filing.*] Shower—Shower—does the name mean anything—to
you, Willie—evoke any reality, I mean—for you, Willie—don't
answer if you don't—feel up to it—you have done more—
than your bit—already—Shower—Shower. [*Inspects filed nails.*]
Bit more like it. [*Raises head, gazes front.*] Keep yourself nice,
Winnie, that's what I always say, come what may, keep yourself
nice. [*Pause. Resumes filing.*] Yes—Shower—Shower—[*stops
filing, raises head, gazes front, pause*]—or Cooker, perhaps I
should say Cooker. [*Turning a little towards Willie.*] Cooker,
Willie, does Cooker strike a chord? [*Pause. Turns a little further.
Louder.*] Cooker, Willie, does Cooker ring a bell, the name
Cooker? [*Pause. She cranes back to look at him. Pause.*] Oh really!
[*Pause.*] Have you no handkerchief, darling? [*Pause.*] Have you
no delicacy? [*Pause.*] Oh, Willie, you're not eating it! Spit it out,
dear, spit it out! [*Pause. Back front.*] Ah well, I suppose it's only
natural. [*Break in voice.*] Human. [*Pause. Do.*] What *is* one to do?
[*Head down. Do.*] All day long. [*Pause. Do.*] Day after day. [*Pause.
Head up. Smile. Calm.*] The old style! [*Smile off. Resumes nails.*]

No, done him. [*Passes on to next.*] Should have put on my glasses. [*Pause.*] Too late now. [*Finishes left hand, inspects it.*] Bit more human. [*Starts right hand. Following punctuated as before.*] Well anyway—this man Shower—or Cooker—no matter— and the woman—hand in hand—in the other hands bags— kind of big brown grips—standing there gaping at me—and at last this man Shower—or Cooker—ends in er anyway— stake my life on that—What's she doing? he says—What's the idea? he says—stuck up to her diddies in the bleeding ground—coarse fellow—What does it mean? he says—What's it meant to mean?—and so on—lot more stuff like that— usual drivel—Do you hear me? he says—I do, she says, God help me—What do you mean, he says, God help you? [*Stops filing, raises head, gazes front.*] And you, she says, what's the idea of you, she says, what are you meant to mean? It is because you're still on your two flat feet, with your old ditty full of tinned muck and changes of underwear, dragging me up and down this fornicating wilderness, coarse creature, fit mate— [*with sudden violence*]—let go of my hand and drop for God's sake, she says, drop! [*Pause. Resumes filing.*] Why doesn't he dig her out? he says—referring to you, my dear—What good is she to him like that?—What good is he to her like that?—and so on—usual tosh—Good! she says, have a heart for God's sake—Dig her out, he says, dig her out, no sense in her like that—Dig her out with what? she says—I'd dig her out with my bare hands, he says—must have been man and—wife. [*Files in silence.*] Next thing they're away—hand in hand—and the bags—dim—then gone—last human kind—to stray this way. [*Finishes right hand, inspects it, lays down file, gazes front.*] Strange thing, time like this, drift up into the mind. [*Pause.*] Strange? [*Pause.*] No, here all is strange. [*Pause.*] Thankful for it in any case. [*Voice breaks.*] Most thankful. [*Head down. Pause. Head up. Calm.*] Bow and raise the head, bow and raise, always that. [*Pause.*] And now? [*Long pause. Starts putting things back in *bag, toothbrush last. This operation, interrupted by pauses as indicated, punctuates following.*] It is perhaps a little soon—to make ready—for the night—[*stops tidying, head up, smile*]—the old style!—[*smile off, resumes tidying*]—and yet I do—make ready for the night—feeling it at hand—the bell for sleep— saying to myself—Winnie—it will not be long now, Winnie— until the bell for sleep. [*Stops tidying, head up.*] Sometimes I am wrong. [*Smile.*] But not often. [*Smile off.*] Sometimes all is over, for the day, all done, all said, all ready for the night, and the day not over, far from over, the night not ready, far, far from ready. [*Smile.*] But not often. [*Smile off.*] Yes, the bell for sleep, when I feel it at hand, and so make ready for the night— [*gesture*]—in this way, sometimes I am wrong—[*smile*]—but not often. [*Smile off. Resumes tidying.*] I used to think—I say I used to think—that all these things—put back into the bag— if too soon—put back too soon—could be taken out again—if necessary—if needed—and so on—indefinitely—back into the bag—back out of the bag—until the bell—went. [*Stops tidying, head up, smile.*] But no. [*Smile broader.*] No no. [*Smile off. Resumes tidying.*] I suppose this—might seem strange—this— what shall I say—this what I have said—yes—[*she takes up revolver*]—strange—[*she turns to put revolver in bag*]—were it not—[*about to put revolver in bag she arrests gesture and turns back front*]—were it not—[*she lays down revolver to her right, stops tidying, head up*]—that all seems strange. [*Pause.*] Most strange. [*Pause.*] Never any change. [*Pause.*] And more and more strange. [*Pause. She bends to mound again, takes up last object, i.e. toothbrush, and turns to put it in bag when her attention is drawn to disturbance from Willie. She cranes back and to her right to see. Pause.*] Weary of your hole, dear? [*Pause.*] Well I can understand that. [*Pause.*] Don't forget your straw. [*Pause.*] Not the crawler you were, poor darling. [*Pause.*] No, not the crawler I gave my heart to. [*Pause.*] The hands and knees, love, try the hands and knees. [*Pause.*] The knees! The knees! [*Pause.*] What a curse,

mobility! [*She follows with eyes his progress towards her behind mound, i.e. towards place he occupied at beginning of act.*] Another foot, Willie, and you're home. [*Pause as she observes last foot.*] Ah! [*Turns back front laboriously, rubs neck.*] Crick in my neck admiring you. [*Rubs neck.*] But it's worth it, well worth it. [*Turning slightly towards him.*] Do you know what I dream sometimes? [*Pause.*] What I dream sometimes, Willie. [*Pause.*] That you'll come round and live this side where I could see you. [*Pause. Back front.*] I'd be a different woman. [*Pause.*] Unrecognizable. [*Turning slightly towards him.*] Or just now and then, come round this side just every now and then and let me feast on you. [*Back front.*] But you can't, I know. [*Head down.*] I know. [*Pause. Head up.*] Well anyway—[*looks at toothbrush in her hand*]—can't be long now [*looks at brush*]—until the bell. [*Top back of Willie's head appears above slope. Winnie looks closer at brush.*] Fully guaranteed . . . [*head up*] . . . what's this it was? [*Willie's hand appears with handkerchief, spreads it on skull, disappears.*] Genuine pure . . . fully guaranteed . . . [*Willie's hand appears with boater, settles it on head, rakish angle, disappears*] . . . genuine pure . . . ah! hog's setae. [*Pause.*] What is a hog exactly? [*Pause. Turns slightly towards Willie.*] What exactly is a hog, Willie, do you know, I can't remember. [*Pause. Turning a little further, pleading.*] What *is* a hog, Willie, please!
[*Pause.*]

WILLIE   Castrated male swine. [*Happy expression appears on Winnie's face.*] Reared for slaughter.
[*Happy expression increases. Willie opens newspaper, hands invisible. Tops of yellow sheets appear on either side of his head. Winnie gazes before her with happy expression.*]

WINNIE   Oh this *is* a happy day! This will have been another happy day! [*Pause.*] After all. [*Pause.*] So far.
[*Pause. Happy expression off. Willie turns page. Pause. He turns another page. Pause.*]

WILLIE   Opening for smart youth.

[*Pause. Winnie takes off hat, turns to put it in bag, arrests gesture, turns back front. Smile.*]

WINNIE   No. [*Smile broader.*] No no. [*Smile off. Puts on hat again, gazes front, pause.*] And now? [*Pause.*] Sing. [*Pause.*] Sing your song, Winnie. [*Pause.*] No? [*Pause.*] Then pray. [*Pause.*] Pray your prayer, Winnie.

[*Pause. Willie turns page. Pause.*]

WILLIE   Wanted bright boy.

[*Pause. Winnie gazes before her. Willie turns page. Pause. Newspaper disappears. Long pause.*]

WINNIE   Pray your old prayer, Winnie.

[*Long pause.*]

Curtain

ACT II

Scene as before.

Winnie imbedded up to neck, hat on head, eyes closed. Her head, which she can no longer turn, nor bow, nor raise, faces front motionless throughout act. Movements of eyes as indicated.

Bag and parasol as before. Revolver conspicuous to her right on mound.

Long pause.

Bell rings loudly. She opens eyes at once. Bell stops. She gazes front. Long pause.

WINNIE   Hail, holy light. [*Long pause. She closes her eyes. Bell rings loudly. She opens eyes at once. Bell stops. She gazes front. Long smile. Smile off. Long pause.*] Someone is looking at me still. [*Pause.*] Caring for me still. [*Pause.*] That is what I find so wonderful. [*Pause.*] Eyes on my eyes. [*Pause.*] What is that unforgettable line? [*Pause. Eyes right.*] Willie. [*Pause. Louder.*] Willie. [*Pause. Eyes front.*] May one still speak of time? [*Pause.*] Say it is a long time now, Willie, since I saw you. [*Pause.*] Since I heard you. [*Pause.*] May one? [*Pause.*] One does. [*Smile.*] The old style! [*Smile off.*] There is so little one can speak of. [*Pause.*] One speaks of it all. [*Pause.*] All one can. [*Pause.*] I used to think ... [*pause*] ... I say I used to think that I would learn to talk alone. [*Pause.*] By that I mean to myself, the wilderness. [*Smile.*] But no. [*Smile broader.*] No no. [*Smile off.*] Ergo you are there. [*Pause.*] Oh no doubt you are dead, like the others, no doubt you have died, or gone away and left me, like the others, it doesn't matter, you are there. [*Pause. Eyes left.*] The bag too is there, the same as ever, I can see it. [*Pause. Eyes right. Louder.*] The bag is there, Willie, as good as ever, the one you gave me that day . . . to go to market. [*Pause. Eyes front.*] That day. [*Pause.*] What day? [*Pause.*] I used to pray. [*Pause.*] I say I used to pray. [*Pause.*] Yes, I must confess I did. [*Smile.*] Not now. [*Smile broader.*] No no. [*Smile off. Pause.*] Then . . . now . . . what difficulties here, for the mind. [*Pause.*] To have been always what I am—and so changed from what I was. [*Pause.*] I am the one, I say the one, then the other. [*Pause.*] Now the one, then the other. [*Pause.*] There is so little one can say, one says it all. [*Pause.*] All one can. [*Pause.*] And no truth in it anywhere. [*Pause.*] My arms. [*Pause.*] My breasts. [*Pause.*] What arms? [*Pause.*] What breasts? [*Pause.*] Willie. [*Pause.*] What Willie? [*Sudden vehement affirmation.*] My Willie! [*Eyes right, calling.*] Willie! [*Pause. Louder.*] Willie! [*Pause. Eyes front.*] Ah well, not to know, not to know for sure, great mercy, all I ask. [*Pause.*] Ah yes . . . then . . . now . . . beechen green . . . this . . . Charlie . . . kisses . . . this . . . all that . . . deep trouble for the mind. [*Pause.*] But it does not trouble mine. [*Smile.*] Not now. [*Smile broader.*] No no. [*Smile off. Long pause. She closes eyes. Bell rings loudly. She opens eyes. Pause.*] Eyes float up that seem to close in peace . . . to see . . . in peace. [*Pause.*] Not mine. [*Smile.*] Not now. [*Smile broader.*] No no. [*Smile off. Long pause.*] Willie. [*Pause.*] Do you think the earth has lost its atmosphere, Willie? [*Pause.*] Do you, Willie? [*Pause.*] You have no opinion? [*Pause.*] Well that is like you, you never had any opinion about anything. [*Pause.*] It's understandable. [*Pause.*] Most. [*Pause.*] The earthball. [*Pause.*] I sometimes wonder. [*Pause.*] Perhaps not quite all. [*Pause.*] There always remains something. [*Pause.*] Of everything. [*Pause.*] Some remains. [*Pause.*] If the mind were

to go. [*Pause.*] It won't of course. [*Pause.*] Not quite. [*Pause.*] Not
mine. [*Smile.*] Not now. [*Smile broader.*] No no. [*Smile off. Long
pause.*] It might be the eternal cold. [*Pause.*] Everlasting
perishing cold. [*Pause.*] Just chance, I take it, happy chance.
[*Pause.*] Oh yes, great mercies, great mercies. [*Pause.*] And now?
[*Long pause.*] The face. [*Pause.*] The nose. [*She squints down.*] I
can see it . . . [*squinting down*] . . . the tip . . . the nostrils . . .
breath of life . . . that curve you so admired [*pouts*] . . . a hint of
lip . . . [*pouts again*] . . . if I pout them out . . . [*sticks out tongue*]
. . . the tongue of course . . . you so admired . . . if I stick it
out . . . [*sticks it out again*] . . . the tip . . . [*eyes up*] . . . suspicion
of brow . . . eyebrow . . . imagination possibly . . . [*eyes left*] . . .
cheek . . . no . . . [*eyes right*] . . . no . . . [*distends cheeks*] . . . even if
I puff them out . . . [*eyes left, distends cheeks again*] . . . no . . . no
damask. [*Eyes front.*] That is all. [*Pause.*] The bag of course . . .
[*eyes left*] . . . a little blurred perhaps . . . but the bag. [*Eyes front.
Offhand.*] The earth of course and sky. [*Eyes right.*] The
sunshade you gave me . . . that day . . . [*pause*] . . . that day . . .
the lake . . . the reeds. [*Eyes front. Pause.*] What day? [*Pause.*]
What reeds? [*Long pause. Eyes close. Bell rings loudly. Eyes open.
Pause. Eyes right.*] Brownie of course. [*Pause.*] You remember
Brownie, Willie, I can see him. [*Pause.*] Brownie is there, Willie,
beside me. [*Pause. Loud.*] Brownie is there, Willie. [*Pause. Eyes
front.*] That is all. [*Pause.*] What would I do without them?
[*Pause.*] What would I do without them, when words fail?
[*Pause.*] Gaze before me, with compressed lips. [*Long pause
while she does so.*] I cannot. [*Pause.*] Ah yes, great mercies, great
mercies. [*Long pause. Low.*] Sometimes I hear sounds. [*Listening
expression. Normal voice.*] But not often. [*Pause.*] They are a boon,
sounds are a boon, they help me . . . through the day. [*Smile.*]
The old style! [*Smile off.*] Yes, those are happy days, when there
are sounds. [*Pause.*] When I hear sounds. [*Pause.*] I used to
think . . . [*pause*] . . . I say I used to think they were in my head.
[*Smile.*] But no. [*Smile broader.*] No no. [*Smile off.*] That was just

logic. [*Pause.*] Reason. [*Pause.*] I have not lost my reason. [*Pause.*] Not yet. [*Pause.*] Not all. [*Pause.*] Some remains. [*Pause.*] Sounds. [*Pause.*] Like little . . . sunderings, little falls . . . apart. [*Pause. Low.*] It's things, Willie. [*Pause. Normal voice.*] In the bag, outside the bag. [*Pause.*] Ah yes, things have their life, that is what I always say, *things* have a life. [*Pause.*] Take my looking-glass, it doesn't need me. [*Pause.*] The bell. [*Pause.*] It hurts like a knife. [*Pause.*] A gouge. [*Pause.*] One cannot ignore it. [*Pause.*] How often . . . [*pause*] . . . I say how often I have said, Ignore it, Winnie, ignore the bell, pay no heed, just sleep and wake, sleep and wake, as you please, open and close the eyes, as you please, or in the way you find most helpful. [*Pause.*] Open and close the eyes, Winnie, open and close, always that. [*Pause.*] But no. [*Smile.*] Not now. [*Smile broader.*] No no. [*Smile off. Pause.*] What now? [*Pause.*] What now, Willie? [*Long pause.*] There is my story of course, when all else fails. [*Pause.*] A life. [*Smile.*] A long life. [*Smile off.*] Beginning in the womb, where life used to begin, Mildred has memories, she will have memories, of the womb, before she dies, the mother's womb. [*Pause.*] She is now four or five already and has recently been given a big waxen dolly. [*Pause.*] Fully clothed, complete outfit. [*Pause.*] Shoes, socks, undies, complete set, frilly frock, gloves. [*Pause.*] White mesh. [*Pause.*] A little white straw hat with a chin elastic. [*Pause.*] Pearly necklet. [*Pause.*] A little picture-book with legends in real print to go under her arm when she takes her walk. [*Pause.*] China blue eyes that open and shut. [*Pause. Narrative.*] The sun was not well up when Milly rose, descended the steep . . . [*pause*] . . . slipped on her nightgown, descended all alone the steep wooden stairs, backwards on all fours, though she had been forbidden to do so, entered the . . . [*pause*] . . . tiptoed down the silent passage, entered the nursery and began to undress Dolly. [*Pause.*] Crept under the table and began to undress Dolly. [*Pause.*] Scolding her . . . the while. [*Pause.*] Suddenly a mouse— [*Long pause.*] Gently,

Winnie. [*Long pause. Calling.*] Willie! [*Pause. Louder.*] Willie!
[*Pause. Mild reproach.*] I sometimes find your attitude a little
strange, Willie, all this time, it is not like you to be wantonly
cruel. [*Pause.*] Strange? [*Pause.*] No. [*Smile.*] Not here. [*Smile
broader.*] Not now. [*Smile off.*] And yet . . . [*Suddenly anxious.*] I do
hope nothing is amiss. [*Eyes right, loud.*] Is all well, dear?
[*Pause. Eyes front. To herself.*] God grant he did not go in head
foremost! [*Eyes right, loud.*] You're not stuck, Willie? [*Pause. Do.*]
You're not jammed, Willie? [*Eyes front, distressed.*] Perhaps he is
crying out for help all this time and I do not hear him! [*Pause.*]
I do of course hear cries. [*Pause.*] But they are in my head
surely. [*Pause.*] Is it possible that . . . [*Pause. With finality.*] No no,
my head was always full of cries. [*Pause.*] Faint confused cries.
[*Pause.*] They come. [*Pause.*] Then go. [*Pause.*] As on a wind.
[*Pause.*] That is what I find so wonderful. [*Pause.*] They cease.
[*Pause.*] Ah yes, great mercies, great mercies. [*Pause.*] The day is
now well advanced. [*Smile. Smile off.*] And yet it is perhaps a
little soon for my song. [*Pause.*] To sing too soon is fatal, I
always find. [*Pause.*] On the other hand it is possible to leave it
too late. [*Pause.*] The bell goes for sleep and one has not sung.
[*Pause.*] The whole day has flown—[*smile, smile off*]—flown by,
quite by, and no song of any class, kind or description. [*Pause.*]
There is a problem here. [*Pause.*] One cannot sing . . . just like
that, no. [*Pause.*] It bubbles up, for some unknown reason, the
time is ill chosen, one chokes it back. [*Pause.*] One says, Now is
the time, it is now or never, and one cannot. [*Pause.*] Simply
cannot sing. [*Pause.*] Not a note. [*Pause.*] Another thing, Willie,
while we are on this subject. [*Pause.*] The sadness after song.
[*Pause.*] Have you run across that, Willie? [*Pause.*] In the course
of your experience. [*Pause.*] No? [*Pause.*] Sadness after intimate
sexual intercourse one is familiar with of course. [*Pause.*] You
would concur with Aristotle there, Willie, I fancy. [*Pause.*] Yes,
that one knows and is prepared to face. [*Pause.*] But after
song . . . [*Pause.*] It does not last of course. [*Pause.*] That is what

I find so wonderful. [*Pause.*] It wears away. [*Pause.*] What are those exquisite lines? [*Pause.*] Go forget me why should something o'er that something shadow fling . . . go forget me . . . why should sorrow . . . brightly smile . . . go forget me . . . never hear me . . . sweetly smile . . . brightly sing . . . [*Pause. With a sigh.*] One loses one's classics. [*Pause.*] Oh not all. [*Pause.*] A part. [*Pause.*] A part remains. [*Pause.*] That is what I find so wonderful, a part remains, of one's classics, to help one through the day. [*Pause.*] Oh yes, many mercies, many mercies. [*Pause.*] And now? [*Pause.*] And now, Willie? [*Long pause.*] I call to the eye of the mind . . . Mr. Shower—or Cooker. [*She closes her eyes. Bell rings loudly. She opens her eyes. Pause.*] Hand in hand, in the other hands bags. [*Pause.*] Getting on . . . in life. [*Pause.*] No longer young, not yet old. [*Pause.*] Standing there gaping at me. [*Pause.*] Can't have been a bad bosom, he says, in its day. [*Pause.*] Seen worse shoulders, he says, in my time. [*Pause.*] Does she feel her legs? he says. [*Pause.*] Is there any life in her legs? he says [*Pause.*] Has she anything on underneath? he says. [*Pause.*] Ask her, he says, I'm shy. [*Pause.*] Ask her what? she says. [*Pause.*] Is there any life in her legs. [*Pause.*] Has she anything on underneath. [*Pause.*] Ask her yourself, she says. [*Pause. With sudden violence.*] Let go of me for Christ sake and drop! [*Pause. Do.*] Drop dead! [*Smile.*] But no. [*Smile broader.*] No no. [*Smile off.*] I watch them recede. [*Pause.*] Hand in hand— and the bags. [*Pause.*] Dim. [*Pause.*] Then gone. [*Pause.*] Last human kind—to stray this way. [*Pause.*] Up to date. [*Pause.*] And now? [*Pause. Low.*] Help. [*Pause. Do.*] Help, Willie. [*Pause. Do.*] No? [*Long pause. Narrative.*] Suddenly a mouse . . . [*Pause.*] Suddenly a mouse ran up her little thigh and Mildred, dropping Dolly in her fright, began to scream—[*Winnie gives a sudden piercing scream*]—and screamed and screamed—[*Winnie screams twice*]—screamed and screamed and screamed and screamed till all came running, in their night attire, papa, mamma, Bibby and . . . old Annie, to see what was the

matter ... [*pause*] ... what on earth could possibly be the
matter. [*Pause.*] Too late. [*Pause.*] Too late. [*Long pause. Just
audible.*] Willie. [*Pause. Normal voice.*] Ah well, not long now,
Winnie, can't be long now, until the bell for sleep. [*Pause.*]
Then you may close your eyes, then you *must* close your
eyes—and keep them closed. [*Pause.*] Why say that again?
[*Pause.*] I used to think ... [*pause*] ... I say I used to think there
was no difference between one fraction of a second and the
next. [*Pause.*] I used to say ... [*pause*] ... I say I used to say,
Winnie, you are changeless, there is never any difference
between one fraction of a second and the next. [*Pause.*] Why
bring that up again? [*Pause.*] There is so little one can bring
up, one brings up all. [*Pause.*] All one can. [*Pause.*] My neck is
hurting me. [*Pause. With sudden violence.*] My neck is hurting
me! [*Pause.*] Ah that's better. [*With mild irritation.*] Everything
within reason. [*Long pause.*] I can do no more. [*Pause.*] Say no
more. [*Pause.*] But I must say more. [*Pause.*] Problem here.
[*Pause.*] No, something must move, in the world, I can't any
more. [*Pause.*] A zephyr. [*Pause.*] A breath. [*Pause.*] What are
those immortal lines? [*Pause.*] It might be the eternal dark.
[*Pause.*] Black night without end. [*Pause.*] Just chance, I take it,
happy chance. [*Pause.*] Oh yes, abounding mercies. [*Long pause.*]
And now? [*Pause.*] And now, Willie? [*Long pause.*] That day.
[*Pause.*] The pink fizz. [*Pause.*] The flute glasses. [*Pause.*] The
last guest gone. [*Pause.*] The last bumper with the bodies
nearly touching. [*Pause.*] The look. [*Long pause.*] What day?
[*Long pause.*] What look? [*Long pause.*] I hear cries. [*Pause.*] Sing.
[*Pause.*] Sing your old song, Winnie.
[*Long pause. Suddenly alert expression. Eyes switch right. Willie's
head appears to her right round corner of mound. He is on all fours,
dressed to kill—top hat, morning coat, striped trousers, etc., white
gloves in hand. Very long bushy white Battle of Britain moustache.
He halts, gazes front, smooths moustache. He emerges completely
from behind mound, turns to his left, halts, looks up at Winnie. He*

*advances on all fours towards centre, halts, turns head front, gazes
front, strokes moustache, straightens tie, adjusts hat, advances a little
further, halts, takes off hat and looks up at Winnie. He is now not far
from centre and within her field of vision. Unable to sustain effort of
looking up he sinks head to ground.*]

WINNIE   [*mondaine*] Well this is an unexpected pleasure! [*Pause.*] Reminds
me of the day you came whining for my hand. [*Pause.*] I
worship you, Winnie, be mine. [*He looks up.*] Life a mockery
without Win. [*She goes off into a giggle.*] What a get up, you do
look a sight! [*Giggles.*] Where are the flowers? [*Pause.*] That
smile today. [*Willie sinks head.*] What's that on your neck, an
anthrax? [*Pause.*] Want to watch that, Willie, before it gets a
hold on you. [*Pause.*] Where were you all this time? [*Pause.*]
What were you doing all this time? [*Pause.*] Changing? [*Pause.*]
Did you not hear me screaming for you? [*Pause.*] Did you get
stuck in your hole? [*Pause. He looks up.*] That's right, Willie,
look at me. [*Pause.*] Feast your old eyes, Willie. [*Pause.*] Does
anything remain? [*Pause.*] Any remains? [*Pause.*] No? [*Pause.*] I
haven't been able to look after it, you know. [*He sinks his head.*]
You are still recognizable, in a way. [*Pause.*] Are you thinking of
coming to live this side now . . . for a bit maybe? [*Pause.*] No?
[*Pause.*] Just a brief call? [*Pause.*] Have you gone deaf, Willie?
[*Pause.*] Dumb? [*Pause.*] Oh I know you were never one to talk, I
worship you Winnie be mine and then nothing from that day
forth only titbits from Reynolds' News. [*Eyes front. Pause.*] Ah
well, what matter, that's what I always say, it will have been a
happy day, after all, another happy day. [*Pause.*] Not long now,
Winnie. [*Pause.*] I hear cries. [*Pause.*] Do you ever hear cries,
Willie? [*Pause.*] No? [*Eyes back on Willie.*] Willie. [*Pause.*] Look at
me again, Willie. [*Pause.*] Once more, Willie. [*He looks up.
Happily.*] Ah! [*Pause. Shocked.*] What ails you, Willie, I never saw
such an expression! [*Pause.*] Put on your hat, dear, it's the sun,
don't stand on ceremony, I won't mind. [*He drops hat and gloves*

and starts to crawl up mound towards her. Gleeful.] Oh I say, this is
terrific! [*He halts, clinging to mound with one hand, reaching up
with the other.*] Come on, dear, put a bit of jizz into it, I'll cheer
you on. [*Pause.*] Is it me you're after, Willie ... or is it
something else? [*Pause.*] Do you want to touch my face ...
again? [*Pause.*] Is it a kiss you're after, Willie ... or is it
something else? [*Pause.*] There was a time when I could have
given you a hand. [*Pause.*] And then a time before that again
when I did give you a hand. [*Pause.*] You were always in dire
need of a hand, Willie. [*He slithers back to foot of mound and lies
with face to ground.*] Brrum! [*Pause. He rises to hands and knees,
raises his face towards her.*] Have another go, Willie, I'll cheer
you on. [*Pause.*] Don't look at me like that! [*Pause. Vehement.*]
Don't look at me like that! [*Pause. Low.*] Have you gone off your
head, Willie? [*Pause. Do.*] Out of your poor old wits, Willie?
[*Pause.*]

WILLIE [*just audible*] Win.

[*Pause. Winnie's eyes front. Happy expression appears, grows.*]

WINNIE Win! [*Pause.*] Oh this *is* a happy day, this will have been another
happy day! [*Pause.*] After all. [*Pause.*] So far.

[*Pause. She hums tentatively beginning of song, then sings softly,
musical-box tune.*]

> Though I say not
> What I may not
> Let you hear,
> Yet the swaying
> Dance is saying,
> Love me dear!
> Every touch of fingers
> Tells me what I know,
> Says for you,
> It's true, it's true,
> You love me so!

[*Pause. Happy expression off. She closes her eyes. Bell rings loudly. She opens her eyes. She smiles, gazing front. She turns her eyes, smiling, to Willie, still on his hands and knees looking up at her. Smile off. They look at each other. Long pause.*]

Curtain

ROUGH FOR RADIO I

HE [*gloomily*] Madam.

SHE Are you all right? [*Pause.*] You asked me to come.

HE I ask no one to come here.

SHE You suffered me to come.

HE I meet my debts.
[*Pause.*]

SHE I have come to listen.

HE When you please.
[*Pause.*]

SHE May I squat on this hassock? [*Pause.*] Thank you. [*Pause.*] May we have a little heat?

HE No, madam.
[*Pause.*]

SHE Is it true the music goes on all the time?

HE Yes.

SHE Without cease?

HE Without cease.

SHE It's unthinkable! [*Pause.*] And the words too? All the time too?

HE All the time.

SHE Without cease?

HE Yes.

SHE It's unimaginable. [*Pause.*] So you are here all the time?

HE   Without cease.

[*Pause.*]

SHE   How troubled you look! [*Pause.*] May one see them?

HE   No, madam.

SHE   I may not go and see them?

HE   No, madam.

[*Pause.*]

SHE   May we have a little light?

HE   No, madam.

[*Pause.*]

SHE   How cold you are! [*Pause.*] Are these the two knobs?

HE   Yes.

SHE   Just push? [*Pause.*] Is it live? [*Pause.*] I ask you is it live.

HE   No, you must twist. [*Pause.*] To the right.

[*Click.*]

MUSIC [*faint*] . . . .

[*Silence.*]

SHE   [*astonished*] But there are more than one!

HE   Yes.

SHE   How many?

[*Pause.*]

HE   To the right, madam, to the right.

[*Click.*]

VOICE [*faint*] . . . .

SHE   [*with voice*] Louder!

VOICE [*no louder*] . . . .

[*Silence.*]

SHE   [*astonished*] But he is alone!

HE   Yes.

SHE   All alone?

HE   When one is alone one is all alone.

[*Pause.*]

SHE   What is it like together?

[*Pause.*]

HE   To the right, madam.

     [*Click.*]

MUSIC   [*faint, brief*] ....

MUSIC ⎫

VOICE ⎭ [*together*] ....

     [*Silence.*]

SHE   They are not together?

HE   No.

SHE   They cannot see each other?

HE   No.

SHE   Hear each other?

HE   No.

SHE   It's inconceivable!

     [*Pause.*]

HE   To the right, madam.

     [*Click.*]

VOICE   [*faint*] ....

SHE   [*with voice*] Louder!

VOICE   [*no louder*] ....

     [*Silence.*]

SHE   And—[*faint stress*]—*you* like that?

HE   It is a need.

SHE   A need? *That* a need?

HE   It has become a need. [*Pause.*] To the right, madam.

     [*Click.*]

MUSIC   [*faint*] ....

SHE   [*with music*] Louder!

MUSIC   [*no louder*] ....

     [*Silence.*]

SHE   That too? [*Pause.*] That a need too?

HE   It has become a need, madam.

SHE   Are they in the same ... situation?

     [*Pause.*]

HE   I don't understand.

SHE   Are they . . . subject to the same . . . conditions?

HE   Yes, madam.

SHE   For instance? [*Pause.*] For instance?

HE   One cannot describe them, madam.

     [*Pause.*]

SHE   Well, I'm obliged to you.

HE   Allow me, this way.

     [*Pause.*]

SHE   [*a little off*] Is that a Turkoman?

HE   [*ditto*] Allow me.

SHE   [*a little further off*] How troubled you look! [*Pause.*] Well, I'll leave
     you. [*Pause.*] To your needs.

HE   [*ditto*] Goodbye, madam. [*Pause.*] To the right, madam, that's the
     garbage—[*faint stress*]—the *house* garbage. [*Pause.*] Goodbye,
     madam.

     [*Long pause. Sound of curtains violently drawn, first one, then the
     other, clatter of the heavy rings along the rods. Pause. Faint ping—as
     sometimes happens—of telephone receiver raised from cradle. Faint
     sound of dialling. Pause.*] Hello . . . Miss . . . is the doctor . . . ah . . .
     yes . . . he to call me . . . Macgillycuddy . . . Mac-gilly-cuddy . . .
     right . . . he'll know . . . and Miss . . . Miss! . . . urgent . . . yes! . . .
     [*shrill*] . . . most urgent!

     [*Pause. Receiver put down with same faint ping. Pause. Click.*]

MUSIC   [*faint*] . . . .

HE   [*with music*] Good God!

MUSIC   [*faint*] . . . .

     [*Silence. Pause. Click.*]

VOICE   [*faint*] . . . .

HE   [*with voice, shrill*] Come on! Come on!

VOICE   [*faint*] . . . .

     [*Silence.*]

HE   [*low*] What'll I do? [*Pause. Faint ping of receiver raised again. Faint
     dialling. Pause.*] Hello . . . Miss . . . Macgillycuddy . . . Mac-gilly-
     cuddy . . . right . . . I'm sorry but . . . ah . . . yes . . . of course . . .

can't reach him ... no idea ... understand ... right ...
immediately ... the moment he gets back ... what? ...
[*shrill*] ... yes! ... I told you so! ... most urgent! ... most
urgent! ... [*Pause. Low.*] Slut!
[*Sound of receiver put down violently. Pause. Click.*]

MUSIC   [*faint, brief*] ....

[*Silence. Click.*]

VOICE   [*faint, brief*]

HE   [*with voice, shrill*] It's crazy! Like one!

MUSIC ⎫
VOICE ⎬ [*together*] ....
       ⎭

[*Telephone rings. Receiver raised immediately, not more than a second's ring.*]

HE   [*with music and voice*] Yes ... wait ... [*Music and voice silent. Very
agitated.*] Yes ... yes ... no matter ... what the trouble is? ...
they're ending ... ENDING ... this morning ... what? ...
no! ... no question! ... ENDING I tell you ... nothing what? ...
to be done? ... I know there's nothing to be done ... what? ...
no! ... it's me ... ME ... what? I tell you they're ending ...
ENDING ... I can't stay like that after ... who? ... but she's left
me ... ah for God's sake ... haven't they all left me? ... did you
not know that? ... all left me ... sure? ... of course I'm sure ...
what? ... in an hour? ... not before? ... wait ... [*low*] ... there's
more ... they're together ... TOGETHER ... yes ... I don't
know ... like ... [*hesitation*] ... one ... the breathing ... I don't
know ... [*vehement*] ... no! ... never! ... meet? ... how could
they meet? ... what? ... what are all alike? ... last what? ...
gasps? ... wait ... don't go yet ... wait! ... [*Pause. Sound of
receiver put down violently. Low.*] Swine!
[*Pause. Click.*]

MUSIC   [*failing*] ....

MUSIC ⎫
VOICE ⎬ [*together, failing*] ....
       ⎭

[*Telephone rings. Receiver immediately raised.*]

HE   [*with music and voice*] Miss . . . what? . . . [*music and voice silent*] . . . a
confinement? . . . [*long pause*] . . . two confinements? . . . [*long
pause*] . . . one what? . . . what? breech? . . . what? . . . [*long
pause*] . . . tomorrow noon? . . .
[*Long pause. Faint ping as receiver put gently down. Long pause.
Click.*]

MUSIC   [*brief, failing*] . . . .

MUSIC ⎫
           ⎬ [*together, ending, breaking off together, resuming together more and
VOICE ⎭   more feebly*] . . . .

[*Silence. Long pause.*]

HE   [*whisper*] Tomorrow . . . noon . . .

ROUGH FOR RADIO II

Animator
Stenographer
Fox
Dick (mute)

A   Ready, miss?

s   And waiting, sir.

A   Fresh pad, spare pencils?

s   The lot, sir.

A   Good shape?

s   Tiptop, sir.

A   And you, Dick, on your toes? [*Swish of bull's pizzle. Admiringly.*] Wow! Let's hear it land. [*Swish and formidable thud.*] Good. Off with his hood. [*Pause.*] Ravishing face, ravishing! Is it not, miss?

s   Too true, sir. We know it by heart and yet the pang is ever new.

A   The gag. [*Pause.*] The blind. [*Pause.*] The plugs. [*Pause.*] Good. [*He thumps on his desk with a cylindrical ruler.*] Fox, open your eyes, readjust them to the light of day and look about you. [*Pause.*] You see, the same old team. I hope—

s   [*aflutter*] Oh!

A   What is it, miss? Vermin in the lingerie?

s   He smiled at me!

A   Good omen. [*Faint hope.*] Not the first time by any chance?

s   Heavens no, sir, what an idea!

A   [*disappointed*] I might have known. [*Pause.*] And yet it still affects you?

s   Why yes, sir, it is so sudden! So radiant! So fleeting!

A   You note it?

s   Oh no, sir, the words alone. [*Pause.*] Should one note the play of feature too?

a   I don't know, miss. Depending perhaps.

s   Me you know—

a   [*trenchant*] Leave it for the moment. [*Thump with ruler.*] Fox, I hope you have had a refreshing night and will be better inspired today than heretofore. Miss.

s   Sir.

a   Let us hear again the report on yesterday's results, it has somewhat slipped my memory.

s   [*reading*] "We the undersigned, assembled under—"

a   Skip.

s   [*reading*] ". . . note yet again with pain that these dicta—"

a   Dicta! [*Pause.*] Read on.

s   ". . . with pain that these dicta, like all those communicated to date and by reason of the same deficiencies, are totally inacceptable. The second half in particular is of such—"

a   Skip.

s   ". . . outlook quite hopeless were it not for our conviction—"

a   Skip. [*Pause.*] Well?

s   That is all, sir.

a   . . . same deficiencies . . . totally inacceptable . . . outlook quite hopeless . . . [*Disgusted.*] Well! [*Pause.*] Well!

s   That is all, sir. Unless I am to read the exhortations.

a   Read them.

s   ". . . instantly renew our standing exhortations, namely:

    1. Kindly to refrain from recording mere animal cries, they serve only to indispose us.

    2. Kindly to provide a strictly literal transcript, the meanest syllable has, or may have, its importance.

    3. Kindly to ensure full neutralization of the subject when not in session, especially with regard to the gag, its permanence and good repair. Thus rigid enforcement of the tube-feed, be it per buccam or be it on the other hand per rectum, is *absolutely*"—one word

underlined—"essential. The least word let fall in solitude and thereby in danger, as Mauthner has shown, of being no longer needed, *may be it*"—three words underlined.

"4. Kindly—"

A Enough! [*Sickened.*] Well! [*Pause.*] Well!

S It is past two, sir.

A [*roused from his prostration*] It is what?

S Past two, sir.

A [*roughly*] Then what are you waiting for? [*Pause. Gently.*] Forgive me, miss, forgive me, my cup is full. [*Pause.*] Forgive me!

S [*coldly*] Shall I open with yesterday's close?

A If you would be so good.

S [*reading*] "When I had done soaping the mole, thoroughly rinsing and drying before the embers, what next only out again in the blizzard and put him back in his chamber with his weight of grubs, at that instant his little heart was beating still I swear, ah my God my God." [*She strikes with her pencil on her desk.*] "My God."
[*Pause.*]

A Unbelievable! And there he jibbed, if I remember aright.

S Yes, sir, he would say no more.

A Dick functioned?

S Let me see . . . Yes, twice.
[*Pause.*]

A Does not the glare incommode you, miss, what if we should let down the blind?

S Thank you, sir, not on my account, it can never be too warm, never too bright, for me. But, with your permission, I shall shed my overall.

A [*with alacrity*] Please do, miss, please do. [*Pause.*] Staggering! Staggering! Ah were I but . . . forty years younger!

S [*rereading*] "Ah my God my God." [*Blow with pencil.*] "My God."

A Crabbed youth! No pity! [*Thump with ruler.*] Do you mark me? On! [*Silence.*] Dick! [*Swish and thud of pizzle on flesh. Faint cry from Fox.*] Off record, miss, remember?

S Drat it! Where's that eraser?

A Erase, miss, erase, we're in trouble enough already. [*Ruler.*] On! [*Silence.*] Dick!

F Ah yes, that for sure, live I did, no denying, all stones all sides—

A One moment.

F —walls no further—

A [*ruler*] Silence! Dick! [*Silence. Musing.*] Live I did . . . [*Pause.*] Has he used that turn before, miss?

S To what turn do you allude, sir?

A Live I did.

S Oh yes, sir, it's a notion crops up now and then. Perhaps not in those precise terms, so far, that I could not say offhand. But allusions to a life, though not common, are not rare.

A His own life?

S Yes, sir, a life all his own.

A [*disappointed*] I might have known. [*Pause.*] What a memory—mine! [*Pause.*] Have you read the Purgatory, miss, of the divine Florentine?

S Alas no, sir. I have merely flipped through the Inferno.

A [*incredulous*] Not read the Purgatory?

S Alas no, sir.

A There all sigh, I was, I was. It's like a knell. Strange, is it not?

S In what sense, sir?

A Why, one would rather have expected, I shall be. No?

S [*with tender condescension*] The creatures! [*Pause.*] It is getting on for three, sir.

A [*sigh*] Good. Where were we?

S ". . . walls no further—"

A Before, that, miss, the house is not on fire.

S ". . . live I did, no denying, all stones all sides"—inaudible—"walls—"

A [*ruler*] On! [*Silence.*] Dick!

S Sir.

A [*impatiently*] What is it, miss, can't you see that old time is aflying?

S I was going to suggest a touch of kindness, sir, perhaps just a hint of kindness.

A So soon? And then? [*Firmly.*] No, miss, I appreciate your sentiment. But
   I have my method. Shall I remind you of it? [*Pause. Pleading.*] Don't
   say no! [*Pause.*] Oh you are an angel! You may sit, Dick. [*Pause.*] In a
   word, REDUCE the pressure instead of increasing it. [*Lyrical.*] Caress,
   fount of resipescence! [*Calmer.*] Dick, if you would. [*Swish and thud of
   pizzle on flesh. Faint cry from Fox.*] Careful, miss.

S Have no fear, sir.

A [*ruler*] . . . walls . . . walls what?

S "no further," sir.

A Right. [*Ruler.*] . . . walls no further . . . [*Ruler.*] On! [*Silence.*] Dick!

F That for sure, no further, and there gaze, all the way up, all the way
   down, slow gaze, age upon age, up again, down again, little lichens of
   my own span, living dead in the stones, and there took to the
   tunnels. [*Silence. Ruler.*] Oceans too, that too, no denying, I drew near
   down the tunnels, blue above, blue ahead, that for sure, and there
   too, no further, ways end, all ends and farewell, farewell and fall,
   farewell seasons, till I fare again. [*Silence. Ruler.*] Farewell.
   [*Silence. Ruler. Pause.*]

A Dick!

F That for sure, no denying, no further, down in Spring, up in Fall, or
   inverse, such summers missed, such winters.
   [*Pause.*]

A Nice! Nicely put! Such summers missed! So sibilant! Don't you agree,
   miss?

F }
    [*together*]   Ah that for sure—
S }   Oh me you know—

A Hsst!

F —fatigue, what fatigue, my brother inside me, my old twin, ah to be he
   and he—but no, no no. [*Pause.*] No no. [*Silence. Ruler.*] Me get up, me
   go on, what a hope, it was he, for hunger. Have yourself opened,
   Maud would say, opened up, it's nothing, I'll give him suck if he's
   still alive, ah but no, no no. [*Pause.*] No no.
   [*Silence.*]

A   [*discouraged*] Ah dear.

S   He is weeping, sir, shall I note it?

A   I really do not know what to advise, miss.

S   Inasmuch as ... how shall I say? ... human trait ... can one say in English?

A   I have never come across it, miss, but no doubt.

F   Scrabble scrabble—

A   Silence! [*Pause.*] No holding him!

S   As such ... I feel ... perhaps ... at a pinch ...
    [*Pause.*]

A   Are you familiar with the works of Sterne, miss?

S   Alas no, sir.

A   I may be quite wrong, but I seem to remember, there somewhere, a tear an angel comes to catch as it falls. Yes, I seem to remember ... admittedly he was grandchild to an archbishop. [*Half rueful, half complacent.*] Ah these old spectres from the days of book reviewing, they lie in wait for one at every turn. [*Pause. Suddenly decided.*] Note it, miss, note it, and come what may. As well as for a sheep ... [*Pause.*] Who is this woman ... what's the name?

S   Maud. I don't know, sir, no previous mention of her has been made.

A   [*excited*] Are you sure?

S   Positive, sir. You see, my nanny was a Maud, so that the name would have struck me, had it been pronounced.
    [*Pause.*]

A   I may be quite wrong, but I somehow have the feeling this is the first time—oh I know it's a far call!—that he has actually ... *named* anyone. No?

S   That may well be, sir. To make sure I would have to check through from the beginning. That would take time.

A   Kith and kin?

S   Never a word, sir. I have been struck by it. Mine play such a part, in my life!

A   And of a sudden, in the same sentence, a woman, with Christian name to boot, and a brother. I ask you!

[*Pause.*]

s   That twin, sir . . .

A   I know, not very convincing.

s   [*scandalized*] But it's quite simply impossible! Inside him! *Him!*

A   No no, such things happen, such things happen. Nature, you know . . .
     [*Faint laugh.*] Fortunately. A world without monsters, just imagine!
     [*Pause for imagining.*] No, that is not what troubles me. [*Warmly.*] Look
     you, miss, what counts is not so much the *thing*, in itself, that would
     astonish me too. No, it's the word, the notion. The notion brother is
     not unknown to him! [*Pause.*] But what really matters is this
     woman—what name did you say?

s   Maud, sir.

A   Maud!

s   And who is in milk, what is more, or about to be.

A   For mercy's sake! [*Pause.*] How does the passage go again?

s   [*rereading*] "Me get up, me go on, what a hope, it was he, for hunger.
     Have yourself opened, Maud would say, opened up, it's nothing, I'll
     give him suck if he's still alive, ah but no, no no." [*Pause.*] "No no."
     [*Pause.*]

A   And then the tear.

s   Exactly, sir. What I call the human trait.
     [*Pause.*]

A   [*low, with emotion*] Miss.

s   Sir.

A   Can it be we near our goal. [*Pause.*] Oh how bewitching you look when
     you show your teeth! Ah were I but . . . thirty years younger.

s   It is well after three, sir.

A   [*sigh*] Good. Where he left off. Once more.

s   "Oh but no, no—"

A   *Ah* but no. No?

s   You are quite right, sir. "Ah but no, no—"

A   [*severely*] Have a care, miss.

s   "Ah but no, no no." [*Pause.*] "No, no."

A   [*ruler*] On! [*Silence.*] Dick!

s   He has gone off, sir.

A   Just a shade lighter, Dick. [*Mild thud of pizzle.*] Ah no, you exaggerate, better than that. [*Swish and violent thud. Faint cry from Fox. Ruler.*] Ah but no, no no. On!

F   [*scream*] Let me out! Peter out in the stones!

A   Ah dear! There he goes again. Peter out in the stones!

s   It's a mercy he's tied.

A   [*gently*] Be reasonable, Fox. Stop—you may sit, Dick—stop jibbing. It's hard on you, we know. It does not lie entirely with us, we know. You might prattle away to your latest breath and still the one . . . thing remain unsaid that can give you back your darling solitudes, we know. But this much is sure: the more you say the greater your chances. Is that not so, miss?

s   It stands to reason, sir.

A   [*as to a backward pupil*] Don't ramble! Treat the subject, whatever it is! [*Snivel.*] More variety! [*Snivel.*] Those everlasting wilds may have their charm, but there is nothing there for us, that would astonish me. [*Snivel.*] Those micaceous schists, if you knew the effect [*snivel*] they can have on one, in the long run. [*Snivel.*] And your fauna! Those fodient rodents! [*Snivel.*] You wouldn't have a handkerchief, miss, you could lend me?

s   Here you are, sir.

A   Most kind. [*Blows nose abundantly.*] Much obliged.

s   Oh you may keep it, sir.

A   No no, now I'll be all right. [*To Fox.*] Of course we do not know, any more than you, what exactly it is we are after, what sign or set of words. But since you have failed so far to let it escape you, it is not by harking on the same old themes that you are likely to succeed, that would astonish me.

s   He has gone off again, sir.

A   [*warming to his point*] Someone, perhaps that is what is wanting, someone who once saw you . . . [*abating*] . . . go by. I may be quite wrong, but try, at least, what do you stand to lose? [*Beside himself.*] Even though it is not true!

s   [*shocked*] Oh sir!

A   A father, a mother, a friend, a . . . Beatrice—no, that is asking too much. Simply someone, anyone, who once saw you . . . go by. [*Pause.*] That woman . . . what's the name?

s   Maud, sir.

A   That Maud, for example, perhaps you once brushed against each other. Think hard!

s   He has gone off, sir.

A   Dick!—no, wait. Kiss him, miss, perhaps that will stir some fibre.

s   Where, sir?

A   In his heart, in his entrails—or some other part.

s   No, I mean kiss him where, sir?

A   [*angry*] Why on his stinker of a mouth, What do you suppose? [*Stenographer kisses Fox. Howl from Fox.*] Till it bleeds! Kiss it white! [*Howl from Fox.*] Suck his gullet!
[*Silence.*]

s   He has fainted away, sir.

A   Ah . . . perhaps I went too far. [*Pause.*] Perhaps I slipped you too soon.

s   Oh no, sir, you could not have waited a moment longer, time is up. [*Pause.*] The fault is mine, I did not go about it as I ought.

A   Come, come, miss! To the marines! [*Pause.*] Up already! [*Pained.*] I chatter too much.

s   Come, come, sir, don't say that, it is part of your rôle, as animator. [*Pause.*]

A   That tear, miss, do you remember?

s   Oh yes, sir, distinctly.

A   [*faint hope*] Not the first time by any chance?

s   Heavens no, sir, what an idea!

A   [*disappointed*] I might have known.

s   Last winter, now I come to think of it, he shed several, do you not remember?

A   Last winter! But, my dear child, I don't remember yesterday, it is down the hatch with love's young dream. Last winter! [*Pause. Low, with emotion.*] Miss.

s [*low*] Sir.

A That . . . Maud.
   [*Pause.*]

s [*encouraging*] Yes, sir.

A Well . . . you know . . . I may be wrong . . . I wouldn't like to . . . I hardly
   dare say it . . . but it seems to me that . . . here . . . possibly . . . we
   have something at last.

s Would to God, sir.

A Particularly with that tear so hard behind. It is not the first, agreed. But
   in such a context!

s And the milk, sir, don't forget the milk.

A The breast! One can almost see it!

s Who got her in that condition, there's another question for us.

A What condition, miss, I fail to follow you.

s Someone has fecundated her. [*Pause. Impatient.*] If she is in milk
   someone must have fecundated her.

A To be sure!

s Who?

A [*very excited*] You mean . . .

s I ask myself.
   [*Pause.*]

A May we have that passage again, miss?

s "Have yourself opened, Maud would say, opened—"

A [*delighted*] That frequentative! [*Pause.*] Sorry, miss.

s "Have yourself opened, Maud would say, opened—"

A Don't skip, miss, the text in its entirety if you please.

s I skip nothing, sir. [*Pause.*] What have I skipped, sir?

A [*emphatically*] ". . . between two kisses . . ." [*Sarcastic.*] That mere trifle!
   [*Angry.*] How can we ever hope to get anywhere if you suppress gems
   of that magnitude?

s But, sir, he never said anything of the kind.

A [*angry*] ". . . Maud would say, *between two kisses*, etc." Amend.

s But, sir, I—

A   What the devil are you deriding, miss? My hearing? My memory? My
    good faith? [*Thunderous.*] Amend!

s   [*feebly*] As you will, sir.

A   Let us hear how it runs now.

s   [*tremulous*] "Have yourself opened, Maud would say, between two
    kisses, opened up, it's nothing, I'll give him suck if he's still alive, ah
    but no, no no." [*Faint pencil.*] "No no."
    [*Silence.*]

A   Don't cry, miss, dry your pretty eyes and smile at me. Tomorrow, who
    knows, we may be free.

WORDS AND MUSIC

A piece for radio

MUSIC   *Small orchestra softly tuning up.*
WORDS   Please! [*Tuning. Louder.*] Please! [*Tuning dies away.*] How much
        longer cooped up here in the dark? [*With loathing.*] With you!
        [*Pause.*] Theme. . . . [*Pause.*] Theme . . . sloth. [*Pause. Rattled off, low.*]
        Sloth is of all the passions the most powerful passion and indeed
        no passion is more powerful than the passion of sloth, this is the
        mode in which the mind is most affected and indeed— [*Burst of
        tuning. Loud, imploring.*] Please! [*Tuning dies away. As before.*] The
        mode in which the mind is most affected and indeed in no mode
        is the mind more affected than in this, by passion we are to
        understand a movement of the soul pursuing or fleeing real or
        imagined pleasure or pain pleasure or pain real or imagined
        pleasure or pain, of all these movements and who can number
        them of all these movements and they are legion sloth is the
        most urgent and indeed by no movement is the soul more
        urged than by this by this by this to and from by no movement
        the soul more urged than by this to and— [*Pause.*] From. [*Pause.*]
        Listen! [*Distant sound of rapidly shuffling carpet slippers.*] At last!
        [*Shuffling louder. Burst of tuning.*] Hsst!
        [*Tuning dies away. Shuffling louder. Silence.*]
CROAK   Joe.
WORDS   [*humble*] My Lord.

CROAK   Bob.

MUSIC   *Humble muted adsum.*

CROAK   My comforts! Be friends! [*Pause.*] Bob.

MUSIC   *As before.*

CROAK   Joe.

WORDS   [*as before*] My Lord.

CROAK   Be friends! [*Pause.*] I am late, forgive. [*Pause.*] The face. [*Pause.*]
           On the stairs. [*Pause.*] Forgive. [*Pause.*] Joe.

WORDS   [*as before*] My Lord.

CROAK   Bob.

MUSIC   *As before.*

CROAK   Forgive. [*Pause.*] In the tower. [*Pause.*] The face. [*Long pause.*]
           Theme tonight. . . . [*Pause.*] Theme tonight . . . love. [*Pause.*] Love.
           [*Pause.*] My club. [*Pause.*] Joe.

WORDS   [*as before*] My Lord.

CROAK   Love. [*Pause. Thump of club on ground.*] Love!

WORDS   [*orotund*] Love is of all the passions the most powerful passion
           and indeed no passion is more powerful than the passion of
           love. [*Clears throat.*] This is the mode in which the mind is most
           strongly affected and indeed in no mode is the mind more
           strongly affected than in this.
           [*Pause.*]

CROAK   *Rending sigh. Thump of club.*

WORDS   [*as before*] By passion we are to understand a movement of the
           mind pursuing or fleeing real or imagined pleasure or pain.
           [*Clears throat.*] Of all—

CROAK   [*anguished*] Oh!

WORDS   [*as before*] Of all these movements then and who can number
           them and they are legion sloth is the LOVE is the most urgent
           and indeed by no manner of movement is the soul more urged
           than by this, to and—
           [*Violent thump of club.*]

CROAK   Bob.

WORDS   From.
           [*Violent thump of club.*]

CROAK   Bob!

MUSIC   *As before.*

CROAK   Love!

MUSIC   *Rap of baton on stand. Soft music worthy of foregoing, great
         expression, with audible groans and protestations— "No!" "Please!"
         etc.—from Words. Pause.*

CROAK   [*anguished*] Oh! [*Thump of club.*] Louder!

MUSIC   *Loud rap of baton and as before fortissimo, all expression gone,
         drowning Words' protestations. Pause.*

CROAK   My comforts! [*Pause.*] Joe sweet.

WORDS   [*as before*] Arise then and go now the manifest unanswerable—

CROAK   *Groans.*

WORDS   —to wit this love what is this love that more than all the cursed
         deadly or any other of its great movers so moves the soul and
         soul what is this soul that more than by any of its great movers
         is by love so moved? [*Clears throat. Prosaic.*] Love of woman, I
         mean, if that is what my Lord means.

CROAK   Alas!

WORDS   What? [*Pause. Very rhetorical.*] Is love the word? [*Pause. Do.*] Is soul
         the word? [*Pause. Do.*] Do we mean love, when we say love?
         [*Pause. Pause. Do.*] Soul, when we say soul?

CROAK   [*anguished*] Oh! [*Pause.*] Bob dear.

WORDS   Do we? [*With sudden gravity.*] Or don't we?

CROAK   [*imploring*] Bob!

MUSIC   *Rap of baton. Love and soul music, with just audible protestations—
         "No!" "Please!" "Peace!" etc.—from Words. Pause.*

CROAK   [*anguished*] Oh! [*Pause.*] My balms! [*Pause.*] Joe.

WORDS   [*humble*] My Lord.

CROAK   Bob.

MUSIC   *Adsum as before.*

CROAK   My balms! [*Pause.*] Age. [*Pause.*] Joe. [*Pause. Thump of club.*] Joe.

WORDS   [*as before*] My Lord.

CROAK   Age!
         [*Pause.*]

WORDS   [*faltering*] Age is . . . age is when . . . old age I mean . . . if that is

what my Lord means . . . is when . . . if you're a man . . . were a man . . . huddled . . . nodding . . . the ingle . . . waiting—
[*Violent thump of club.*]

CROAK   Bob. [*Pause.*] Age. [*Pause. Violent thump of club.*] Age!

MUSIC   *Rap of baton. Age music, soon interrupted by violent thump.*

CROAK   Together. [*Pause. Thump.*] Together! [*Pause. Violent thump.*] Together, dogs!

MUSIC   *Long la.*

WORDS   [*imploring*] No!
[*Violent thump.*]

CROAK   Dogs!

MUSIC   *La.*

WORDS   [*trying to sing*] Age is when . . . to a man . . .

MUSIC   *Improvement of above.*

WORDS   [*trying to sing this*] Age is when to a man . . .

MUSIC   *Suggestion for following.*

WORDS   [*trying to sing this*] Huddled o'er . . . the ingle. . . . [*Pause. Violent thump. Trying to sing.*] Waiting for the hag to put the . . . pan in the bed . . .

MUSIC   *Improvement of above.*

WORDS   [*trying to sing this*] Waiting for the hag to put the pan in the bed.

MUSIC   *Suggestion for following.*

WORDS   [*trying to sing this*] And bring the . . . arrowroot. . . . [*Pause. Violent thump. As before.*] And bring the toddy. . . .
[*Pause. Tremendous thump.*]

CROAK   Dogs!

MUSIC   *Suggestion for following.*

WORDS   [*trying to sing this*] She comes in the ashes. . . . [*Imploring.*] No!

MUSIC   *Repeats suggestion.*

WORDS   [*trying to sing this*] She comes in the ashes who loved could not be . . . won or . . .
[*Pause.*]

MUSIC   *Repeats end of previous suggestion.*

WORDS   [*trying to sing this*] Or won not loved . . . [*wearily*] . . . or some other trouble.... [*Pause. Trying to sing.*] Comes in the ashes like in that old—

MUSIC   *Interrupts with improvement of this and brief suggestion.*

WORDS   [*trying to sing this*] Comes in the ashes like in that old light ... her face ... in the ashes....

         [*Pause.*]

CROAK   *Groans.*

MUSIC   *Suggestion for following.*

WORDS   [*trying to sing this*] That old moonlight ... on the earth ... again.

         [*Pause.*]

MUSIC   *Further brief suggestion.*

         [*Silence.*]

CROAK   *Groans.*

MUSIC   *Plays air through alone, then invites Words with opening, pause, invites again and finally accompanies very softly.*

WORDS   [*trying to sing, softly*]

         Age is when to a man

         Huddled o'er the ingle

         Shivering for the hag

         To put the pan in the bed

         And bring the toddy

         She comes in the ashes

         Who loved could not be won

         Or won not loved

         Or some other trouble

         Comes in the ashes

         Like in that old light

         The face in the ashes

         That old starlight

         On the earth again.

         [*Long pause.*]

CROAK   [*murmur*] The face. [*Pause.*] The face. [*Pause.*] The face. [*Pause.*] The face.

MUSIC   *Rap of baton and warmly sentimental, about one minute.*

[*Pause.*]

CROAK   The face.

WORDS   [*cold*] Seen from above in that radiance so cold and faint. . . .
[*Pause.*]

MUSIC   *Warm suggestion from above for above.*

WORDS   [*disregarding, cold*] Seen from above at such close quarters in that
radiance so cold and faint with eyes so dimmed by . . . what had
passed, its quite . . . piercing beauty is a little. . . .
[*Pause.*]

MUSIC   *Renews timidly previous suggestion.*

WORDS   [*interrupting, violently*] Peace!

CROAK   My comforts! Be friends!
[*Pause.*]

WORDS   . . . blunted. Some moments later however, such are the powers
of recuperation at this age, the head is drawn back to a distance
of two or three feet, the eyes widen to a stare and begin to feast
again. [*Pause.*] What then is seen would have been better seen in
the light of day, that is incontestable. But how often it has, in
recent months, how often, at all hours, under all angles, in
cloud and shine, been seen I mean. And there is, is there not, in
that clarity of silver . . . that clarity of silver . . . is there not . . .
my Lord. . . . [*Pause.*] Now and then the rye, swayed by a light
wind, casts and withdraws its shadow.
[*Pause.*]

CROAK   *Groans.*

WORDS   Leaving aside the features or lineaments proper, matchless
severally and in their ordonnance—

CROAK   *Groans.*

WORDS   —flare of the black disordered hair as though spread wide on
water, the brows knitted in a groove suggesting pain but simply
concentration more likely all things considered on some
consummate inner process, the eyes of course closed in
keeping with this, the lashes . . . [*pause*] . . . the nose . . .
[*pause*] . . . nothing, a little pinched perhaps, the lips. . . .

CROAK   [*anguished*] Lily!

WORDS ... tight, a gleam of tooth biting on the under, no coral, no swell, whereas normally. . . .

CROAK *Groans.*

WORDS ... the whole so blanched and still that were it not for the great white rise and fall of the breasts, spreading as they mount and then subsiding to their natural ... aperture—

MUSIC *Irrepressible burst of spreading and subsiding music with vain protestations— "Peace!" "No!" "Please!" etc. —from Words. Triumph and conclusion.*

WORDS [*gently expostulatory*] My Lord! [*Pause. Faint thump of club.*] I resume, so wan and still and so ravished away that it seems no more of the earth than Mira in the Whale, at her tenth and greatest magnitude on this particular night shining coldly down—as we say, looking up. [*Pause.*] Some moments later however, such are the powers—

CROAK [*anguished*] No!

WORDS —the brows uncloud, the lips part and the eyes ... [*pause*] ... the brows uncloud, the nostrils dilate, the lips part and the eyes ... [*pause*] ... a little colour comes back into the cheeks and the eyes ... [*reverently*] ... open. [*Pause.*] Then down a little way ... [*Pause. Change to poetic tone. Low.*]

    Then down a little way
    Through the trash
    To where ... towards where. . . .

[*Pause.*]

MUSIC *Discreet suggestion for above.*

WORDS [*trying to sing this*]

    Then down a little way
    Through the trash
    Towards where ...

[*Pause.*]

MUSIC *Discreet suggestion for following.*

WORDS [*trying to sing this*]

    All dark no begging
    No giving no words
    No sense no need. . . .

[*Pause.*]

MUSIC   *More confident suggestion for following.*

WORDS   [*trying to sing this*]

> Through the scum
> Down a little way
> To where one glimpse
> Of that wellhead.

[*Pause.*]

MUSIC   *Invites with opening, pause, invites again and finally accompanies very softly.*

WORDS   [*trying to sing, softly*]

> Then down a little way
> Through the trash
> Towards where
> All dark no begging
> No giving no words
> No sense no need
> Through the scum
> Down a little way
> To whence one glimpse
> Of that wellhead.

[*Pause. Shocked.*] My Lord! [*Sound of club let fall. As before.*] My Lord! [*Shuffling slippers, with halts. They die away. Long pause.*] Bob. [*Pause.*] Bob!

MUSIC   *Brief rude retort.*

WORDS   Music. [*Imploring.*] Music!

[*Pause.*]

MUSIC   *Rap of baton and statement with elements already used or wellhead alone.*

[*Pause.*]

WORDS   Again. [*Pause. Imploring.*] Again!

MUSIC   *As before or only very slightly varied.*

[*Pause.*]

WORDS   *Deep sigh.*

Curtain

CASCANDO

A radio piece for music and voice

OPENER [*cold*] It is the month of May . . . for me.
[*Pause.*]
Correct.
[*Pause.*]
I open.

VOICE [*low, panting*] —story . . . if you could finish it . . . you could
rest . . . sleep . . . not before . . . oh I know . . . the ones I've
finished . . . thousands and one . . . all I ever did . . . in my
life . . . with my life . . . saying to myself . . . finish this one . . .
it's the right one . . . then rest . . . sleep . . . no more stories . . .
no more words . . . and finished it . . . and not the right one . . .
couldn't rest . . . straight away another . . . to begin . . . to
finish . . . saying to myself . . . finish this one . . . then rest . . .
this time . . . it's the right one . . . this time . . . you have it . . .
and finished it . . . and not the right one . . . couldn't rest . . .
straight away another . . . but this one . . . it's different . . . I'll
finish it . . . I've got it . . . Woburn . . . I resume . . . a long
life . . . already . . . say what you like . . . a few misfortunes . . .
that's enough . . . five years later . . . ten . . . I don't know . . .
Woburn . . . he's changed . . . not enough . . . recognizable . . .
in the shed . . . yet another . . . waiting for night . . . night to
fall . . . to go out . . . go on . . . elsewhere . . . sleep elsewhere . . .

it's slow . . . he lifts his head . . . now and then . . . his eyes . . .
to the window . . . it's darkening . . . earth darkening . . . it's
night . . . he gets up . . . knees first . . . then up . . . on his
feet . . . slips out . . . Woburn . . . same old coat . . . right the
sea . . . left the hills . . . he has the choice . . . he has only—

OPENER   [*with Voice*] And I close.

[*Silence.*]

I open the other.

MUSIC   . . . .

OPENER   [*with Music*] And I close.

[*Silence.*]

I open both.

VOICE ⎫
        ⎬ [*together*] —on . . . getting on . . . finish . . . don't
MUSIC ⎭ . . . .

give up . . . then rest . . . sleep . . . not before . . . finish
. . . .
this time . . . it's the right one . . . you have it . . . you've got
. . . .
it . . . it's there . . . somewhere . . . you've got him . . . follow . . .
. . . .
him . . . don't lose him . . . Woburn story . . . getting on . . .
. . . .
finish . . . then sleep . . . no more stories . . . no more words
. . . .
. . . come on . . . next thing . . . he—
. . . .

OPENER   [*with Voice and Music*] And I close.

[*Silence.*]

I start again.

VOICE   —down . . . gentle slopes . . . boreen . . . giant aspens . . . wind in
the boughs . . . faint sea . . . Woburn . . . same old coat . . . he
goes on . . . stops . . . not a soul . . . not yet . . . night too
bright . . . say what you like . . . he goes on . . . hugging the
bank . . . same old stick . . . he goes down . . . falls . . . on

purpose or not . . . can't see . . . he's down . . . that's what
counts . . . face in the mud . . . arms spread . . . that's the
idea . . . already . . . there already . . . no not yet . . . he gets
up . . . knees first . . . hands flat . . . in the mud . . . head
sunk . . . then up . . . on his feet . . . huge bulk . . . come on . . .
he goes on . . . he goes down . . . come on . . . in his head . . .
what's in his head . . . a hole . . . a shelter . . . a hollow . . . in the
dunes . . . a cave . . . vague memory . . . in his head . . . of a
cave . . . he goes down . . . no more trees . . . no more bank . . .
he's changed . . . not enough . . . night too bright . . . soon the
dunes . . . no more cover . . . not a soul . . . not—
[*Silence.*]

MUSIC . . . .

[*Silence.*]

VOICE ⎱
      ⎰ [*together*] —rest . . . sleep . . . no more stories . . .
MUSIC
. . . .

no more words . . . don't give up . . . this time . . . it's the
. . . .

right one . . . we're there . . . I'm there . . . somewhere . . .
. . . .

Woburn . . . I've got him . . . don't lose him . . . follow him
. . . .

. . . to the end . . . come on . . . this time . . . it's the right one
. . . .

. . . finish . . . sleep . . . Woburn . . . come on—
. . . .

[*Silence.*]

OPENER So, at will.
They say, It's in his head.
No. I open.

VOICE —falls . . . again . . . on purpose or not . . . can't see . . . he's
down . . . that's what matters . . . face in the sand . . . arms
spread . . . bare dunes . . . not a scrub . . . same old coat . . .
night too bright . . . say what you like . . . sea louder . . .

thunder . . . manes of foam . . . Woburn . . . his head . . . what's in his head . . . peace . . . peace again . . . in his head . . . no further . . . no more searching . . . sleep . . . no not yet . . . he gets up . . . knees first . . . hands flat . . . in the sand . . . head sunk . . . then up . . . on his feet . . . huge bulk . . . same old broadbrim . . . jammed down . . . come on . . . he goes on . . . ton weight . . . in the sand . . . knee-deep . . . he goes down . . . sea—

OPENER   [*with Voice*] And I close.

[*Silence.*]

I open the other.

MUSIC   . . . .

OPENER   [*with Music*] And I close.

[*Silence.*]

So, at will.

It's my life, I live on that.

[*Pause.*]

Correct.

[*Pause.*]

What do I open?

They say, He opens nothing, he has nothing to open, it's in his head.

They don't see me, they don't see what I do, they don't see what I have, and they say, He opens nothing, he has nothing to open, it's in his head.

I don't protest any more, I don't say any more,

There is nothing in my head.

I don't answer any more.

I open and close.

VOICE   —lights . . . of the land . . . the island . . . the sky . . . he need only . . . lift his head . . . his eyes . . . he'd see them . . . shine on him . . . but no . . . he—

[*Silence.*]

MUSIC   [*brief*] . . . .

[*Silence.*]

OPENER   They say, That is not his life, he does not live on that. They don't see me, they don't see what my life is, they don't see what I live on, and they say, That is not his life, he does not live on that.
[*Pause.*]
I have lived on it . . . till I'm old.
Old enough.
Listen.

VOICE   [*weakening*] —this time . . . I'm there . . . Woburn . . . it's him . . . I've seen him . . . I've got him . . . come on . . . same old coat . . . he goes down . . . falls . . . falls again . . . on purpose or not . . . can't see . . . he's down . . . that's what counts . . . come on—

OPENER   [*with Voice*] Full strength.

VOICE   —face . . . in the stones . . . no more sand . . . all stones . . . that's the idea . . . we're there . . . this time . . . no not yet . . . he gets up . . . knees first . . . hands flat . . . in the stones . . . head sunk . . . then up . . . on his feet . . . huge bulk . . . Woburn . . . faster . . . he goes on . . . he goes down . . . he—
[*Silence.*]

MUSIC   [*weakening*] . . . .

OPENER   [*with Music*] Full strength.

MUSIC   . . . .
[*Silence.*]

OPENER   That's not all.
I open both.
Listen.

VOICE ⎱
   [*together*] —sleep . . . no further . . . no more
MUSIC ⎰
   . . . .

searching . . . to find him . . . in the dark . . . to see him . . .
. . . .

to say to him . . . for whom . . . that's it . . . no matter . . .
. . . .

never him . . . never right . . . start again . . . in the dark . . .
. . . .

done with that . . . this time . . . it's the right one . . . we're

....

there ... nearly ... finish—

....

[*Silence.*]

OPENER   From one world to another, it's as though they drew together.
We have not much further to go. Good.

VOICE ⎱
        [*together*]   —nearly ... I've got him ... I've seen
MUSIC ⎰ ....

him ... I've said him ... we're there ... nearly ... no more

....

stories ... all false ... this time ... it's the right one ... I

....

have it ... finish ... sleep ... Woburn ... it's him ... I've

....

got him ... follow him ... to—

....

[*Silence.*]

OPENER   Good.

[*Pause.*]

Yes, correct, the month of May.

You know, the reawakening.

[*Pause.*]

I open.

VOICE   —no tiller ... no thwarts ... no oars ... afloat ... sucked out ...
then back ... aground ... drags free ... out ... Woburn ... he
fills it ... flat out ... face in the bilge ... arms spread ... same
old coat ... hands clutching ... the gunnels ... no ... I don't
know ... I see him ... he clings on ... out to sea ... heading
nowhere ... for the island ... then no more ... else—

[*Silence.*]

MUSIC   ....

[*Silence.*]

OPENER   They said, It's his own, it's his voice, it's in his head.

[*Pause.*]

VOICE —faster ... out ... driving out ... rearing ... plunging ...
heading nowhere ... for the island ... then no more ...
elsewhere ... anywhere ... heading anywhere ... lights—
[*Pause.*]

OPENER No resemblance.
I answered, And that ...

MUSIC [*brief*] ....
[*Silence.*]

OPENER ... is that mine too?
But I don't answer any more.
And they don't say anything any more.
They have quit.
Good.
[*Pause.*]
Yes, correct, the month of May, the close of May.
The long days.
[*Pause.*]
I open.
[*Pause.*]
I'm afraid to open.
But I must open.
So I open.

VOICE —come on ... Woburn ... arms spread ... same old coat ... face
in the bilge ... he clings on ... island gone ... far astern ...
heading out ... open sea ... land gone ... his head ... what's
in his head ... Woburn—

OPENER [*with Voice*] Come on! Come on!

VOICE —at last ... we're there ... no further ... no more searching
... in the dark ... elsewhere ... always elsewhere ... we're
there ... nearly ... Woburn ... hang on ... don't let go ... lights
gone ... of the land ... all gone ... nearly all ... too far ... too
late ... of the sky ... those ... if you like ... he need only ...
turn over ... he'd see them ... shine on him ... but no ... he
clings on ... Woburn ... he's changed ... nearly enough—

[*Silence.*]

MUSIC   ....

OPENER   [*with Music*] God.

MUSIC   ....

[*Silence.*]

OPENER   God God.

[*Pause.*]

There was a time I asked myself, What is it.

There were times I answered, It's the outing.

Two outings.

Then the return.

Where?

To the village.

To the inn.

Two outings, then at last the return, to the village, to the inn,

by the only road that leads there.

An image, like any other.

But I don't answer any more.

I open.

VOICE ⎫
          ⎬ [*together*]   —don't let go ... finish ... it's the
MUSIC ⎭   ....

right one ... this time ... I have it ... we're there ...

....

Woburn ... nearly—

....

OPENER   [*with Voice and Music*] As though they had linked their arms.

VOICE ⎫
          ⎬ [*together*]   —sleep ... no more stories ... come on
MUSIC ⎭   ....

... Woburn ... it's him ... see him ... say him ... to the

....

end ... don't let go—

OPENER   [*with Voice and Music*] Good.

VOICE ⎫
          ⎬ [*together*]   —nearly ... just a few more ... a few
MUSIC ⎭   ....

more . . . I'm there . . . nearly . . . Woburn . . . it's him . . . it

. . . .

was him . . . I've got him . . . nearly—

OPENER [*with Voice and Music, fervently*] Good!

VOICE ⎫
            ⎬ [*together*] —this time . . . it's the right one . . .
MUSIC ⎭

. . . .

finish . . . no more stories . . . sleep . . . we're there . . . nearly

. . . .

. . . just a few more . . . don't let go . . . Woburn . . . he clings . . .

. . . .

on . . . come on . . . come on—

. . . .

[*Silence.*]

Curtain

PLAY

A play in one act

Front centre, touching one another, three identical grey urns (see page 367) about one yard high. From each a head protrudes, the neck held fast in the urn's mouth. The heads are those, from left to right as seen from auditorium, of W 2, M and W 1. They face undeviatingly front throughout the play. Faces so lost to age and aspect as to seem almost part of urns. But no masks.

Their speech is provoked by a spotlight projected on faces alone (see page 366).

The transfer of light from one face to another is immediate. No blackout, i.e. return to almost complete darkness of opening, except where indicated.

The response to light is immediate.

Faces impassive throughout. Voices toneless except where an expression is indicated.

Rapid tempo throughout.

The curtain rises on a stage in almost complete darkness. Urns just discernible. Five seconds.

Faint spots simultaneously on three faces. Three seconds. Voices faint, largely unintelligible.

W1   Yes, strange, darkness best, and the darker the worse, till all dark, then all well, for the time, but it will come, the time will come, the thing is there, you'll see it, get off me, keep off me, all dark, all still, all over, wiped out—

W2   Yes, perhaps, a shade gone, I suppose, some might say,

[*together,*   poor thing, a shade gone, just a shade, in the head—[*faint*

see   *wild laugh*]—just a shade, but I doubt it, I doubt it, not

page   really, I'm all right, still all right, do my best, all I can—

M   *367*]   Yes, peace, one assumed, all out, all the pain, all as if . . . never been, it will come—[*hiccup*]—pardon, no sense in this, oh I know . . . none the less, one assumed, peace . . . I mean . . . not merely all over, but as if . . . never been—

[*Spots off. Blackout. Five seconds. Strong spots simultaneously on three faces. Three seconds. Voices normal strength.*]

W1   I said to him, Give her up—

W2   [*together*]   One morning as I was sitting—

M   We were not long together—

[*Spots off. Blackout. Five seconds. Spot on W1.*]

W1   I said to him, Give her up. I swore by all I held most sacred—

[*Spot from W1 to W2.*]

W2   One morning as I was sitting stitching by the open window she burst in and flew at me. Give him up, she screamed, he's mine. Her photographs were kind to her. Seeing her now for the first time full length in the flesh I understood why he preferred me.

[*Spot from W2 to M.*]

M   We were not long together when she smelled the rat. Give up that whore, she said, or I'll cut my throat—[*hiccup*] pardon—so help me God. I knew she could have no proof. So I told her I did not know what she was talking about.

[*Spot from M to W2.*]

W2   What are you talking about? I said, stitching away. Someone yours? Give up whom? I smell you off him, she screamed, he stinks of bitch.

[*Spot from W2 to W1.*]

W1   Though I had him dogged for months by a first-rate man, no shadow of proof was forthcoming. And there was no denying that he continued as . . . assiduous as ever. This, and his horror of the merely Platonic thing, made me sometimes wonder if I were not accusing him unjustly. Yes.

[*Spot from W1 to M.*]

M   What have you to complain of? I said. Have I been neglecting you? How could we be together in the way we are if there were someone else? Loving her as I did, with all my heart, I could not but feel sorry for her.

[*Spot from M to W2.*]

W2   Fearing she was about to offer me violence I rang for Erskine and had her shown out. Her parting words, as he could testify, if he is still living, and has not forgotten, coming and going on the earth, letting people in, showing people out, were to the effect that she would settle my hash. I confess this did alarm me a little, at the time.

[*Spot from W2 to M.*]

M   She was not convinced. I might have known. I smell her off you, she kept saying. There was no answer to this. So I took her in my arms and swore I could not live without her. I meant it, what is more. Yes, I am sure I did. She did not repulse me.

[*Spot from M to W1.*]

W1   Judge then of my astonishment when one fine morning, as I was sitting stricken in the morning room, he slunk in, fell on his knees before me, buried his face in my lap and . . . confessed.

[*Spot from W1 to M.*]

M   She put a bloodhound on me, but I had a little chat with him. He was glad of the extra money.

[*Spot from M to W2.*]

W2   Why don't you get out, I said, when he started moaning about his home life, there is obviously nothing between you any more. Or is there?

[*Spot from W2 to W1.*]

W1   I confess my first feeling was one of wonderment. What a male!
      [*Spot from W1 to M. He opens his mouth to speak. Spot from M to W2.*]

W2   Anything between us, he said, what do you take me for, a
      something machine? And of course with him no danger of the . . .
      spiritual thing. Then why don't you get out? I said. I sometimes
      wondered if he was not living with her for her money.
      [*Spot from W2 to M.*]

M   The next thing was the scene between them. I can't have her
      crashing in here, she said, threatening to take my life. I must have
      looked incredulous. Ask Erskine, she said, if you don't believe me.
      But she threatens to take her own, I said. Not yours? she said. No, I
      said, hers. We had fun trying to work this out.
      [*Spot from M to W1.*]

W1   Then I forgave him. To what will love not stoop! I suggested a little
      jaunt to celebrate, to the Riviera or our darling Grand Canary. He
      was looking pale. Peaked. But this was not possible just then.
      Professional commitments.
      [*Spot from W1 toW2.*]

W2   She came again. Just strolled in. All honey. Licking her lips. Poor
      thing. I was doing my nails, by the open window. He has told me
      all about it, she said. Who he, I said filing away, and what it? I know
      what torture you must be going through, she said, and I have
      dropped in to say I bear you no ill-feeling. I rang for Erskine.
      [*Spot from W2 to M.*]

M   Then I got frightened and made a clean breast of it. She was
      looking more and more desperate. She had a razor in her vanity-
      bag. Adulterers, take warning, never admit.
      [*Spot from M to W1.*]

W1   When I was satisfied it was all over I went to have a gloat. Just a
      common tart. What he could have found in her when he had me—
      [*Spot from W1 to W2.*]

W2   When he came again we had it out. I felt like death. He went on
      about why he had to tell her. Too risky and so on. That meant he
      had gone back to her. Back to that!
      [*Spot from W2 to W1.*]

W1   Pudding face, puffy, spots, blubber mouth, jowls, no neck, dugs you could—

[Spot from W1 to W2.]

W2   He went on and on. I could hear a mower. An old hand mower. I stopped him and said that whatever I might feel I had no silly threats to offer—but not much stomach for her leavings either. He thought that over for a bit.

[spot from W2 to W1.]

W1   Calves like a flunkey—

[Spot from W1 to M.]

M   When I saw her again she knew. She was looking—*[hiccup]*— wretched. Pardon. Some fool was cutting grass. A little rush, then another. The problem was how to convince her that no . . . revival of intimacy was involved. I couldn't. I might have known. So I took her in my arms and said I could not go on living without her. I don't believe I could have.

[Spot from M to W2.]

W2   The only solution was to go away together. He swore we should as soon as he had put his affairs in order. In the meantime we were to carry on as before. By that he meant as best we could.

[Spot from W2 to W1.]

W1   So he was mine again. All mine. I was happy again. I went about singing. The world—

[Spot from W1 to M.]

M   At home all heart to heart, new leaf and bygones bygones. I ran into your ex-doxy, she said one night, on the pillow, you're well out of that. Rather uncalled for, I thought. I am indeed, sweetheart, I said, I am indeed. God what vermin women. Thanks to you, angel, I said.

[Spot from M to W1.]

W1   Then I began to smell her off him again. Yes.

[Spot from W1 to W2.]

W2   When he stopped coming I was prepared. More or less.

[Spot from W2 to M.]

M   Finally it was all too much. I simply could no longer—

[Spot from M to W1.]

W1   Before I could do anything he disappeared. That meant she had won. That slut! I couldn't credit it. I lay stricken for weeks. Then I drove over to her place. It was all bolted and barred. All grey with frozen dew. On the way back by Ash and Snodland—
[Spot from W1 to M.]

M   I simply could no longer—
[Spot from M to W2.]

W2   I made a bundle of his things and burnt them. It was November and the bonfire was going. All night I smelt them smouldering.
[Spot off W2. Blackout. Five seconds. Spots half previous strength simultaneously on three faces. Three seconds. Voices proportionately lower.]

W1 ⎫   Mercy, mercy—
W2 ⎬ *[together]*   To say I am—
M ⎭   When first this change—

[Spots off. Blackout. Five seconds. Spot on M.]

M   When first this change I actually thanked God. I thought, It is done, it is said, now all is going out—
[Spot from M to W1.]

W1   Mercy, mercy, tongue still hanging out for mercy. It will come. You haven't seen me. But you will. Then it will come.
[Spot from W1 to W2.]

W2   To say I am not disappointed, no, I am. I had anticipated something better. More restful.
[Spot from W2 to W1.]

W1   Or you will weary of me.
[Spot from W1 to M.]

M   Down, all going down, into the dark, peace is coming, I thought, after all, at last, I was right, after all, thank God, when first this change.
[Spot from M to W2.]

W2   Less confused. Less confusing. At the same time I prefer this to . . . the other thing. Definitely. There are endurable moments.
[Spot from W2 to M.]

M   I thought.

[Spot from M to W2.]

W2 When you go out—and I go out. Some day you will tire of me and
go out . . . for good.

[Spot from W2 to W1.]

W1 Hellish half-light.

[Spot from W1 to M.]

M Peace, yes, I suppose, a kind of peace, and all that pain as if . . .
never been.

[Spot from M to W2.]

W2 Give me up, as a bad job. Go away and start poking and pecking at
someone else. On the other hand—

[Spot from W2 to W1.]

W1 Get off me! Get off me!

[Spot from W1 to M.]

M It will come. Must come. There is no future in this.

[Spot from M to W2.]

W2 On the other hand things may disimprove, there is that danger.

[Spot from W2 to M.]

M Oh of course I know now—

[Spot from M to W1.]

W1 Is it that I do not tell the truth, is that it, that some day somehow I
may tell the truth at last and then no more light at last, for the truth?

[Spot from W1 to W2.]

W2 You might get angry and blaze me clean out of my wits. Mightn't
you?

[Spot from W2 to M.]

M I know now, all that was just . . . play. And all this? When will all
this—

[Spot from M to W1.]

W1 Is that it?

[Spot from W1 to W2.]

W2 Mightn't you?

[Spot from W2 to M.]

M All this, when will all this have been . . . just play?

[*Spot from M to W1.*]

W1   I can do nothing . . . for anybody . . . any more . . . thank God. So it
must be something I have to say. How the mind works still!
[*Spot from W1 to W2.*]

W2   But I doubt it. It would not be like you somehow. And you must
know I am doing my best. Or don't you?
[*Spot from W2 to M.*]

M   Perhaps they have become friends. Perhaps sorrow—
[*Spot from M to W1.*]

W1   But I have said all I can. All you let me. All I—
[*Spot from W1 to M*]

M   Perhaps sorrow has brought them together.
[*Spot from M to W2.*]

W2   No doubt I make the same mistake as when it was the sun that
shone, of looking for sense where possibly there is none.
[*Spot from W2 to M.*]

M   Perhaps they meet, and sit, over a cup of that green tea they both
so loved, without milk or sugar, not even a squeeze of lemon—
[*Spot from M to W2.*]

W2   Are you listening to me? Is anyone listening to me? Is anyone
looking at me? Is anyone bothering about me at all?
[*Spot from W2 to M.*]

M   Not even a squeeze of—
[*Spot from M to W1.*]

W1   Is it something I should do with my face, other than utter? Weep?
[*Spot from W1 to W2.*]

W2   Am I taboo, I wonder. Not necessarily, now that all danger is
averted. That poor creature—I can hear her—that poor creature—
[*Spot from W2 to W1.*]

W1   Bite off my tongue and swallow it? Spit it out? Would that placate
you? How the mind works still to be sure!
[*Spot from W1 to M.*]

M   Meet, and sit, now in the one dear place, now in the other, and
sorrow together, and *compare*—[*hiccup*]—pardon—happy memories.

[Spot from M to W1.]

W1   If only I could think, There is no sense in this . . . either, none whatsoever. I can't.

[Spot from W1 to W2.]

W2   That poor creature who tried to seduce you, what ever became of her, do you suppose?—I can hear her. Poor thing.

[Spot from W2 to M.]

M   Personally I always preferred Lipton's.

[Spot from M to W1.]

W1   And that all is falling, all fallen, from the beginning, on empty air. Nothing being asked at all. No one asking me for anything at all.

[Spot from W1 to W2.]

W2   They might even feel sorry for me, if they could see me. But never so sorry as I for them.

[Spot from W2 to W1.]

W1   I can't.

[Spot from W1 to W2.]

W2   Kissing their sour kisses.

[Spot from W2 to M.]

M   I pity them in any case, yes, compare my lot with theirs, however blessed, and—

[Spot from M to W1.]

W1   I can't. The mind won't have it. It would have to go. Yes.

[Spot from W1 to M.]

M   Pity them.

[Spot from M to W2.]

W2   What do you do when you go out? Sift?

[Spot from W2 to M.]

M   Am I hiding something? Have I lost—

[Spot from M to W1.]

W1   She had means, I fancy, though she lived like a pig.

[Spot from W1 to W2.]

W2   Like dragging a great roller, on a scorching day. The strain . . . to get it moving, momentum coming—

[*Spot off* W2. *Blackout. Three seconds. Spot on* W2.]

W2   Kill it and strain again.

[*Spot from* W2 *to* M.]

M   Have I lost . . . the thing you want? Why go out? Why go—

[*Spot from* M *to* W2.]

W2   And you perhaps pitying me, thinking, Poor thing, she needs a rest.

[*Spot from* W2 *to* W1.]

W1   Perhaps she has taken him away to live . . . somewhere in the sun.

[*Spot from* W1 *to* M.]

M   Why go down? Why not—

[*Spot from* M *to* W2.]

W2   I don't know.

[*Spot from* W2 *to* W1.]

W1   Perhaps she is sitting somewhere, by the open window, her hands folded in her lap, gazing down out over the olives—

[*Spot from* W1 *to* M.]

M   Why not keep on glaring at me without ceasing? I might start to rave and—[*hiccup*]—bring it up for you. Par—

[*Spot from* M *to* W2.]

W2   No.

[*Spot from* W2 *to* M.]

M   —don.

[*Spot from* M *to* W1.]

W1   Gazing down out over the olives, then the sea, wondering what can be keeping him, growing cold. Shadow stealing over everything. Creeping. Yes.

[*Spot from* W1 *to* M.]

M   To think we were never together.

[*Spot from* M *to* W2.]

W2   Am I not perhaps a little unhinged already?

[*Spot from* W2 *to* W1.]

W1   Poor creature. Poor creatures.

[*Spot from* W1 *to* M.]

M   Never woke together, on a May morning, the first to wake to wake the other two. Then in a little dinghy—

[*Spot from M to W1.*]

W1 Penitence, yes, at a pinch, atonement, one was resigned, but no, that does not seem to be the point either.

[*Spot from W1 to W2.*]

W2 I say, Am I not perhaps a little unhinged already? [*Hopefully.*] Just a little? [*Pause.*] I doubt it.

[*Spot from W2 to M.*]

M A little dinghy—

[*Spot from M to W1.*]

W1 Silence and darkness were all I craved. Well, I get a certain amount of both. They being one. Perhaps it is more wickedness to pray for more.

[*Spot from W1 to M.*]

M A little dinghy, on the river, I resting on my oars, they lolling on air-pillows in the stern . . . sheets. Drifting. Such fantasies.

[*Spot from M to W1.*]

W1 Hellish half-light.

[*Spot from W1 to W2.*]

W2 A shade gone. In the head. Just a shade. I doubt it.

[*Spot from W2 to M.*]

M We were not civilized.

[*Spot from M to W1.*]

W1 Dying for dark—and the darker the worse. Strange.

[*Spot from W1 to M.*]

M Such fantasies. Then. And now—

[*Spot from M to W2.*]

W2 I doubt it.

[*Pause. Peal of wild low laughter from W2 cut short as spot from her to W1.*]

W1 Yes, and the whole thing there, all there, staring you in the face. You'll see it. Get off me. Or weary.

[*Spot from W1 to M.*]

M And now, that you are . . . mere eye. Just looking. At my face. On and off.

[*Spot from M to W1.*]

W1 Weary of playing with me. Get off me. Yes.

[*Spot from W1 to M.*]

M   Looking for something. In my face. Some truth. In my eyes. Not
even.

[*Spot from M to W2. Laugh as before from W2 cut short as spot from her
to M.*]

M   Mere eye. No mind. Opening and shutting on me. Am I as much—

[*Spot off M. Blackout. Three seconds. Spot on M.*]

Am I as much as . . . being seen?

[*Spot off M. Blackout. Five seconds. Faint spots simultaneously on three
faces. Three seconds. Voices faint, largely unintelligible.*]

W1 ⎫   Yes, strange, etc.

W2 ⎬ [*together*] Yes, perhaps, etc.

M ⎭   Yes, peace, etc.

[*Repeat play.*]

M   [*Closing repeat.*] Am I as much as . . . being seen?

[*Spot off M. Blackout. Five seconds. Strong spots simultaneously on three
faces. Three seconds. Voices normal strength.*]

W1 ⎫   I said to him, Give her up—

W2 ⎬ [*together*] One morning as I was sitting—

M ⎭   We were not long together—

[*Spots off. Blackout. Five seconds. Spot on M.*]

M   We were not long together—

[*Spot off M. Blackout. Five seconds.*]

                                         Curtain

LIGHT

The source of light is single and must not be situated outside the ideal
space (stage) occupied by its victims.

The optimum position for the spot is at the centre of the footlights,
the faces being thus lit at close quarters and from below.

When exceptionally three spots are required to light the three faces
simultaneously, they should be as a single spot branching into three.

Apart from these moments a single mobile spot should be used,
swivelling at maximum speed from one face to another as required.

The method consisting in assigning to each face a separate fixed spot is unsatisfactory in that it is less expressive of a unique inquisitor than the single mobile spot.

CHORUS

w1	Yes strange	darkness best	and the darker	the worse
w2	Yes perhaps	a shade gone	I suppose	some might say
M	Yes peace	one assumed	all out	all the pain

w1	till all dark	then all well	for the time	but it will come
w2	poor thing	a shade gone	just a shade	in the head
M	all as if	never been	it will come	[*Hiccup.*] pardon

w1	the time will come	the thing is there	you'll see it
w2	[*Laugh ------*]	just a shade	but I doubt it
M	no sense in this	oh I know	none the less

w1	get off me	keep off me	all dark	all still
w2	*I* doubt it	not really	I'm all right	still all right
M	one assumed	peace I mean	not merely	all over

w1	all over	wiped out—
w2	do my best	all I can—
M	but as if	never been—

URNS

In order for the urns to be only one yard high, it is necessary either that traps be used, enabling the actors to stand below stage level, or that they kneel throughout play, the urns being open at the back.

Should traps be not available, and the kneeling posture found impracticable, the actors should stand, the urns be enlarged to full length and moved back from front to mid-stage, the tallest actor setting the height, the broadest the breadth, to which the three urns should conform.

The sitting posture results in urns of unacceptable bulk and is not to be considered.

REPEAT

The repeat may be an exact replica of first statement or it may present an element of variation.

In other words, the light may operate the second time exactly as it did the first (exact replica) or it may try a different method (variation).

The London production (and in a lesser degree the Paris production) opted for the variation with following deviations from first statement:

1. Introduction of an abridged chorus, cut short on laugh of W2, to open fragment of second repeat.

2. Light less strong in repeat and voices correspondingly lower, giving the following schema, where A is the highest level of light and voice and E the lowest:

    C First chorus.   ⎫
    A First part of 1.   ⎬ 1
    B Second part of 1. ⎭

    D Second chorus.   ⎫
    B First part of Repeat 1. ⎬   Repeat 1
    C Second part of Repeat 1. ⎭

    E Abridged chorus.   ⎫
    C Fragment of Repeat 2 ⎭   Fragment of Repeat 2

3. Breathless quality in voices from beginning of Repeat 1 and increasing to end of play.

4. Changed order of speeches in repeat as far as this is compatible with unchanged continuity for actors. E.g. the order of interrogation W1, W2, M, W2, W1, M at opening of 1 becomes W2, W1, M, W2, M, W1 at opening of repeat, and so on if and as desired.

FILM

*Throughout first two parts all perception is E's. E is the camera. But in third part
there is O's perception of room and contents and at the same time E's continued
perception of O. This poses a problem of images which I cannot solve without
technical help. See below, note 8.*

*The film is divided into three parts. 1. The street (about eight minutes).
2. The stairs (about five minutes). 3. The room (about seventeen minutes).*

The film is entirely silent except for the "sssh!" in part one.

*Climate of film comic and unreal. O should invite laughter throughout by
his way of moving. Unreality of street scene (see notes to this section).*

GENERAL

Esse est percipi.

All extraneous perception suppressed, animal, human, divine, self-
perception maintains in being.

Search of non-being in flight from extraneous perception breaking
down in inescapability of self-perception.

No truth value attaches to above, regarded as of merely structural and
dramatic convenience.

In order to be figured in this situation the protagonist is sundered
into object (O) and eye (E), the former in flight, the latter in pursuit.

It will not be clear until end of film that pursuing perceiver is not
extraneous, but self.

Until end of film O is perceived by E from behind and at an angle not exceeding 45°. Convention: O enters *percipi* = experiences anguish of perceivedness, only when this angle is exceeded.

O not in perceivedness:

$$O \nearrow \\ 45 \searrow E$$

O in perceivedness:

$$O \nearrow \\ 46 \searrow E$$

E is therefore at pains, throughout pursuit, to keep within this "angle of immunity" and only exceeds it (1) inadvertently at beginning of part one when he first sights O (2) inadvertently at beginning of part two when he follows O into vestibule and (3) deliberately at end of part three when O is cornered. In first two cases he hastily reduces angle.

OUTLINE

1. The street

Dead straight. No sidestreets or intersections. Period: about 1929. Early summer morning. Small factory district. Moderate animation of workers going unhurriedly to work. All going in same direction and all in couples. No automobiles. Two bicycles ridden by men with girl passengers (on crossbar). One cab, cantering nag, driver standing brandishing whip. All persons in opening scene to be shown in some way perceiving—one another, an object, a shop window, a poster, etc., i.e. all contentedly in *percipere* and *percipi*. First view of above is by E motionless and searching with his eyes for O. He may be supposed at street edge of wide (4 yards) sidewalk. O finally comes into view hastening blindly along sidewalk, hugging the wall on his left, in opposite direction to all the others. Long dark overcoat (whereas all others in light summer dress) with collar up, hat pulled down over eyes, briefcase in left hand, right hand shielding exposed side of face. He storms along in comic foundered precipitancy. E's searching eye, turning left from street to sidewalk, picks him up at an angle exceeding that of immunity (O's unperceivedness according to convention) (1). O, entering perceivedness, reacts (after just sufficient onward movement for his gait to be established) by halting and cringing aside towards wall. E immediately draws back to close the angle (2) and O, released from perceivedness, hurries on. E lets him get about 10 yards ahead and then starts after him (3). Street elements from now on incidental (except for episode of couple) in the sense that only registered in so far as they happen to enter field of pursuing eye fixed on O.

Episode of couple (4). In his blind haste O jostles an elderly couple of shabby genteel aspect, standing on sidewalk, peering together at a newspaper. They should be discovered by E a few yards before collision. The woman is holding a pet monkey under her left arm. E follows O an instant as he hastens blindly on, then registers couple recovering from shock, comes up with them, passes them slightly and halts to observe them (5). Having recovered they turn and look after O, the woman raising a lorgnon to her eyes, the man taking off his pince-nez fastened to his coat by a ribbon. They then look at each other, she lowering her lorgnon, he resuming his pince-nez. He opens his mouth to vituperate. She checks him with a gesture and soft "sssh!" He turns again, taking off his pince-nez, to look after O. She feels the gaze of E upon them and turns, raising her lorgnon, to look at him. She nudges her companion who turns back towards her, resuming his pince-nez, follows direction of her gaze and, taking off his pince-nez, looks at E. As they both stare at E the expression gradually comes over their faces which will be that of the flower-woman in the stairs scene and that of O at the end of film, an expression only to be described as corresponding to an agony of perceivedness. Indifference of monkey, looking up into face of its mistress. They close their eyes, she lowering her lorgnon, and hasten away in direction of all the others, i.e. that opposed to O and E (6).

E turns back towards O by now far ahead and out of sight. Immediate acceleration of E in pursuit (blurred transit of encountered elements). O comes into view, grows rapidly larger until E settles down behind him at same angle and remove as before. O disappears suddenly through open housedoor on his left. Immediate acceleration of E who comes up with O in vestibule at foot of stairs.

2. Stairs

Vestibule about 4 yards square with stairs at inner righthand angle. Relation of streetdoor to stairs such that E's first perception of O (E near door, O motionless at foot of stairs, right hand on banister, body shaken by panting) is from an angle a little exceeding that of immunity. O, entering perceivedness (according to convention), transfers right hand from banister to exposed side of face and cringes aside towards wall on his left. E immediately draws back to close the angle and O, released, resumes his pose at foot of stairs, hand on banister. O mounts a few steps (E remaining near door), raises head, listens, redescends hastily backwards and crouches down in angle of stairs and wall on his right, invisible to one descending (7). E registers him there, then transfers to stairs. A frail old woman appears on bottom landing. She carries a tray of flowers slung from her neck by a strap. She descends slowly, with fumbling feet, one hand steadying the tray, the other holding the banister. Absorbed by difficulty of descent she does not become aware of E until she is quite down and making for the door. She halts and looks full at E. Gradually same expression as that of couple in street. She closes her eyes, then sinks to the ground and lies with face in scattered flowers. E lingers on this a moment, then transfers to where O last registered. He is no longer there, but hastening up the stairs. E transfers to stairs and picks up O as he reaches first landing. Bound forward and up of E who overtakes O on second flight and is literally at his heels when he reaches second landing and opens with key door of room. They enter room together, E turning with O as he turns to lock the door behind him.

3. The room

Here we assume problem of dual perception solved and enter O's perception (8). E must so manoeuvre throughout what follows, until investment proper, that O is always seen from behind, at most convenient remove, and from an angle never exceeding that of immunity, i.e. preserved from perceivedness.

Small barely furnished room (9). Side by side on floor a large cat and small dog. Unreal quality. Motionless till ejected. Cat bigger than dog. On a table against wall a parrot in a cage and a goldfish in a bowl. This room sequence falls into three parts.

1. Preparation of room (occlusion of window and mirror, ejection of dog and cat, destruction of God's image, occlusion of parrot and goldfish).

2. Period in rocking-chair. Inspection and destruction of photographs.

3. Final investment of O by E and dénouement.

1. O stands near door with case in hand and takes in room. Succession of images: dog and cat, side by side, staring at him; mirror; window; couch with rug; dog and cat staring at him; parrot and goldfish, parrot staring at him; rocking-chair; dog and cat staring at him. He sets down case, approaches window from side and draws curtain. He turns towards dog and cat, still staring at him, then goes to couch and takes up rug. He turns towards dog and cat, still staring at him. Holding rug before him he approaches mirror from side and covers it with rug. He turns towards parrot and goldfish, parrot still staring at him. He goes to rocking-chair, inspects it from front. Insistent image of curiously carved headrest (10). He turns towards dog and cat still staring at him. He puts them out of room (11). He takes up case and is moving towards chair when rug falls from mirror. He drops briefcase, hastens to wall between couch and mirror, follows walls past window, approaches mirror from side, picks up rug and, holding it before him, covers mirror with it again. He returns to briefcase, picks it up, goes to chair, sits down and is opening case when disturbed by print, pinned to wall before him, of the face of God the Father, the eyes staring at him severely. He sets down case on floor to his left, gets up and inspects print. Insistent image of wall, paper hanging off in strips (10). He tears print from wall, tears it in four, throws down the pieces and grinds them underfoot. He turns back to chair, image again of its curious headrest, sits down, image again of tattered wall-paper, takes case on his knees, takes out a folder, sets down case on floor to his left and is opening folder when disturbed by parrot's eye. He lays folder on case, gets up, takes off overcoat, goes to parrot, close-up of parrot's eye, covers cage with coat, goes back to chair, image again of headrest, sits down, image again of tattered wall-paper, takes up folder and is opening it when

disturbed by fish's eye. He lays folder on case, gets up, goes to fish, close-up of fish's eye, extends coat to cover bowl as well as cage, goes back to chair, image again of headrest, sits down, image again of wall, takes up folder, takes off hat and lays it on case to his left. Scant hair or bald to facilitate identification of narrow black elastic encircling head.

When O sits up and back his head is framed in headrest which is a narrower extension of backrest. Throughout scene of inspection and destruction of photographs E may be supposed immediately behind chair looking down over O's left shoulder (12).

2. O opens folder, takes from it a packet of photographs (13), lays folder on case and begins to inspect photographs. He inspects them in order 1 to 7. When he has finished with 1 he lays it on his knees, inspects 2, lays it on top of 1, and so on, so that when he has finished inspecting them all 1 will be at the bottom of the pile and 7—or rather 6, for he does not lay down 7—at the top. He gives about six seconds each to 1–4, about twice as long to 5 and 6 (trembling hands). Looking at 6 he touches with fore-finger little girl's face. After six seconds of 7 he tears it in four and drops pieces on floor on his left. He takes up 6 from top of pile on his knees, looks at it again for about three seconds, tears it in four and drops pieces on floor to his left. So on for the others, looking at each again for about three seconds before tearing it up. 1 must be on tougher mount for he has difficulty in tearing it across. Straining hands. He finally succeeds, drops pieces on floor and sits, rocking slightly, hands holding armrests (14).

3. Investment proper. Perception from now on, if dual perception feasible, E's alone, except perception of E by O at end. E moves a little back (image of headrest from back), then starts circling to his left, approaches maximum angle and halts. From this open angle, beyond which he will enter *percipi*, O can be seen beginning to doze off. His visible hand relaxes on armrest, his head nods and falls forward, the rock approaches stillness. E advances, opening angle beyond limit of immunity, his gaze pierces the light sleep and O starts awake. The start revives the rock, immediately arrested by foot to floor. Tension of hand on armrest. Turning his head to right, O cringes away from perceivedness. E draws back to reduce the angle and after a moment, reassured, O turns back front and resumes his

pose. The rock resumes, dies down slowly as O dozes off again. E now begins a much wider encirclement. Images of curtained window, walls and shrouded mirror to indicate his path and that he is not yet looking at O. Then brief image of O seen by E from well beyond the angle of immunity, i.e. from near the table with shrouded bowl and cage. O is now seen to be fast asleep, his head sunk on his chest and his hands, fallen from the armrests, limply dangling. E resumes his cautious approach. Images of shrouded bowl and cage and tattered wall adjoining, with same indication as before. Halt and brief image, not far short of full-face, of O still fast asleep. E advances last few yards along tattered wall and halts directly in front of O. Long image of O, full-face, against ground of headrest, sleeping. E's gaze pierces the sleep, O starts awake, stares up at E. Patch over O's left eye now seen for the first time. Rock revived by start, stilled at once by foot to ground. Hand clutches armrests. O half starts from chair, then stiffens, staring up at E. Gradually that look. Cut to E, of whom this very first image (face only, against ground of tattered wall). It is O's face (with patch) but with very different expression, impossible to describe, neither severity nor benignity, but rather acute *intentness*. A big nail is visible near left temple (patch side). Long image of the unblinking gaze. Cut back to O, still half risen, staring up, with that look. O closes his eyes and falls back in chair, starting off rock. He covers his face with his hands. Image of O rocking, his head in his hands but not yet bowed. Cut back to E. As before. Cut back to O. He sits, bowed forward, his head in his hands, gently rocking. Hold it as the rocking dies down.

End

NOTES

1.   Wall
       O→   Sidewalk   First sight of O
     E
         Street

2.
       O→   O released from perceivedness   ⊢——⊣
     E   = 2 yds

3.
E   → O→   Relation E–O during pursuit

4. The purpose of this episode, undefendable except as a dramatic convenience, is to suggest as soon as possible unbearable quality of E's scrutiny.
Reinforced by episode of flower-woman in stairs sequence.

5.   Wall
     He Couple   O →   ⊢——⊣ = 2 yds
     She E   Sidewalk
           Street

6. Expression of this episode, like that of animals' ejection in part three,
should be as precisely stylized as possible. The purpose of the monkey,
either unaware of E or indifferent to him, is to anticipate behaviour of
animals in part three, attentive to O exclusively.

7. Suggestion for vestibule with (1) O in *percipi* (2) released (3) hiding from
flower-woman. Note that even when E exceeds angle of immunity O's
face never really seen because of immediate turn aside and (here) hand
to shield face.

1   S|tairs   2   S|tairs   3   S|tairs
      O.   O.→   O.
   E.   E.   E.
     Entry   Entry   Entry

8. Up till now the perceptions of O, hastening *blindly* to illusory sanctuary, have been neglected and must in fact have been negligible. But in the room, until he falls asleep and the investment begins, they must be recorded. And at the same time E's perceiving of O must continue to be given. E is concerned only with O, not with the room, or only incidentally with the room in so far as its elements happen to enter the field of his gaze fastened on O. We see O in the room thanks to E's perceiving and the room itself thanks to O's perceiving. In other words this room sequence, up to the moment of O's falling asleep, is composed of two independent sets of images. I feel that any attempt to express them in simultaneity (composite images, double frame, superimposition, etc.) must prove unsatisfactory. The presentation in a single image of O's perception of the print, for example, and E's perception of O perceiving it—no doubt feasible technically—would perhaps

make impossible for the spectator a clear apprehension of either. The solution might be in a succession of images of different *quality*, corresponding on the one hand to E's perception of O and on the other to O's perception of the room. This difference of quality might perhaps be sought in different degrees of development, the passage from the one to the other being from greater to lesser and lesser to greater definition or luminosity. The dissimilarity, however obtained, would have to be flagrant. Having been up till now exclusively in the E quality, we would suddenly pass, with O's first survey of the room, into this quite different O quality. Then back to the E quality when O is shown moving to the window. And so on throughout the sequence, switching from the one to the other as required. Were this the solution adopted it might be desirable to establish, by means of brief sequences, the O quality in parts one and two.

This seems to be the chief problem of the film, though I perhaps exaggerate its difficulty through technical ignorance.

9.

Suggestion for room.

This obviously cannot be O's room. It may be supposed it is his mother's room, which he has not visited for many years and is now to occupy momentarily, to look after the pets, until she comes out of hospital. This has no bearing on the film and need not be elucidated.

10. At close of film face E and face O can only be distinguished (1) by different expressions (2) by fact of O looking up and E down and (3) by difference of ground (for O headrest of chair, for E wall). Hence insistence on headrest and tattered wall.

11. Foolish suggestion for eviction of cat and dog. Also see Note 6.

12. Chair from front during photo sequence.

13. Description of photographs.

1. Male infant. 6 months. His mother holds him in her arms. Infant smiles front. Mother's big hands. Her severe eyes devouring him. Her big old-fashioned beflowered hat.

2. The same. 4 years. On a veranda, dressed in loose nightshirt, kneeling on a cushion, attitude of prayer, hands clasped, head bowed, eyes closed. Half profile. Mother on chair beside him, big hands on knees, head bowed towards him, severe eyes, similar hat to 1.

3. The same. 15 years. Bareheaded. School blazer. Smiling. Teaching a dog to beg. Dog on its hind legs looking up at him.

4. The same. 20 years. Graduation day. Academic gown. Mortar-board under arm. On a platform, receiving scroll from Rector. Smiling. Section of public watching.

5. The same. 21 years. Bareheaded. Smiling. Small moustache. Arm round fiancée. A young man takes a snap of them.

6. The same. 25 years. Newly enlisted. Bareheaded. Uniform. Bigger moustache. Smiling. Holding a little girl in his arms. She looks into his face, exploring it with finger.

7. The same. 30 years. Looking over 40. Wearing hat and overcoat. Patch over left eye. Cleanshaven. Grim expression.

14. Profit by rocking-chair to emotionalize inspection, e.g. gentle steady rock for 1 to 4, rock stilled (foot to ground) after two seconds of 5, rock resumed between 5 and 6, rock stilled after two seconds of 6, rock resumed after 6 and for 7 as for 1–4.

COME AND GO

A dramaticule

For John Calder

Flo
Vi
Ru
(Ages undeterminable)

Sitting centre side by side stage right to left Flo, Vi and Ru.
  Very erect, facing front, hands clasped in laps.
  Silence.

VI   Ru.

RU   Yes.

VI   Flo.

FLO Yes.

VI   When did we three last meet?

RU   Let us not speak.
     [*Silence.*
     Exit Vi right.
     Silence.]

FLO Ru.

RU   Yes.

FLO What do you think of Vi?

RU   I see little change. [*Flo moves to centre seat, whispers in Ru's ear.*
     Appalled.] Oh! [*They look at each other. Flo puts her finger to her lips.*]
     Does she not realize?

FLO God grant not.
     [*Enter Vi. Flo and Ru turn back front, resume pose. Vi sits right. Silence.*]
     Just sit together as we used to, in the playground at Miss Wade's.

RU   On the log.

[*Silence.*

Exit Flo left.

Silence.]

Vi.

VI   Yes.

RU   How do you find Flo?

VI   She seems much the same. [*Ru moves to centre seat, whispers in Vi's ear. Appalled.*] Oh! [*They look at each other. Ru puts her finger to her lips.*] Has she not been told?

RU   God forbid.

[*Enter Flo. Ru and Vi turn back front, resume pose. Flo sits left.*]

Holding hands . . . that way.

FLO   Dreaming of . . . love.

[*Silence.*

Exit Ru right.

Silence.]

VI   Flo.

FLO   Yes.

VI   How do you think Ru is looking?

FLO   One sees little in this light. [*Vi moves to centre seat, whispers in Flo's ear. Appalled.*] Oh! [*They look at each other. Vi puts her finger to her lips.*] Does she not know?

VI   Please God not.

[*Enter Ru. Vi and Flo turn back front, resume pose. Ru sits right.*

Silence.]

May we not speak of the old days? [*Silence.*] Of what came after? [*Silence.*] Shall we hold hands in the old way?

[*After a moment they join hands as follows: Vi's right hand with Ru's right hand. Vi's left hand with Flo's left hand, Flo's right hand with Ru's left hand, Vi's arms being above Ru's left arm and Flo's right arm. The three pairs of clasped hands rest on the three laps. Silence.*]

FLO   I can feel the rings.

[*Silence.*]

                                                             Curtain

NOTES

Successive positions

1	Flo	Vi	Ru
2 ⎡	Flo		Ru
⎣		Flo	Ru
3	Vi	Flo	Ru
4 ⎡	Vi		Ru
⎣	Vi	Ru	
5	Vi	Ru	Flo
6 ⎡	Vi		Flo
⎣		Vi	Flo
7	Ru	Vi	Flo

Hands

Ru	Vi	Flo

Lighting

Soft, from above only and concentrated on playing area. Rest of stage as dark as possible.

Costume

Full-length coats, buttoned high, dull violet (Ru), dull red (Vi), dull yellow (Flo). Drab nondescript hats with enough brim to shade faces. Apart from colour differentiation three figures as alike as possible. Light shoes with rubber soles. Hands made up to be as visible as possible. No rings apparent.

Seat

Narrow benchlike seat, without back, just long enough to accommodate three figures almost touching. As little visible as possible. It should not be clear what they are sitting on.

Exits

The figures are not seen to go off stage. They should disappear a few steps from lit area. If dark not sufficient to allow this, recourse should be had to screens or drapes as little visible as possible. Exits and entrances slow, without sound of feet.

Ohs

Three very different sounds.

Voices

As low as compatible with audibility. Colourless except for three "ohs" and two lines following.

EH JOE

A piece for television

Joe, late fifties, grey hair, old dressing-gown, carpet slippers, in his room.

1. Joe seen from behind sitting on edge of bed, intent pose, getting up, going to window, opening window, looking out, closing window, drawing curtain, standing intent.

2. Joe do. (= from behind) going from window to door, opening door, looking out, closing door, locking door, drawing hanging before door, standing intent.

3. Joe do. going from door to cupboard, opening cupboard, looking in, closing cupboard, locking cupboard, drawing hanging before cupboard, standing intent.

4. Joe do. going from cupboard to bed, kneeling down, looking under bed, getting up, sitting down on edge of bed as when discovered, beginning to relax.

5. Joe seen from front sitting on edge of bed, relaxed, eyes closed. Hold, then dolly slowly in to close-up of face. First word of text stops this movement.

Camera

Joe's opening movements followed by camera at constant remove, Joe full length in frame throughout. No need to record room as whole. After this opening pursuit, between first and final close-up of face, camera has nine slight moves in towards face, say four inches each time. Each move is stopped by voice resuming, never camera move and voice together. This would give position of camera when dolly stopped by first word of text as one yard from maximum close-up of face. Camera does not move between paragraphs till clear that pause (say three seconds) longer than between phrases. Then four inches in say four seconds when movement stopped by voice resuming.

Voice

Low, distinct, remote, little colour, absolutely steady rhythm, slightly slower than normal. Between phrases a beat of one second at least. Between paragraphs about seven, i.e. three before camera starts to advance and four for advance before it is stopped by voice resuming.

Face

Practically motionless throughout, eyes unblinking during paragraphs, impassive except in so far as it reflects mounting tension of listening. Brief zones of relaxation between paragraphs when perhaps voice has relented for the evening and intentness may relax variously till restored by voice resuming.

WOMAN'S VOICE

Joe ...

[*Eyes open, resumption of intentness.*]

Joe ...

[*Full intentness.*]

Thought of everything? ... Forgotten nothing? ... You're all right now, eh? ... No one can see you now.... No one can get at you now.... Why don't you put out that light? ... There might be a louse watching you.... Why don't you go to bed? ... What's wrong with that bed, Joe? ... You changed it, didn't you? ... Made no difference? ... Or is the heart already? ... Crumbles when you lie down in the dark.... Dry rotten at last.... Eh Joe?

Camera move 1

The best's to come, you said, that last time.... Hurrying me into my coat.... Last I was favoured with from you.... Say it you now, Joe, no one'll hear you.... Come on, Joe, no one can say it like you, say it again now and listen to yourself.... The best's to come.... You were right for once.... In the end.

Camera move 2

You know that penny farthing hell you call your mind. . . . That's where you think this is coming from, don't you? . . . That's where you heard your father. . . . Isn't that what you told me? . . . Started in on you one June night and went on for years. . . . On and off. . . . Behind the eyes. . . . That's how you were able to throttle him in the end. . . . Mental thuggee you called it. . . . One of your happiest fancies. . . . Mental thuggee. . . . Otherwise he'd be plaguing you yet. . . . Then your mother when her hour came. . . . "Look up, Joe, look up, we're watching you." . . . Weaker and weaker till you laid her too. . . . Others. . . . All the others. . . . Such love he got. . . . God knows why. . . . Pitying love. . . . None to touch it. . . . And look at him now. . . . Throttling the dead in his head.

Camera move 3

Anyone living love you now, Joe? . . . Anyone living sorry for you now? . . . That slut that comes on Saturday, you pay her, don't you? . . . Penny a hoist tuppence as long as you like. . . . Watch yourself you don't run short, Joe. . . . Ever think of that? . . . Eh Joe? . . . What it'd be if you ran out of us. . . . Not another soul to still. . . . Sit there in his stinking old wrapper hearing himself. . . . That lifelong adorer. . . . Weaker and weaker till not a gasp left there either. . . . Is it that you want? . . . Well preserved for his age and the silence of the grave. . . . That old paradise you were always harping on. . . . No Joe. . . . Not for the likes of us.

Camera move 4

I was strong myself when I started. . . . In on you. . . . Wasn't I, Joe? . . . Normal strength. . . . Like those summer evenings in the Green. . . . In the early days. . . . Of our idyll. . . . When we sat watching the ducks. . . . Holding hands exchanging vows. . . . How you admired my elocution! . . . Among other charms. . . . Voice like flint glass. . . . To borrow your expression. . . . Powerful grasp of language you had. . . . Flint glass. . . . You could have listened to it for ever. . . . And now this. . . . Squeezed down to this. . . . How much longer would you say? . . . Till the whisper. . . . You know. . . . When you can't hear the words. . . . Just the odd one here and there. . . . That's the worst. . . . Isn't it, Joe? . . . Isn't that what you told me. . . . Before we expire. . . . The odd word. . . . Straining to hear. . . . Why must you do that? . . . When you're nearly home. . . . What matter then. . . . What we mean. . . . It should be the best. . . . Nearly home again. . . . Another stilled. . . . And it's the worst. . . . Isn't that what you said? . . . The whisper. . . . The odd word. . . . Straining to hear. . . . Brain tired squeezing. . . . It stops in the end. . . . You stop it in the end. . . . Imagine if you couldn't. . . . Ever think of that? . . . If it went on. . . . The whisper in your head. . . . Me whispering at you in your head. . . . Things you can't catch. . . . On and off. . . . Till you join us. . . . Eh Joe?

Camera move 5

How's your Lord these days? . . . Still worth having? . . . Still lapping it up? . . . The passion of our Joe. . . . Wait till He starts talking to you. . . . When you're done with yourself. . . . All your dead dead. . . . Sitting there in your foul old wrapper. . . . Very fair health for a man of your years. . . . Just that lump in your bubo. . . . Silence of the grave without the maggots. . . . To crown your labours. . . . Till one night. . . . "Thou fool thy soul." . . . Put your thugs on that. . . . Eh Joe? . . . Ever think of that? . . . When He starts in on you. . . . When you're done with yourself. . . . If you ever are.

Camera move 6

Yes, great love God knows why. . . . Even me. . . . But I found a better. . . . As I hope you heard. . . . Preferable in all respects. . . .

Kinder. . . . Stronger. . . . More intelligent. . . . Better looking. . . .
Cleaner. . . . Truthful. . . . Faithful. . . . Sane. . . . Yes. . . . I did all right.

Camera move 7

But there was one didn't. . . . You know the one I mean, Joe. . . . The
green one. . . . The narrow one. . . . Always pale. . . . The pale eyes. . . .
Spirit made light. . . . To borrow your expression. . . . The way they
opened after. . . . Unique. . . . Are you with me now? . . . Eh Joe? . . .
There was love for you. . . . The best's to come, you said. . . . Bundling
her into her Avoca sack. . . . Her fingers fumbling with the big horn
buttons. . . . Ticket in your pocket for the first morning flight. . . .
You've had her, haven't you? . . . You've laid her? . . . Of course he
has. . . . She went young. . . . No more old lip from her.

Camera move 8

Ever know what happened? . . . She didn't say? . . . Just the
announcement in the *Independent*. . . . "On Mary's beads we plead her
needs and in the Holy Mass." . . . Will I tell you? . . . Not
interested? . . . Well I will just the same. . . . I think you should
know. . . . That's right, Joe, squeeze away. . . . Don't lose heart now. . . .
When you're nearly home. . . . I'll soon be gone. . . . The last of
them. . . . Unless that poor old slut loves you. . . . Then yourself. . . .
That old bonfire. . . . Years of that stink. . . . Then the silence. . . . A
dollop of that. . . . To crown all. . . . Till His Nibs. . . . One dirty winter
night. . . . "Mud thou art."

Camera move 9

All right. . . . Warm summer night. . . . All sleeping. . . . Sitting on the
edge of her bed in her lavender slip. . . . You know the one. . . . Ah she
knew you, heavenly powers! . . . Faint lap of sea through open
window. . . . Gets up in the end and slips out as she is. . . . Moon. . . .

Stock. . . . Down the garden and under the viaduct. . . . Sees from the seaweed the tide is flowing. . . . Goes on down to the edge and lies down with her face in the wash. . . . Cut a long story short doesn't work. . . . Gets up in the end sopping wet and back up to the house. . . . Gets out the Gillette. . . . The make you recommended for her body hair. . . . Back down the garden and under the viaduct. . . . Takes the blade from the holder and lies down at the edge on her side. . . . Cut another long story short doesn't work either. . . . You know how she always dreaded pain. . . . Tears a strip from the slip and ties it round the scratch. . . . Gets up in the end and back up to the house. . . . Slip clinging the way wet silk will. . . . This all new to you, Joe? . . . Eh Joe? . . . Gets the tablets and back down the garden and under the viaduct. . . . Takes a few on the way. . . . Unconscionable hour by now. . . . Moon going off the shore behind the hill. . . . Stands a bit looking at the beaten silver. . . . Then starts along the edge to a place further down near the Rock. . . . Imagine what in her mind to make her do that. . . . Imagine. . . . Trailing her feet in the water like a child. . . . Takes a few more on the way. . . . Will I go on, Joe? . . . Eh Joe? . . . Lies down in the end with her face a few feet from the tide. . . . Clawing at the shingle now. . . . Has it all worked out this time. . . . Finishes the tube. . . . There's love for you. . . . Eh Joe? . . . Scoops a little cup for her face in the stones. . . . The green one. . . . The narrow one. . . . Always pale. . . . The pale eyes. . . . The look they shed before. . . . The way they opened after. . . . Spirit made light. . . . Wasn't that your description, Joe? . . .
[*Voice drops to whisper, almost inaudible except words in italics.*]
All right. . . . You've had the best. . . . Now *imagine*. . . . Before she goes. . . . Face in the cup. . . . Lips on a *stone*. . . . Taking Joe with her. . . . Light gone. . . . *"Joe Joe."* . . . No sound. . . . To the *stones*. . . . Say it you now, no one'll hear you. . . . Say "Joe" it parts the *lips*. . . . *Imagine* the hands. . . . The *solitaire*. . . . Against a *stone*. . . . Imagine the *eyes*. . . . Spiritlight. . . . Month of June. . . . What year of your Lord? . . . *Breasts* in the stones. . . . And the *hands*. . . . Before they

go. . . . *Imagine* the hands. . . . What are they at? . . . In the *stones.* . . .
[*Image fades, voice as before.*]
What are they fondling? . . . Till they go. . . . *There's love for you.* . . .
Isn't it, Joe? . . . Wasn't it, Joe? . . . *Eh Joe?* . . . Wouldn't you say? . . .
Compared to us. . . . Compared to Him. . . . *Eh Joe?* . . .
[*Voice and image out. End.*]

BREATH

Curtain

1. Faint light on stage littered with miscellaneous rubbish. Hold about five seconds.

2. Faint brief cry and immediately inspiration and slow increase of light together reaching maximum together in about ten seconds. Silence and hold about five seconds.

3. Expiration and slow decrease of light together reaching minimum together (light as in 1) in about ten seconds and immediately cry as before. Silence and hold about five seconds.

Curtain

RUBBISH

No verticals, all scattered and lying.

CRY

Instant of recorded vagitus. Important that two cries be identical, switching on and off strictly synchronized light and breath.

BREATH

Amplified recording.

MAXIMUM LIGHT

Not bright. If 0 = dark and 10 = bright, light should move from about 3 to 6 and back.

NOT I

NOTE

Movement: this consists in simple sideways raising of arms from sides and their falling back, in a gesture of helpless compassion. It lessens with each recurrence till scarcely perceptible at third. There is just enough pause to contain it as Mouth recovers from vehement refusal to relinquish third person.

Stage in darkness but for Mouth, upstage audience right, about 8 feet above stage level, faintly lit from close-up and below, rest of face in shadow. Invisible microphone.

    Auditor, downstage audience left, tall standing figure, sex undeterminable, enveloped from head to foot in loose black djellaba, with hood, fully faintly lit, standing on invisible podium about 4 feet high shown by attitude alone to be facing diagonally across stage intent on Mouth, dead still throughout but for four brief movements where indicated. See Note. As house lights down Mouth's voice unintelligible behind curtain. House lights out. Voice continues unintelligible behind curtain, 10 seconds. With rise of curtain ad-libbing from text as required leading when curtain fully up and attention sufficient into:

MOUTH   ... out ... into this world ... this world ... tiny little thing ...
                     before its time ... in a godfor— ... what? ... girl? ... yes ...
                     tiny little girl ... into this ... out into this ... before her

time . . . godforsaken hole called . . . called . . . no matter . . .
parents unknown . . . unheard of . . . he having vanished . . .
thin air . . . no sooner buttoned up his breeches . . . she
similarly . . . eight months later . . . almost to the tick . . . so no
love . . . spared that . . . no love such as normally vented on
the . . . speechless infant . . . in the home . . . no . . . nor indeed
for that matter any of any kind . . . no love of any kind . . . at
any subsequent stage . . . so typical affair . . . nothing of any
note till coming up to sixty when— . . . what? . . seventy? . . .
good God! . . . coming up to seventy . . . wandering in a field . . .
looking aimlessly for cowslips . . . to make a ball . . . a few steps
then stop . . . stare into space . . . then on . . . a few more . . .
stop and stare again . . . so on . . . drifting around . . . when
suddenly . . . gradually . . . all went out . . . all that early April
morning light . . . and she found herself in the— . . . what? . . .
who? . . . no! . . . she! . . . [*pause and movement 1*] . . . found
herself in the dark . . . and if not exactly . . . insentient . . .
insentient . . . for she could still hear the buzzing . . . so-
called . . . in the ears . . . and a ray of light came and went . . .
came and went . . . such as the moon might cast . . . drifting . . .
in and out of cloud . . . but so dulled . . . feeling . . . feeling so
dulled . . . she did not know . . . what position she was in . . .
imagine! . . . what position she was in! . . . whether standing . . .
or sitting . . . but the brain— . . . what? . . . kneeling? . . . yes . . .
whether standing . . . or sitting . . . or kneeling . . . but the
brain— . . . what? . . . lying? . . . yes . . . whether standing . . . or
sitting . . . or kneeling . . . or lying . . . but the brain still . . .
still . . . in a way . . . for her first thought was . . . oh long
after . . . sudden flash . . . brought up as she had been to
believe . . . with the other waifs . . . in a merciful . . . [*Brief
laugh.*] . . . God . . . [*Good laugh.*] . . . first thought was . . . oh
long after . . . sudden flash . . . she was being punished . . . for
her sins . . . a number of which then . . . further proof if proof
were needed . . . flashed through her mind . . . one after

another ... then dismissed as foolish ... oh long after ... this
thought dismissed ... as she suddenly realized ... gradually
realized ... she was not suffering ... imagine! ... not
suffering! ... indeed could not remember ... off-hand ...
when she had suffered less ... unless of course she was ...
meant to be suffering ... ha! ... *thought* to be suffering ... just
as the odd time ... in her life ... when clearly intended to be
having pleasure ... she was in fact ... having none ... not the
slightest ... in which case of course ... that notion of
punishment ... for some sin or other ... or for the lot ... or
no particular reason ... for its own sake ... thing she
understood perfectly ... that notion of punishment ... which
had first occurred to her ... brought up as she had been to
believe ... with the other waifs ... in a merciful ... [*Brief
laugh.*] ... God ... [*Good laugh.*] ... first occurred to her ...
then dismissed ... as foolish ... was perhaps not so foolish ...
after all ... so on ... all that ... vain reasonings ... till another
thought ... oh long after ... sudden flash ... very foolish
really but— ... what? ... the buzzing? ... yes ... all the time
the buzzing ... so-called ... in the ears ... though of course
actually ... not in the ears at all ... in the skull ... dull roar in
the skull ... and all the time this ray or beam ... like
moonbeam ... but probably not ... certainly not ... always the
same spot ... now bright ... now shrouded ... but always the
same spot ... as no moon could ... no ... no moon ... just all
part of the same wish to ... torment ... though actually in
point of fact ... not in the least ... not a twinge ... so far ...
ha! ... so far ... this other thought then ... oh long after ...
sudden flash ... very foolish really but so like her ... in a
way ... that she might do well to ... groan ... on and off ...
writhe she could not ... as if in actual agony ... but could
not ... could not bring herself ... some flaw in her make-
up ... incapable of deceit ... or the machine ... more likely
the machine ... so disconnected ... never got the message ...

or powerless to respond . . . like numbed . . . couldn't make the
sound . . . not any sound . . . no sound of any kind . . . no
screaming for help for example . . . should she feel so
inclined . . . scream . . . [*screams*] . . . then listen . . . [*silence*] . . .
scream again . . . [*screams again*] . . . then listen again . . .
[*silence*] . . . no . . . spared that . . . all silent as the grave . . . no
part— . . . what? . . . the buzzing? . . . yes . . . all silent but for
the buzzing . . . so-called . . . no part of her moving . . . that she
could feel . . . just the eyelids . . . presumably . . . on and off . . .
shut out the light . . . reflex they call it . . . no feeling of any
kind . . . but the lids . . . even best of times . . . who feels
them? . . . opening . . . shutting . . . all that moisture . . . but the
brain still . . . still sufficiently . . . oh very much so! . . . at this
stage . . . in control . . . under control . . . to question even
this . . . for on that April morning . . . so it reasoned . . . that
April morning . . . she fixing with her eye . . . a distant bell . . .
as she hastened towards it . . . fixing it with her eye . . . lest it
elude her . . . had not all gone out . . . all that light . . . of
itself . . . without any . . . any . . . on her part . . . so on . . . so on
it reasoned . . . vain questionings . . . and all dead still . . . sweet
silent as the grave . . . when suddenly . . . gradually . . . she
realiz— . . . what? . . . the buzzing? . . . yes . . . all dead still but
for the buzzing . . . when suddenly she realized . . . words
were— . . . what? . . . who? . . . no! . . . she! . . . [*pause and
movement 2*] . . . realized . . . words were coming . . . imagine!
. . . words were coming . . . a voice she did not recognize . . . at
first . . . so long since it had sounded . . . then finally had to
admit . . . could be none other . . . than her own . . . certain
vowel sounds . . . she had never heard . . . elsewhere . . . so that
people would stare . . . the rare occasions . . . once or twice a
year . . . always winter some strange reason . . . stare at her
uncomprehending . . . and now this stream . . . steady
stream . . . she who had never . . . on the contrary . . .
practically speechless . . . all her days . . . how she survived! . . .

even shopping . . . out shopping . . . busy shopping centre . . .
supermart . . . just hand in the list . . . with the bag . . . old
black shopping bag . . . then stand there waiting . . . any length
of time . . . middle of the throng . . . motionless . . . staring
into space . . . mouth half open as usual . . . till it was back in
her hand . . . the bag back in her hand . . . then pay and go . . .
not as much as goodbye . . . how she survived! . . . and now this
stream . . . not catching the half of it . . . not the quarter . . . no
idea . . . what she was saying . . . imagine! . . . no idea what she
was saying! . . . till she began trying to . . . delude herself . . . it
was not hers at all . . . not her voice at all . . . and no doubt
would have . . . vital she should . . . was on the point . . . after
long efforts . . . when suddenly she felt . . . gradually she
felt . . . her lips moving . . . imagine! . . . her lips moving! . . .
as of course till then she had not . . . and not alone the
lips . . . the cheeks . . . the jaws . . . the whole face . . . all
those—. . . what? . . . the tongue? . . . yes . . . the tongue in the
mouth . . . all those contortions without which . . . no speech
possible . . . and yet in the ordinary way . . . not felt at all . . . so
intent one is . . . on what one is saying . . . the whole being . . .
hanging on its words . . . so that not only she had . . . had
she . . . not only had she . . . to give up . . . admit hers alone . . .
her voice alone . . . but this other awful thought . . . oh long
after . . . sudden flash . . . even more awful if possible . . . that
feeling was coming back . . . imagine! . . . feeling coming
back! . . . starting at the top . . . then working down . . . the
whole machine . . . but no . . . spared that . . . the mouth
alone . . . so far . . . ha! . . . so far . . . then thinking . . . oh long
after . . . sudden flash . . . it can't go on . . . all this . . . all
that . . . steady stream . . . straining to hear . . . make something of it . . . and her own thoughts . . . make something of
them . . . all—. . . what? . . . the buzzing? . . . yes . . . all the time
the buzzing . . . so-called . . . all that together . . . imagine! . . .
whole body like gone . . . just the mouth . . . lips . . . cheeks . . .

jaws . . . never— . . . what? . . . tongue? . . . yes . . . lips . . .
cheeks . . . jaws . . . tongue . . . never still a second . . . mouth
on fire . . . stream of words . . . in her ear . . . practically in her
ear . . . not catching the half . . . not the quarter . . . no idea
what she's saying . . . imagine! . . . no idea what she's saying! . . .
and can't stop . . . no stopping it . . . she who but a moment
before . . . but a moment! . . . could not make a sound . . . no
sound of any kind . . . now can't stop . . . imagine! . . . can't stop
the stream . . . and the whole brain begging . . . something
begging in the brain . . . begging the mouth to stop . . . pause a
moment . . . if only for a moment . . . and no response . . . as if
it hadn't heard . . . or couldn't . . . couldn't pause a second . . .
like maddened . . . all that together . . . straining to hear . . .
piece it together . . . and the brain . . . raving away on its
own . . . trying to make sense of it . . . or make it stop . . . or in
the past . . . dragging up the past . . . flashes from all over . . .
walks mostly . . . walking all her days . . . day after day . . . a few
steps then stop . . . stare into space . . . then on . . . a few
more . . . stop and stare again . . . so on . . . drifting around . . .
day after day . . . or that time she cried . . . the one time she
could remember . . . since she was a baby . . . must have cried
as a baby . . . perhaps not . . . not essential to life . . . just the
birth cry to get her going . . . breathing . . . then no more till
this . . . old hag already . . . sitting staring at her hand . . .
where was it? . . . Croker's Acres . . . one evening on the way
home . . . home! . . . a little mound in Croker's Acres . . .
dusk . . . sitting staring at her hand . . . there in her lap . . .
palm upward . . . suddenly saw it wet . . . the palm . . . tears
presumably . . . hers presumably . . . no one else for miles . . .
no sound . . . just the tears . . . sat and watched them dry . . . all
over in a second . . . or grabbing at straw . . . the brain . . .
flickering away on its own . . . quick grab and on . . . nothing
there . . . on to the next . . . bad as the voice . . . worse . . . as
little sense . . . all that together . . . can't— . . . what? . . . the

buzzing? . . . yes . . . all the time the buzzing . . . dull roar like
falls . . . and the beam . . . flickering on and off . . . starting to
move around . . . like moonbeam but not . . . all part of the
same . . . keep an eye on that too . . . corner of the eye . . . all
that together . . . can't go on . . . God is love . . . she'll be
purged . . . back in the field . . . morning sun . . . April . . . sink
face down in the grass . . . nothing but the larks . . . so on . . .
grabbing at the straw . . . straining to hear . . . the odd word . . .
make some sense of it . . . whole body like gone . . . just the
mouth . . . like maddened . . . and can't stop . . . no stopping
it . . . something she— . . . something she had to— . . .
what? . . . who? . . . no! . . . she! . . . [*pause and movement 3*] . . .
something she had to— . . . what? . . . the buzzing? . . . yes . . .
all the time the buzzing . . . dull roar . . . in the skull . . . and
the beam . . . ferreting around . . . painless . . . so far . . . ha! . . .
so far . . . then thinking . . . oh long after . . . sudden flash . . .
perhaps something she had to . . . had to . . . tell . . . could that
be it? . . . something she had to . . . tell . . . tiny little thing . . .
before its time . . . godforsaken hole . . . no love . . . spared
that . . . speechless all her days . . . practically speechless . . .
how she survived! . . . that time in court . . . what had she to say
for herself . . . guilty or not guilty . . . stand up woman . . .
speak up woman . . . stood there staring into space . . . mouth
half open as usual . . . waiting to be led away . . . glad of the
hand on her arm . . . now this . . . something she had to tell . . .
could that be it? . . . something that would tell . . . how it
was . . . how she— . . . what? . . . had been? . . . yes . . .
something that would tell how it had been . . . how she had
lived . . . lived on and on . . . guilty or not . . . on and on . . . to
be sixty . . . something she— . . . what? . . . seventy? . . . good
God! . . . on and on to be seventy . . . something she didn't
know herself . . . wouldn't know if she heard . . . then
forgiven . . . God is love . . . tender mercies . . . new every
morning . . . back in the field . . . April morning . . . face in the

grass ... nothing but the larks ... pick it up there ... get on
with it from there ... another few— ... what? ... not that? ...
nothing to do with that? ... nothing she could tell? ... all
right ... nothing she could tell ... try something else ... think
of something else ... oh long after ... sudden flash ... not
that either ... all right ... something else again ... so on ...
hit on it in the end ... think everything keep on long
enough ... then forgiven ... back in the— ... what? ... not
that either? ... nothing to do with that either? ... nothing she
could think? ... all right ... nothing she could tell ... nothing
she could think ... nothing she— ... what? ... who? ...
no! ... she! ... [*pause and movement 4*] ... tiny little thing ...
out before its time ... godforsaken hole ... no love ... spared
that ... speechless all her days ... practically speechless ...
even to herself ... never out loud ... but not completely ...
sometimes sudden urge ... once or twice a year ... always
winter some strange reason ... the long evenings ... hours of
darkness ... sudden urge to ... tell ... then rush out stop the
first she saw ... nearest lavatory ... start pouring it out ...
steady stream ... mad stuff ... half the vowels wrong ... no
one could follow ... till she saw the stare she was getting ...
then die of shame ... crawl back in ... once or twice a year ...
always winter some strange reason ... long hours of
darkness ... now this ... this ... quicker and quicker ... the
words ... the brain ... flickering away like mad ... quick grab
and on ... nothing there ... on somewhere else ... try
somewhere else ... all the time something begging ...
something in her begging ... begging it all to stop ...
unanswered ... prayer unanswered ... or unheard ... too
faint ... so on ... keep on ... trying ... not knowing what ...
what she was trying ... what to try ... whole body like gone ...
just the mouth ... like maddened ... so on ... keep— ...
what? ... the buzzing? ... yes ... all the time the buzzing ...
dull roar like falls ... in the skull ... and the beam ... poking

around ... painless ... so far ... ha! ... so far ... all that ...
keep on ... not knowing what ... what she was— ... what? ...
who? ... no! ... she! ... SHE! ... [*pause*] ... what she was
trying ... what to try ... no matter ... keep on ... [*curtain starts
down*] ... hit on it in the end ... then back ... God is love ...
tender mercies ... new every morning ... back in the field ...
April morning ... face in the grass ... nothing but the
larks ... pick it up—

[*Curtain fully down. House dark. Voice continues behind curtain,
unintelligible, 10 seconds, ceases as house lights up.*]

THAT TIME

Moments of one and the same voice A B C relay one another without solution of continuity—apart from the two 10-second breaks. Yet the switch from one to another must be clearly faintly perceptible. If threefold source and context prove insufficient to produce this effect it should be assisted mechanically (e.g. threefold pitch).

Curtain. Stage in darkness. Fade up to Listener's Face about 10 feet above stage level midstage off centre.

Old white face, long flaring white hair as if seen from above outspread.

Voices A B C are his own coming to him from both sides and above. They modulate back and forth without any break in general flow except where silence indicated. See note. Silence 7 seconds. Listener's Eyes are open. His breath audible, slow and regular.

A that time you went back that last time to look was the ruin still there where you hid as a child when was that [*eyes close*] grey day took the eleven to the end of the line and on from there no no trams then all gone long ago that time you went back to look was the ruin still there where you hid as a child that last time not a tram left in the place only the old rails when was that

C when you went in out of the rain always winter then always raining that time in the Portrait Gallery in off the street out of the cold and

rain slipped in when no one was looking and through the rooms
shivering and dripping till you found a seat marble slab and sat
down to rest and dry off and on to hell out of there when was that

B   on the stone together in the sun on the stone at the edge of the little
wood and as far as eye could see the wheat turning yellow vowing
every now and then you loved each other just a murmur not
touching or anything of that nature you one end of the stone she the
other long low stone like millstone no looks just there on the stone
in the sun with the little wood behind gazing at the wheat or eyes
closed all still no sign of life not a soul abroad no sound

A   straight off the ferry and up with the nightbag to the high street
neither right nor left not a curse for the old scenes the old names
straight up the rise from the wharf to the high street and there not a
wire to be seen only the old rails all rust when was that was your
mother ah for God's sake all gone long ago that time you went back
that last time to look was the ruin still there where you hid as a child
someone's folly

C   was your mother ah for God's sake all gone long ago all dust the lot
you the last huddled up on the slab in the old green greatcoat with
your arms round you whose else hugging you for a bit of warmth to
dry off and on to hell out of there and on to the next not a living
soul in the place only yourself and the odd attendant drowsing
around in his felt shufflers not a sound to be heard only every now
and then a shuffle of felt drawing near then dying away

B   all still just the leaves and ears and you too still on the stone in a daze
no sound not a word only every now and then to vow you loved each
other just a murmur one thing could ever bring tears till they dried
up altogether that thought when it came up among the others
floated up that scene

A   Foley was it Foley's Folly bit of a tower still standing all the rest rubble
and nettles where did you sleep no friend all the homes gone was it
that kip on the front where you no she was with you then still with
you then just the one night in any case off the ferry one morning
and back on her the next to look was the ruin still there where none

ever came where you hid as a child slip off when no one was looking and hide there all day long on a stone among the nettles with your picture-book

C till you hoisted your head and there before your eyes when they opened a vast oil black with age and dirt someone famous in his time some famous man or woman or even child such as a young prince or princess some young prince or princess of the blood black with age behind the glass where gradually as you peered trying to make it out gradually of all things a face appeared had you swivel on the slab to see who it was there at your elbow

B on the stone in the sun gazing at the wheat or the sky or the eyes closed nothing to be seen but the wheat turning yellow and the blue sky vowing every now and then you loved each other just a murmur tears without fail till they dried up altogether suddenly there in whatever thoughts you might be having whatever scenes perhaps way back in childhood or the womb worst of all or that old Chinaman long before Christ born with long white hair

C never the same after that never quite the same but that was nothing new if it wasn't this it was that common occurrence something you could never be the same after crawling about year after year sunk in your lifelong mess muttering to yourself who else you'll never be the same after this you were never the same after that

A or talking to yourself who else out loud imaginary conversations there was childhood for you ten or eleven on a stone among the giant nettles making it up now one voice now another till you were hoarse and they all sounded the same well on into the night some moods in the black dark or moonlight and they all out on the roads looking for you

B or by the window in the dark harking to the owl not a thought in your head till hard to believe harder and harder to believe you ever told anyone you loved them or anyone you till just one of those things you kept making up to keep the void out just another of those old tales to keep the void from pouring in on top of you the shroud

[*Silence 10 seconds. Breath audible. After 3 seconds eyes open.*]

c never the same but the same as what for God's sake did you ever say I
to yourself in your life come on now [*eyes close*] could you ever say I
to yourself in your life turning-point that was a great word with you
before they dried up altogether always having turning-points and
never but the one the first and last that time curled up worm in
slime when they lugged you out and wiped you off and straightened
you up never another after that never looked back after that was that
the time or was that another time

B muttering that time altogether on the stone in the sun or that time
together on the towpath or that time together in the sand that time
that time making it up from there as best you could always together
somewhere in the sun on the towpath facing downstream into the
sun sinking and the bits of flotsam coming from behind and
drifting on or caught in the reeds the dead rat it looked like came
on you from behind and went drifting on till you could see it no
more

A that time you went back to look was the ruin still there where you hid
as a child that last time straight off the ferry and up the rise to the
high street to catch the eleven neither right nor left only one
thought in your head not a curse for the old scenes the old names
just head down press on up the rise to the top and there stood
waiting with the nightbag till the truth began to dawn

c when you started not knowing who you were from Adam trying how
that would work for a change not knowing who you were from Adam
no notion who it was saying what you were saying whose skull you
were clapped up in whose moan had you the way you were was that
the time or was that another time there alone with the portraits of
the dead black with dirt and antiquity and the dates on the frames in
case you might get the century wrong not believing it could be you
till they put you out in the rain at closing-time

B no sight of the face or any other part never turned to her nor she to
you always parallel like on an axle-tree never turned to each other
just blurs on the fringes of the field no touching or anything of that
nature always space between if only an inch no pawing in the

manner of flesh and blood no better than shades no worse if it wasn't for the vows

A   no getting out to it that way so what next no question of asking not another word to the living as long as you lived so foot it up in the end to the station bowed half double get out to it that way all closed down and boarded up Doric terminus of the Great Southern and Eastern all closed down and the colonnade crumbling away so what next

C   the rain and the old rounds trying making it up that way as you went along how it would work that way for a change never having been how never having been would work the old rounds trying to wangle you into it tottering and muttering all over the parish till the words dried up and the head dried up and the legs dried up whosever they were or it gave up whoever it was

B   stock still always stock still like that time on the stone or that time in the sand stretched out parallel in the sand in the sun gazing up at the blue or eyes closed blue dark blue dark stock still side by side scene float up and there you were wherever it was

A   gave it up gave up and sat down on the steps in the pale morning sun no those steps got no sun somewhere else then gave up and off somewhere else and down on a step in the pale sun a doorstep say someone's doorstep for it to be time to get on the night ferry and out to hell out of there no need sleep anywhere not a curse for the old scenes the old names the passers pausing to gape at you quick gape then pass pass on pass by on the other side

B   stock still side by side in the sun then sink and vanish without your having stirred any more than the two knobs on a dumbbell except the lids and every now and then the lips to vow and all around all still all sides wherever it might be no stir or sound only faintly the leaves in the little wood behind or the ears or the bent or the reeds as the case might be of man no sight of man or beast no sight or sound

C   always winter then always raining always slipping in somewhere when no one would be looking in off the street out of the cold and rain in

the old green holeproof coat your father left you places you hadn't to
pay to get in like the Public Library that was another great thing free
culture far from home or the Post Office that was another another
place another time

A   huddled on the doorstep in the old green greatcoat in the pale sun
with the nightbag needless on your knees not knowing where you
were little by little not knowing where you were or when you were or
what for place might have been uninhabited for all you knew like
that time on the stone the child on the stone where none ever came
[*Silence 10 seconds. Breath audible. After 3 seconds eyes open.*]

B   or alone in the same the same scenes making it up that way to keep it
going keep it out on the stone [*eyes close*] alone on the end of the
stone with the wheat and blue or the towpath alone on the towpath
with the ghosts of the mules the drowned rat or bird or whatever it
was floating off into the sunset till you could see it no more nothing
stirring only the water and the sun going down till it went down and
you vanished all vanished

A   none ever came but the child on the stone among the giant nettles
with the light coming in where the wall had crumbled away poring
on his book well on into the night some moods the moonlight and
they all out on the roads looking for him or making up talk breaking
up two or more talking to himself being together that way where
none ever came

C   always winter then endless winter year after year as if it couldn't end
the old year never end like time could go no further that time in the
Post Office all bustle Christmas bustle in off the street when no one
was looking out of the cold and rain pushed open the door like
anyone else and straight for the table neither right nor left with all
the forms and the pens on their chains sat down first vacant seat and
were taking a look round for a change before drowsing away

B   or that time alone on your back in the sand and no vows to break the
peace when was that an earlier time a later time before she came
after she went or both before she came after she was gone and you
back in the old scene wherever it might be might have been the

same old scene before as then then as after with the rat or the wheat
the yellowing ears or that time in the sand the glider passing over
that time you went back soon after long after

A eleven or twelve in the ruin on the flat stone among the nettles in the
dark or moonlight muttering away now one voice now another there
was childhood for you till there on the step in the pale sun you
heard yourself at it again not a curse for the passers pausing to gape
at the scandal huddled there in the sun where it had no warrant
clutching the nightbag drooling away out loud eyes closed and the
white hair pouring out down from under the hat and so sat on in
that pale sun forgetting it all

C perhaps fear of ejection having clearly no warrant in the place to say
nothing of the loathsome appearance so this look round for once at
your fellow bastards thanking God for once bad and all as you were
you were not as they till it dawned that for all the loathing you were
getting you might as well not have been there at all the eyes passing
over you and through you like so much thin air was that the time or
was that another time another place another time

B the glider passing over never any change same blue skies nothing ever
changed but she with you there or not on your right hand always the
right hand on the fringe of the field and every now and then in the
great peace like a whisper so faint she loved you hard to believe you
even you made up that bit till the time came in the end

A making it all up on the doorstep as you went along making yourself all
up again for the millionth time forgetting it all where you were and
what for Foley's Folly and the lot the child's ruin you came to look
was it still there to hide in again till it was night and time to go till
that time came

C the Library that was another place another time that time you slipped
in off the street out of the cold and rain when no one was looking
what was it then you were never the same after never again after
something to do with dust something the dust said sitting at the big
round table with a bevy of old ones poring on the page and not a
sound

B   that time in the end when you tried and couldn't by the window in the
    dark and the owl flown to hoot at someone else or back with a shrew
    to its hollow tree and not another sound hour after hour hour after
    hour not a sound when you tried and tried and couldn't any more no
    words left to keep it out so gave it up gave up there by the window in
    the dark or moonlight gave up for good and let it in and nothing the
    worse a great shroud billowing in all over you on top of you and
    little or nothing the worse little or nothing

A   back down to the wharf with the nightbag and the old green greatcoat
    your father left you trailing the ground and the white hair pouring
    out down from under the hat till that time came on down neither
    right nor left not a curse for the old scenes the old names not a
    thought in your head only get back on board and away to hell out of
    it and never come back or was that another time all that another
    time was there ever any other time but that time away to hell out of
    it all and never come back

C   not a sound only the old breath and the leaves turning and then
    suddenly this dust whole place suddenly full of dust when you
    opened your eyes from floor to ceiling nothing only dust and not a
    sound only what was it it said come and gone was that it something
    like that come and gone come and gone no one come and gone in
    no time gone in no time

[*Silence 10 seconds. Breath audible. After 3 seconds eyes open. After 5 seconds
smile, toothless for preference. Hold 5 seconds till fade out and curtain.*]

FOOTFALLS

May (M), *dishevelled grey hair, worn grey wrap hiding feet, trailing.*
Woman's Voice (V) *from dark upstage.*

Strip: downstage, parallel with front, length nine steps, width one metre, a little off centre audience right.

$$\text{L}\ \frac{\text{r}\quad\text{l}\quad\text{r}\quad\text{l}\quad\text{r}\quad\text{l}\quad\text{r}\quad\text{l}\quad\text{r}\ \leftarrow}{\rightarrow\text{l}\quad\text{r}\quad\text{l}\quad\text{r}\quad\text{l}\quad\text{r}\quad\text{l}\quad\text{r}\quad\text{l}}\ \text{R}$$

Pacing: starting with right foot (r), from right (R) to left (L), with left foot (l) from L to R.

Turn: rightabout at L, leftabout at R.

Steps: clearly audible rhythmic tread.

Lighting: dim, strongest at floor level, less on body, least on head.

Voices: both low and slow throughout.

Curtain. Stage in darkness.

Faint single chime. Pause as echoes die.

Fade up to dim on strip. Rest in darkness.

M discovered pacing towards L. Turns at L. paces three more lengths, halts, facing front at R.

Pause.

M   Mother. [*Pause. No louder.*] Mother.

    [*Pause.*]

V   Yes, May.

M   Were you asleep?

V   Deep asleep. [*Pause.*] I heard you in my deep sleep. [*Pause.*] There is no sleep so deep I would not hear you there. [*Pause. M resumes pacing.*

Four lengths. After first length, synchronous with steps.] One two three four five six seven wheel one two three four five six seven wheel. [*Free.*] Will you not try to snatch a little sleep?

[*M halts facing front at R. Pause.*]

M   Would you like me to inject you again?

V   Yes, but it is too soon.

[*Pause.*]

M   Would you like me to change your position again?

V   Yes, but it is too soon.

[*Pause.*]

M   Straighten your pillows? [*Pause.*] Change your drawsheet? [*Pause.*] Pass you the bedpan? [*Pause.*] The warming-pan? [*Pause.*] Dress your sores? [*Pause.*] Sponge you down? [*Pause.*] Moisten your poor lips? [*Pause.*] Pray with you? [*Pause.*] For you? [*Pause.*] Again.

[*Pause.*]

V   Yes, but it is too soon.

[*Pause.*]

M   What age am I now?

V   And I? [*Pause. No louder.*] And I?

M   Ninety.

V   So much?

M   Eighty-nine, ninety.

V   I had you late. [*Pause.*] In life. [*Pause.*] Forgive me again. [*Pause. No louder.*] Forgive me again.

[*M resumes pacing. After one length halts facing front at L. Pause.*]

M   What age am I now?

V   In your forties.

M   So little?

V   I'm afraid so. [*Pause. M resumes pacing. After first turn at L.*] May. [*Pause. No louder.*] May.

M   [*pacing*] Yes, Mother.

V   Will you never have done? [*Pause.*] Will you never have done ... revolving it all?

M [*halting*] It?

V It all. [*Pause.*] In your poor mind. [*Pause.*] It all. [*Pause.*] It all.
[*M resumes pacing. Five seconds. Fade out on strip.*
All in darkness. Steps cease.
Pause.
Chime a little fainter. Pause for echoes.
Fade up to a little less on strip. Rest in darkness.
M discovered facing front at R.
Pause.]

V I walk here now. [*Pause.*] Rather I come and stand. [*Pause.*] At nightfall.
[*Pause.*] She fancies she is alone. [*Pause.*] See how still she stands, how
stark, with her face to the wall. [*Pause.*] How outwardly unmoved.
[*Pause.*] She has not been out since girlhood. [*Pause.*] Not out since
girlhood. [*Pause.*] Where is she, it may be asked. [*Pause.*] Why, in the
old home, the same where she— [*Pause.*] The same where she began.
[*Pause.*] Where it began. [*Pause.*] It all began. [*Pause.*] But this, this,
when did this begin? [*Pause.*] When other girls of her age were out
at . . . lacrosse she was already here. [*Pause.*] At this. [*Pause.*] The floor
here, now bare, once was— [*M begins pacing. Steps a little slower.*] But
let us watch her move, in silence. [*M paces. Towards end of second*
length.] Watch how feat she wheels. [*M turns, paces. Synchronous with*
steps third length.] Seven, eight, nine, wheel. [*M turns at L, paces one*
more length, halts facing front at B.] I say the floor here, now bare, this
strip of floor, once was carpeted, a deep pile. Till one night, while
still little more than a child, she called her mother and said, Mother,
this is not enough. The mother: Not enough? May—the child's given
name—May: Not enough. The mother: What do you mean, May, not
enough, what can you possibly mean, May, not enough? May: I mean,
Mother, that I must hear the feet, however faint they fall. The
mother: The motion alone is not enough? May: No, Mother, the
motion alone is not enough, I must hear the feet, however faint they
fall. [*Pause. M resumes pacing. With pacing.*] Does she still sleep, it may
be asked? Yes, some nights she does, in snatches, bows her poor head
against the wall and snatches a little sleep. [*Pause.*] Still speak? Yes,

some nights she does, when she fancies none can hear. [*Pause.*] Tells
how it was. [*Pause.*] Tries to tell how it was. [*Pause.*] It all. [*Pause.*] It all.
[*M continues pacing. Five seconds. Fade out on strip.*
All in darkness, steps cease.
Pause.
Chime a little fainter still. Pause for echoes.
Fade up to a little less still on strip. Rest in darkness.
M discovered facing front at R.
Pause.]

M   Sequel. [*Pause. Begins pacing. Steps a little slower still. After two lengths*
halts facing front at R. Pause.] Sequel. A little later, when she was quite
forgotten, she began to— [*Pause.*] A little later, when as though she
had never been, it never been, she began to walk. [*Pause.*] At
nightfall. [*Pause.*] Slip out at nightfall and into the little church by
the north door, always locked at that hour, and walk, up and down,
up and down, his poor arm. [*Pause.*] Some nights she would halt, as
one frozen by some shudder of the mind, and stand stark still till
she could move again. But many also were the nights when she
paced without pause, up and down, up and down, before vanishing
the way she came. [*Pause.*] No sound. [*Pause.*] None at least to be
heard. [*Pause.*] The semblance. [*Pause. Resumes pacing. After two*
lengths halts facing front at R. Pause.] The semblance. Faint, though by
no means invisible, in a certain light. [*Pause.*] Given the right light.
[*Pause.*] Grey rather than white, a pale shade of grey. [*Pause.*]
Tattered. [*Pause.*] A tangle of tatters. [*Pause.*] Watch it pass—[*pause*]—
watch her pass before the candelabrum, how its flames, their
light . . . like moon through passing rack. [*Pause.*] Soon then after
she was gone, as though never there, began to walk, up and down,
up and down, that poor arm. [*Pause.*] At nightfall. [*Pause.*] That is to
say, at certain seasons of the year, during Vespers. [*Pause.*]
Necessarily. [*Pause. Resumes pacing. After one length halts facing front at*
L. Pause.] Old Mrs. Winter, whom the reader will remember, old
Mrs. Winter, one late autumn Sunday evening, on sitting down to

supper with her daughter after worship, after a few half-hearted mouthfuls laid down her knife and fork and bowed her head. What is it, Mother, said the daughter, a most strange girl, though scarcely a girl any more ... [*brokenly*] ... dreadfully un— ... [*Pause. Normal voice.*] What is it, Mother, are you not feeling yourself? [*Pause.*] Mrs. W. did not at once reply. But finally, raising her head and fixing Amy—the daughter's given name, as the reader will remember— raising her head and fixing Amy full in the eye she said—[*pause*]— she murmured, fixing Amy full in the eye she murmured, Amy did you observe anything ... strange at Evensong? Amy: No, Mother, I did not. Mrs. W: Perhaps it was just my fancy. Amy: Just what exactly, Mother, did you perhaps fancy it was? [*Pause.*] Just what exactly, Mother, did you perhaps fancy this ... strange thing was you observed? [*Pause.*] Mrs. W: You yourself observed nothing ... strange? Amy: No, Mother, I myself did not, to put it mildly. Mrs. W: What do you mean, Amy, to put it mildly, what can you possibly mean, Amy, to put it mildly? Amy: I mean, Mother, that to say I observed nothing ... strange is indeed to put it mildly. For I observed nothing of any kind, strange or otherwise. I saw nothing, heard nothing, of any kind. I was not there. Mrs. W: Not there? Amy: Not there. Mrs. W: But I heard you respond. [*Pause.*] I heard you say Amen. [*Pause.*] How could you have responded if you were not there? [*Pause.*] How could you possibly have said Amen if, as you claim, you were not there? [*Pause.*] The love of God, and the fellowship of the Holy Ghost, be with us all, now, and for evermore. Amen. [*Pause.*] I heard you distinctly. [*Pause. Resumes pacing. After three steps halts without facing front. Long pause. Resumes pacing, halts facing front at R. Long pause.*] Amy. [*Pause. No louder.*] Amy. [*Pause.*] Yes, Mother. [*Pause.*] Will you never have done? [*Pause.*] Will you never have done ... revolving it all? [*Pause.*] It? [*Pause.*] It all. [*Pause.*] In your poor mind. [*Pause.*] It all. [*Pause.*] It all.
[*Pause. Fade out on strip. All in darkness.*
Pause.

Chime even a little fainter still. Pause for echoes.
Fade up to even a little less still on strip.
No trace of May.
Hold ten seconds.
Fade out.]

Curtain

GHOST TRIO

A play for television

Female Voice (V)
Male Figure (F)

A   Room: 6 m × 5 m

1 Door.
2 Window.
3 Mirror.
4 Pallet.
5 F seated by door.
6 F at window.
7 F at head of pallet.
A Position general view.
B Position medium shot.
C Position near shot of 5 and 1, 6 and 2, 7 and 3.

I

1.   *Fade up to general view from A. 10 seconds.*

2. v Good evening. Mine is a faint voice. Kindly tune accordingly.
     [*Pause.*] Good evening. Mine is a faint voice. Kindly tune accord-
     ingly. [*Pause.*] It will not be raised, nor lowered, whatever hap-
     pens. [*Pause.*] Look. [*Long pause.*] The familiar chamber. [*Pause.*]
     At the far end a window. [*Pause.*] On the right the indispens-
     able door. [*Pause.*] On the left, against the wall, some kind of pal-
     let. [*Pause.*] The light: faint, omnipresent. No visible source. As if
     all luminous. Faintly luminous. No shadow. [*Pause.*] No shadow.
     Colour: none. All grey. Shades of grey. [*Pause.*] The colour grey
     if you wish, shades of the colour grey. [*Pause.*] Forgive my stat-
     ing the obvious. [*Pause.*] Keep that sound down. [*Pause.*] Now look
     closer. [*Pause.*] Floor.

3.   *Cut to close-up of floor. Smooth grey rectangle 0.70 m × 1.50 m. 5 seconds.*

4. v Dust. [*Pause.*] Having seen that specimen of floor you have seen it
     all. Wall.

5.   *Cut to close-up of wall. Smooth grey rectangle 0.70 m × 1.50 m. 5 seconds.*

6. v Dust. [*Pause.*] Knowing this, the kind of wall—

7.   *Close-up of wall continued. 5 seconds.*

8. v The kind of floor—

9.   *Cut to close-up of floor. 5 seconds.*

10. v Look again.

11.   *Cut to general view from A. 5 seconds.*

12. v Door.

13.   *Cut to close-up of whole door. Smooth grey rectangle 0.70 m × 2 m.*
     Imperceptibly ajar. No knob. Faint music. 5 seconds.

14. v Window.

15.   *Cut to close-up of whole window. Opaque sheet of glass 0.70 m × 1.50 m.*
     Imperceptibly ajar. No knob. 5 seconds.

16. v Pallet.

17.   *Cut to close-up from above of whole pallet. 0.70 m × 2 m. Grey sheet.*
     Grey rectangular pillow at window end. 5 seconds.

18. v Knowing all this, the kind of pallet—

19. *Close-up of whole pallet continued. 5 seconds.*

20. v The kind of window—

21. *Cut to close-up of whole window. 5 seconds.*

22. v The kind of door—

23. *Cut to close-up of whole door. Faint music. 5 seconds.*

24. v The kind of wall—

25. *Cut to close-up of wall as before. 5 seconds.*

26. v The kind of floor.

27. *Cut to close-up of floor as before. 5 seconds.*

28. v Look again.

29. *Cut to general view. 5 seconds.*

30. v Sole sign of life a seated figure.

31. *Move in slowly from A to B whence medium shot of F and door. F is seated on a stool, bowed forward, face hidden, clutching with both hands a small cassette not identifiable as such at this range. Faint music. 5 seconds.*

32. *Move in from B to C whence near shot of F and door. Cassette now identifiable. Music slightly louder, 5 seconds.*

33. *Move in from C to close-up of head, hands, cassette. Clutching hands, head bowed, face hidden. Music slightly louder. 5 seconds.*

34. *Move slowly back to A via C and B (no stops). Music progressively fainter till at level of B it ceases to be heard.*

35. *General view from A. 5 seconds.*

II

All from A except 26–29

  1. v He will now think he hears her.

  2.   *F raises head sharply, turns still crouched to door, fleeting face, tense pose. 5 seconds.*

  3. v No one.

  4.   *F relapses into opening pose, bowed over cassette. 5 seconds.*

  5. v Again.

  6.   *Same as 2.*

  7. v Now to door.

  8.   *F gets up, lays cassette on stool, goes to door, listens with right ear against door, back to camera. 5 seconds.*

  9. v No one. [*Pause 5 seconds.*] Open.

10.   *With right hand F pushes door open halfway clockwise, looks out, back to camera. 2 seconds.*

11. v No one.

12.   *F removes hand from door which closes slowly of itself, stands irresolute, back to camera. 2 seconds.*

13. v Now to window.

14.   *F goes to window, stands irresolute, back to camera. 5 seconds.*

15. v Open.

16.   *With right hand F pushes window open halfway clockwise, looks out, back to camera. 5 seconds.*

17. v No one.

18.   *F removes hand from window which closes slowly of itself, stands irresolute, back to camera. 2 seconds.*

19. v Now to pallet.

20.   *F goes to head of pallet (window end), stands looking down at it. 5 seconds.*

21.   *F turns to wall at head of pallet, goes to wall, looks at his face in mirror hanging on wall, invisible from A.*

22. v [*surprised*] Ah!

23.   *After 5 seconds F bows his head, stands before mirror with bowed head. 2 seconds.*

24. v Now to door.

25.   *F goes to stool, takes up cassette, sits, settles into opening pose, bowed over cassette. 2 seconds.*

26.   *Same as I.31.*

27.   *Same as I.32.*

28.   *Same as I.33.*

29.   *Same as I.34.*

30.   *Same as I.35.*

31. v He will now again think he hears her.

32.   *Same as II.2.*

33.   *F gets up, lays cassette on stool, goes to door, opens it as before, looks out, stoops forward. 10 seconds.*

34.   *F straightens up, releases door which closes slowly of itself, stands irreso-lute, goes to stool, takes up cassette, sits irresolute, settles finally into opening pose, bowed over cassette. 5 seconds.*

35.   *Faint music audible for first time at A. It grows louder. 5 seconds.*

36. v *Stop.*

37.   *Music stops. General view from A. 5 seconds.*

38. v *Repeat.*

III

1. *Immediately after "Repeat" cut to near shot from C of F and door. Music audible. 5 seconds.*

2. *Move in to close-up of head, hands, cassette. Music slightly louder. 5 seconds.*

3. *Music stops. Action II.2. 5 seconds.*

4. *Action II.4. Music resumes. 5 seconds.*

5. *Move back to near shot from C of F and door. Music audible. 5 seconds.*

6. *Music stops. Action II.2. Near shot from C of F and door. 5 seconds.*

7. *Action II.8. Near shot from C of stool, cassette, F with right ear to door. 5 seconds.*

8. *Action II.10. Crescendo creak of door opening. Near shot from C of stool, cassette, F with right hand holding door open. 5 seconds.*

9. *Cut to view of corridor seen from door. Long narrow (0.70 m) grey rectangle between grey walls, empty, far end in darkness. 5 seconds.*

10. *Cut back to near shot from C of stool, cassette, F holding door open. 5 seconds.*

11. *Action II.12. Decrescendo creak of door slowly closing. Near shot from C of stool, cassette, F standing irresolute, door. 5 seconds.*

12. *Cut to close-up from above of cassette on stool, small grey rectangle on larger rectangle of seat. 5 seconds.*

13. *Cut back to near shot of stool, cassette, F standing irresolute, door. 5 seconds.*

14. *Action II.14 seen from C. Near shot from C of F and window. 5 seconds.*

15. *Action II.16 seen from C. Crescendo creak of window opening. Faint sound of rain. Near shot from C of F with right hand holding window open. 5 seconds.*

16. *Cut to view from window. Night. Rain falling in dim light. Sound of rain slightly louder. 5 seconds.*

17. *Cut back to near shot from C of F with right hand holding window open. Faint sound of rain. 5 seconds.*

18. *Action II.18 seen from C. Decrescendo creak of window slowly closing. Near shot from C of F and window. 5 seconds.*

19. *Action II.20 seen from C. Near shot from C of F, mirror, head of pallet.*

20.   *Cut to close-up from above of whole pallet.*

21.   *Move down to tighter close-up of pallet moving slowly from pillow to foot and back to pillow. 5 seconds on pillow.*

22.   *Move back to close-up from above of whole pallet. 5 seconds.*

23.   *Cut back to near shot from C of F, mirror, head of pallet. 5 seconds.*

24.   *Cut to close-up of mirror reflecting nothing. Small grey rectangle (same dimensions as cassette) against larger rectangle of wall. 5 seconds.*

25.   *Cut back to near shot from C of F, mirror, head of pallet. 5 seconds.*

26.   *Action II.21 seen from C. Near shot from C of F and mirror. 5 seconds.*

27.   *Cut to close-up of F's face in mirror. 5 seconds. Eyes close. 5 seconds. Eyes open. 5 seconds. Head bows. Top of head in mirror. 5 seconds.*

28.   *Cut back to near shot from C of F with bowed head, mirror, head of pallet. 5 seconds.*

29.   *Action II.25 seen from C. Near shot from C of F settling into opening pose. Music audible once settled. 10 seconds.*

30.   *Music stops. Action II.2 seen from C. Faint sound of steps approaching. They stop. Faint sound of knock on door. 5 seconds. Second knock, no louder. 5 seconds.*

31.   *Action II.33 seen from C. Crescendo creak of door slowly opening. Near shot from C of stool, cassette, F holding door open, stooping forward. 10 seconds.*

32.   *Cut to near shot of small boy full length in corridor before open door. Dressed in black oilskin with hood glistening with rain. White face raised to invisible F. 5 seconds. Boy shakes head faintly. Face still, raised. 5 seconds. Boy shakes head again. Face still, raised. 5 seconds. Boy turns and goes. Sound of receding steps. Register from the same position his slow recession till he vanishes in dark at end of corridor. 5 seconds on empty corridor.*

33.   *Cut back to near shot from C of stool, cassette, F holding door open. 5 seconds.*

34.   *Action II.34 seen from C. Decrescendo creak of door slowly closing. 5 seconds.*

35.   *Cut to general view from A. 5 seconds.*

36.   *Music audible at A. It grows. 10 seconds.*

37. *With growing music move in slowly to close-up of head bowed right down over cassette now held in arms and invisible. Hold till end of Largo.*

38. *Silence. F raises head. Face seen clearly for second time. 10 seconds.*

39. *Move slowly back to A.*

40. *General view from A. 5 seconds.*

41. *Fade out.*

MUSIC

From Largo of Beethoven's Fifth Piano Trio (*The Ghost*):

I.13	*beginning bar 47*
I.23	*beginning bar 49*
I.31–34	*beginning bar 19*
II.26–29	*beginning bar 64*
II.35–36	*beginning bar 71*
III.1–2, 4–5	*beginning bar 26*
III.29	*beginning bar 64*
III.36 to end	*beginning bar 82*

...but the clouds...

A play for television

M   Near shot from behind of man sitting on invisible stool bowed over invisible table. Light grey robe and skullcap. Dark ground. Same shot throughout.

M1   M in set. Hat and greatcoat dark, robe and skullcap light.

W   Close-up of woman's face reduced as far as possible to eyes and mouth. Same shot throughout.

S   Long shot of set empty or with M1. Same shot throughout.

V   M's voice.

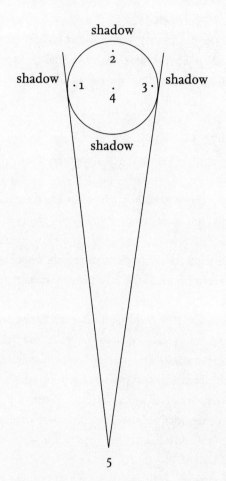

Set: circular, about 5 m diameter, surrounded by deep shadow.

Lighting: a gradual lightening from dark periphery to maximum light at centre.

1. West, roads.
2. North, sanctum.
3. East, closet.
4. Standing position.
5. Camera.

1.   *Dark. 5 seconds.*

2.   *Fade up to M. 5 seconds.*

3. v When I thought of her it was always night. I came in—

4.   *Dissolve to S empty. 5 seconds. M1 in hat and greatcoat emerges from west shadow, advances five steps and stands facing east shadow. 2 seconds.*

5. v No—

6.   *Dissolve to M. 2 seconds.*

7. v No, that is not right. When she appeared it was always night. I came in—

8.   *Dissolve to S empty. 5 seconds. M1 in hat and greatcoat emerges from west shadow, advances five steps and stands facing east shadow. 5 seconds.*

9. v Right. Came in, having walked the roads since break of day, brought night home, stood listening [5 seconds], finally went to closet—

10.   *M1 advances five steps to disappear in east shadow. 2 seconds.*

11. v Shed my hat and greatcoat, assumed robe and skull, reappeared—

12.   *M1 in robe and skullcap emerges from east shadow, advances five steps and stands facing west shadow. 5 seconds.*

13. v Reappeared and stood as before, only facing the other way, exhibiting the other outline [5 seconds], finally turned and vanished—

14.   *M1 turns right and advances five steps to disappear in north shadow. 5 seconds.*

15. v Vanished within my little sanctum and crouched, where none could see me, in the dark.

16.   *Dissolve to M. 5 seconds.*

17. v Let us now make sure we have got it right.

18.   *Dissolve to S empty. 2 seconds. M1 in hat and greatcoat emerges from west shadow, advances five steps and stands facing east shadow. 2 seconds. He advances five steps to disappear in east shadow. 2 seconds. He emerges in robe and skullcap from east shadow, advances five steps and stands facing west shadow. 2 seconds. He turns right and advances five steps to disappear in north shadow. 2 seconds.*

19. V Right.

20. *Dissolve to M. 2 seconds.*

21. V Then crouching there, in my little sanctum, in the dark, where none could see me, I began to beg, of her, to appear, to me. Such had long been my use and wont. No sound, a begging of the mind, to her, to appear, to me. Deep down into the dead of night, until I wearied, and ceased. Or of course until—

22. *Dissolve to W. 2 seconds.*

23. *Dissolve to M. 2 seconds.*

24. V For had she never once appeared, all that time, would I have, could I have, gone on begging, all that time? Not just vanished within my little sanctum and busied myself with something else, or with nothing, busied myself with nothing? Until the time came, with break of day, to issue forth again, shed robe and skull, resume my hat and greatcoat, and issue forth again, to walk the roads.

25. *Dissolve to S empty. 2 seconds. M1 in robe and skullcap emerges from north shadow, advances five steps and stands facing camera. 2 seconds. He turns left and advances five steps to disappear in east shadow. 2 seconds. He emerges in hat and greatcoat from east shadow, advances five steps and stands facing west shadow. 2 seconds. He advances five steps to disappear in west shadow. 2 seconds.*

26. V Right.

27. *Dissolve to M. 5 seconds.*

28. V Let us now distinguish three cases. One: she appeared and—

29. *Dissolve to W. 2 seconds.*

30. *Dissolve to M. 2 seconds.*

31. V In the same breath was gone. 2 *seconds.* Two: she appeared and—

32. *Dissolve to W. 5 seconds.*

33. V Lingered. 5 *seconds.* With those unseeing eyes I so begged when alive to look at me. 5 *seconds.*

34. *Dissolve to M. 2 seconds.*

35. V Three: she appeared and—

36. *Dissolve to W. 5 seconds.*

37. v After a moment—

38.   *W's lips move, uttering inaudibly:* "... clouds ... but the clouds ... of the sky ...," *V murmuring, synchronous with lips:* "... but the clouds ..." *Lips cease. 5 seconds.*

39. v Right.

40.   *Dissolve to M. 5 seconds.*

41. v Let us now run through it again.

42.   *Dissolve to S empty. 2 seconds. M1 in hat and greatcoat emerges from west shadow, advances five steps and stands facing east shadow. 2 seconds. He advances five steps to disappear in east shadow. 2 seconds. He emerges in robe and skullcap from east shadow, advances five steps and stands facing west shadow. 2 seconds. He turns right and advances five steps to disappear in north shadow. 2 seconds.*

43.   *Dissolve to M. 5 seconds.*

44.   *Dissolve to W. 2 seconds.*

45.   *Dissolve to M. 2 seconds.*

46.   *Dissolve to W. 5 seconds.*

47. v Look at me. *5 seconds.*

48.   *Dissolve to M. 5 seconds.*

49.   *Dissolve to W. 2 seconds. W's lips move, uttering inaudibly:* "... clouds ... but the clouds ... of the sky ...," *V murmuring, synchronous with lips:* "... but the clouds ..." *Lips cease. 5 seconds.*

50. v Speak to me. *5 seconds.*

51.   *Dissolve to M. 5 seconds.*

52. v Right. There was of course a fourth case, or case nought, as I pleased to call it, by far the commonest, in the proportion say of nine hundred and ninety-nine to one, or nine hundred and ninety-eight to two, when I begged in vain, deep down into the dead of night, until I wearied, and ceased, and busied myself with something else, more ... rewarding, such as ... such as ... cube roots, for example, or with nothing, busied myself with nothing, that MINE, until the time came, with break of day, to issue forth again, void my little sanctum, shed robe and skull,

resume my hat and greatcoat, and issue forth again, to walk the
roads. [*Pause.*] The back roads.

53.   *Dissolve to S empty. 2 seconds. M1 in robe and skullcap emerges from
north shadow, advances five steps and stands facing camera. 2 seconds.
He turns left and advances five steps to disappear in east shadow.
2 seconds. He emerges in hat and greatcoat from east shadow, advances
five steps and stands facing west shadow. 2 seconds. He advances five
steps to disappear in west shadow. 2 seconds.*

54. v   Right.

55.   *Dissolve to M. 5 seconds.*

56.   *Dissolve to W. 5 seconds.*

57. v   "... but the clouds of the sky ... when the horizon fades ... or a
bird's sleepy cry ... among the deepening shades ..." *5 seconds.*

58.   *Dissolve to M. 5 seconds.*

59.   *Fade out on M.*

60.   *Dark. 5 seconds.*

A PIECE OF MONOLOGUE

Curtain.

Faint diffuse light.

Speaker stands well off centre downstage audience left.

White hair, white nightgown, white socks.

Two metres to his left, same level, same height, standard lamp, skull-sized white globe, faintly lit.

Just visible extreme right, same level, white foot of pallet bed.

Ten seconds before speech begins.

Thirty seconds before end of speech lamplight begins to fail.

Lamp out. Silence. Speaker, globe, foot of pallet, barely visible in diffuse light.

Ten seconds.

Curtain.

SPEAKER   Birth was the death of him. Again. Words are few. Dying too.
Birth was the death of him. Ghastly grinning ever since. Up
at the lid to come. In cradle and crib. At suck first fiasco. With
the first totters. From mammy to nanny and back. All the
way. Bandied back and forth. So ghastly grinning on. From
funeral to funeral. To now. This night. Two and a half billion
seconds. Again. Two and a half billion seconds. Hard to
believe so few. From funeral to funeral. Funerals of . . . he all
but said of loved ones. Thirty thousand nights. Hard to

believe so few. Born dead of night. Sun long sunk behind the larches. New needles turning green. In the room dark gaining. Till faint light from standard lamp. Wick turned low. And now. This night. Up at nightfall. Every nightfall. Faint light in room. Whence unknown. None from window. No. Next to none. No such thing as none. Gropes to window and stares out. Stands there staring out. Stock still staring out. Nothing stirring in that black vast. Gropes back in the end to where the lamp is standing. Was standing. When last went out. Loose matches in right-hand pocket. Strikes one on his buttock the way his father taught him. Takes off milk white globe and sets it down. Match goes out. Strikes a second as before. Takes off chimney. Smoke-clouded. Holds it in left hand. Match goes out. Strikes a third as before and sets it to wick. Puts back chimney. Match goes out. Puts back globe. Turns wick low. Backs away to edge of light and turns to face east. Blank wall. So nightly. Up. Socks. Nightgown. Window. Lamp. Backs away to edge of light and stands facing blank wall. Covered with pictures once. Pictures of . . . he all but said of loved ones. Unframed. Unglazed. Pinned to wall with drawing-pins. All shapes and sizes. Down one after another. Gone. Torn to shreds and scattered. Strewn all over the floor. Not at one sweep. No sudden fit of . . . no word. Ripped from the wall and torn to shreds one by one. Over the years. Years of nights. Nothing on the wall now but the pins. Not all. Some out with the wrench. Some still pinning a shred. So stands there facing blank wall. Dying on. No more no less. No. Less. Less to die. Ever less. Like light at nightfall. Stands there facing east. Blank pinpocked surface once white in shadow. Could once name them all. There was father. That grey void. There mother. That other. There together. Smiling. Wedding day. There all three. That grey blot. There alone. He alone. So on. Not now. Forgotten. All gone so long. Gone. Ripped off and torn to shreds. Scattered all over the floor.

Swept out of the way under the bed and left. Thousand
shreds under the bed with the dust and spiders. All the . . . he
all but said the loved ones. Stands there facing the wall
staring beyond. Nothing there either. Nothing stirring there
either. Nothing stirring anywhere. Nothing to be seen
anywhere. Nothing to be heard anywhere. Room once full of
sounds. Faint sounds. Whence unknown. Fewer and fainter
as time wore on. Nights wore on. None now. No. No such
thing as none. Rain some nights still slant against the panes.
Or dropping gentle on the place beneath. Even now. Lamp
smoking though wick turned low. Strange. Faint smoke
issuing through vent in globe. Low ceiling stained by night
after night of this. Dark shapeless blot on surface elsewhere
white. Once white. Stands facing wall after the various
motions described. That is up at nightfall and into gown and
socks. No. In them already. In them all night. All day. All day
and night. Up at nightfall in gown and socks and after a
moment to get his bearings gropes to window. Faint light in
room. Unutterably faint. Whence unknown. Stands stock still
staring out. Into black vast. Nothing there. Nothing stirring.
That he can see. Hear. Dwells thus as if unable to move
again. Or no will left to move again. Not enough will left to
move again. Turns in the end and gropes to where he knows
the lamp is standing. Thinks he knows. Was last standing.
When last went out. Match one as described for globe. Two
for chimney. Three for wick. Chimney and globe back on.
Turns wick low. Backs away to edge of light and turns to face
wall. East. Still as the lamp by his side. Gown and socks white
to take faint light. Once white. Hair white to take faint light.
Foot of pallet just visible edge of frame. Once white to take
faint light. Stands there staring beyond. Nothing. Empty
dark. Till first word always the same. Night after night the
same. Birth. Then slow fade up of a faint form. Out of the
dark. A window. Looking west. Sun long sunk behind the

larches. Light dying. Soon none left to die. No. No such thing
as no light. Starless moonless heaven. Dies on to dawn and
never dies. There in the dark that window. Night slowly
falling. Eyes to the small pane gaze at that first night. Turn
from it in the end to face the darkened room. There in the
end slowly a faint hand. Holding aloft a lighted spill. In the
light of spill faintly the hand and milkwhite globe. Then
second hand. In light of spill. Takes off globe and disappears.
Reappears empty. Takes off chimney. Two hands and
chimney in light of spill. Spill to wick. Chimney back on.
Hand with spill disappears. Second hand disappears.
Chimney alone in gloom. Hand reappears with globe. Globe
back on. Turns wick low. Disappears. Pale globe alone in
gloom. Glimmer of brass bedrail. Fade. Birth the death of
him. That nevoid smile. Thirty thousand nights. Stands at
edge of lamplight staring beyond. Into dark whole again.
Window gone. Hands gone. Light gone. Gone. Again and
again. Again and again gone. Till dark slowly parts again.
Grey light. Rain pelting. Umbrellas round a grave. Seen from
above. Streaming black canopies. Black ditch beneath. Rain
bubbling in the black mud. Empty for the moment. That
place beneath. Which . . . he all but said which loved one?
Thirty seconds. To add to the two and a half billion odd.
Then fade. Dark whole again. Blest dark. No. No such thing
as whole. Stands staring beyond half hearing what he's
saying. He? The words falling from his mouth. Making do
with his mouth. Lights lamp as described. Backs away to edge
of light and turns to face wall. Stares beyond into dark. Waits
for first word always the same. It gathers in his mouth. Parts
lips and thrusts tongue forward. Birth. Parts the dark. Slowly
the window. That first night. The room. The spill. The hands.
The lamp. The gleam of brass. Fade. Gone. Again and again.
Again and again gone. Mouth agape. A cry. Stifled by nasal.
Dark parts. Grey light. Rain pelting. Streaming umbrellas.

Ditch. Bubbling black mud. Coffin out of frame. Whose? Fade. Gone. Move on to other matters. Try to move on. To other matters. How far from wall? Head almost touching. As at window. Eyes glued to pane staring out. Nothing stirring. Black vast. Stands there stock still staring out as if unable to move again. Or gone the will to move again. Gone. Faint cry in his ear. Mouth agape. Closed with hiss of breath. Lips joined. Feel soft touch of lip on lip. Lip lipping lip. Then parted by cry as before. Where is he now? Back at window staring out. Eyes glued to pane. As if looking his last. Turns away at last and gropes through faint unaccountable light to unseen lamp. White gown moving through that gloom. Once white. Lights and moves to face wall as described. Head almost touching. Stands there staring beyond waiting for first word. It gathers in his mouth. Birth. Parts lips and thrusts tongue between them. Tip of tongue. Feel soft touch of tongue on lips. Of lips on tongue. Fade up in outer dark of window. Stare beyond through rift in dark to other dark. Further dark. Sun long sunk behind the larches. Nothing stirring. Nothing faintly stirring. Stock still eyes glued to pane. As if looking his last. At that first night. Of thirty thousand odd. Turn away in the end to darkened room. Where soon to be. This night to be. Spill. Hands. Lamp. Gleam of brass. Pale globe alone in gloom. Brass bedrail catching light. Thirty seconds. To swell the two and a half billion odd. Fade. Gone. Cry. Snuffed with breath of nostrils. Again and again. Again and again gone. Till whose grave? Which . . . he all but said which loved one's? He? Black ditch in pelting rain. Way out through the grey rift in dark. Seen from on high. Streaming canopies. Bubbling black mud. Coffin on its way. Loved one . . . he all but said loved one on his way. Her way. Thirty seconds. Fade. Gone. Stands there staring beyond. Into dark whole again. No. No such thing as whole. Head almost touching wall. White hair catching light.

White gown. White socks. White foot of pallet edge of frame stage left. Once white. Least . . . give and head rests on wall. But no. Stock still head haught staring beyond. Nothing stirring. Faintly stirring. Thirty thousand nights of ghosts beyond. Beyond that black beyond. Ghost light. Ghost nights. Ghost rooms. Ghost graves. Ghost . . . he all but said ghost loved ones. Waiting on the rip word. Stands there staring beyond at that black veil lips quivering to half-heard words. Treating of other matters. Trying to treat of other matters. Till half hears there are no other matters. Never were other matters. Never two matters. Never but the one matter. The dead and gone. The dying and the going. From the word go. The word begone. Such as the light going now. Beginning to go. In the room. Where else? Unnoticed by him staring beyond. The globe alone. Not the other. The unaccountable. From nowhere. On all sides nowhere. Unutterably faint. The globe alone. Alone gone.

ROCKABY

NOTES
Light

Subdued on chair. Rest of stage dark.

Subdued spot on face constant throughout, unaffected by successive fades. Either wide enough to include narrow limits of rock or concentrated on face when still or at mid-rock. Then throughout speech face slightly swaying in and out of light. Opening fade-up: first spot on face alone, long pause, then light on chair.

Final fade-out: first chair, long pause with spot on face alone, head slowly sinks, come to rest, fade out spot.

W

Prematurely old. Unkempt grey hair. Huge eyes in white expressionless face. White hands holding ends of armrests.

Eyes

Now closed, now open in unblinking gaze. About equal proportions section 1, increasingly closed 2 and 3, closed for good halfway through 4.

Costume

Black lacy high-necked evening gown. Long sleeves. Jet sequins to glitter when rocking. Incongruous flimsy head-dress set askew with extravagant trimming to catch light when rocking.

Attitude

Completely still till fade-out of chair. Then in light of spot head slowly inclined.

Chair

Pale wood highly polished to gleam when rocking. Footrest. Vertical back. Rounded inward curving arms to suggest embrace.

Rock

Slight. Slow. Controlled mechanically without assistance from W.

Voice

Towards end of 4, say from "saying to herself" on, gradually softer. Lines in italics spoken by W with V. A little softer each time. W's "more" a little softer each time.

W: *Woman in chair.*

V: *Her recorded voice.*

Fade up on W in rocking-chair facing front downstage slightly off centre audience left.

Long pause.

w More.

[*Pause. Rock and voice together.*]

v till in the end
   the day came
   in the end came
   close of a long day
   when she said
   to herself
   whom else
   time she stopped
   time she stopped
   going to and fro
   all eyes

all sides
high and low
for another
another like herself
another creature like herself
a little like
going to and fro
all eyes
all sides
high and low
for another
till in the end
close of a long day
to herself
whom else
time she stopped
time she stopped
going to and fro
all eyes
all sides
high and low
for another
another living soul
going to and fro
all eyes like herself
all sides
high and low
for another
another like herself
a little like
going to and fro
till in the end
close of a long day
to herself

whom else
time she stopped
going to and fro
time she stopped
time she stopped
[*Together: echo of "time she stopped," coming to rest of rock, faint fade of light.*
Long pause.]

w More.

[*Pause. Rock and voice together.*]

v so in the end
close of a long day
went back in
in the end went back in
saying to herself
whom else
time she stopped
time she stopped
going to and fro
time she went and sat
at her window
quiet at her window
facing other windows
so in the end
close of a long day
in the end went and sat
went back in and sat
at her window
let up the blind and sat
quiet at her window
only window
facing other windows
other only windows
all eyes
all sides

high and low
for another
at her window
another like herself
a little like
another living soul
one other living soul
at her window
gone in like herself
gone back in
in the end
close of a long day
saying to herself
whom else
time she stopped
time she stopped
going to and fro
time she went and sat
at her window
quiet at her window
only window
facing other windows
other only windows
all eyes
all sides
high and low
for another
another like herself
a little like
another living soul
one other living soul
[*Together: echo of "living soul," coming to rest of rock, faint fade of light.
Long pause.*]

w   More.

[*Pause. Rock and voice together.*]

v   till in the end
     the day came
     in the end came
     close of a long day
     sitting at her window
     quiet at her window
     only window
     facing other windows
     other only windows
     all blinds down
     never one up
     hers alone up
     till the day came
     in the end came
     close of a long day
     sitting at her window
     quiet at her window
     all eyes
     all sides
     high and low
     for a blind up
     one blind up
     no more
     never mind a face
     behind the pane
     famished eyes
     like hers
     to see
     be seen
     no
     a blind up
     like hers
     a little like

one blind up no more
another creature there
somewhere there
behind the pane
another living soul
one other living soul
till the day came
in the end came
close of a long day
when she said
to herself
whom else
time she stopped
time she stopped
sitting at her window
quiet at her window
only window
facing other windows
other only windows
all eyes
all sides
high and low
time she stopped
time she stopped
[*Together: echo of "time she stopped," coming to rest of rock, faint fade of light.*
Long pause.]

w   More.
[*Pause. Rock and voice together.*]
v   so in the end
close of a long day
went down
in the end went down
down the steep stair

let down the blind and down
right down
into the old rocker
mother rocker
where mother rocked
all the years
all in black
best black
sat and rocked
rocked
till her end came
in the end came
off her head they said
gone off her head
but harmless
no harm in her
dead one day
no
night
dead one night
in the rocker
in her best black
head fallen
and the rocker rocking
rocking away
so in the end
close of a long day
went down
in the end went down
down the steep stair
let down the blind and down
right down
into the old rocker
those arms at last

and rocked
rocked
with closed eyes
closing eyes
she so long all eyes
famished eyes
all sides
high and low
to and fro
at her window
to see
be seen
till in the end
close of a long day
to herself
whom else
time she stopped
let down the blind and stopped
time she went down
down the steep stair
time she went right down
was her own other
own other living soul
so in the end
close of a long day
went down
let down the blind and down
right down
into the old rocker
and rocked
rocked
saying to herself
no
done with that

the rocker
those arms at last
saying to the rocker
rock her off
stop her eyes
fuck life
stop her eyes
rock her off
rock her off

[*Together: echo of "rock her off," coming to rest of rock, slow fade out.*]

OHIO IMPROMPTU

L = Listener.
R = Reader.
As alike in appearance as possible.
Light on table midstage. Rest of stage in darkness.
Plain white deal table say 8' × 4'.
Two plain armless white deal chairs.
L seated at table facing front towards end of long side audience right. Bowed head propped on right hand. Face hidden. Left hand on table. Long black coat. Long white hair.
R seated at table in profile centre of short side audience right. Bowed head propped on right hand. Left hand on table. Book on table before him open at last pages. Long black coat. Long white hair.
Black wide-brimmed hat at centre of table.
Fade up.
Ten seconds.
R turns page.
Pause.

R [*reading*] Little is left to tell. In a last—
    [*L knocks with left hand on table.*]
    Little is left to tell.
    [*Pause. Knock.*]

In a last attempt to obtain relief he moved from where they had been so long together to a single room on the far bank. From its single window he could see the downstream extremity of the Isle of Swans.

[*Pause.*]

Relief he had hoped would flow from unfamiliarity.

Unfamiliar room. Unfamiliar scene. Out to where nothing ever shared. Back to where nothing ever shared. From this he had once half hoped some measure of relief might flow.

[*Pause.*]

Day after day he could be seen slowly pacing the islet. Hour after hour. In his long black coat no matter what the weather and old world Latin Quarter hat. At the tip he would always pause to dwell on the receding stream. How in joyous eddies its two arms conflowed and flowed united on. Then turn and his slow steps retrace.

[*Pause.*]

In his dreams—

[*Knock.*]

Then turn and his slow steps retrace.

[*Pause. Knock.*]

In his dreams he had been warned against this change. Seen the dear face and heard the unspoken words, Stay where we were so long alone together, my shade will comfort you.

[*Pause.*]

Could he not—

[*Knock.*]

Seen the dear face and heard the unspoken words, Stay where we were so long alone together, my shade will comfort you.

[*Pause. Knock.*]

Could he not now turn back? Acknowledge his error and return to where they were once so long alone together. Alone together so much shared. No. What he had done alone could not be undone. Nothing he had ever done alone could ever be undone. By him alone.

[*Pause.*]

In this extremity his old terror of night laid hold on him again. After so long a lapse that as if never been. [*Pause. Looks closer.*] Yes, after so long a lapse that as if never been. Now with redoubled force the fearful symptoms described at length page forty paragraph four. [*Starts to turn back the pages. Checked by L's left hand. Resumes relinquished page.*] White nights now again his portion. As when his heart was young. No sleep no braving sleep till—[*turns page*]—dawn of day. [*Pause.*]

Little is left to tell. One night—

[*Knock.*]

Little is left to tell.

[*Pause. Knock.*]

One night as he sat trembling head in hands from head to foot a man appeared to him and said, I have been sent by—and here he named the dear name—to comfort you. Then drawing a worn volume from the pocket of his long black coat he sat and read till dawn. Then disappeared without a word.

[*Pause.*]

Some time later he appeared again at the same hour with the same volume and this time without preamble sat and read it through again the long night through. Then disappeared without a word.

[*Pause.*]

So from time to time unheralded he would appear to read the sad tale through again and the long night away. Then disappear without a word.

[*Pause.*]

With never a word exchanged they grew to be as one.

[*Pause.*]

Till the night came at last when having closed the book and dawn at hand he did not disappear but sat on without a word.

[*Pause.*]

Finally he said, I have had word from—and here he named the dear name—that I shall not come again. I saw the dear face and heard the unspoken words, No need to go to him again, even were it in your power.

[*Pause.*]

So the sad—

[*Knock.*]

Saw the dear face and heard the unspoken words, No need to go to him again, even were it in your power.

[*Pause. Knock.*]

So the sad tale a last time told they sat on as though turned to stone. Through the single window dawn shed no light. From the street no sound of reawakening. Or was it that buried in who knows what thoughts they paid no heed? To light of day. To sound of reawakening. What thoughts who knows. Thoughts, no, not thoughts. Profounds of mind. Buried in who knows what profounds of mind. Of mindlessness. Whither no light can reach. No sound. So sat on as though turned to stone. The sad tale a last time told.

[*Pause.*]

Nothing is left to tell.

[*Pause. R makes to close book.*

Knock. Book half closed.]

Nothing is left to tell.

[*Pause. R closes book.*

Knock.

Silence. Five seconds.

Simultaneously they lower their right hands to table, raise their heads and look at each other. Unblinking. Expressionless:

Ten seconds.

Fade out.]

QUAD

A piece for four players, light and percussion.

The players (1, 2, 3, 4) pace the given area, each following his particular course.

Area: square. Length of side: 6 paces.

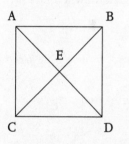

Course 1: AC, CB, BA, AD, DB, BC, CD, DA
Course 2: BA, AD, DB, BC, CD, DA, AC, CB
Course 3: CD, DA, AC, CB, BA, AD, DB, BC
Course 4: DB, BC, CD, DA, AC, CB, BA, AD

1 enters at A, completes his course and is joined by 3. Together they complete their courses and are joined by 4. Together all three complete their courses and are joined by 2. Together all four complete their courses. Exit 1. 2, 3 and 4 continue and complete their courses. Exit 3. 2 and 4 continue and complete their courses. Exit 4. End of 1st series. 2 continues,

opening 2nd series, completes his course and is joined by 1. Etc. Unbroken movement.

    1st series (as above): 1, 13, 134, 1342, 342, 42

    2nd series: 2, 21, 214, 2143, 143, 43

    3rd series: 3, 32, 321, 3214, 214, 14

    4th series: 4, 43, 432, 4321, 321, 21

Four possible solos all given.

Six possible duos all given (two twice).

Four possible trios all given twice.

Without interruption begin repeat and fade out on 1 pacing alone.

Light (2)

Dim on area from above fading out into dark.

    Four sources of differently coloured light clustered together.

    Each player has his particular light, to be turned on when he enters, kept on while he paces, turned off when he exits.

    Say 1 white, 2 yellow, 3 blue, 4 red. Then

    1st series: white, white + blue, white + blue + red, white + blue + red + yellow, blue + red + yellow, red + yellow.

    2nd series: yellow, yellow + white, yellow + white + red etc.

    All possible light combinations given.

Percussion

Four types of percussion, say drum, gong, triangle, wood block.

    Each player has his particular percussion, to sound when he enters, continue while he paces, cease when he exits.

    Say 1 drum, 2 gong, 3 triangle, 4 wood block. Then

    1st series: drum, drum + triangle, drum + triangle + wood block etc. Same system as for light.

    All possible percussion combinations given.

    Percussion intermittent in all combinations to allow footsteps alone to be heard at intervals.

Pianissimo throughout.

Percussionists barely visible in shadow on raised podium at back of set.

Footsteps

Each player has his particular sound.

Costumes

Gowns reaching to ground, cowls hiding faces.

Each player has his particular colour corresponding to his light. 1 white, 2 yellow, 3 blue, 4 red.

All possible costume combinations given.

Players

As alike in build as possible. Short and slight for preference.

Some ballet training desirable. Adolescents a possibility. Sex indifferent.

Camera

Raised frontal. Fixed. Both players and percussionists in frame.

Time (3)

On basis of one pace per second and allowing for time lost at angles and centre approximately 25 minutes.

Problem (4)

Negotiation of E without rupture of rhythm when three or four players cross paths at this point. Or, if ruptures accepted, how best exploit?

1. This original scenario (*Quad I*) was followed in the Stuttgart production by a variation (*Quad II*). (5)

2. Abandoned as impracticable. Constant neutral light throughout.

3. Overestimated. *Quad I*, fast tempo. 15' approx. *Quad II*, slow tempo, series 1 only, 5' approx.

4. E supposed a danger zone. Hence deviation. Manoeuvre established at outset by first solo at first diagonal (CB). E.g. series 1:

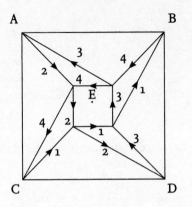

5. No colour, all four in identical white gowns, no percussion, footsteps only sound, slow tempo, series 1 only.

CATASTROPHE

For Václav Havel

Director (D).
His female assistant (A).
Protagonist (P).
Luke, in charge of the lighting, offstage (L).

Rehearsal. Final touches to the last scene. Bare stage. A and L have just set the
lighting. D has just arrived.

D in an armchair downstairs audience left. Fur coat. Fur toque to match.
Age and physique unimportant.

A standing beside him. White overall. Bare head. Pencil on ear. Age and
physique unimportant.

P midstage standing on a black block 18 inches high. Black wide-brimmed
hat. Black dressing-gown to ankles. Barefoot. Head bowed. Hands in pockets.
Age and physique unimportant.

D and A contemplate P. Long pause.

A [*finally*] Like the look of him?
D So so. [*Pause.*] Why the plinth?
A To let the stalls see the feet.
   [*Pause.*]
D Why the hat?
A To help hide the face.
   [*Pause.*]
D Why the gown?
A To have him all black.
   [*Pause.*]
D What has he on underneath? [*A moves towards P.*] Say it.

[*A halts.*]

A   His night attire.

D   Colour?

A   Ash.

[*D takes out a cigar.*]

D   Light. [*A returns, lights the cigar, stands still. D smokes.*]
   How's the skull?

A   You've seen it.

D   I forget. [*A moves towards P.*] Say it.

[*A halts.*]

A   Moulting. A few tufts.

D   Colour?

A   Ash.

[*Pause.*]

D   Why hands in pockets?

A   To help have him all black.

D   They mustn't.

A   I make a note. [*She takes out a pad, takes pencil, notes.*]
   Hands exposed.
   [*She puts back pad and pencil.*]

D   How are they? [*A at a loss. Irritably.*] The hands, how are the hands?

A   You've seen them.

D   I forget.

A   Crippled. Fibrous degeneration.

D   Clawlike?

A   If you like.

D   Two claws?

A   Unless he clench his fists.

D   He mustn't.

A   I make a note. [*She takes out pad, takes pencil, notes.*]
   Hands limp.
   [*She puts back pad and pencil.*]

D   Light. [*A returns, relights the cigar, stands still. D smokes.*]
   Good. Now let's have a look. [*A at a loss. Irritably.*] Get going. Lose that
   gown. [*He consults his chronometer.*] Step on it, I have a caucus.

[*A goes to P, takes off the gown. P submits, inert. A steps back, the gown over her arm. P in old grey pyjamas, head bowed, fists clenched. Pause.*]

A   Like him better without? [*Pause.*] He's shivering.

D   Not all that. Hat.
[*A advances, takes off hat, steps back, hat in hand. Pause.*]

A   Like that cranium?

D   Needs whitening.

A   I make a note. [*She takes out pad, takes pencil, notes.*] Whiten cranium.
[*She puts back pad and pencil.*]

D   The hands. [*A at a loss. Irritably.*] The fists. Get going. [*A advances, unclenches fists, steps back.*] And whiten.

A   I make a note. [*She takes out pad, takes pencil, notes.*] Whiten hands.
[*She puts back pad and pencil. They contemplate P.*]

D   [*finally*] Something wrong. [*Distraught.*] What is it?

A   [*timidly*] What if we were . . . were to . . . join them?

D   No harm trying. [*A advances, joins the hands, steps back.*] Higher. [*A advances, raises waist-high the joined hands, steps back.*] A touch more. [*A advances, raises breast-high the joined hands.*] Stop! [*A steps back.*] Better. It's coming. Light.
[*A returns, relights cigar, stands still. D smokes.*]

A   He's shivering.

D   Bless his heart.
[*Pause.*]

A   [*timidly*] What about a little . . . a little . . . gag?

D   For God's sake! This craze for explicitation! Every i dotted to death! Little gag! For God's sake!

A   Sure he won't utter?

D   Not a squeak. [*He consults his chronometer.*] Just time. I'll go and see how it looks from the house.
[*Exit D, not to appear again. A subsides in the armchair, springs to her feet no sooner seated, takes out a rag, wipes vigorously back and seat of chair, discards rag, sits again. Pause.*]

D   [*off, plaintive*] I can't see the toes. [*Irritably.*] I'm sitting in the front row of the stalls and can't see the toes.

A   [*rising*] I make a note. [*She takes out a pad, takes pencil, notes.*] Raise pedestal.

D   There's a trace of face.

A   I make a note.

[*She takes out pad, takes pencil, makes to note.*]

D   Down the head. [*A at a loss. Irritably.*] Get going. Down his head. [*A puts back pad and pencil, goes to P, bows his head further, steps back.*] A shade more. [*A advances, bows the head further.*] Stop! [*A steps back.*] Fine. It's coming. [*Pause.*] Could do with more nudity.

A   I make a note.

[*She takes out pad, makes to take her pencil.*]

D   Get going! Get going! [*A puts back the pad, goes to P, stands irresolute.*] Bare the neck. [*A undoes top buttons, parts the flaps, steps back.*] The legs. The shins. [*A advances, rolls up to below knee one trouser-leg, steps back.*] The other. [*Same for other leg, steps back.*] Higher. The knees. [*A advances, rolls up to above knees both trouser-legs, steps back.*] And whiten.

A   I make a note. [*She takes out pad, takes pencil, notes.*] Whiten all flesh.

D   It's coming. Is Luke around?

A   [*calling*] Luke! [*Pause. Louder.*] Luke!

L   [*off, distant*] I hear you. [*Pause. Nearer.*] What's the trouble now?

A   Luke's around.

D   Blackout stage.

L   What?

[*A transmits in technical terms. Fade-out of general light. Light on P alone. A in shadow.*]

D   Just the head.

L   What?

[*A transmits in technical terms. Fade-out of light on P's body. Light on head alone. Long pause.*]

D   Lovely.

[*Pause.*]

A   [*timidly*] What if he were to . . . were to . . . raise his head . . . an instant . . . show his face . . . just an instant.

D   For God's sake! What next? Raise his head? Where do you think we are? In Patagonia? Raise his head? For God's sake! [*Pause.*] Good. There's our catastrophe. In the bag. Once more and I'm off.

A   [*to L*] Once more and he's off.

[*Fade-up of light on P's body. Pause. Fade-up of general light.*]

D   Stop! [*Pause.*] Now . . . let 'em have it. [*Fade-out of general light. Pause. Fade-out of light on body. Light on head alone. Long pause.*] Terrific! He'll have them on their feet. I can hear it from here.

[*Pause. Distant storm of applause. P raises his head, fixes the audience. The applause falters, dies.*

Long pause.

Fade-out of light on face.]

NACHT UND TRÄUME

Elements.
Evening light.
Dreamer (A).
His dreamt self (B).
Dreamt hands R (right) and L (left).
Last 7 bars of Schubert's lied "Nacht und Träume."

1. Fade up on a dark empty room lit only by evening light from a
   window set high in back wall.
   Left foreground, faintly lit, a man seated at a table. Right profile,
   head bowed, grey hair, hands resting on table.
   Clearly visible only head and hands and section of table on which
   they rest.
2. Softly hummed, male voice, last 7 bars of Schubert's lied "Nacht
   und Träume."
3. Fade out evening light.
4. Softly sung, with words, last 3 bars of lied, beginning "Holde
   Träume . . ."
5. Fade down A as he bows his head further to rest on hands. Thus
   minimally lit he remains just visible throughout dream as first
   viewed.
6. A dreams. Fade up on B on an invisible podium about 4 feet
   above floor level, middle ground, well right of centre. He is
   seated at a table in the same posture as A dreaming, bowed
   head resting on hands, but left profile, faintly lit by kinder light
   than A's.
7. From dark beyond and above B's head L appears and rests gently
   on it.
8. B raises his head, L withdraws and disappears.

9. From same dark R appears with a cup, conveys it gently to B's lips. B drinks, R disappears.

10. R reappears with a cloth, wipes gently B's brow, disappears with cloth.

11. B raises his head further to gaze up at invisible face.

12. B raises his right hand, still gazing up, and holds it raised palm upward.

13. R reappears and rests gently on B's right hand, B still gazing up.

14. B transfers gaze to joined hands.

15. B raises his left hand and rests it on joined hands.

16. Together hands sink to table and on them B's head.

17. L reappears and rests gently on B's head.

18. Fade out dream.

19. Fade up A and evening light.

20. A raises head to its opening position.

21. Lied as before (2).

22. Fade out evening light.

23. Close of lied as before (4).

24. Fade down A as before (5).

25. A dreams. Fade up on B as before (6).

26. Move in slowly to close-up of B, losing A.

27. Dream as before (7–16) in close-up and slower motion.

28. Withdraw slowly to opening viewpoint, recovering A.

29. Fade out dream.

30. Fade out A.

WHAT WHERE

Bam

Bem

Bim

Bom

Voice of Bam (V)

NOTE

Players as alike as possible.

Same long grey gown.

Same long grey hair.

V *in the shape of a small megaphone at head level.*

Playing area (P) rectangle 3 m × 2 m, dimly lit, surrounded by shadow, stage right as seen from house. Downstage left, dimly lit, surrounded by shadow, V.

General dark.
Light on V.
Pause.

    v   We are the last five.
        In the present as were we still.
        It is spring.
        Time passes.
        First without words.
        I switch on.

[Light on P.
Bam at 3 head haught, Bom at 1 head bowed.
Pause.]
Not good.
I switch off.
[Light off P.]
I start again.
We are the last five.
It is spring.
Time passes.
First without words.
I switch on.
[Light on P.
Bam alone at 3 head haught.
Pause.]
Good.
I am alone.
It is spring.
Time passes.
First without words.
In the end Bom appears.
Reappears.
[Bom enters at N, halts at 1 head bowed.
Pause.
Bim enters at E, halts at 2 head haught.
Pause.
Bim exits at E followed by Bom.
Pause.
Bim enters at E, halts at 2 head bowed.
Pause.
Bem enters at N, halts at 1 head haught.
Pause.
Bem exits at N followed by Bim.
Pause.

Bem enters at N, halts at 1 head bowed.
Pause.
Bam exits at W followed by Bem.
Pause.
Bam enters at W, halts at 3 head bowed.
Pause.]
Good.
I switch off.
[*Light off P.*]
I start again.
We are the last five.
It is spring.
Time passes.
I switch on.
[*Light on P.*
Bam alone at 3 head haught.
Pause.]
Good.
I am alone.
It is spring.
Time passes.
Now with words.
In the end Bom appears.
Reappears.
[*Bom enters at N, halts at 1 head bowed.*]

BAM   Well?

BOM   [*Head bowed throughout.*] Nothing.

BAM   He didn't say anything?

BOM   No.

BAM   You gave him the works?

BOM   Yes.

BAM   And he didn't say anything?

BOM   No.

BAM   He wept?

BOM   Yes.

BAM   Screamed?

BOM   Yes.

BAM   Begged for mercy?

BOM   Yes.

BAM   But didn't say anything?

BOM   No.

V   Not good.

      I start again.

BAM   Well?

BOM   Nothing.

BAM   He didn't say it?

V   Good.

BOM   No.

BAM   You gave him the works?

BOM   Yes.

BAM   And he didn't say it?

BOM   No.

BAM   He wept?

BOM   Yes.

BAM   Screamed?

BOM   Yes.

BAM   Begged for mercy?

BOM   Yes.

BAM   But didn't say it?

BOM   No.

BAM   Then why stop?

BOM   He passed out.

BAM   And you didn't revive him?

BOM   I tried.

BAM   Well?

BOM   I couldn't.

      [*Pause.*]

BAM   It's a lie. [*Pause.*] He said it to you.

[*Pause.*] Confess he said it to you. [*Pause.*] You'll be given the works until you confess.

v   Good.

In the end Bim appears.

[*Bim enters at E, halts at 2 head haught.*]

BAM   [*to Bim*] Are you free?

BIM   Yes.

BAM   Take him away and give him the works until he confesses.

BIM   What must he confess?

BAM   That he said it to him.

BIM   Is that all?

BAM   Yes.

v   Not good.

I start again.

BAM   Take him away and give him the works until he confesses.

BIM   What must he confess?

BAM   That he said it to him.

BIM   Is that all?

BAM   And what.

v   Good.

BIM   Is that all?

BAM   Yes.

BIM   Then stop?

BAM   Yes.

BIM   Good. [*To Bom.*] Come.

[*Bim exits at E followed by Bom.*]

v   Good.

I am alone.

It is summer.

Time passes.

In the end Bim appears.

Reappears.

[*Bim enters at E, halts at 2 head bowed.*]

BAM   Well?

BIM   [*Head bowed throughout.*] Nothing.

BAM   He didn't say it?

BIM   No.

BAM   You gave him the works?

BIM   Yes.

BAM   And he didn't say it?

BIM   No.

V   Not good.

   I start again.

BAM   Well?

BIM   Nothing.

BAM   He didn't say where?

V   Good.

BIM   Where?

V   Ah!

BAM   Where.

BIM   No.

BAM   You gave him the works?

BIM   Yes.

BAM   And he didn't say where?

BIM   No.

BAM   He wept?

BIM   Yes.

BAM   Screamed?

BIM   Yes.

BAM   Begged for mercy?

BIM   Yes.

BAM   But didn't say where?

BIM   No.

BAM   Then why stop?

BIM   He passed out.

BAM   And you didn't revive him?

BIM   I tried.

BAM   Well?

BIM   I couldn't.

     [*Pause.*]

BAM   It's a lie. [*Pause.*] He said where to you. [*Pause.*] Confess he said where to you. [*Pause.*] You'll be given the works until you confess.

  V   Good.

     In the end Bem appears.

     [*Bem enters at N, halts at 1 head haught.*]

BAM   [*to Bem*] Are you free?

BEM   Yes.

BAM   Take him away and give him the works until he confesses.

BEM   What must he confess?

BAM   That he said where to him.

BEM   Is that all?

BAM   Yes.

  V   Not good.

     I start again.

BAM   Take him away and give him the works until he confesses.

BEM   What must he confess?

BAM   That he said where to him.

BEM   Is that all?

BAM   And where.

  V   Good.

BEM   Is that all?

BAM   Yes.

BEM   Then stop?

BAM   Yes.

BEM   Good. [*to Bim*] Come.

     [*Bem exits at N followed by Bim.*]

  V   Good.

     I am alone.

     It is autumn.

     Time passes.

     In the end Bem appears.

     Reappears.

[*Bem enters at N, halts at 1 head bowed.*]

BAM　Well?

BEM　[*Head bowed throughout.*] Nothing.

BAM　He didn't say where?

BEM　No.

　V　So on.

BAM　It's a lie. [*Pause.*] He said where to you. [*Pause.*] Confess he said
　　　where to you. [*Pause.*] You'll be given the works until you confess.

BEM　What must I confess?

BAM　That he said where to you.

BEM　Is that all?

BAM　And where.

BEM　Is that all?

BAM　Yes.

BEM　Then stop?

BAM　Yes. Come.

　　　[*Bam exits at W followed by Bem.*]

　V　Good.

　　　It is winter.

　　　Time passes.

　　　In the end I appear.

　　　Reappear.

　　　[*Bam enters at W, halts at 3 head bowed.*]

　V　Good.

　　　I am alone.

　　　In the present as were I still.

　　　It is winter.

　　　Without journey.

　　　Time passes.

　　　That is all.

　　　Make sense who may.

　　　I switch off.

　　　[*Light off P.*
　　　Pause.
　　　Light off V.]

NOTES

Waiting for Godot. Written in French between October 9, 1948, and January 29, 1949 (*En attendant Godot*). Published by Éditions de Minuit, October 1952. First performed on January 5, 1953, at the Théâtre Babylone, Paris. First Grove edition of Beckett's English translation, 1954. First English-language performance at the Arts Theatre Club, London, August 3, 1955. First American performance at the Coconut Grove Playhouse, Miami Beach, Florida, January 3, 1956.

Endgame. Written in French between 1953 and 1957 (*Fin de partie*). First French-language performance at the Royal Court Theatre, London, April 3, 1957. After six nights, the production closed, then moved to the Studio des Champs-Élysées in Paris, where it reopened on April 26. Published by Minuit under the title *Fin de partie suivi de Acte sans paroles*, 1957. Beckett translated the text into English in the spring of 1957. First English-language performance at the Cherry Lane Theater, New York, January 28, 1958. First Grove edition, *Endgame, Followed by Act Without Words*, 1958.

All That Fall. Written in English, 1956. First broadcast by the BBC Third Programme, January 13, 1957. First American broadcast, by National Public Radio, took place on Beckett's eightieth birthday, April 13, 1986. First publication by Grove in *Krapp's Last Tape and Other Dramatic Pieces*, 1960.

Act Without Words I. Written in French, 1956. (*Acte sans paroles I*). First performed with *Fin de partie* (*Endgame*) at the Royal Court Theatre, London, April 3, 1957, with music by John Beckett (a cousin). Published in *Fin de partie suivi de Acte sans paroles*. First publication by Grove in *Endgame, Followed by Act Without Words*.

Embers. Written in English, 1957. First broadcast by the BBC Third Programme, June 24, 1959. Appeared in *The Evergreen Review*, 1959. First publication by Grove in *Krapp's Last Tape and Other Dramatic Pieces.*

Act Without Words II. Written in French, 1958 (*Acte sans paroles II*). First performed at the Institute of Contemporary Arts, London, January 25, 1960. First publication by Grove in *Krapp's Last Tape and Other Dramatic Pieces.* In France, it appeared in *Comédie et actes divers* (Minuit, 1966).

Krapp's Last Tape. Written in English, 1958. First British performance at the Royal Court Theatre, London, October 28, 1958. Published in *The Evergreen Review*, 1958. First American performance at the Provincetown Playhouse, New York, January 14, 1960 (part of a double bill with Edward Albee's *The Zoo Story*). First publication by Grove in *Krapp's Last Tape and Other Dramatic Pieces.*

Rough for Theatre I. Written in French in the late fifties or early sixties (*Fragment de théâtre*). First publication by Grove in *Ends and Odds*, 1977.

Rough for Theatre II. Written in French in the late fifties or early sixties (*Fragment de théâtre*). First publication by Grove in *Ends and Odds.*

The Old Tune. Beckett's English adaptation of *La Manivelle*, a play for radio by Robert Pinget. First broadcast by the BBC Third Programme, August 23, 1960. Published in *The Evergreen Review*, 1961. A stage version was first performed at the Royal Playhouse, New York, March 23, 1961. First publication by Grove in *Collected Shorter Plays*, 1984.

Happy Days. Written in English, 1960. World premiere at the Cherry Lane Theater, New York, September 17, 1961. First Grove edition, 1961.

Rough for Radio I. Written in French, 1961 (*Esquisse radiophonique*). Appeared as "Sketch for Radio Play" in *Stereo Headphones*, 1976. First publication by Grove in *Ends and Odds.*

Rough for Radio II. Written in French some time in the early sixties (*Pochade radiophonique*). First broadcast, in Beckett's English translation, by the BBC on April 13, 1976 (the author's seventieth birthday). First publication by Grove in *Ends and Odds.*

Words and Music. Written in English, 1961. First broadcast by the BBC on December 7, 1962, with music composed by John Beckett. Appeared in

The Evergreen Review, 1962. First publication by Grove in *Cascando and Other Short Dramatic Pieces*, 1969.

Cascando. Written in French, with the subtitle "Invention radiophonique pour musique et voix," early sixties. First broadcast on France Culture, April 3, 1963, with music composed by Marcel Mihalovici. Beckett's translation was published in *The Evergreen Review*, 1963. First British broadcast on the BBC Third Programme, October 6, 1964. First publication by Grove in *Cascando and Other Short Dramatic Pieces.*

Play. Written in English, 1962–63. The world premiere was in German (*Spiel*) at the Ulmer Theater, Ulm-Donau, June 14, 1963. First American performance at the Cherry Lane Theater, New York, January 4, 1964. Published in *The Evergreen Review*, 1964. First publication by Grove in *Cascando and Other Short Dramatic Pieces.*

Film. Written in English, 1963. Beckett's only screenplay, which was shot in New York in the summer of 1964 and led to his only visit to the United States. Directed by Alan Schneider; starring Buster Keaton. Shown at the Venice and New York Film Festivals, 1965. First Grove edition (with illustrations, production shots, and an essay by Alan Schneider), 1969. Also in *Cascando and Other Short Dramatic Pieces.*

Come and Go. Written in English, 1965. The world premiere was in German (*Kommen und Gehen*) at the Schiller-Theater, Berlin, January 14, 1966. First English-language performance at the Peacock Theatre, Dublin, February 28, 1968. First American performance at the Theater for the New City, New York, October 23, 1975. First publication by Grove in *Cascando and Other Short Dramatic Pieces.*

Eh Joe. Written in English, spring 1965. Beckett's first work for television and also his directorial debut. First broadcast in German (*He, Joe*) by Süddeutscher Rundfunk, April 13, 1966 (the author's sixtieth birthday). The first English-language production was broadcast by BBC 2, July 4, 1966. First publication by Grove in *Cascando and Other Short Dramatic Pieces.*

Breath. Written in English, composition date unknown. First performed (in a version altered without Beckett's permission) at the Eden Theater, New York, June 16, 1969, as a curtain-raiser to Jacques Levy and

Kenneth Tynan's review *Oh! Calcutta!* (the title is a pun on the French "O quel cul t'as," "Oh what an ass you have"). First publication by Grove in *First Love and Other Shorts*, 1974.

Not I. Written in English, spring 1972. First performed at the Repertory Theater of Lincoln Center, New York, November 22, 1972, as part of a Samuel Beckett Festival. First publication by Grove in *Ends and Odds.*

That Time. Written in English between June 1974 and August 1975. First performed at the Royal Court Theatre, London, May 20, 1976. First American production at the Arena Stage, Kreeger Theater, Washington, D.C., December 3 of the same year. First publication by Grove in *I Can't Go On, I'll Go On,* edited by Richard Seaver, 1976. Later included in *Ends and Odds.*

Footfalls. Written in English, 1975. First performed with *That Time* at the Royal Court Theatre, London, May 20, 1976. First American performance as above. First publication by Grove in *Ends and Odds.*

Ghost Trio. Written in English, 1975. First televised on BBC 2, April 17, 1977. First publication by Grove in *Ends and Odds.*

... but the clouds ... Written in English, October–November 1976. First televised on BBC 2, April 17, 1977. First publication by Grove in the expanded edition of *Ends and Odds,* 1981.

A Piece of Monologue. Written in English, 1977–79, for the American actor David Warrilow. It premiered at the Annex of La Mama, ETC, New York, December 14, 1979. The text appeared in *The Kenyon Review* that same year. First publication by Grove in *Rockaby and Other Short Pieces,* 1981.

Rockaby. Written in English, 1980. First performed at the Center for Theatre Research (SUNY Buffalo), April 8, 1981, as part of the university's Beckett Festival. First publication by Grove in *Rockaby and Other Short Pieces.*

Ohio Impromptu. Written in English, 1981, for a symposium at Ohio State University in honor of Beckett's seventy-fifth birthday. First performed in the Drake Union, Stadium 2 Theater, May 9, 1981. First publication by Grove in *Rockaby and Other Short Pieces.*

Quad. Written in English, 1981. A work for television, first broadcast in Germany (*Quadrat 1 + 2*) by Süddeutscher Rundfunk, October 8, 1981, directed by Beckett. First publication by Grove in *Collected Shorter Plays.*

Catastrophe. Written in French, 1982, in support of imprisoned playwright Václav Havel, who later became president of the Czech Republic. First performed in French at the Avignon Festival, July 12, 1982. First American production opened at the Harold Clurman Theater, New York, June 15, 1983. Beckett's English translation appeared in *The New Yorker,* January 1983. First publication by Grove in *Three Plays,* 1984.

Nacht und Träume. Written in English, 1982 (*Night and Dreams*). A work for television, first broadcast in Germany by Süddeutscher Rundfunk, May 19, 1983. First publication by Grove in *Collected Shorter Plays.*

What Where. Written in French, 1983 (*Quoi où*). Beckett's English version premiered with *Catastrophe* and *Ohio Impromptu* at the Harold Clurman Theater, New York, June 15, 1983. First publication by Grove in *Three Plays.*